The Complete Idiot's Reference Card

General Windows Keyboard Shortcuts

Press	To
Alt+Print Screen	Copy the active window's image to the Clipboard.
Print Screen	Copy the entire screen image to the Clipboard.
Ctrl+Alt+Delete	Display the Windows Task Manager.
Ctrl+Esc	Open the Start menu.
Ctrl+Z	Undo the most recent action.

Keyboard Shortcuts for Programs

Press	To

Working with Program Windows

Alt+Esc	Cycle through the open program windows.
Alt+Tab	Cycle through the active programs.
Alt+F4	Close the active program window.
F1	Display context-sensitive Help.

Working with Documents

Ctrl+N	Create a new document.
Ctrl+O	Display the Open dialog box.
Ctrl+P	Display the Print dialog box.
Ctrl+S	Save the current file. If the file is new, display the Save As dialog box.

Keyboard Shortcuts for Working with Data

Press	To
Backspace	Delete the character to the left of the insertion point.
Delete	Delete the selected data or the character to the right of the insertion point.
Ctrl+A	Select all the data in the current window.
Ctrl+C	Copy the selected data.
Ctrl+X	Cut the selected data.
Ctrl+V	Paste the most recently cut or copied data.

Keyboard Shortcuts for Dialog Boxes

Hold Down	To
Tab	Move forward through the dialog box controls.
Shift+Tab	Move backward through the dialog box controls.
Ctrl+Tab	Move forward through the dialog box tabs.
Alt+Down arrow	Display the list in a drop-down list box.
Spacebar	Toggle a check box on and off; select the active option button or command button.
Enter	Select the default command button or the active command button.
Esc	Close the dialog box without making any changes.

ALPHA

P9-CJZ-139

Keys to Hold Down While Dragging-and-Dropping

Hold Down	To
Ctrl	Copy the dragged object.
Ctrl+Shift	Display a shortcut menu after dropping a dragged object.
Esc	Cancel the current drag.
Shift	Move the dragged object.

Windows Explorer Keyboard Shortcuts

Press	To
+ (numeric keypad)	Display the next level of subfolders for the current folder.
– (numeric keypad)	Hide the current folder's subfolders.
* (numeric keypad)	Display all levels of subfolders for the current folder.
Backspace	Navigate to the parent folder of the current folder.
Delete	Delete the selected object.
Ctrl+A	Select all the objects in the current folder.
Shift+Delete	Delete the currently selected objects without sending them to the Recycle Bin.
F2	Rename the selected object.
F3	Display the Find dialog box with the current folder displayed in the Look In list.
F4	Open the Address toolbar's drop-down list.

Internet Explorer Keyboard Shortcuts

Press	To
Alt+Left arrow	Navigate backward to a previously displayed Web page.
Alt+Right arrow	Navigate forward to a previously displayed Web page.
Ctrl+A	Select the entire Web page.
Ctrl+B	Display the Organize Favorites dialog box.
Ctrl+D	Add the current page to the Favorites list.
Esc	Stop downloading the Web page.
F4	Open the Address toolbar's drop-down list.
F5	Refresh the Web page.
F11	Toggle between full screen mode and the regular window.

Shortcuts That Use the Windows Logo (⊞) Key

Press	To
⊞	Open the Start menu.
⊞+E	Open Windows Explorer.
⊞+F	Find a file or folder.
⊞+M	Minimize all open windows.
⊞+Shift+M	Undo minimize all.
⊞+R	Display the Run dialog box.

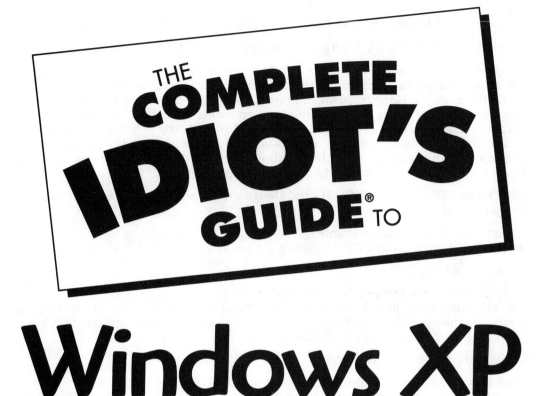

THE COMPLETE IDIOT'S GUIDE® TO

Windows XP

by Paul McFedries

ALPHA

A member of Penguin Group (USA) Inc.

To Karen and Gypsy, who are always happy to see me.

Copyright © 2002 by Penguin Group (USA) Inc.

International Standard Book Number: 0-02-864232-5
Library of Congress Catalog Card Number: 2001094730

04   03   11

Interpretation of the printing code: The rightmost number of the first series of numbers is the year of the book's printing; the rightmost number of the second series of numbers is the number of the book's printing. For example, a printing code of 02-1 shows that the first printing occurred in 2002.

Printed in the United States of America

Note: This publication contains the opinions and ideas of its author. It is intended to provide helpful and informative material on the subject matter covered. It is sold with the understanding that the author and publisher are not engaged in rendering professional services in the book. If the reader requires personal assistance or advice, a competent professional should be consulted.

Publisher
Marie Butler-Knight

Product Manager
Phil Kitchel

Managing Editor
Jennifer Chisholm

Acquisitions Editor
Eric Heagy

Development Editor
Nancy D. Warner

Production Editor
Billy Fields

Copy Editor
Michael Dietsch

Illustrator
Jody Schaeffer

Cover Designers
Mike Freeland
Kevin Spear

Book Designers
Scott Cook and Amy Adams of DesignLab

Indexer
Lisa Wilson

Layout/Proofreading
Svetlana Dominguez
Ayanna Lacey

Contents at a Glance

Contents

7 Installing and Uninstalling Programs and Devices   83

Part 2: Windows XP at Home   97

8 Playing with Pictures   99

9 Graphics Gadgetry: Working with Scanners and Digital Cameras   111

xvii

Introduction

Never let a computer know you're in a hurry.

—Anonymous

The world's gardeners have told us for years that if you want to keep your plants healthy and happy, then you should talk to them in a kindly, soothing voice. The world's gardeners are, I suspect, an eccentric bunch, but who can argue with their success?

Certainly not me, so perhaps that's why I've taken to talking to my computer using the same gentle, comforting tones. "Now, my good fellow, I have a *very* important deadline tomorrow, oh yes, and I just need you to be a good boy and not crash between now and then. Okey-doke?" (This is made *much* easier by the fact that I work at home.)

I think that, subconsciously, I view my computer as though it's the electronic equivalent of some deranged lunatic who'll snap at the least provocation. Or perhaps I see it as more of a fragile, high-strung, Southern belle type, a digital Blanche DuBois who is depending on the kindness of a stranger (that is to say, me) to keep it together.

Of course, what's really happening here is that years of using various incarnations of Windows have made me certifiably paranoid. I've simply come to expect that Windows will do something weird or toss me some semicomprehensible message that will have me scratching my head for hours. So even though it has been well over 10 years since Windows 3.0 was foisted upon an unsuspecting world, Windows remains both devilishly difficult and fiendishly fickle. Windows can, in other words, make any of us feel, temporarily, like a complete idiot.

That, in the end, is why I wrote *The Complete Idiot's Guide to Windows XP*. My goal here is to help you and Windows XP get along. If you aren't a computer wizard (and don't even want to be one), this book is for you; if you have a job to do—a job that includes working with Windows XP—and you just want to get it done as quickly and painlessly as possible, this book is for you; if you don't want to learn about Windows XP using absurdly serious, put-a-crease-in-your-brow-and-we'll-begin tutorials, this book is for you.

No experience with Windows XP? No problem. In fact, this book doesn't assume you have *any* previous experience with *any* version of Windows. I begin each topic at the beginning and build your knowledge from there. So even if you've never used a computer before, this book will get you through those crucial (and scary) early stages.

No time? No problem. With *The Complete Idiot's Guide to Windows XP*, you get just the facts you need—not everything there is to know. This means I avoid long-winded discussions of boring, technical details. Instead, you get all the information in short, easy-to-digest chunks that you can quickly skim through to find just the tidbits you need.

How This Book Is Organized

With Windows, *anything* can happen (and often does). So my best advice as you cross over into Windows XP territory is to expect (you guessed it) the unexpected. However, the last thing you need is to be thrown a few curve balls by the book that's supposed to be your trusted guide in this newfound land. So, to get you better prepared for the journey to come, let's bone up on some of the flora and fauna you'll be seeing along the way.

First, the itinerary. *The Complete Idiot's Guide to Windows XP* is organized into six reasonably sensible parts. To help you locate what you need fast, here's a summary of what you'll find in each part.

Part 1: "Windows XP Everywhere: A Few Things You Need to Know." The lucky seven chapters that open the book are designed to help you get your Windows XP travels off on the right foot. Chapter 1 runs through what's new in Windows XP. New Windows users will want to start with Chapter 2, which gives you a tour of the Windows XP screen and offers some mouse and keyboard basics. From there, you learn about controlling programs (Chapter 3), working with windows (Chapter 4), dealing with documents (Chapter 5), working with files and folders (Chapter 6), and installing and uninstalling programs and devices (Chapter 7).

Part 2: "Windows XP at Home." Using a computer at home, we tend more toward the fun end of the computer spectrum. (Yes, there *is* a fun end.) With that in mind, I structured Part 2 to cover some of the more fun features that can be found in Windows XP. This includes working with pictures (Chapter 8); using scanners and digital cameras (Chapter 9); creating images with the Paint program (Chapter 10); working with music, videos, and other multimedia (Chapter 11); and creating digital movies (Chapter 12). For good measure, I also show you an easy way to share your computer with other family members (Chapter 13).

Part 3: "Windows XP at Work." This part is short but sweet (assuming that using Windows at work could be described as "sweet," that is). The three chapters in Part 3 cover workaday tasks such as using Windows XP's writing programs (Chapter 14), sending and receiving faxes (Chapter 15), and using Windows XP's notebook computer features (Chapter 16).

Part 4: "Windows XP on the Internet." There are plenty of days when it seems that our computers are just one giant communications terminal. Electronic communication in all its forms is a huge part of our daily lives, and Part 4 devotes no less than seven chapters to Windows XP Internet and communications goodies. You'll learn step-by-step how to get connected to the Internet (Chapter 17), how to surf the World Wide Web with Internet Explorer (Chapters 18 and 19), how to exchange Internet e-mail with Outlook Express (Chapters 20 and 21), how to participate in newsgroups (Chapter 22), and how to send those newfangled instant messages that everyone's talking about (Chapter 23).

Part 5: "Windows XP at the Shop: Customizing, Maintaining, and Trouble-shooting." Like people living in row houses who paint their doors and windowpanes to stand out from the crowd, most Windows' users like to personalize their computing experience by adjusting the screen colors, changing the background, and performing other individualistic tweaks. The first three chapters in Part 5 show you how to perform these customizations in Windows XP. You'll learn how to customize the desktop (Chapter 24), the Start menu and taskbar (Chapter 25), and the My Computer program (Chapter 26).

Thanks to higher-quality parts and improved manufacturing, modern computers are fairly reliable and will often run for years without so much as an electronic hiccup. However, that doesn't mean some disaster—be it a nasty computer virus, an ill-timed power failure, or some other spawn of Murphy's Law—can't strike at any time. The other three chapters in Part 5 can help you to prepare for problems. You'll get the goods on using Windows XP's collection of system maintenance tools (Chapter 27), backing up your precious-as-gold data (Chapter 28), and troubleshooting common Windows problems (Chapter 29).

Part 6: "Windows XP on the Network." The final part of the book takes you into the mysterious and arcane world of networking. However, you'll see that for the small networks that Windows XP is ideally suited for, networking doesn't have to be an esoteric pursuit. On the contrary, I even take the fairly radical step of actually showing you how to put together your own small network (Chapter 30). From there, you'll learn how to use the Windows XP networking features and how to dial up your network from remote locations (Chapter 31).

Some Things to Help Out Along the Way

In a book such as this, I believe that it's not only important *what* you say, but also *how* you say it. So I've gone to great lengths to present the info in easy-to-digest tidbits that can be absorbed quickly. I've also liberally sprinkled the book with features that I hope will make it easier for you to understand what's going in. Here's a rundown:

➤ Stuff that you have to type will appear in a `monospaced font`, like that.

➤ Menus, commands, and dialog box controls that you have to select, as well as keys you have to press, appear in a **bold font.**

➤ Whenever I tell you to select a menu command, I separate the various menu and command names with commas. For example, instead of saying "click the **Start** button, then click **All Programs**, and then click **Internet Explorer**," I just say this: "select **Start, All Programs, Internet Explorer.**"

➤ Many Windows XP commands have equivalent keyboard shortcuts, and most of them involve holding down one key while you press another key. For example, in most Windows programs, you save your work by holding down the **Ctrl** key, pressing the **S** key, and then releasing **Ctrl.** I'm *way* too lazy to write all that out each time, so I'll just plop a plus sign (+) in between the two keys, like so: **Ctrl+S.**

I've also populated each chapter with several different kinds of sidebars (some appear in the middle of the page and others appear in the margin):

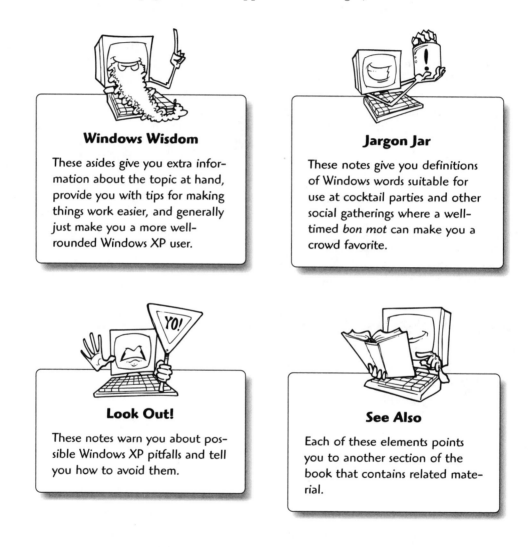

Windows Wisdom

These asides give you extra information about the topic at hand, provide you with tips for making things work easier, and generally just make you a more well-rounded Windows XP user.

Jargon Jar

These notes give you definitions of Windows words suitable for use at cocktail parties and other social gatherings where a well-timed *bon mot* can make you a crowd favorite.

Look Out!

These notes warn you about possible Windows XP pitfalls and tell you how to avoid them.

See Also

Each of these elements points you to another section of the book that contains related material.

Acknowledgments

Substitute damn every time you're inclined to write very; your editor will delete it and the writing will be just as it should be.

—*Mark Twain*

I didn't follow Mark Twain's advice in this book (the word *very* appears throughout), but if my writing still appears "just as it should be," then it's because of the keen minds and sharp linguistic eyes of the editors at Alpha Books. Near the front of the book you'll find a long list of the hard-working professionals whose fingers made it into this particular paper pie. However, there are a few folks that I worked with directly, so I'd like to single them out for extra credit. A big, heaping helping of thanks goes out to acquisitions editor Eric Heagy, development editor Nancy Warner, production editor Billy Fields, copy editor Michael Dietsch, and technical editor Bill Bruns.

Special Thanks to the Tech Reviewer

The Complete Idiot's Guide to Windows XP was reviewed by an expert who double-checked the accuracy of what you'll learn here. Thanks are extended to Bill Bruns.

Bill Bruns is a veteran of finance and data retrieval in the information age. Bill is the chief financial officer for Jacob Marlie Financial, Inc. (www.jacobmarlie.com), a Web-based invoicing and collections agency for fraternal organizations. Currently, he is the Assistant Director for Business Systems at the University of Illinois College of Medicine. For six years, he has been a technical editor, working on at least 125 books relating to the Internet, Web servers, HTML, operating systems and Office applications. You can reach him at bill@jacobmarlie.com.

About the Author

Paul McFedries has been wrestling with computers (metaphorically speaking) for over 25 years. He has a degree in mathematics, can swap out a computer circuit board in seconds flat, and once even used the phrase "paradigm shift" in a sentence. Despite all of this, McFedries still, inexplicably, has a life.

He is the author of more than 40 computer books that have sold over two million copies throughout the solar system. His most recent titles include *The Complete Idiot's Guide to Windows Me*, *The Complete Idiot's Guide to Creating a Web Page*, and *Special Edition Using JavaScript*.

When asked what made him an expert on Windows XP, McFedries responded:

> ➤ "If XP crashes, I know how to get it started again with a well-aimed kick."
> ➤ "My mouse skills are terrifyingly advanced."
> ➤ "I'm a close, personal friend of a guy who almost went to the same high school as a woman who has the same last name as Bill Gates."

Although primarily a freelance writer by day, at night McFedries wears other hats, including president of Logophilia Limited and head spy of the world-famous Word Spy Web site (check out www.logophilia.com/WordSpy/). He lives with Karen, the love of his life, and Gypsy, the kissing dog. His favorite hobbies are building large wooden structures, taking naps, and talking about himself in the third person.

He can be reached via the Internet (compliments and kudos preferred) by sending an e-mail missive to this book's address: WindowsXP@mcfedries.com.

You—yes, *you*—are also encouraged to drop by his Web site: www.mcfedries.com.

Trademarks

All terms mentioned in this book that are known to be or are suspected of being trademarks or service marks have been appropriately capitalized. Alpha Books and Penguin Group (USA) Inc. cannot attest to the accuracy of this information. Use of a term in this book should not be regarded as affecting the validity of any trademark or service mark.

Part 1

Windows XP Everywhere: A Few Things You Need to Know

One of the great things about Windows XP is what technoid types refer to as its "consistent interface." In plain English, this just means that a lot of the techniques you learn in one Windows program today can also be used in another Windows program tomorrow. These techniques are things you'll be using day in and day out: starting programs, using menus and toolbars, manipulating windows, opening and printing documents, and installing programs and devices. The seven chapters that populate Part 1 take you through all of these techniques and quite a few more.

Chapter 1

New News Is Good News: New Windows XP Features

In This Chapter

➤ The new Windows XP system requirements

➤ Changes to the Windows XP look and feel

➤ A review of the new multimedia stuff in Windows XP

➤ A look at what's new with Windows XP and the Internet

➤ A sneak preview of the new Windows XP attractions

Over the past few years, whenever Microsoft shipped yet another new version of Windows, the release was greeted by an ever-louder chorus of yawns. Windows Me, for example, took not even the tiniest portion of the world by storm.

Why the Windows weariness? Part of the reason is that Microsoft, with its ravenous appetite for revenues, began picking up the pace and releasing new Windows versions faster than ever. It used to be that you could expect three years or more between versions, now they come at you every 12 or 18 months. People and businesses have only just grown used to the existing version and are reluctant to start from scratch after such a short time.

Another reason is that the Microsoft marketers and other mucky-mucks don't seem to have the faintest idea what they're doing when it comes to naming Windows. Windows 95 and Windows 98 made sense, but Windows 2000 wasn't a direct descendant of them. And don't get me started on the name Windows Me. People are confused about which Windows is the right one for them.

Finally, I also think that people are suffering from what I call "upgrade fatigue." They're simply tired of jumping on each new Windows bandwagon that lurches by. Sure, the new versions fix many of the problems in the old versions, but they invariably come with a few gremlins of their own. And, of course, it's always a hassle to move your settings and files from one version of Windows to another.

So does all this means that the release of Windows XP will also be relegated to the "Paint Drying" shelf in the Excitement Store? On the surface it would seem so: Windows XP made its debut only a little over a year since Windows Me; the XP moniker doesn't tell you a whole lot about what you're getting; and there's no reason to believe that people are any less reluctant to move to a new operating system. Ergo, yawnsville, right?

Maybe not. Speaking personally, this is the first version of Windows since Windows 95 that I installed on my main computer as soon as it came out. Why? Mostly because, having lived with pre-release versions of XP for about a year, I can see that XP combines the best of the old "consumer" line (Windows 95, 98, and Me) and the "business" line (Windows NT and 2000):

➤ It has the stability of Windows 2000, which has been praised far and wide for being solid as a rock.

➤ It has the hardware support and ease-of-use of Windows Me, which was friendly to almost any device manufactured in the recent past.

Note, though, that this doesn't mean there's now only one version of Windows. No, there are still two, but they've been amalgamated somewhat so that they share the same innards. The two versions are Windows XP Home Edition, which is aimed at people who use a computer at home, and Windows XP Professional, which is designed for working stiffs.

In the end, you'll have to make up your own mind about the relative worth of Windows XP. Part of that will be listening to others and, if you've taken the plunge, living with XP and your devices and applications for a while. But it also means understanding and appreciating what's new in XP so that you can take advantage of the improvements.

This chapter will help as it describes some of the many new and noteworthy features that Windows XP brings to your desktop. You'll be happy to know that I completely ignore all the high-end features that would warm the cockles of those hearts found only in system administrators, IT jocks, and other geeks. Instead, my focus here (as it is in the entire book) is on those features that are helpful and useful for normal people who just want to get their work or play done. This will be, by necessity, only a brief overview of these features. Happily, everything I discuss here is explained in more detail elsewhere in the book.

If you're just starting out with Windows, then *everything* in Windows XP will seem new to you. You can still read this chapter to get some idea of what to expect.

However, you might find that your time is better spent poring over Chapters 2 through 7.

More Windows Equals More Computer

With each new version of Windows, Microsoft puts together a "minimum system requirements" list, which tells you about the bare-bones system you need to have to run the new version. Unfortunately, these minimal requirements get beefed up with each new release, which may be yet another reason why people don't upgrade right away. In any case, Windows XP is no different and comes with its own requirements:

➤ **Processor**   The minimum is 233 MHz, and Microsoft recommends 300 MHz.

➤ **Memory**   Windows XP can run on a system with 64 megabytes (MB), but it's not pretty. The real minimum is 128MB.

➤ **Hard disk space**   You must have at least 1.5 gigabytes (GB) available to install and run Windows XP.

➤ **Display**   You must have a video card that supports the 800 × 600 resolution.

In all cases, the more you have, the better and faster Windows XP will run.

Some Spit and Polish on the Fit and Finish

Every version of Windows since Windows 95 has looked more or less the same. Sure, there were tweaks here and there, but the basic look went unchanged for about six years. Not so with Windows XP, which sports a snappy new outfit:

➤ **The desktop**   The boring sea of blue or green that usually covers the desktop area is gone in favor of a snappy looking image. Note, too, that the new desktop is almost totally devoid of icons, the lone exception now being the Recycle Bin in the lower right corner. Even if you put icons on the desktop, the new Desktop Cleanup Wizard will offer to hide any that you haven't used in a while.

➤ **The taskbar**   The taskbar looks and works more or less the same, but it has a few small and reasonable updates. First, the area on the right where the clock resides—the notification area, as it's called—now comes with the welcome ability to hide any icons that you haven't used it a while. Also, the taskbar can be "locked" into place, which should help prevent the accidental resizes and moves that plague new users. Finally, the taskbar is also now smart enough to combine similar program buttons into a single button, which helps to reduce taskbar clutter. The one change I'm against is the hiding of the handy Quick Launch toolbar, which is one of my favorite Windows features. Fortunately, it's easy to bring it back.

Figure 1.1

The new Windows XP desktop (this is the professional flavor).

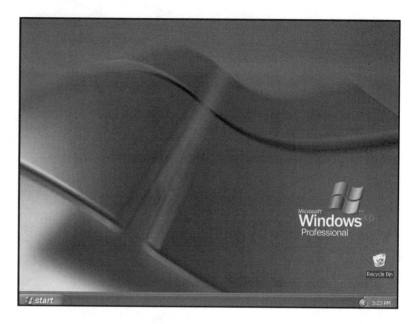

➤ **The Start menu**   The Start menu offers what may well be the biggest "look-and-feel" difference between XP and the Windows versions of yore. As you can see in Figure 1.2, clicking **Start** produces a menu that's unlike anything you've seen before. The icons on the left side offer one-click access to programs: **Internet** and **E-mail** are permanent members, and then cast of icons below them represent the programs you launch most often. The icons on the right side give you easy access to folders (such as **My Documents**) and XP features (such as the **Control Panel**). All your other programs and XP doodads are accessible via the **All Programs** icon.

➤ **The Control Panel**   The Control Panel—the place where you change Windows XP settings and options—has been given a total makeover in Windows XP. Similar to Windows Me, the XP Control Panel is organized into categories that cover broad areas such as Printers and Other Hardware, Performance and Maintenance, and Appearance and Themes.

➤ **The WebView panel**—When you open a folder in Windows XP, the left side of the window displays a WebView template, which is a collection of links to tasks and locations that are related to the contents of the folder. For example, when

Windows Wisdom

The new Control Panel looks good, but it isn't a total success because it's often hard to remember where things are stored. To help you out, I've summarized how to find every Control Panel icon in this book's inside back cover.

you select a file in the My Documents folder, the WebView panel sprouts links for renaming, moving, copying, printing, and deleting the file (see Figure 1.3).

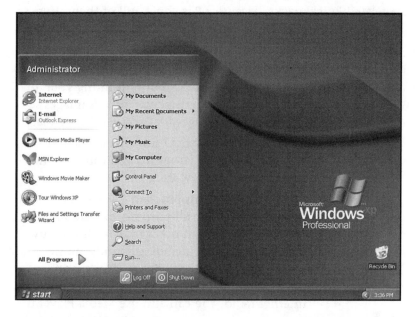

Figure 1.2

The Start menu has been totally retooled for Windows XP.

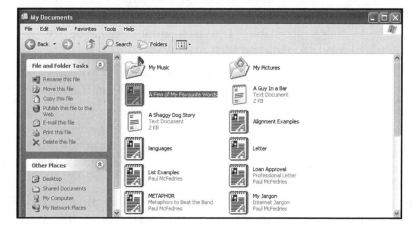

Figure 1.3

Windows XP's folder windows have a WebView panel on the left that contains links to common tasks and places.

➤ **Specialized folders**   Speaking of folders, Windows XP also comes with a number of specialized folders that are designed to store specific types of files. There are My Pictures for image files, My Music for audio files, My Movies for video files, and more. Each of these folders has a WebView panel that's tailored to the type of file the folder specializes in. Even better, it's possible to customize any other folder so that it behaves just like one of these specialized folders.

New Multimedia Bells and Whistles

It looks to me as though the Windows XP programmers spent the bulk of their time working on multimedia-related knickknacks, because XP is chock-full of them. Here's a brief summary of what's noteworthily new:

➤ **Graphics**   Besides the My Pictures folder that I mentioned earlier, Windows XP also enables you to order prints of image files over the Internet. There's also a Photo Printing Wizard that takes a lot of the guesswork out of printing your photos, and new Filmstrip view that enables you to display a folder's images sequentially, and the ability to reduce the size of images that you send via e-mail.

Jargon Jar

To **burn** files means to copy them to a CD-R or CD-RW disc.

➤ **CDs**   Wndows XP now supports CD-R and CD-RW drives, which means you can *burn* files to CD-R and CD-RW discs.

➤ **Media Player**   This program (it's version 8) has now become a true all-purpose, one-stop multimedia shop. You can use it to play almost any kind of media file, including sounds, music files, audio CDs, digital videos, DVDs, and media streamed over the Internet, including Internet radio. You can also use Media Player to copy music tracks from an audio CD to your hard disk, and you can write tracks back to a recordable CD or to a portable music device (such as an MP3 player).

➤ **Music**   Besides the music features found in Media Player, the new My Music folder enables you to organize your music by artist, album, genre, and more.

➤ **Document scanners**   For most newer scanners, Windows XP recognizes the device as soon as you plug it in and then makes it available to almost any program on your computer. That is, when you go to "open" a file, you can also choose to capture it straight from your scanner. Also, the revamped Scanner and Camera Wizard offers a wider range of features for controlling the scan.

➤ **Digital cameras**   Windows XP can work with most newer digital cameras, and the aforementioned Scanner and Camera Wizard makes it easy to grab the images you want. However, the best new camera feature in Windows XP is its ability to treat the camera storage module as a disk drive, which means you can work with the images directly from My Computer.

What's New on the Internet Front

The Internet has been a Big Deal for a while now, and Windows XP reflects that because all of its Internet tools are "mature" (that is, they've been through a number of versions) and most experts rank these tools among the best in the business. Here's a summary of what to expect:

➤ **Internet Explorer 6**   This version of Microsoft's World Wide Web browser feels a bit faster than its predecessors and has been given a bit of a facelift to make it look like the rest of Windows XP. Probably the most welcome new feature is its support for the management of "cookies," those little files that Web sites plant on your hard disk. You can set up cookie restrictions and Internet Explorer even offers an easy way to delete some or all of your cookie files. Finally, Internet Explorer also has a new Media bar that gives you easier access to Internet media.

➤ **Outlook Express 6**   This is Windows XP's Internet e-mail program. There isn't a whole lot that's new in this program, unfortunately. The most significant change is the ability to stop attachments that may contain viruses from being launched.

➤ **Windows Messenger**   This is the new name that's been given to MSN Messenger, Microsoft's instant messaging program. The messaging portion of the program is still basically the same, but Windows Messenger also includes features that enable you to share programs and to run "video chats" (although I don't talk about these more advanced features in this book).

➤ **.NET Passport**   Windows Messenger is also your gateway to a .NET Passport, which is administered through a Microsoft e-mail account. This gives you easier access to certain Web sites, and it will be a must if you plan on using any of Microsoft upcoming .NET services.

➤ **Internet Connection** *Firewall*   This new feature sets up a kind of digital roadblock that prevents malicious hackers from breaking into your computer while it's connected to the Internet.

A Few More Nouveau Riches

To wind up this look at what's shiny and new in Windows XP, here's a mixed bag of things that I discuss in the book:

➤ **User accounts**   This new feature is Windows XP's way of promoting inter-family and inter-office harmony. If you share a computer with

Jargon Jar

A **firewall** is a program that acts as a kind of sentry between you and the Internet. It lets you go out to the Internet, but it doesn't let any strange–looking data come in from the Internet.

other people, you can set everyone up with their own user account, which means they get their own desktop, Start menu, My Documents folder, Internet Explorer favorites, and Outlook Express e-mail accounts. You can also password-protect your stuff to ensure that no one peeks where they shouldn't.

➤ **Fast-user switching** This handy new feature supports the user accounts. What it does is allow you and your peers to switch immediately from one user to another while keeping each user's programs and windows open and ready for action.

➤ **Product activation** This is one of the more controversial of the new Windows XP features. What it means is that you have 15 days after installing Windows XP to "activate" the product with Microsoft (you can do this over the phone or over the Internet). If you don't, then Windows XP will refuse to run until you do. This activation is tied to a specific computer, so it means you can't install the same copy of Windows on multiple computers at the same time.

➤ **Files and Settings Transfer Wizard** This welcome new wizard enables you to take your settings from an existing Windows system—your e-mail data, Web favorites, desktop settings, and more—and copy them to your new Windows XP machine.

➤ **Network Setup Wizard** This wizard makes it easier than ever to set up a small-scale network in your home or small office. It's more streamlined than the Home Networking Wizard in Windows Me, and it does a better job of detecting things such as which computer has an Internet connection.

Chapter 2

A Field Guide to Windows XP

In This Chapter

➤ Checking out the Windows XP screen

➤ Handy mouse and keyboard techniques

➤ A cautionary tale about shutting Windows down

Thrill-seeking types enjoy diving into the deep end of any new pool they come across. The rest of us, however, prefer to check things out first by dipping a toe or two into the waters and then slipping ever-so-gently into the shallow end. The latter is the most sensible approach when it comes to Windows waters, which can be cold and murky to the uninitiated. You need to ease into the pool by learning a few basics about the layout of the screen and a few useful mouse and keyboard techniques. That's exactly what you'll do here in this chapter.

Note, however, that this chapter assumes your Windows XP pool has already been built and filled with water. That is, I assume that either your computer came with Windows XP already installed or else you have (or a nearby computer wonk has) up-graded your computer to Windows XP.

Starting Windows XP

After you poke your computer's power switch, Windows XP begins pulling itself up by its own bootstraps. This takes a few minutes on most machines, so this is an excellent time to grab a cup of coffee or tea and review your copy of *Feel the Fear and Do It Anyway*.

Windows Wisdom

The idea of Windows pulling it-self up by its own bootstraps is actually a pretty good way to describe the whole process of Windows starting itself up from scratch. In fact, it's the source of the verb *boot*, which means "to start a computer."

After your machine has churned through a few behind-the-scenes (and happily ignorable) chores, Windows XP's next move depends on which version you're using and on how it has been set up.

If you have Windows XP Home Edition, one of two things will happen:

➤ You end up at the Windows XP "desktop," which is the screen shown a bit later in Figure 2.3. If that's the case, you get a free pass to the next section of this chapter ("What's What in the Windows Screen").

➤ You're left staring at the "Welcome" screen, which will be similar to the one shown in Figure 2.1. In this case, just press the **Enter** key on your keyboard. I'll talk more about the Welcome screen later in the book (see Chapter 13, "Avoiding Fistfights While Sharing Your Coomputer").

Figure 2.1

This box might come your way while Windows XP Home Edition loads.

Gypsy

Karen

Paul

To begin, click your user name

Turn off computer

After you log on, you can add or change accounts.
Just go to Control Panel and click User Accounts.

If you're running Windows XP Professional, instead, then you'll see a box titled Welcome to Windows. Here's what you do from here:

1. The box asks you to **Press Ctrl+Alt+Delete to begin.** This arcane instruction means that you press and hold down both the **Ctrl** key and the **Alt** key on your keyboard, and then tap the **Delete** key. This gets you to another box that's titled

Log On to Windows, as shown in Figure 2.2. (At this point, you can release the **Ctrl** and **Alt** keys if you've still got them held down for dear life.)

2. What's happening here is that Windows XP wants you to supply the appropriate password before going any further. (The person who set up your system, or the person at work who administers your computer system, should have told you what your password is.) Go ahead and type your password in the **Password** box. (The letters you type will appear as dots, but that's okay. It's a security feature that prevents some snoop from eyeballing your password.) Then press **Enter** to continue loading Windows XP.

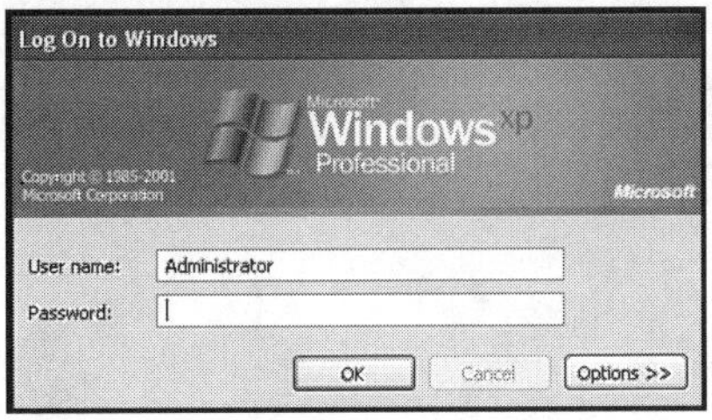

Figure 2.2

This box might come your way while Windows XP Professional loads.

A few seconds later, the dust clears and—voilà!—Windows XP is ready to roll.

What's What in the Windows Screen

The screen shown in Figure 2.3 is typical of the face that Windows XP Home Edition presents to the world. (The screen for XP Pro looks a bit different. Note, too, that your screen might have a different look, depending on how your computer manufacturer chose to set up your machine.) If you're new to Windows XP, you need to get comfortable with the lay of the Windows land. To that end, let's examine the vista you now see before you, which I divide into two sections: the desktop and the taskbar.

The Desktop

Ivory-tower computer types enjoy inventing metaphors for the way the rest of us use a computer. The idea is that more people will put up with a computer's shenanigans if using the computer reflects the way we do things in real life.

For Windows, the metaphor of choice is the humble desktop. The idea is that the Windows screen is comparable to the top of a real desk in a real office or den. Starting a program is like taking a folder full of papers out of storage and placing it on the desk. To do some work, of course, you need to pull papers out of a folder and place them on the desk. This is just like opening a file within the program (it could be a letter, a drawing, an e-mail message, or whatever). To extend the metaphor a

13

little, most programs also come with tools, such as a ruler, a calculator, and a calendar, that are the electronic equivalents of the tools you use at your desk.

Figure 2.3

The Windows XP Home Edition landscape.

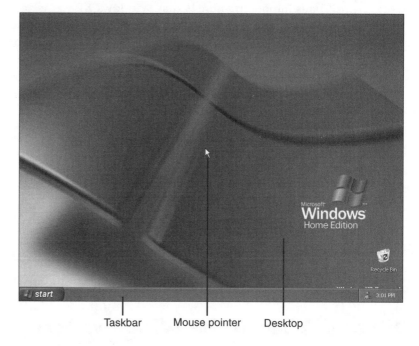

Taskbar   Mouse pointer   Desktop

So, officially, the vast expanse that takes up the bulk of the screen real estate is the Windows XP desktop, and it's where you'll do your work. (If looking at the same old screen all day long makes you feel a bit batty, changing to a different image, color, or psychedelic pattern is no sweat. I'll tell you how in Chapter 24, "Refurbishing the Desktop.")

The Taskbar

The multicolored strip along the bottom of the Windows XP screen is called the *taskbar*. The taskbar sports three distinct features (pointed out in Figure 2.4).

Start button   Notification area

Figure 2.4

The features of the Windows XP Home Edition taskbar.

Clock

14

➤ **Start button** Believe it or not, this tiny chunk of screen real estate is one of the most important features in all of Windows XP. As its name implies, the Start button is your starting point for most of the Windows XP features and goodies. I discuss the Start button in depth in Chapter 3, "Making Your Programs Do What You Want Them to Do."

➤ **Notification area** Windows XP populates this area with even more icons. In this case, these icons tell you a bit about what's happening with your machine. For example, an icon appears here when you add new hardware to your machine and another icon shows up while you're connected to the Internet.

➤ **Clock** The clock's purpose is obvious enough: It simply tells you the current time.

Windows Wisdom

The system tray's clock can also show you the date. To try it, move your mouse pointer until it sits over the time. After a second or two, the date pops up, just like that. If you ever need to change the time or date, double-click the clock.

The rest of the taskbar is empty right now, but that will change soon enough. As you'll see in the next chapter when I show you how to start programs, Windows XP uses the taskbar to keep track of all your running programs. You can use the taskbar to switch between the programs, shut them down, and do other handy things.

NEW! As a final note on the taskbar, Windows XP comes with a new feature for the notification area. This feature automatically hides those notification icons that you haven't used in a while. (I'll explain how you "use" a notification icon in various places throughout this book.) One fine day you'll start your computer and see a notice that tells you your unused icons have been hidden from view. If you want to see those icons, click the left-pointing arrow, as shown in Figure 2.5.

Click here to see your hidden icons ⌐

Figure 2.5

Windows XP hides your unused notification icons.

Some Mouse and Keyboard Fundamentals

Windows XP is supposed to have all kinds of fancy-schmancy features. How do I get at 'em?

Ah, that's where your mouse and keyboard come in. You use them as "input devices" to give Windows XP its marching orders. The next few sections show you the basic mouse and keyboard techniques you need to do just that.

15

Basic Mouse Maneuvers

If you're unfamiliar with Windows, there's a good chance that you're also unfamiliar with the mouse, the electromechanical (and, thankfully, toothless) mammal attached to your machine. If so, this section presents a quick look at a few mouse moves, which is important because much of what you do in Windows will involve the mouse in some way.

For starters, be sure the mouse is sitting on its pad or on your desk with the cord facing away from you. (If you have one of those newfangled cordless mice, move the mouse so that the buttons are facing away from you.) Rest your hand lightly on the mouse with your index finger on (but not pressing down) the left button and your middle finger on the right button (or the rightmost button). Southpaws need to reverse the fingering.

Figure 2.3, displayed earlier, showed you the *mouse pointer*. Find the pointer on your screen and then slowly move the mouse on its pad. As you do this, notice that the pointer moves in the same direction (although it will stop dead in its tracks when it hits the edge of the screen). Take a few minutes to practice moving the pointer to and fro using slow, easy movements.

To new users, the mouse seems an unnatural device that confounds common sense and often reduces the strongest among us to tears of frustration. The secret to mastering the mouse is twofold. First, use the same advice as was given to the person who wanted to get to Carnegie Hall: practice, practice, practice. Fortunately, with Windows XP being so mouse-dependent, you'll get plenty of chances to perfect your skills.

Second, understand all the basic mouse moves that are required of the modern-day mouse user. There are a half-dozen in all:

➤ **Point** This means that you move the mouse pointer so that it's positioned over some specified part of the screen. For example, "point at the Start button" means that you move the mouse pointer over the taskbar's Start button.

➤ **Click** This means that you press and immediately release the left mouse button to initiate some kind of action. Need a "fer instance"? Okay, point at the Start button and then click it. Instantly, a menu sprouts up in response to the click. (This is Windows XP's Start menu. I'll discuss it in detail in the next chapter. For now, you can get rid of the menu by clicking an empty section of the desktop.)

➤ **Double-click** This means that you press and release the left mouse button *twice*, one press right after the other (there should be little or no delay between each press). To give it a whirl, point at the time in the lower-right corner and then double-click. If all goes well, Windows XP will toss a box titled Date and Time Properties onto the desktop. You use this box to change the current date and time. To return this box from whence it came, click the button labeled **Cancel.** If nothing happens when you double-click, try to click as quickly as you can, and try not to move the mouse while you're clicking.

Windows Wisdom

Okay, so clicking initiates some kind of action, but so does double-clicking. What's the diff? The whole single-click versus double-click conundrum is one of the most confusing and criticized traits in Windows, and I'm afraid there's no easy answer. Some things require just a click to get going, whereas other things require a double-click. With experience, you'll eventually come to know which clicking technique is needed. Note, too, that if Windows seems to be missing some of your double-clicks, it's possible to change some settings to fix this. See Chapter 29, "When Windows Won't Work: Troubleshooting Common Problems."

➤ **Right-click** This means that you press and immediately release the *right* mouse button. In Windows XP, the right-click is used almost exclusively to display a creature called the *shortcut menu*. To see one, right-click an empty part of the desktop. Windows XP displays a menu with a few common commands related to the desktop. To remove this menu, *left*-click the desktop.

➤ **Drag** This means that you point at some object, press and *hold down* the left mouse button, move the mouse, and then release the button. You almost always use this technique to move an object from one place to another. For example, try dragging any of the desktop icons. (To restore apple-pie order to the desktop, right-click the desktop, click **Arrange Icons** in the shortcut menu, and then click **By Name.**)

➤ **Scroll** This means that you turn the little wheel that's nestled in between the left and right mouse buttons. In programs that support scrolling, you use this technique to move up and down within a document. The wheel is a relatively new innovation, so your mouse might not have one. If not, never fear, as Windows provides other ways to navigate a document. I tell you about those other ways to navigate a document in Chapter 4, "Your Twenty-Minute Window Workout."

Common Keyboard Conveniences

I mentioned earlier that getting comfy with your mouse is crucial if you want to make your Windows XP life as easy as possible. That's not to say, however, that the keyboard never comes in handy as a timesaver. On the contrary, Windows XP is chock-full of keyboard shortcuts that are sometimes quicker than the standard mouse techniques. I'll tell you about these shortcuts as we go along. For now, let's run through some of the standard keyboard parts and see how they fit into the Windows way of doing things.

➤ **The Ctrl and Alt keys**   If you press **Ctrl** (it's pronounced "control") or **Alt** (it's pronounced "alt"), nothing much happens, but that's okay because nothing much is supposed to happen. You don't use these keys by themselves, but as part of *key combinations*. (The Shift key often gets into the act as well.) For example, hold down the **Ctrl** key with one hand, use your other hand to tap the **Esc** key, and then release **Ctrl**. Like magic, you see a menu of options sprout from the Start button. (To hide this menu again, press **Esc** by itself.)

Windows Wisdom

Windows XP has all kinds of keyboard combo shortcuts, so they pop up regularly throughout the book. Because I'm *way* too lazy to write out something like "Hold down the **Ctrl** key with one hand, use your other hand to tap the **Esc** key, and then release **Ctrl**" each time, however, I use the following shorthand notation instead: "Press **Hold+Tap**," where **Hold** is the key you hold down and **Tap** is the key you tap. In other words, instead of the previous long-winded sentence, I say this: "Press **Ctrl+Esc**." (On rare occasions, a third key joins the parade, so you might see something like "Press **Ctrl+Alt+Delete**." In this case, you hold down the first two keys and then tap the third key.)

➤ **The Esc key**   Your keyboard's Esc (or Escape) key is your all-purpose get-me-the-heck-out-of-here key. For example, you just saw that you can get rid of the Start menu by pressing Esc. In many cases, if you do something in Windows XP that you didn't want to do, you can reverse your tracks with a quick tap (or maybe two or three) on Esc.

➤ **The numeric keypad**   On a standard keyboard layout, the numeric keypad is the separate collection of numbered keys on the right. The numeric keypad usually serves two functions, and you toggle between these functions by pressing the **Num Lock** key. (Most keyboards have a Num Lock indicator light that tells you when Num Lock is on.) When Num Lock is on, you can use the numeric keypad to type numbers. When Num Lock is off, the other symbols on the keys become active. For example, the 8 key's upward-pointing arrow becomes active, which means you can use it to move up within a program. Some keyboards (called *extended keyboards*) have a separate keypad for the insertion point movement keys, and you can keep Num Lock on all the time.

Making It Legit: Activating Your Copy of Windows XP

NEW! After you've had Windows XP (or a new computer that came with Windows XP) for a short time (a day or two), one of two things will happen:

➤ When you start Windows XP, a message will appear on your screen telling you that **Your Windows product must be activated within X day(s)** (where X is some number between 1 and 15).

➤ When Windows XP is running, a message will pop up from the taskbar's notification areas telling you that you have **X days until activation**.

What your computer is trying to tell you is that you have to "activate" Windows XP with Microsoft or else Windows will simply stop working. This is Microsoft's way of checking for illegal copies of Windows. What happens is that Windows checks the hardware configuration of your computer and ties it to the Product ID of your copy of Windows XP. Don't worry: no personal information is ever sent to Microsoft and there are no fees or other hidden goings-on. Here's what you have to do:

1. If you see the dialog box at startup, click **Yes;** if, instead, you see the taskbar message, click the message.

2. In the window that appears, click **Next.** If your computer is set up to access the Internet, the activation process will happen automatically, so skip to step 4. Otherwise, another window will show up to let you know that Windows XP will dial a telephone number to process the activation.

3. Click **Next.** The activation program elbows your computer's modem and asks it to dial a number. When the call goes through, try to ignore the very strange noises that your modem makes while it contacts the "activation server."

4. When the activation is done, you'll see a message telling you the good news. Click **Finish.**

Quittin' Time: Shutting Down Windows

When you've stood just about all you can stand of your computer for one day, it's time to close up shop. Please tape the following to your cat's forehead so that you never forget it: *Never, I repeat, never, turn off your computer's power while Windows XP is still running.* Doing so can lead to data loss, a trashed configuration, and accelerated hair loss that those new pills don't help.

Now that I've scared the daylights out of you, let's see the proper procedure for shutting down your computer. To begin, click the **Start** button to pop up the Windows XP Start menu. The route you take from here depends on a couple of different factors:

> ➤ If you have Windows XP Home, or if you have Windows XP Professional that isn't running on a corporate network, then click the **Turn off computer** option. Windows XP displays the little box shown in Figure 2.6. Use your mouse to click the option you want (I explain them in a sec).

Figure 2.6

In Windows XP Home Edition, when you click the Start menu's Turn off computer option, you see this dialog box.

> ➤ If you're running Windows XP Professional on a corporate network, click **Shut Down** to see the box shown in Figure 2.7. Use the **What do you want the computer to do?** list to choose the action you want (they're explained below) and then click **OK**. If you're not sure how to work the list, see "Dealing with the Dialog Boxes" section in Chapter 3.

Figure 2.7

In Windows XP Professional, when you click the Start menu's Shut Down option, you see this dialog box.

Now click one of the following choices:

> ➤ **Stand By** Choose this option (which is only available on some computers) to put your machine in *standby mode*, which powers down just the monitor and hard disk.

20

➤ **Turn Off** (XP Home) or **Shut Down** (XP Pro)   Choose this option if you're going to turn off the computer's power.

➤ **Restart**   Choose this option if you want to start Windows XP all over again. For example, if you find that Windows is acting strangely, restarting can often put things right.

➤ **Log Off** *User* (XP Pro only)   Choose this option to log off your network.

➤ **Hibernate** (in Windows XP Home, hold down the **Shift** key to see this option) Choose this option (which, again, is only available on newer computers) if you're going to shut down your computer, but you also want Windows XP to re-member all your open windows and documents and to restore them the next time you crank things up. If you go this route, it takes a bit longer for Windows XP to prepare itself for bed, but your machine will rouse from its slumbers much faster the next time you start it.

The Least You Need to Know

➤ **Screen anatomy**   The Windows XP screen is carved into two main areas: the *desktop*—the large area that covers most of your monitor—and the *taskbar*—the thin strip along the bottom of the screen.

➤ **Taskbar features**   The taskbar consists of the Start button, a space for run-ning program icons, and the notification area.

➤ **Standard mouse dance steps**   The three most-used mouse movements are the *click* (quickly pressing and releasing the left mouse button), the *double-click* (two quick clicks), and the *drag* (holding down the left button and mov-ing the mouse).

➤ **Keyboard shorthand**   A *key combination* involves holding down one key, pressing a second key, and then releasing the first key. I signify such a combo with the notation **Hold+Tap** (where **Hold** is the key you hold down and **Tap** is the key you tap); For example, **Ctrl+Esc.**

➤ **Shutting down Windows**   Click **Start**, click **Turn off computer,** and then click **Turn Off.**

Chapter 3

Making Your Programs Do What You Want Them to Do

In This Chapter

➤ A couple of ways to get a program off the ground

➤ Learning about pull–down menus, toolbars, and dialog boxes

➤ Getting the hang of the taskbar

➤ Techniques for switching between programs

➤ Shutting down a program

If you want to get your computer to do anything even remotely nonpaperweight-like, you need to launch and work with a program or three. For example, if you want to write a memo or a letter, you need to fire up a word processing program; if you want to draw pictures, you need to crank up a graphics program. If you want to use the Windows spreadsheet program, well … there isn't one. Windows XP comes with a passel of programs, but a spreadsheet isn't among them. If you want to crunch numbers, you need to get a third-party spreadsheet program such as Microsoft Excel or Lotus 1-2-3.

On the other hand, Windows XP *does* come with a decent collection of programs that enable you to perform most run-of-the-mill computing tasks. This chapter shows you how to get at those programs as well as how to mess with them after they're up and running.

How to Start a Program

If you're interested in starting a program, then you might think that the Start button in the lower-left corner of the screen would be a promising place to begin. If so, give yourself a pat on the back (or have a nearby loved one do it) because that's exactly right. Go ahead and use your mouse to point at the Start button and then click. As you can see in Figure 3.1, Windows XP responds by tossing a rather large box onto the screen. This is called the *Start menu*, and you'll be visiting this particular place a lot in your Windows XP travels.

Figure 3.1

The Start menu: your Windows XP launch pad.

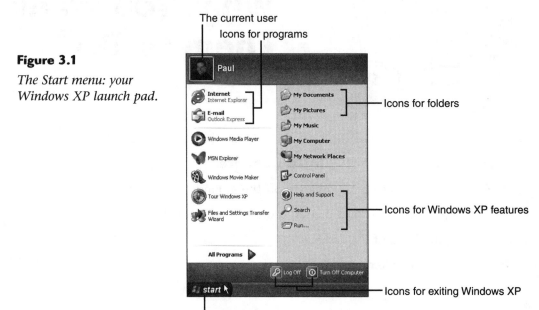

A Start Menu Summary

The Start menu is populated with all kinds of interesting-looking pictures and text. Each little picture and the text beside it is called an *icon* in the Windows world. An icon is a representation of something that exists on your computer. To see what I mean, let's run through the various icons that exist on the Start menu. (Again, however, I need to point out that computer manufacturers can and will customize the Start menu, so yours may be populated with a different set of icons.) As pointed out in Figure 3.1, I divide the icons into four general categories: programs, folders, features, and exiting.

For the programs, the initial Start menu has eight icons:

➤ **Internet**   This icon represents the Internet Explorer program, which you use to make your way around the World Wide Web. I talk about this program in Chapter 18, "It's a Small Web After All: Using Internet Explorer."

Windows Wisdom

Clicking the Start button is probably the most common way to get at the Start menu, but Windows XP also offers a couple of keyboard methods that you should have in your arsenal. No matter what kind of keyboard you have, you can press **Ctrl+Esc.** But, if you have the Microsoft Natural Keyboard—the one with the alphanumeric keys split down the middle and the curvaceous look—press the key with the Windows logo on it (▦). Most recent keyboards sport the Windows logo key. In almost all cases, the key is located between the Ctrl and Alt keys.

➤ **E-mail** This icon represents the Outlook Express program, which you use to send and read e-mail messages. You can get the scoop on this program in Chapter 20, "Sending and Receiving E-Mail Missives."

➤ **Windows Media Player** This icon represents the Windows Media Player program, which you use to play music, watch DVD movies, create audio CDs, and perform other multimedia tricks. (See Chapter 11, "Sights and Sounds: Music and Other Multimedia.")

➤ **MSN Explorer** This is yet another Web browser. I don't talk about this program in this book.

➤ **Windows Movie Maker** This icon represents the Windows Movie Maker program, which enables you to capture and edit digital video footage. (See Chapter 12, "Creating Movies with Windows Movie Maker.")

➤ **Tour Windows XP** This icon represents a multimedia tour of what Windows XP has to offer.

➤ **Files and Settings Transfer Wizard** This icon represents a program that makes it easy for you to transfer your documents and settings from an old computer to Windows XP. (See Chapter 27, "Smooth System Sailing: Wielding the System Tools.")

➤ **All Programs** This icon represents another menu that lists all the other programs installed on your computer. (See the next section, "Maneuvering Around the Start Menu," to learn more about this icon.)

You should know, as well, that the space below and including the Windows Media Player icon will soon be filled with more icons that represent the last six programs you've worked with most often.

Before I talk about the folder icons, the first thing you should know is that a *folder* is a storage location on your computer's hard disk. What do you store in a folder? You store files, which generally come in two flavors: *documents* that you create yourself and *program files* that run the programs installed on your computer. The Start menu is loaded with five icons:

➤ **My Documents**   This icon represents the folder where you'll store most of the documents that you create. (See Chapter 5, "Saving, Opening, Printing, and Other Document Lore.")

➤ **My Pictures**   This icon represents the folder where you'll store your picture files (which are also known as graphics file and image files). (Check out Chapter 8, "Playing with Pictures.")

➤ **My Music**   This icon represents the folder where you'll store your music files. (See Chapter 11 for more info.)

➤ **My Computer**   This icon represents the folder that contains everything on your computer, including your hard disk, CD-ROM or DVD-ROM drive, floppy disk drive, and so on. (To get the details, head for Chapter 6, "Using My Computer to Fiddle with Files and Folders.")

➤ **My Network Places**   This icon represents your local area network, if your computer is attached to one. (See Chapter 31, "Using Windows XP's Networking Features.")

For the Windows XP features, the Start menu is home to four icons:

➤ **Control Panel**   This icon represents the Windows XP Control Panel feature, which you use to customize Windows XP. I talk about the Control Panel throughout this book. For a summary of what's in the Control Panel, see this book's inside back cover.

➤ **Help and Support**   This icon represents the Windows XP Help feature, which offers guidance and instruction on the various Windows XP bits and pieces.

➤ **Search**   This icon represents the Search feature, which you use to search for files on your hard disk, people in your Windows address book, information on the Internet, and more. I discuss file searching in Chapter 6 and Internet searching in Chapter 18.

➤ **Run**   This icon represents the Run feature, which you use to start programs that aren't accessible via the Start menu, and sometimes to install programs. Chapter 6 is the place to go to find out how this works.

Last and quite possibly least, for exiting Windows XP, the Start menu lines up two icons:

➤ **Log Off**   This icon represents the logging off process, which enables another person to use Windows XP with their own settings and program. I talk about setting up Windows XP for different users in Chapter 13, "Avoiding Fistfights While Sharing Your Computer."

➤ **Turn Off Computer** (Windows XP Home) or **Shut Down** (Windows XP Professional)   This icon represents the shutdown process, which you can use to either turn off or restart your computer. (See Chapter 2, "A Field Guide to Windows XP," for the specifics.)

Maneuvering Around the Start Menu

Now that you've met the denizens of the Start menu, you need to know how to make them do something useful. To launch an icon, you have two possibilities:

➤ For every icon except All Programs, you need only click the icon, and Windows XP launches the program, folder, or feature without further ado.

➤ Clicking the **All Programs** icon brings up another menu, as shown in Figure 3.2. As you can see, this new menu is filled with even more icons, some of which are duplicates of icons on the Start menu (Internet Explorer, Outlook Express, and Windows Media Player). To launch one of these icons, click it with your mouse.

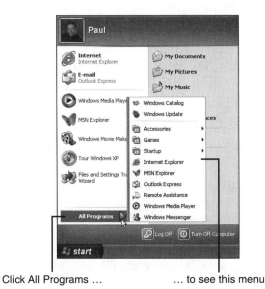

Click All Programs …   … to see this menu

Figure 3.2

Launching the All Programs icon displays a menu of programs.

Notice, however, that two of the icons (Accessories and Startup) have little arrow on the right. When you click either one of these icons, a new menu (called a *submenu*) slides out to the right of the icon. For example, clicking the Accessories icon displays the submenu shown in Figure 3.3.

Figure 3.3

Some icons exist only to display a submenu that contains even more icons.

When you click Accessories ...

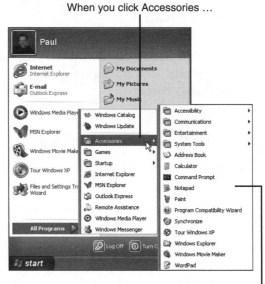

... Windows yanks out this submenu

Don't be surprised if you find yourself wading through two or three of these submenus to get the program you want. For example, here are the steps you'd follow to fire up Solitaire, one of Windows XP's addictive card games:

1. Click the **Start** button to display the Start menu.

2. Click **All Programs** to open the menu.

3. Click **Accessories** to open the submenu.

4. Click **Games** to open yet another submenu.

5. Click **Solitaire.** Windows XP launches the Solitaire program.

In the future, I abbreviate these long-winded Start menu procedures by using a comma (,) to separate each item you click, like so: "Select **Start, All Programs, Accessories, Games, Solitaire.**"

Windows Wisdom

Here's a bonus: To display a submenu, you don't even need to click the icon. Instead, just point at the icon with your mouse and in a second or two the submenu will drift out automatically.

Now What? Getting a Program to Do Something Useful

Okay, so I know how to get a program running. What's next?

Ah, now you get to go on a little personal power trip because this section shows you how to boss around your programs. Specifically, you learn how to work with pull-down menus, toolbars, and dialog boxes.

Making It Go: Selecting Commands from Pull-Down Menus

Each program you work with has a set of commands and features that define the majority of what you can do with the program. Most of these commands and features are available via the program's *drop-down menus*. Oh sure, there are easier ways to tell a program what to do (I talk about some of them later in this chapter), but pull-down menus are special because they offer a complete road map for any program. This section gets you up to speed on this crucial Windows topic.

I'm going to use the My Computer program as an example for the next page or two. If you feel like following along, go ahead and launch the program by selecting **Start, My Computer.**

The first thing you need to know is that a program's pull-down menus are housed in the *menu bar*, the horizontal strip that runs just beneath the blue title bar. Each word in the menu bar represents a pull-down menu. Figure 3.4 points out the menu bar in My Computer.

The various items that run across the menu bar (such as File, Edit, and View in My Computer) are the names of the menus. To see (that is, *pull down*) one of these menus, use either of the following techniques:

➤ Use your mouse to click the menu name. For example, click **View** to pull down the View menu.

➤ Hold down the **Alt** key and examine the menu bar once again. See how each menu name sprouts an underline under one letter. That underline tells you that you can pull down the menu by holding down **Alt** and pressing the underlined letter on your keyboard. For example, the "V" in View gets underlined when you hold down Alt, so you can pull down this menu by pressing **Alt+V.**

The menu bar

When you click View
in the menu bar ...

... Windows pulls
down the View menu

Figure 3.4

My Computer's View menu.

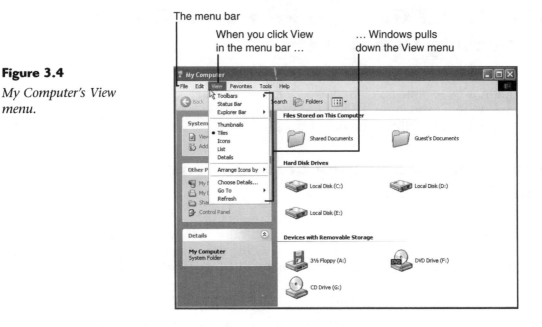

The various items you see in the menu are called *commands*. From here, you use any of the following techniques to select a command:

Windows Wisdom

What if you don't want to select the commands from a menu you already opened? Remove the menu by clicking any empty part of the program's window; pull down a different menu by clicking its name in the menu bar; press **Alt** by itself; press the **Esc** key twice; or press **Alt** plus the underlined letter of the new menu.

➤ Use your mouse to click the command you want.

➤ From your keyboard, use the down arrow key (↓) or the up arrow key (↑) to highlight the command, and then press **Enter**.

➤ Press the underlined letter in the command. For example, the "R" in the View menu's Refresh command is underlined, so you can select this command by pressing **R**. (Go ahead and try this example; you won't hurt anything.)

Throughout this book, I tell you to select a pull-down menu command by separating the menu name and command name with a comma (,), like this: "Select the **View, Refresh** command."

What happens next depends on which command you picked. Here's a summary of the various possibilities:

➤ **The command runs without further fuss**
This is the simplest scenario, and it just means

that the program carries out the command, no questions asked. For example, clicking the Refresh command updates My Computer's display automatically.

➤ **Another menu appears**   As shown in Figure 3.5, when you click the **View** menu's **Arrange Icons** command, a submenu appears on the right (similar to what you saw earlier with the Start menu). You then click the command you want to execute from the new menu.

➤ **The command is toggled on or off**   Some commands operate like light switches: They toggle certain features of a program on and off. When the feature is on, a small check mark appears to the left of the command to let you know. Selecting the command turns off the feature and removes the check mark. If you select the command again, the feature turns back on and the check mark reappears. For example, click the **View** menu's **Status Bar** command, which activates the status bar at the bottom of the My Computer window (see Figure 3.5).

➤ **An option is activated**   Besides having features that you can toggle on and off, some programs have flexible features that can assume three or more different states. My Computer, for example, gives you five ways to display the contents of your computer, according to your choice of one of the following View menu commands: Thumbnails, Tiles, Icons, List, and Details (see Chapter 26, "Renovating My Computer"). Because these states are mutually exclusive (you can select only one at a time), you need some way of knowing which of the four commands is currently active. That's the job of the *option mark:* a small dot that appears to the left of the active command (see the Tiles command in Figure 3.5).

➤ **A dialog box appears**   Dialog boxes are pesky little windows that show up whenever the program needs to ask you for more information. You learn more about them in the "Dealing with Dialog Boxes" section, later in this chapter.

Windows Wisdom

Many Windows programs (and Windows XP itself) use **shortcut menus** to give you quick access to oft-used commands. The idea is that you right-click something and the program pops up a small menu of commands, each of which is somehow related to whatever it is you right-clicked. If you see the command you want, great: Just click it (using the left button this time). If you don't want to select a command from the menu, either left-click an empty part of the window or press **Esc.**

The check mark indicates an activated feature

Select a command that has an arrow …

… and Windows coughs up a submenu

Figure 3.5

A few pull-down menu features.

The option mark indicates the activated command in this group

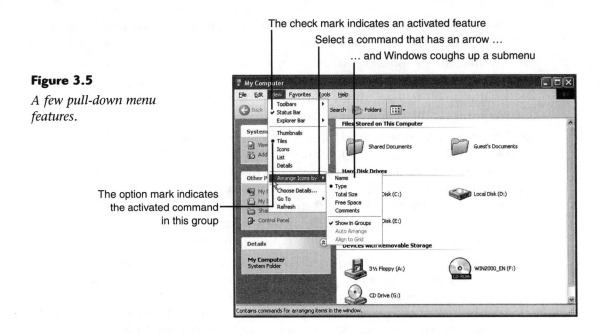

Your Click Is My Command: Toolbar Basics

One of their most useful inventions has to be the *toolbar*. This is a collection of easily accessible icons designed to give you push-button access to common commands and features. No unsightly key combinations to remember; no pull-down menu forests to get lost in.

Toolbars play a big role in Windows XP, and you can reap some big dividends if you get to know how they work. Although most Windows XP components have a toolbar or two as standard equipment, let's stick with My Computer. As you can see in Figure 3.6, the toolbar is the horizontal strip located just south of the menu bar.

Most toolbar icons are buttons that represent commands you'd normally access by using the pull-down menus. All you have to do is click a button, and the program runs the command, no questions asked.

Here's a summary of a few other toolbar-related techniques you ought to know:

➤ **Toolbar text**   Most toolbar buttons advertise what they do using nothing more than an icon. Rather than trying to decipher the icon, some toolbars let you display text that at least gives you the name of each button. In My Computer, for example, select **View, Toolbars, Customize** to display the Customize Toolbar dialog box. Now use the **Text options** list to select **Show text labels**, and then click **Close**.

➤ **Button banners**   If the toolbar doesn't offer text labels, you can still find out the name of a particular button by pointing at it with your mouse. After a second or two, a banner—sometimes called a *tooltip*—with the button name pops up.

➤ **Hiding and showing toolbars**   In most programs, you toggle a toolbar on and off by selecting the **View, Toolbar** command. If a program offers multiple toolbars (as does My Computer), select the **View, Toolbars** command to display a submenu of the available toolbars, and then select the one you want.

➤ **Drop-down buttons**   You'll occasionally come across toolbar buttons that are really drop-down menu wannabes. In My Computer, the View "button" is an example of the species. As shown in Figure 3.6, you click the downward-pointing arrow to see a list of commands.

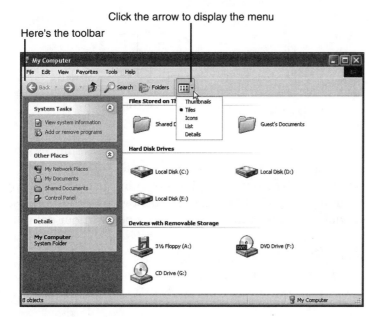

Click the arrow to display the menu

Here's the toolbar

Figure 3.6

Like most Windows XP components, My Computer comes with a toolbar.

Dealing with Dialog Boxes

I mentioned earlier that after you select some menu commands, the program might require more info from you. For example, if you run a Print command, the program might want to know how many copies of the document you want to print.

In these situations, the program sends an emissary to parley with you. These emissaries, called *dialog boxes*, are one of the most ubiquitous features in the Windows world. This section preps you for your dialog box conversations by showing you how to work with every type of dialog box control you're likely to encounter. (They're called *controls* because you use them to manipulate the different dialog box settings.)

Before starting, it's important to keep in mind that most dialog boxes like to monopolize your attention. When one is on the screen, you usually can't do anything else in the program (such as select a pull-down menu). Deal with the dialog box first, and then you can move on to other things.

Conveniently, the WordPad program offers a wide variety of dialog boxes, so I use it for most of the examples in this section. If you're following along, launch the program by selecting **Start, All Programs, Accessories, WordPad.** Begin by selecting WordPad's **View, Options** command to have the Options dialog box report for duty, as shown in Figure 3.7.

Figure 3.7

WordPad's Options dialog box demonstrates quite a few dialog box features.

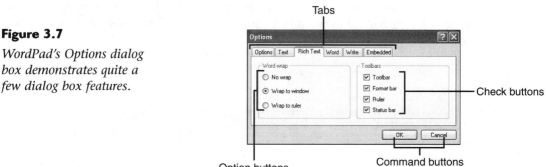

Okay, let's get started:

➤ **Command buttons**   Clicking one of these buttons executes whatever command is written on the button. The two examples shown in the Options dialog box are the most common. You click **OK** to close the dialog box and put the settings into effect, and you click **Cancel** to close the dialog box without doing anything.

➤ **Check boxes**   Windows uses a check box to toggle program features on and off. Clicking the check box either adds a check mark (meaning the feature will get turned on when you click **OK**) or removes the check mark (meaning the feature gets turned off when you click **OK**).

➤ **Option buttons**   If a program feature offers three or more possibilities, the dialog box will offer an option button for each state, and only one button can be activated (that is, have a black dot inside its circle) at a time. You activate an option button by clicking it.

➤ **Tabs**   Click any of the tabs displayed across the top of some dialog boxes and you see a new set of controls. (At this point, you no longer need the Options dialog box, so click **Cancel** to shut it down.)

➤ **Text boxes**   You use these controls to type text data. To see some examples, select WordPad's **Format, Paragraph** command to get to the Paragraph dialog box, shown in Figure 3.8. The **Left, Right,** and **First line** controls are all text boxes. (The Paragraph dialog box has served its purpose, so click **Cancel**.)

34

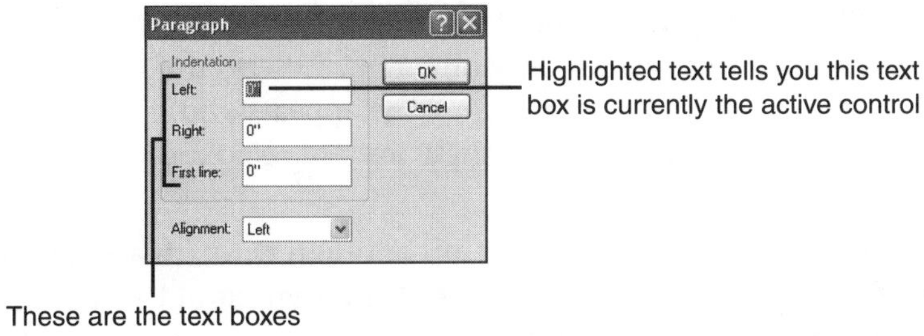

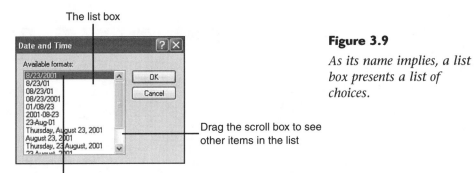

Figure 3.8

Some sample text boxes.

Highlighted text tells you this text box is currently the active control

These are the text boxes

➤ **List boxes**   These controls display a list of items and you select an item by clicking it. An example can be seen if you select WordPad's **Insert**, **Date and Time** command, shown in Figure 3.9. (After you've played around a bit, click **Cancel** to close this dialog box.)

The list box

Figure 3.9

As its name implies, a list box presents a list of choices.

Drag the scroll box to see other items in the list

The highlight shows you the currently selected item

➤ **Combo boxes**   These hybrid controls combine a list box and a text box. You can either select the item you want from the list or type it in the text box. In Figure 3.10, WordPad's Font dialog box shows several examples (select **Format**, **Font** to get there).

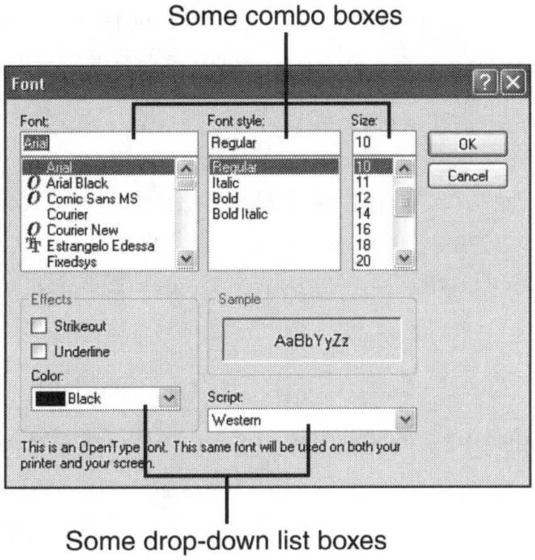

Some combo boxes

Figure 3.10

WordPad's Font dialog box offers several examples of both combo boxes and drop-down list boxes.

Some drop-down list boxes

35

➤ **Drop-down list boxes** These controls represent yet another example of the list box genre. In this case, at first you see only one item. However, if you click the downward-pointing arrow on the right, the full list appears and it becomes much like a regular list box. (That's enough of the Font dialog box, so click **Cancel.**)

➤ **Spin boxes** These controls enable you to cycle up or down through a series of numbers. To see an example, select WordPad's **File, Print** command to wake up the Print dialog box, shown in Figure 3.11. The spin box is named **Number of copies.** The left part of the spin box is a simple text box into which you can type a number; however, the right part of the spin box has tiny up and down arrow buttons. You click the up arrow to increase the value, and you click the down arrow to decrease the value. (When you're finished, click **Cancel** to return the Print dialog box from whence it came.)

Figure 3.11

Click the spin box arrows to cycle up or down through a range of values.

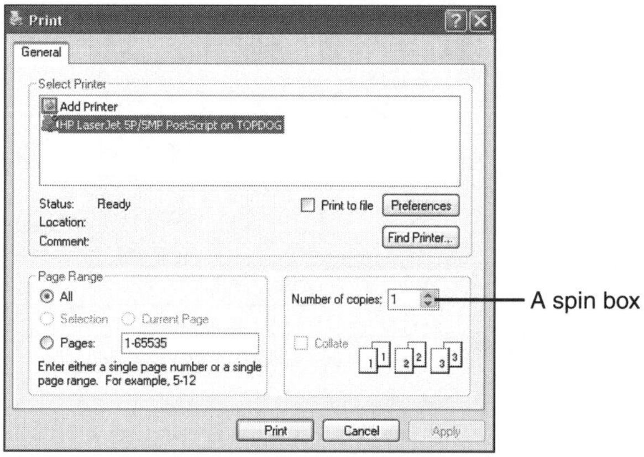

A spin box

Switching from One Program to Another

When you fire up a program, Windows XP marks the occasion by adding a button to the taskbar. If you then coax another program or two onto the screen (remember, Windows XP is capable of *multitasking*—running multiple programs simultaneously), each one gets its own taskbar button.

For example, Figure 3.12 shows Windows XP with two programs up and running: WordPad and Paint. (To run the latter, select **Start, All Programs, Accessories, Paint.**) It looks as though Paint has lopped off a good portion of the WordPad window, but in reality Windows XP is just displaying Paint "on top" of WordPad. In addition, the taskbar has changed in two ways:

➤ There are now buttons for both WordPad and Paint in the taskbar.

➤ In the taskbar, the *active* program's button (the Paint button in this figure) looks as though it's been pressed. (The active program is the one you're currently slaving away in.)

Windows Wisdom

Although it's true that Windows XP is happy to deal with multiple running programs—think of it as the electronic equivalent of walking and chewing gum at the same time—that doesn't mean you can just start every program you have and leave them running all day. The problem is that because each open program usurps a chunk of Windows' resources, the more programs you run, the slower each program performs, including Windows itself. The number of applications you can fire up at any one time depends on how much horsepower your computer has. You probably need to play around a bit to see just how many applications you can launch before things get too slow.

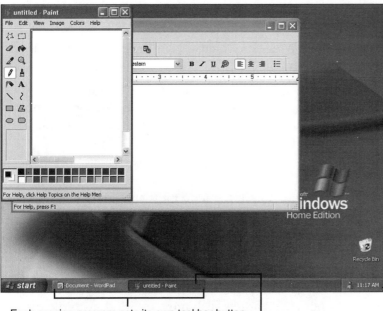

Figure 3.12

Windows XP with two programs on the go.

Each running program gets its own taskbar button

The button for the active program appears pressed

The taskbar has another trick up its digital sleeve: You can switch from one running program to another by clicking the latter's taskbar button. For example, when I click the WordPad button, the WordPad window comes to the fore, as shown in Figure 3.13.

37

Figure 3.13

You can use the taskbar buttons to switch from one program to another.

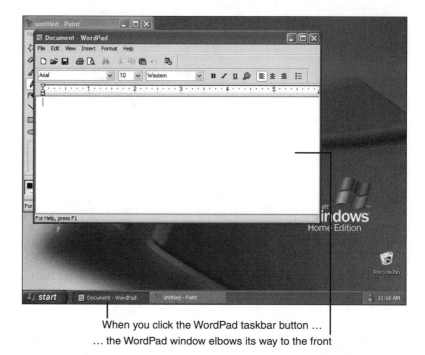

When you click the WordPad taskbar button ...
... the WordPad window elbows its way to the front

Besides clicking the taskbar buttons, Windows XP gives you three other ways to leap from one running program to another:

➤ **Click the program's window**   This is perhaps the simplest and most obvious method. All you do is point the mouse inside the program's window and then click. This method is most useful if your hand is already on the mouse and you can see at least part of the window you want to activate.

➤ **Hold down Alt and tap Tab**   When you do this, Windows XP displays a box that boasts an icon for each running program. Each time you press Tab, the next icon gets highlighted. After you highlight the icon for the program you want, release the Alt key, and Windows XP then switches to the program. This technique is useful if your hands are on the keyboard and you have only a few programs running.

➤ **Hold down Alt and tap Esc**   This method is similar to the Alt+Tab method in that Windows XP cycles through the open programs. The difference is that with each tap of the Esc key, Windows XP brings each program window to the fore. Use this method when you want to check out the contents of each window before you decide which program you want to work with.

When Enough's Enough: Quitting a Program

When you're finished with a particular program, you should close it to keep your screen uncluttered and to reduce the load on Windows' resources. The easiest way to do this is to click the Close button—the × in the upper-right corner of the program's window.

You can also use a few other methods, which you may find faster under certain circumstances:

➤ Press **Alt+F4**.

➤ Pull down the program's **File** menu and select the **Exit** command (or, more rarely, the **Close** command).

➤ Right-click the program's taskbar button and then click **Close** in the little menu that appears.

Depending on the program you're closing and the work you were doing with it, you might be asked whether you want to "save" some files.

See Also

I tell you how to handle saving documents in Chapter 5, "Saving, Opening, Printing, and Other Document Lore." See the section titled "The All-Important Save Command."

The Least You Need to Know

➤ **Starting a program**   Click the **Start** button to display the Start menu, and then click the command or submenus required to launch the program.

➤ **Selecting a pull-down menu command**   First display the menu by clicking its name in the menu bar, and then click the command.

➤ **Dialog box command buttons**   Click **OK** to put dialog box settings into effect; click **Cancel** to bail out of a dialog box without doing anything; click **Help** to view the program's Help system.

➤ **Switching between running programs**   Click the taskbar buttons. Alternatively, click the program window if you can see a chunk of it, or else press **Alt+Tab**.

➤ **Quitting a program**   Click the **Close** × button. You can also usually get away with selecting the program's **File, Exit** command or pressing **Alt+F4.**

Chapter 4

Your Twenty-Minute Window Workout

In This Chapter

➤ Window gadgets and gewgaws

➤ Minimizing and maximizing windows

➤ Moving and sizing windows

➤ How to wield window scrollbars

Windows gets its name because, as you saw in the previous chapter, each program that you launch shows up on the screen in a box, and that box is called a *window*. Why they named them "windows" instead of, say, "boxes" or "frames," I can't imagine. After all, have *you* ever seen a window on the top of a desk? I thought not.

Nincompoop nomenclature concerns aside, you're going to have to build up some window stamina because they'll come at you from the four corners of the screen. Fortunately, such stamina can be had without resorting to smelly workout clothes or Stairmasters. As you see in this chapter, all that's required is practicing a few handy mouse techniques.

Warming Up: A Window Walkabout

Your average window is a kind of mini Nautilus machine brimming with various gadgets that you push and pull. The secret to a successful window workout is to get to know where these gadgets are and what you use them for. To that end, let's take a tour of a typical window, as shown in Figure 4.1. This is a Notepad window. To get it on-screen, select **Start, All Programs, Accessories, Notepad.** (More on the Notepad program in Chapter 14, "Prose Programs: Windows XP's Faxing Features.")

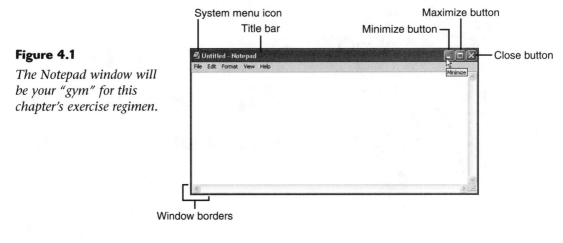

Figure 4.1

The Notepad window will be your "gym" for this chapter's exercise regimen.

Here's a rundown of the various trinkets pointed out in Figure 4.1:

➤ **Title bar**   This is the band (it's usually blue) that forms the top portion of the window. As its name implies, the title bar's job is to tell you the name of the currently open document. (In Figure 4.1, the document is new, so it has the temporary—and decidedly uninspiring—name "Untitled." See Figure 4.7 for a better example.) The title bar also usually shows the name of the program (with a dash in between the two names).

Windows Wisdom

With all those buttons crowded into the upper-right corner of a window, it's tough keeping them straight. To help us out, Windows XP has a feature that tells you the name of each button. To check it out, move your mouse pointer over a button. A second or two later a little "tooltip" shows up with the button's name (as shown in Figure 4.1 by the word "Minimize").

➤ **Buttons, galore**   The right side of the title bar is populated with three buttons: the two blue buttons are named Minimize and Maximize, and the red button is named Close. I fill you in on what they do a bit later (see the section "Breaking a Sweat: Window Exercises").

➤ **Borders**   Most windows are surrounded by four borders that you can manipulate, with your mouse, to change the size of the window (I show you how to do this later in this chapter; see "Breaking a Sweat: Window Exercises").

➤ **System menu icon**   The system menu sports several commands that enable keyboard users to perform routine window maintenance. If you're dealing with a program window, you drop down the system menu by pressing **Alt+spacebar;** for a document window, the system menu sprouts in response to **Alt+-** (**hyphen**).

42

Now just hold on a cotton-picking second. What's the diff between a "program window" and a "document window"?

Gee, you *are* paying attention, aren't you? Here you go:

➤ **Program window**   This is the window in which the program as a whole appears.

➤ **Document window**   This is a window that appears inside the program window and it contains a single, open document. This isn't something you have to worry about if you run only the programs that come with Windows XP because they're only capable of opening one document at a time. However, lots of other programs—such as those that come with Microsoft Office—are capable of working with two or more documents at once. In this case, each document appears inside its own window.

Breaking a Sweat: Window Exercises

Let's see how the four main window techniques—minimizing, maximizing, moving, and sizing—can solve some niggling Windows problems and help you work better:

Problem #1: You have an open program that you know you won't need for a while. It's taking up desktop space, but you don't want to close it. The solution is to *minimize* the program's window, which means that it's cleared off the desktop, but it remains open and appears only as a taskbar button.

Problem #2: You want the largest possible work area for a program. The solution here is to *maximize* the program's window. This enlarges the window so that it fills the entire desktop area.

Problem #3: You have multiple programs on the go and their windows overlap each other so some data gets covered up. The way to fix this is to *move* one or more of the windows so that they don't overlap (or so that they overlap less).

Problem #4: No matter how much you move your windows, they still overlap. In this case, you need to resort to more drastic measures: *sizing* the windows. For example, you can reduce the size of less important windows and increase the size of windows in which you do the most work.

Look Out!

You can't move or size a window if it's either maximized or minimized.

The next few sections discuss these techniques and a few more, for good measure.

Minimizing a Window

When you click a window's Minimize button, the window disappears from view. The window isn't closed, however, because its taskbar button remains in place, as you can see in Figure 4.2.

Figure 4.2

When you minimize a program's window, the program remains running, but all you see is its taskbar button.

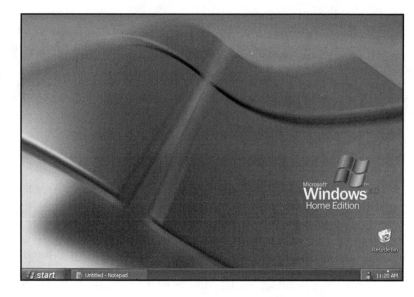

Maximizing a Window

Clicking a window's Maximize button is a whole different kettle of window fish. In this case, the window grows until it fills the entire desktop, as you can see in Figure 4.3. Note that the Maximize button has, without warning, morphed into a new entity: the Restore button. I talk about this new creature in the next section.

Windows Wisdom

With Windows XP, Microsoft has made the Minimize, Maximize, Restore, and Close buttons a bit bigger, but they're still smallish targets. Here are some techniques that can help: minimize the current window by clicking its taskbar button; maximize a window by double-clicking its title bar; restore a maximized window by double-clicking its title bar; close a window by double-clicking its system menu icon.

44

Restoring a Window

In Windows parlance, *restoring* a window means that you put the window back exactly the way it was before minimizing it or maximizing it. How you do this depends on what action you inflicted on the window:

➤ If you minimized the window, click its taskbar button.

➤ If you maximized the window, click the Restore button (pointed out in Figure 4.3).

The Restore button

Figure 4.3

When you maximize a window, it takes over the entire desktop.

The taskbar remains conveniently visible

Moving a Window

Moving a window from one part of the desktop to another takes a simple mouse maneuver. Here are the steps to follow:

1. Make sure the window isn't maximized (or that it's not, duh, minimized).

2. Position the mouse pointer inside the window's title bar (but not over the system menu icon or any of the buttons on the right).

3. Press and hold down the left mouse button. You can now drag the title bar. As you drag, the window moves along with your mouse. (Although it may lag behind slightly if you have a slower system.)

4. When the window is in the position you want, release the mouse button.

45

Windows Wisdom

If you want to change both the height and width of a window, you can save yourself a bit of effort by sizing two sides in one fell swoop. To do this, move the mouse pointer over a window corner. (The pointer will change to a diagonal two-sided arrow.) When you drag the mouse, Windows XP sizes the two sides that create the corner.

Sizing a Window

If you want to change the size of a window, instead, you need to plow through these steps:

1. Make sure the window isn't maximized or minimized.

2. Point the mouse at the window border you want to adjust. For example, if you want to expand the window toward the bottom of the screen, point the mouse at the bottom border. When you've positioned the pointer correctly, it becomes a two-headed arrow, as shown in Figure 4.4.

3. Drag the border to the position you want.

4. Release the mouse button to set the new border position.

5. Repeat steps 2 through 4 for any other borders you want to size.

Figure 4.4

You resize a window by dragging the window borders hither and yon.

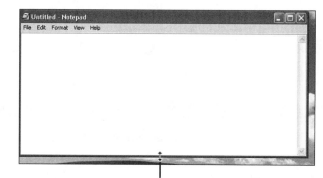

At a window border, the mouse pointer morphs into a two-headed arrow

Cascading and Tiling Windows

If you're pressed for time, you can take advantage of some Windows XP features that can save you a ton of time. To get at these features, right-click an empty section of the taskbar. The shortcut menu that slides into view contains (among others) the following commands:

➤ **Cascade Windows** This command automatically arranges all your nonminimized windows in a diagonal pattern that lets you see the title bar of each window. Figure 4.5 shows three cascaded windows.

Figure 4.5

The Cascade Windows command arranges your windows neatly in a diagonal pattern.

➤ **Tile Windows Horizontally** This feature automatically arranges all your nonminimized windows into horizontal strips so that each of them gets an equal amount of desktop real estate without overlapping each other. Figure 4.6 shows the same three windows arranged horizontally.

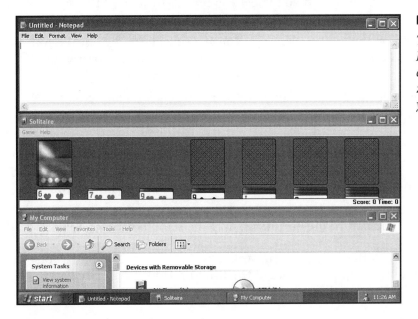

Figure 4.6

The Tile Windows Horizontally command carves out equal-size horizontal desktop chunks for your windows.

47

➤ **Tile Windows Vertically** This command is similar to the Tile Windows Horizontally command, except that it arranges the windows into vertical strips.

➤ **Bring Desktop to Front** This command hides all the nonminimized windows so that you can see the full desktop. After you run this command, it changes to Send Desktop to Back which restores all your windows.

Window Weightlifting: Using Scrollbars

Depending on the program you're using, you often find that the document you're dealing with won't fit entirely inside the window's boundaries, even when you maximize the window. When this happens, you need some way to move to the parts of the document you can't see.

From the keyboard, you can use the basic navigation keys (the arrow keys, Page Up, and Page Down). Mouse users, as usual, have all the fun. To navigate through a document, they get to learn a new skill: how to use scrollbars. The *scrollbar* is the narrow strip that runs along the right side of most windows. Using the Notepad window shown in Figure 4.7, I've pointed out the major features of the average scrollbar. Here's how to use these features to get around inside a document:

➤ The position of the scroll box gives you an idea of where you are in the document. For example, if the scroll box is about halfway down, you know you're somewhere near the middle of the document. Similarly, if the scroll box is near the bottom of the scrollbar, then you know you're near the end of the document.

➤ To scroll down through the document one line at a time, click the down scroll arrow. To scroll continuously, press and hold down the left mouse button on the down scroll arrow.

➤ To scroll up through the document one line at a time, click the up scroll arrow. To scroll continuously, press and hold down the left mouse button on the up scroll arrow.

➤ To leap through the document one screen at a time, click inside the scrollbar between the scroll box and the scroll arrows. For example, to move down one screen, click inside the scrollbar between the scroll box and the down scroll arrow.

➤ To move to a specific part of the document, drag the scroll box up or down.

Note, as well, that many of the windows you work in will also sport a second scrollbar that runs horizontally along the bottom of the window. Horizontal scrollbars work the same as their vertical cousins, except that they let you move left and right in wide documents.

Up scroll arrow

Scroll box

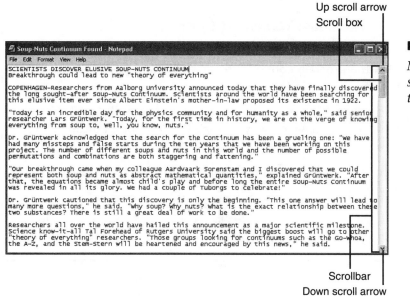

Figure 4.7

Mouse fans get to use the scrollbar to traipse through a document.

Scrollbar

Down scroll arrow

Scrolling with a "Wheel" Mouse

In early 1997, Microsoft introduced a radical new mouse design that incorporates a little wheel between the two buttons. If you have one of these rotary rodents (or one of the knockoffs that many other mouse makers have put out), you can scroll up and down through a document by rotating the wheel forward or backward.

Some applications (such as Microsoft's Internet Explorer and the Microsoft Office 97/2000/XP programs) also support a feature called *panning* that lets you scroll automatically through a document and control the speed. To enable panning, click the wheel button. The application will then display an *origin mark* (the position of this mark varies from application to application). Drag the pointer above the origin mark to scroll up; drag the pointer below the origin mark to scroll down. Note also that the farther the pointer is from the origin mark, the faster you scroll. To turn off panning, click the wheel again.

The Least You Need to Know

➤ **Minimizing a window**   This means that the window disappears from the desktop, although the program continues to run. You minimize a window by clicking the Minimize button in the upper-right corner.

➤ **Maximizing a window**   This means that the window expands to fill the entire desktop. You maximize a window by clicking the Maximize button in the upper-right corner.

➤ **Moving a window**   Use your mouse to drag the title bar to and fro.

➤ **Sizing a window**   Use your mouse to drag any of the window's borders.

➤ **Letting Windows do the work**   Right-click an empty part of the taskbar to eyeball several commands for cascading, tiling, and minimizing all windows.

Chapter 5

Saving, Opening, Printing, and Other Document Lore

In This Chapter

➤ Forging a fresh document

➤ Saving a document for posterity

➤ Closing a document and opening it back up again

➤ Handy document editing techniques

➤ Printing a document

The purpose of Part 1, "XP Everywhere: A Few Things You Need to Know," of the book is to help you get comfortable with Windows XP, and if you've been following along and practicing what you've learned, you and Windows should be getting along famously by now. However, there's another concept you need to immerse yourself in before you're ready to fully explore the Windows universe: documents.

This chapter plugs that gap in your Windows education by teaching you all the basic techniques for manipulating documents. This will include creating, saving, closing, opening, editing, and printing documents, plus much more.

"What's Up, Doc(ument)?"

Most folks think a document is a word processing file. That's certainly true, as far as it goes, but I'm talking about a bigger picture in this chapter. Specifically, when I say "document," what I really mean is *any* file that you create by cajoling a program into doing something useful.

So, yes, a file created within the confines of a word processing program (such as Windows' WordPad) is a document. However, these are also documents: text notes you type into a text editor; images you draw in a graphics program; e-mail missives you compose in an e-mail program; spreadsheets you construct with a spreadsheet program; and presentations you cobble together with a presentation graphics program. In other words, if you can create it or edit it yourself, it's a document.

Manufacturing a New Document

Lots of Windows programs—including WordPad, Notepad, and Paint—are courteous enough to offer up a new, ready-to-roll, document when you start the program. This means you can just dive right in to your typing or drawing or whatever. Later on, however, you may need to start another new document. To do so, use one of the following techniques:

➤ Select the **File, New** command.

➤ Click the **New** button in the program's toolbar, pointed out in Figure 5.1. (This is the WordPad program. If you want to follow along, open WordPad by selecting **Start, All Programs, Accessories, WordPad.**)

➤ In many Windows programs, you can spit out a new document by pressing **Ctrl+N.**

In most cases, the program will then toss a fresh document onscreen. Some programs (WordPad is one) display a dialog box that asks you what kind of new document you want.

Figure 5.1

Most Windows programs offer toolbar buttons for easy access to document commands.

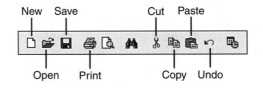

The All-Important Save Command

Save your work as soon as you can and as often as you can.

Without even a jot of hyperbole, I'm telling you right here and now that this deceptively simple slogan is probably the single most important piece of advice that you'll stumble on in this book.

Why all the fuss? Because when you work with a new document (or with an existing document), all the changes you make are stored temporarily in your computer's memory. The bad news is that memory is a fickle and transient medium that, despite its name, forgets all of its contents when you shut down Windows. If you haven't saved your document to your hard disk (which maintains its contents even when Windows isn't running and even if your computer is turned off), you lose all the changes you've made and it's impossible to get them back. Scary!

To guard against such a disaster, remember my "saving slogan" from before and keep the following in mind:

➤ When you create a new document, save it as soon as you've entered any data that's worth keeping.

➤ After the new document is saved, keep right on saving it as often as you can. When I'm writing a book, I typically save my work every 30 to 60 seconds (I'm paranoid!), but a reasonable schedule is to save your work every 5 minutes or so.

Look Out!

If your computer's memory doesn't go into clean slate mode until you shut down Windows, you may be wondering why you can't just wait to save until you're ready to close up shop for the night. If a power failure shuts off your system, or if Windows crashes, all your unsaved work is toast. By saving constantly, you greatly lessen the chance of that happening.

Saving a New Document

Saving a new document takes a bit of extra work, but after that's out of the way, subsequent saves require only a mouse click or two. To save a new document, use either of the following techniques:

➤ Select the **File, Save** command.

➤ Click the **Save** button in the program's toolbar (see Figure 5.1).

Most programs will display a Save As dialog box like the one shown in Figure 5.2.

From here, there's an easy road and a hard road you can take to get your document saved.

The easy road is when you see **My Documents** in the **Save in** list (as shown in Figure 5.2). As its name implies, My Documents is a built-in *folder* that Windows provides for storing your documents. If you want to use it (which I highly recommend), all you need to do is enter a name for the document in the **File name** text box, and then click **Save**. Note, however, that Windows places a few restrictions on file names; see step 3 in the steps that follow.

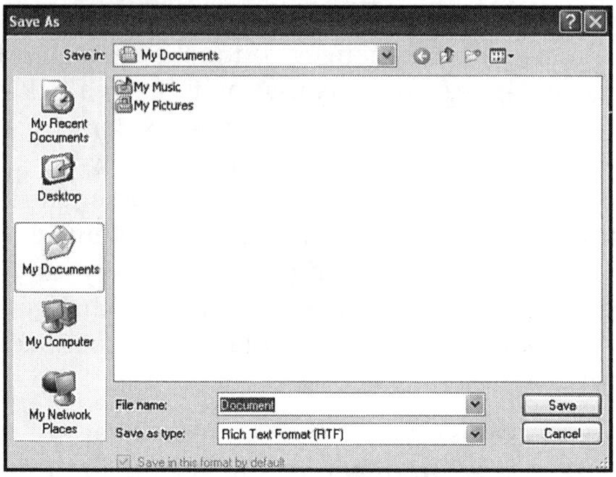

Figure 5.2

The Save As dialog box appears when you're saving a new document.

The ever-so-slightly-harder road is when you're working with images or music files. In this case, you first perform an extra step in the Save As dialog box:

➤ If you're saving an image, double-click the **My Pictures** icon to open the My Pictures folder, which is a special folder for storing graphics files. (I tell you more about it in Chapter 8, "Playing with Pictures.")

➤ If you're saving a music file or sound file, double-click the **My Music** icon to open the My Music folder, which is (as you've probably guessed by now) a special folder for storing music and sound files. (You learn about it in Chapter 11, "Sights and Sounds: Music and Other Multimedia.")

The hard road is when you want to use some other folder to store you document. Here are the steps you need to walk through to get your document safely stowed somewhere else:

1. The **Save in** drop-down list tells you the name of the current folder. To choose a different folder, first drop down the list and choose the disk drive that contains the folder you want to use to store the file.

2. The Save As dialog box then shows you a list of the folders on the selected disk drive. Double-click the folder you want to open. You may need to repeat this several times to get to the folder you want.

3. Use the **File name** text box to enter a name for your document. Note that the name you choose must be different from any other document in the folder. Also, Windows XP lets you enter file names that are up to 255 characters long. Your names can include spaces, commas, and apostrophes, but not the following characters: \ , ? : * " < > .

4. Now use the **Save as type** drop-down list to choose the type of document you want to create. In the vast majority of cases you won't have to bother with this

because the default type is best. Many programs can create different document types, however, and this capability often comes in handy.

5. Click the **Save** button. The program makes a permanent copy of the document on your hard disk.

Here are some notes about saving new documents:

➤ Happily, you won't have to go through the rigmarole of choosing a folder every time you save a new document. Most programs are smart enough to "remember" the most recent folder you worked with and will select it for you automatically the next time you're in the Save As dialog box. (Unfortunately, this only applies to the current session with the program. If you exit the program and then restart it, you have to reselect the folder.)

➤ If you want your new document to replace an existing document, open the folder that contains the document and then double-click the file name. The program will ask whether you want to replace the document, and you then click **Yes**.

➤ The rub with long file names is that DOS programs and programs meant to work with Windows 3.1 will scoff at your attempts to break through the old "8.3" file name barrier (eight characters for the file name and a three-character extension). What happens if you create a document with a long name, using a Windows XP program, and then try to open that document in an older program? Well, the document will probably open just fine, but you'll notice that the file name has been knocked down in size. You see, Windows XP actually keeps track of *two* names for each document: the long name and a shorter DOS-compatible name. The latter is just the first six characters of the long name (sans spaces), followed by a tilde (~), followed by a number. For example, a file named Fiscal 2001 - First Quarter Budget Spreadsheet would also use the DOS alias FIS-CAL~1.

See Also

Confused about folders? Don't worry, I tell you all about them in Chapter 6, "Using My Computer to Fiddle with Files and Folders."

Saving an Existing Document

After all that hard work saving a new document, you'll be happy to know that subsequent saves are much easier. That's because when you select the **File, Save** command, the program simply updates the existing hard disk copy of the document. This takes just a second or two (usually) and no dialog box shows up to pester you for information. Because this is so easy, there's no excuse not to save your work regularly. If you're a fan of keyboard shortcuts, here's one to memorize for the ages: Press **Ctrl+S** to save your document. If you're a fan of toolbar buttons, click the **Save** toolbar button that you saw in Figure 5.1.

Taking Advantage of the My Documents Folder

See Also

For more information about how to back up your documents, see the section in Chapter 28, "Getting a Good Nights Sleep: Preparing for Trouble," titled "Backing Up Your Precious Data with Windows XP Professional."

I mentioned earlier that I highly recommend you use the prefab My Documents folder, which is designed to be a central storage area for all your documents. Using this folder is a good idea for three reasons:

➤ It makes your documents easy to find because they're all stored in one place.

➤ When you want to back up your documents, you need to only select a single folder (rather than hunting around your hard disk for all your documents).

➤ It's easy to get to: Select **Start, My Documents.** (You can also get there by opening My Documents folder within My Computer or Windows Explorer.)

Using the Save As Command to Make a Copy of a Document

As you slave away in Windows XP, you sometimes find that you need to create a second, slightly different, copy of a document. For example, you might create a letter and then decide that you need a second copy to send to someone else. Rather than re-creating the entire letter from scratch, it's much easier to make a copy of the existing document and then change just the address and salutation.

The easiest way to go about this is to use the Save As command. This command is a lot like Save, except that it enables you to save the document with a new name or to a new location. (Think of it as the don't-reinvent-the-wheel command.) To use Save As to create a new document, follow these steps:

1. Open the original document (not a new one). (If you're not sure how to go about this, skip ahead to section titled "Opening an Existing Document" to find out.)

2. Select the **File, Save As** command. The program displays the same Save As dialog box that you saw earlier in Figure 5.2.

3. Either select a different storage location for the new document or enter a different name (or both).

4. Click **Save**. The program closes the original document, makes a copy, and then opens the new document.

5. Make your changes to the new document (see the next section).

Getting It Right: Text Editing for Beginners

As you create your document, you have to delete text, move text chunks to different locations, and so on. To make your electronic writing life easier, it's crucial to get these basic editing chores down pat. To that end, here's a summary of some editing techniques you can use in most any program that deals with text (including Notepad, WordPad, Outlook Express, and MSN Messenger):

➤ **Highlighting text with the mouse**   Before you can do something to existing text, you need to *highlight* it. To highlight text with a mouse, drag the mouse over the characters you want. That is, you first position the mouse pointer a teensy bit to the left of the first character you want to highlight. Then you press and hold down the left mouse button and move the mouse to the right. As you do, the characters you pass over become highlighted. While you drag, you can also move the mouse down to highlight multiple lines. When you release the mouse button, the text remains highlighted.

➤ **Highlighting text with the keyboard**   To highlight text by using the keyboard, position the cursor to the left of the first character, hold down the **Shift** key, and then press the right-arrow key until the entire selection is highlighted. Use the down-arrow key (or even Page Down if you have a lot of ground to cover) when you need to highlight multiple lines.

➤ **Copying highlighted text**   To make a copy of the highlighted text, select the **Edit, Copy** command. (Alternatively, you can also press **Ctrl+C** or click the **Copy** toolbar button, shown in Figure 5.1). Then position the cursor where you want to place the copy, and select

Look Out!

If you highlight some text and then press a character on your keyboard, your entire selection will disappear and be replaced by the character you typed! (If you press the Enter key, the highlighted text just disappears entirely.) This is normal behavior that can cause trouble for even experienced document jockeys. To get your text back, immediately select the **Edit, Undo** command or press **Ctrl+Z.**

the **Edit, Paste** command. (Your other choices are to press **Ctrl+V** or click the **Paste** toolbar button; again, see Figure 5.1). A perfect copy of your selection appears instantly. Note that you can paste this text as many times as you need.

➤ **Moving highlighted text**   When you need to move something from one part of a document to another, you *could* do it by making a copy, pasting it, and then going back to delete the original. If you do this, however, your colleagues will certainly make fun of you because there's an easier way. After you highlight what you want to move, select the **Edit, Cut** command (the shortcuts are pressing **Ctrl+X** or clicking the **Cut** toolbar button; see Figure 5.1). Your selection disappears from the screen, but don't panic; Windows XP saves it for you. Position the cursor where you want to place the text, and then select **Edit, Paste.** Your stuff miraculously reappears in the new location.

➤ **Deleting text**   Because even the best typists make occasional typos, knowing how to delete is a necessary editing skill. Put away the Wite-Out, though, because deleting a character or two is easier (and less messy) if you use either of the following techniques: 1) position the cursor to the right of the offending character and press the **Backspace** key; position the cursor to the left of the character and press the **Delete** key. If you have a large chunk of material you want to expunge from the document, highlight it and press the **Delete** key or the **Backspace** key.

Windows Wisdom

All this cut, copy, and paste moonshine is a bit mysterious. Where does cut text (or whatever) go? How does Windows XP know what to paste? Does Windows XP have some kind of digital hip pocket that it uses to store and retrieve cut or copied data? Truth be told, that's not a bad analogy. This "hip pocket" is actually a chunk of your computer's memory called the *clipboard*. Whenever you run the Cut or Copy command, Windows XP heads to the clipboard, removes whatever currently resides there, and stores the cut or copied data. When you issue the Paste command, Windows XP grabs whatever is on the clipboard and tosses it into your document.

➤ **To err is human, to undo divine**   What do you do if you paste text to the wrong spot or consign a vital piece of an irreplaceable document to deletion purgatory? Happily, Notepad, WordPad, and many other Windows XP programs have an Undo feature to get you out of these jams. To reverse your most recent action, select the **Edit, Undo** command to restore everything to the way it was before you made your blunder. And, yes, there are shortcuts you can use: Try either pressing **Ctrl+Z** or clicking the **Undo** toolbar button (pointed out, as usual, in Figure 5.1).

It's important to remember that most of the time the Undo command usually only undoes your most recent action. So if you delete something, perform some other task, and then try to undo the deletion, chances are the program won't let you do it. Therefore, always try to run Undo immediately after making your error. Note, however, that some programs are more flexible and will let you undo several actions. In this case, you just keep selecting the Undo command until your document is back the way you want it.

Closing a Document

Some weakling Windows programs (such as WordPad and Paint) allow you to open only one document at a time. In such programs, you can close the document you're currently working on by starting a new document, by opening another document, or by quitting the program altogether.

However, most full-featured Windows programs let you open as many documents as you want (subject to the usual memory limitations that govern all computer work). In this case, each open document appears inside its own window—called a *document window,* not surprisingly. These document windows have their own versions of the Minimize, Maximize, Restore, and Close buttons. Also, the name of each document appears on the program's Window menu, which you can use to switch from one document to another.

Because things can get crowded pretty fast, though, you probably want to close any documents you don't need at the moment. To do this, activate the document you want to close and select the **File, Close** command, or click the document window's **Close** button. If you made changes to the document since last saving it, a dialog box appears asking whether you want to save those changes. Click **Yes** to save, **No** to discard the changes, or **Cancel** to leave the document open. In most programs that support multiple open documents, you also can close the current document by pressing **Ctrl+F4.**

Opening an Existing Document

After you've saved a document or two, you often need to get one of them back on-screen to make changes or review your handiwork. To do that, you need to *open* the document by using any of the following techniques:

➤ **Use the Open dialog box**   Select the program's **File, Open** command. (Alternatively, slam **Ctrl+O** or click the **Open** toolbar button, shown in Figure 5.1.) The Open dialog box that appears is similar to the Save As dialog box you messed with earlier. Find the document you want to open, highlight it, and then click **Open.**

See Also

Before you can print, you may need to tell Windows XP what type of printer you have. I tell you how to go about this in Chapter 7, "Installing and Uninstalling Programs and Devices." See the section titled "Installing Specific Devices."

➤ **Use the My Documents folder**   If you're using the My Documents folder to store your stuff, you can open a document by displaying My Documents and then double-clicking the document's icon. You can also highlight the document and then select **File, Open.** If the appropriate application isn't running, Windows XP will start it for you and load the document automatically.

➤ **Use My Computer or Windows Explorer** Along similar lines, you can also use My Computer or Windows Explorer (located under **Start, All Programs, Accessories**) to open a document. Again, find the document you want and launch its icon.

It's possible to convince the Start menu to display a list of the most recent documents you've worked on. I'll show you how to do this in Chapter 25, "Revamping the Start Menu and Taskbar."

Sending a Document to the Printer

The nice thing about printing in Windows XP is that the basic steps you follow are more or less identical in each and every Windows program. After you learn the fundamentals, you can apply them to all your Windows applications. Here are the steps you need to follow:

1. In your program, open the document you want to print.

2. Select the **File, Print** command. You see a Print dialog box similar to the one shown in Figure 5.3 for the WordPad word processor.

   If your fingers are poised over your keyboard, you may find that in most applications pressing **Ctrl+P** is a faster way to get to the Print dialog box. If you just want a single copy of the document, click the **Print** toolbar button (see Figure 5.1) to bypass the Print dialog box and print the document directly.

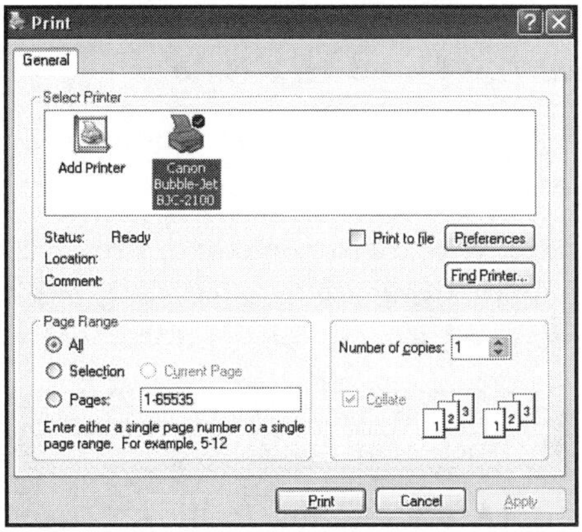

Figure 5.3

WordPad's Print dialog box is a typical example of the species.

3. The options in the Print dialog box vary slightly from application to application, but you almost always see three things:

   ➤ A list for selecting the printer to use. In WordPad's Print dialog box, for example, use the **Select Printer** list to select the printer.

   ➤ A text box or spin box to enter the number of copies you want. In the WordPad Print dialog box, use the **Number of copies** text box.

   ➤ Some controls for selecting how much of the file to print. You normally have the option of printing the entire document or a specific range of pages. (WordPad's Print dialog box also includes a **Selection** option button that you can activate to print only the currently highlighted text.)

4. When you've chosen your options, click the **Print** button to start printing (some Print dialog boxes have an **OK** button, instead).

Keep watching the information area of the taskbar (the area to the left of the clock). After a few seconds (depending on the size of the document), a printer icon appears, as shown in Figure 5.4. This tells you that Windows XP is hard at work farming out the document to your printer. This icon disappears after the printer is finished with its job. If you have an exceptionally speedy printer, this icon may come and go without you ever laying eyes on it. If the printer icon shows up with a red question mark icon superimposed on it, it means there's a problem with the printer. In this case, see Chapter 29, "When Windows Won't Work: Troubleshooting Common Problems."

Here's the printer icon

Figure 5.4

The printer icon tells you that Windows XP is printing.

The Least You Need to Know

➤ **Forging a new document**   Select the **File, New** command, press **Ctrl+N,** or click the toolbar's **New** button.

➤ **Saving a document**   Select the **File, Save** command, press **Ctrl+S,** or click the toolbar's **Save** button. If you're saving a new document, use the Save As dialog box to pick out a location and a name for the document.

➤ **Make My Documents your own**   You'll simplify your life immeasurably if you store all your files in the My Documents folder.

➤ **Editing a document**   Press **Backspace** to delete the character to the left of the cursor; press **Delete** to wipe out the character to the right; press **Ctrl+Z** to undo your most recent mistake.

➤ **Shutting down a document**   Select the **File, Close** command or press **Ctrl+F4.**

➤ **Opening a document**   Select the **File, Open** command, press **Ctrl+O,** or click the toolbar's **Open** button.

➤ **Printing a document**   Select the **File, Print** command, press **Ctrl+P,** or click the toolbar's **Print** button.

Chapter 6

Using My Computer to Fiddle with Files and Folders

In This Chapter

➤ Navigating your system using My Computer

➤ Creating, selecting, copying, moving, renaming, and deleting files and folders

➤ Searching for long-lost files

➤ "Burning" files to a CD

➤ A fistful of useful file and folder factoids

In Chapter 5, "Saving, Opening, Printing, and Other Document Lore," you learned that it's off-the-scale crucial to save your documents as soon and as often as you can. That way, you preserve your documents within the stable confines of your computer's hard disk. You also learned that it's best to use your hard disk's My Documents folder as a central storage location for your documents.

You learned, in other words, that your hard disk is a vital chunk of digital real estate. So, as a responsible landowner, it's important for you to tend your plot and keep your grounds well maintained. That's the purpose of this chapter as it shows you how to use some of Windows XP's built-in tools to work with your hard disk's files and folders. You get the scoop on creating new folders, copying and moving files from one folder to another, renaming and deleting files and folders, and much more.

My, Oh, My: Learning About Your Computer Using My Computer

Windows XP has an annoying habit of appending the word "My" onto the front of things. On the Start menu alone you spy four of these exercises in self-absorption: My Documents, My Pictures, My Music, and My Computer. This "My-opic" point of view is a bit cutesy, but it serves a more serious purpose: To remind you that what's truly important on your system is what you create yourself.

With that in mind, let's take a closer look at the main "My" machine: My Computer. From the name, you might be tempted to think that it represents your entire computer caboodle. Well, that's close, but there's no cigar for you. My Computer really represents only the areas of your computer where files can be stored: your hard disk, your floppy disk, your CD-ROM or DVD-ROM drive, "removable" disks such as those that work with Zip or Jaz drives, folders on a network, and so on.

You can prove this for yourself by opening the Start menu and then clicking the **My Computer** icon. You end up eyeballing a window that looks suspiciously like the one shown in Figure 6.1. (Your version of My Computer may look a bit different if your computer has a different configuration than mine.)

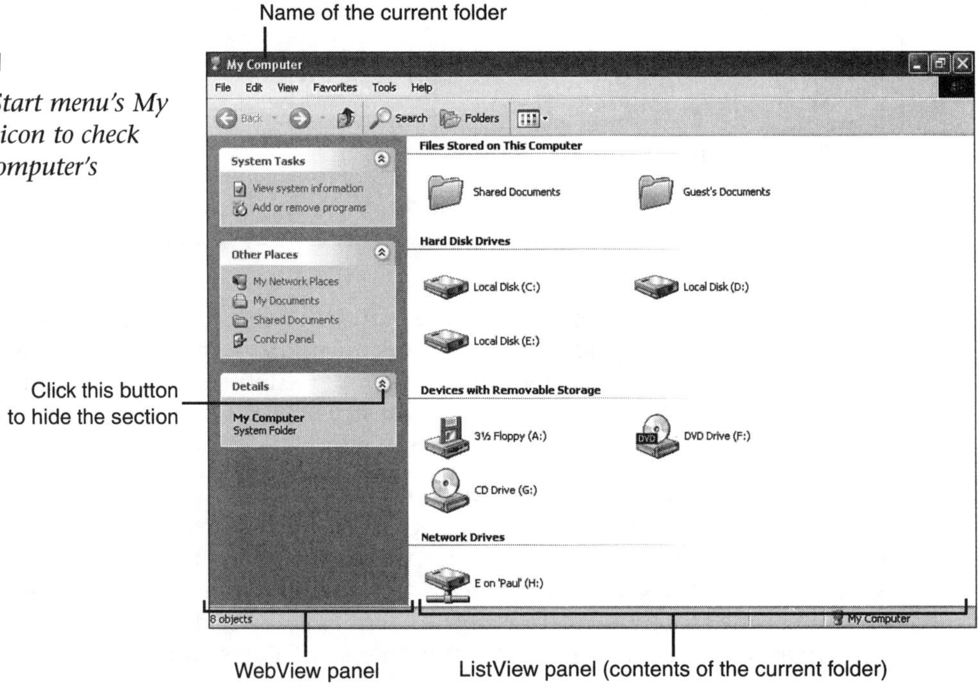

Name of the current folder

Figure 6.1

Click the Start menu's My Computer icon to check out your computer's goodies.

Click this button to hide the section

WebView panel   ListView panel (contents of the current folder)

My Computer's job is to display the contents of a given folder so that you can check out what's in the folder or muck about with those contents in some way (such as renaming one of your files; see the "Renaming a File or Folder" section later in this chapter). So the My Computer window is set up to help you do just that. First, notice that the title bar shows you the name of the current folder that My Computer is displaying. (You always see "My Computer" at first, but the title changes as you jump from folder to folder.)

Next, after you get below the usual window suspects (the title bar, the menu bar, and the toolbar), you see that the My Computer window is divided into two sections:

➤ **WebView panel** The left side of the window offers a collection of icons that are related to the current folder. Depending on the folder that's currently displayed, these icons will be separated into three or four different sections. Here are the four most common sections that you'll stumble upon:

System Tasks The icons in this section initiate broad, system-level actions. For example, in My Computer, this section includes the **Add or remove programs** icon for installing or uninstalling software.

File and Folder Tasks The icons in this section run commands related to files and folder (such as renaming a folder or deleting a file).

Other Places The icons in this section represent other folders on your computer.

Details The text in this section gives you information about the current folder or about a file inside the folder (if you click the file to highlight it).

For the icons in the WebView panel, you can run the task or display the folder by clicking the icon. Note, too, that you can hide a section's icons (or the text in the Details section) by clicking the double-arrow button in the top-right corner (see Figure 6.1).

➤ **ListView panel** The right side of the window displays the contents of the current folder. The My Computer folder stores your

Windows Wisdom

Although my definition of a *folder* as a slice of a disk used for storage is accurate, Windows takes this idea of storage to great lengths. That is, in the Windows worldview, anything that can store anything is considered to be a folder. So even though My Computer isn't technically a slice of any disk, it's treated as a folder because it stores various icons.

Windows Wisdom

If your CD or DVD drive is empty, My Computer shows the icon with **CD Drive** or **DVD Drive.** However, if you insert a CD or DVD disc in the drive, then My Computer's display changes to show whatever title and icon the manufacturer assigned to the disc.

computer's disk drives, so that's mostly what you see in this area. The text associated with each icon tells you what kind of disk drive you're dealing with.

Navigating to a File

One of the most common chores associated with My Computer is navigating through various folders and subfolders to get to a particular file. How you go about this depends on whether the file you want is housed in My Documents (or one of its subfolders) or in some other part of your system.

The My Documents route is easiest, so let's start with that. If you're in the My Computer window, click **My Documents** in the **Other Places** section. (Remember, however, that you can bypass My Computer and go to My Documents directly by selecting **Start, My Documents.**) Figure 6.2 shows the My Documents on my system, which is populated with a few of my files.

Figure 6.2

Opening a folder reveals the contents of that folder.

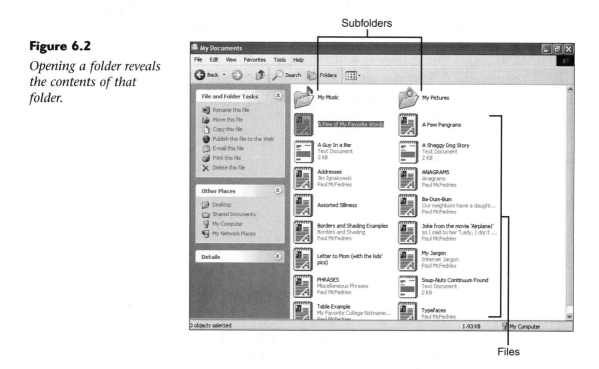

As you can see, this folder contains a couple of icons that represent subfolders, and the rest of the icons represent files. If the file you want is in one of the subfolders, double-click the subfolder's icon. Repeat this as often as necessary to reach the file you want.

If your file isn't in My Documents or one of its subfolders, then you need to hunt it down in some other part of your computer. To do that, follow these steps:

1. In My Computer, double-click the icon for the disk drive that contains the file you want. (If you plan on looking for your file on a floppy drive, CD or DVD drive, or a removable disk drive, be sure you have a disk inside the drive, or Windows XP will reprimand you with an error message.)

2. If Windows doesn't display the contents of the disk drive (for example, you might instead see the message **Looking for your programs?**), then in the **System Tasks** section, click the **Show the contents of this drive** icon.

3. If your file isn't in the current folder, double-click the icon for the subfolder that contains the file.

4. Repeat step 3 until you get to the file.

Look Out!

Certain drives and folders that contain Windows XP system files don't show their contents right away. Note that unless you're given specific instructions, under no circumstances should you play around with (rename, delete, move, and so on) any of the files in these system drives and folders.

You may have noticed by now that the icons in the various folders have all kinds of different pictures. For example, most folders have a yellow icon that looks suspiciously like a file folder. Makes sense. Files are another story, however, because they have all kinds of different icons. The reason is that each icon tells you what kind of file you're dealing with and which program will run if you open (double-click) the file. Back in Figure 6.2, for example, the files named A Few of My Favorite Words and A Few Pangrams are WordPad documents, and the files named A Guy In a Bar and A Shaggy Dog Story are Notepad documents.

Getting Around in My Computer

My Computer's toolbar is chock-full of one-click wonders, but it's sometimes difficult to tell which button does what. To help out, you can force My Computer to display the name of each button (see Figure 6.3). To do this, select **View**, **Toolbars**, **Customize** (or right-click the toolbar and then click **Customize**). In the Customize Toolbar dialog box, use the **Text options** list to choose **Show text labels**, and then click **OK**.

Here are a few pointers for navigating from folder to folder in My Computer:

➤ To go back to the previous folder, either click the **Back** button in the toolbar or select **View, Go To, Back**. (There's also a keyboard shortcut that you can use: **Alt+Left Arrow**.)

➤ After you've gone back to a previous folder, you can move forward again either by clicking the **Forward** button or by selecting **View, Go To, Forward**. (The keyboard shortcut for this is **Alt+Right Arrow**.)

Click this arrow to display the Back list

Figure 6.3

The Back and Forward buttons maintain lists of the places you've been.

➤ Rather than stepping back and forward one folder at a time, you can leap over multiple folders in a single bound. To do this, click the downward-pointing arrow beside either the **Back** or **Forward** toolbar button. In the list that appears (see Figure 6.4), click the folder you want to visit. (You also can do this by selecting **View, Go To** and then choosing the folder from the list at the bottom of the menu.)

➤ If a folder has subfolders, the folder is called the *parent* and each subfolder is called a *child*. (Strange terms, I know.) If you're viewing a child folder, you can go to its parent folder either by clicking the **Up** button in the toolbar or by selecting **View, Go To, Up One Level**. (Keyboard fans can press **Backspace** instead.)

Windows Wisdom

When you combine My Computer with the Folders list, the resulting window is exactly the same as the one you see when you launch another Windows XP program: Windows Explorer. You fire up the latter by selecting **Start, All Programs, Accessories, Windows Explorer.**

Taking Advantage of the Handy Folders List

The thing I dislike the most about My Computer is that it shows only one folder at a time, so you often end up "drilling down" through a series of subfolders to get where you want to go. Too slow! To speed things up, activate My Computer's Folders list either by clicking the **Folders** toolbar button or by selecting **View, Explorer Bar, Folders.** (To get rid of the Folders list, repeat the same procedure.)

As you can see in Figure 6.4, the result is that the WebView panel is replaced by a list of folders. When you highlight a folder in this list, the folder's contents appear in the ListView panel on the right. To view subfolders within the Folders list, use the following techniques:

➤ **To view subfolders**   Click the **plus sign** (+) beside the folder name. The plus sign changes to a minus sign (–).

➤ **To hide subfolders**   Click the **minus sign** (–) beside the folder name.

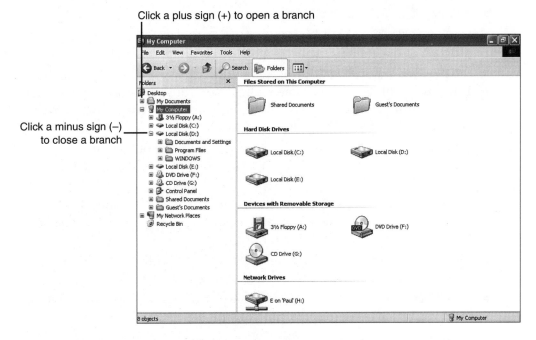

Figure 6.4

My Computer modified to show the handy Folders list.

Workaday File and Folder Maintenance

Now that you and My Computer are getting along famously, it's time to put this digital domestic to good use. Specifically, I show you how to use My Computer to perform no fewer than six workaday chores for files and folders: creating, copying, moving, renaming, deleting, and compressing.

69

Creating a New File or Folder

If you want to manufacture a shiny, new file for yourself, the best way to go about it is to run the appropriate application and select that program's **File, New** command. (Note, too, that most programs—including Windows XP's WordPad and Notepad accessories—create a new file for you automatically when you start them.) You then select the **File, Save** command to save the file to your hard disk.

However, it *is* possible to create a new file within My Computer. Here's how:

1. Open the folder in which you want to create the file. If you're not sure which folder to use, open the handy My Documents folder.

2. Select the **File, New** command. This displays another menu with at least the following file flavors (your system may have more):

   ➤ **Folder**   This command creates a new subfolder.

   ➤ **Shortcut**   This command creates a shortcut, which acts as a pointer to a program or document. (I tell you more about shortcuts in Chapter 25, "Revamping the Start Menu and Taskbar.")

   ➤ **Briefcase**   This command creates a Briefcase, which is a special folder you use for transferring files between two computers. See Chapter 16, "Moveable Feast: Windows XP and Your Notebook Computer."

   ➤ **Bitmap Image**   This command creates an image file of the same type as those you create using Windows XP's Paint program. See Chapter 10, "Giving Your Right Brain a Workout with Paint."

   ➤ **WordPad Document**   This command creates a file of the same type as those you create using Windows XP's WordPad program. See Chapter 14, "Prose Programs: Windows XP's Writing Tools."

   ➤ **Rich Text Document**   This command creates a slightly different type of WordPad file. Again, head for Chapter 14 to get more info.

   ➤ **Text Document**   This command creates a plain text file that's the same as what you create using the Notepad program. See Chapter 14.

   ➤ **Wave Sound**   This command creates a sound file. I tell you more about sound files in Chapter 11, "Sights and Sounds: Music and Other Multimedia."

   ➤ **Compressed (Zipped) Folder**   This command creates a special folder that compresses multiple files into a smaller package suitable for sending over the Internet. I talk more about this type of file later in this chapter in the section "Creating a Compressed Folder."

3. Select the type of file you want. Windows XP creates the new file and displays a generic (read: boring) name—such as "New Text Document"—in a text box.

4. Edit the name and then press **Enter** or click some of the blank real estate inside the window.

If you misspell the file name or simply change your mind, just hold tight and I'll teach you how to change the file name later in this chapter. If Windows XP complains about a particular character that you try to use, leave it out for now. I'll tell you about the rules for file names a bit later. (In both cases, see the "Renaming a File or Folder" section later in this chapter.)

Selecting Files and Folders

Before getting to the rest of the file-maintenance fun, you need to know how to select the files or folders that you want to horse around with.

Let's begin with the simplest case: selecting a single file or folder. This is a two-step procedure:

1. Open the folder that contains the file or subfolder you want to horse around with.

2. In the ListView panel, click the file's icon.

So far, so good. However, there will be plenty of times when you need to deal with two or more files or folders. For example, you might want to herd several files onto a floppy disk. Rather than doing this one item at a time, you can do the whole thing in one fell swoop by first selecting all the items and then moving (or copying, or whatever) them as a group. Windows XP offers the following methods:

➤ **Selecting consecutive items**   If the files or folders you want to select are listed consecutively, say "Ooh, how convenient!" and then do this: Select the first item, hold down the **Shift** key, select the last item, and then release **Shift**. Windows XP kindly does the dirty work of selecting all the items in between.

➤ **Selecting nonconsecutive items**   If the files or folders you want to select are listed willy-nilly, say "Oy!" and then do this: Select the first item, hold down the **Ctrl** key, select each of the other items, and then release **Ctrl**.

➤ **Selecting all items**   If you want to select everything inside a folder, choose the **Edit, Select All** command, or press **Ctrl+A**.

Copying and Moving a File or Folder

A copy of a file or folder is an exact replica of the original that you store on another part of your hard disk or on a removable disk (such as a floppy disk). Copies are useful for making backups or if you want to transport a file or folder to another computer.

Note, too, that the location of the files and folders you create isn't set in stone. If you're not happy with the current location, there's no problem moving a file or folder somewhere else.

Windows XP offers two basic methods for copying and moving files and folders: the Copy to Folder and Move to Folder commands, and the "drag-and-drop" mouse technique.

To use the Copy to Folder or Move to Folder command, follow these steps:

1. Select the files or folders you want to transport.

2. Pull down the **Edit** menu and choose one of the following commands:

   Copy to Folder   This is the command to choose if you're copying files or folders. Alternatively, click **Copy this file** (or **Copy the selected items** if you have multiple files or folders selected) in the WebView panel's **File and Folder Tasks** section.

   Move to Folder   This is the command to choose if you're moving files or folders. Alternatively, click **Move this file** (or **Move the selected items** if you have multiple files or folders selected) in the WebView panel's **File and Folder Tasks** section.

3. Either way, you end up with a version of the Browse for Folder dialog box on-screen. Use the folder "tree" to locate and select the destination folder or disk drive.

4. Click **Copy** or **Move** (depending on which View menu command you chose).

Windows Wisdom

Windows XP has a special Send To menu that contains commonly used destinations, such as your floppy disk or your My Documents folder. To see this menu, either select **File, Send To** or right-click an item and then click **Send To.** Now select the destination you want, and Windows XP copies the selected items lickety-split.

Mouse fans will enjoy the alternative drag-and-drop method:

1. Display the Folders list, as described earlier.

2. Use the ListView panel to select the files or folders you want to copy or move.

3. Move the mouse pointer over any selected item and hold down the right mouse button (yes, you read that correctly: the *right* mouse button).

4. With the button held down for dear life, move the mouse pointer toward the destination folder in the Folders list (this is the "dragging" part).

5. Position the mouse pointer over the destination folder (wait until you see it highlighted) and then release the mouse button (this is the "dropping" part). Windows XP displays a shortcut menu.

6. Click **Copy Here** or **Move Here**, as appropriate.

To get the most out of this drag-and-drop method, you need to first set up the My Computer window so that your destination folder is visible in the Folders list. If you're in mid-drag and you realize you forgot to do this, here are two tips that can help:

➤ If you need to scroll down the Folders list, drag the mouse and highlight the bottom item in the Folders list; similarly, you can scroll up the list by dragging the mouse so that it highlights the top item in the list.

➤ If the destination is a subfolder in an unopened folder, drag the mouse into the Folders list and place it over the folder. After a few seconds, Windows kindly opens the folder.

Renaming a File or Folder

Windows XP supports file and folder names up to about 255 characters long, so you don't have to settle for boring monikers on the files and folders you create. If you don't like a name, feel free to rename it. Follow these simple steps to rename a file or folder:

1. Select the file or folder you want to rename. (You can work with only one item at a time for this.)

2. Run the **File, Rename** command. (You can also press **F2** or click **Rename this file** in the WebView panel's **File and Folder Tasks** section.) Windows XP creates a text box around the name.

3. Edit the name as you see fit.

4. When you're done, press **Enter**.

Bear in mind that although Windows XP likes long filenames and accepts most keyboard characters (including spaces), there are nine characters that are strictly *verboten:* *, \ : " < > ? / .

Deleting a File or Folder

Although most of today's hard disks boast a mammoth amount of real estate, you could still run out of room one day if you don't delete the debris that you no longer use. Deleting unwanted files and folders is fairly easy:

1. Select the files or folders you want to blow away.

2. Run the **File, Delete** command. (Alternatively, press **Delete** or click **Delete this file** or **Delete the selected items** in the WebView panel's **File and Folder Tasks** section.) Windows XP asks whether you're sure you want to consign these poor things to the cold, cruel Recycle Bin.

3. Say "But of course, my good fellow!" and click **Yes**.

What happens if you nuke some crucial file or folder that you'd give your right arm to have back? Assuming you need your right arm, Windows XP offers an alternative method to save your bacon: the *Recycle Bin*.

Windows Wisdom

Another way to delete a file or folder is to drag it from My Computer and drop it on the desktop's Recycle Bin icon.

You should know, first off, that if the deletion was the last thing you did, you don't have to bother with the Recycle Bin. Just pull down the **Edit** menu and select the **Undo Delete** command (or press **Ctrl+Z**) to salvage the file. Note that it will be placed back in the folder where you originally deleted it, not necessarily in the folder you are currently in.

In fact, Windows XP is only too happy to let you reverse the last *10* actions you performed. Again, you pull down the **Edit** menu and select the **Undo Whatever** command (where **Whatever** is the name of the command, such as Delete).

Otherwise, you have to trudge through these steps:

1. Double-click the desktop's **Recycle Bin** icon. The folder that appears contains a list of all the stuff you've expunged recently.

2. Select the files or folders you want to recover.

3. Select the **File, Restore** command (or click **Restore this item** or **Restore the selected items** in the WebView panel). Windows XP marches the items right back to where they came from. Whew!

How the heck can the Recycle Bin restore a deleted file?

Good question. You can get part of the answer by looking at the Recycle Bin icon on your Windows XP desktop. It looks like a garbage can, and that's sort of what the Recycle Bin is. Think about it: If you toss a piece of paper in the garbage, there's nothing to stop you from reaching in and pulling it back out. The Recycle Bin operates the same way: It's really just a special hidden folder (called Recycled) on your hard disk. When you delete a file, Windows XP actually moves the file into the Recycled folder. So restoring a file is a simple matter of "reaching into" the folder and "pulling out" the file. The Recycle Bin handles all this for you (and even returns your file sans wrinkles and coffee grounds). However, just like when you hand your trash out to the garbage man, after you empty the Recycle Bin (covered later), there is no retrieving the lost files.

Creating a Compressed Folder

When you download files from the Internet, they often arrive as ZIP files. These are compressed archive files that contain one or more files that have been compressed for faster downloading. In Windows XP, a ZIP file is called a *compressed folder*. Why a "folder"? Because a ZIP file contains one or more files, just like a regular folder. As you'll see, this makes it easy to deal with the files within the ZIP, and it enables Windows XP to offer a few useful compression and decompression features.

To create a ZIP file, there are two methods you can use:

➤ Select the items you want to store in the ZIP file and then run the **File, Send To, Compressed (Zipped) Folder** command. Windows XP creates a ZIP file with the same name as the first selected file.

➤ Create a new, empty ZIP file by running the **File, New Compressed (Zipped) Folder** command. Windows XP creates a new ZIP file with an active text box. Edit the name and press Enter. You can then drag the files you want to archive and drop them on the ZIP file's icon.

To see what's inside a ZIP file, double-click it. Windows XP opens the file as a folder that the files within the ZIP in the ListView panel. From here, use the following techniques to work with the archived files:

➤ To extract some of the files, select them, drag them out of the compressed folder, and then drop them on the destination folder.

➤ To extract all of the files, select them and then drag and drop them on the destination. Alternatively, select **File, Extract All** (or click the WebView panel's **Extract all files** icon) to launch the Extraction Wizard. Click **Next** and then click **Browse** to select a destination for the extracted files. Finally, click **Next** to extract the files. In the next wizard dialog box, activate the **Show extracted files** check box to open a window for the destination folder (this is optional), and then click **Finish**.

75

"Burning" Files to a CD-R or CD-RW Disc

NEW! CD-ROM drives are great, but the ROM part stands for "read-only memory," which means that you can't use them to, say, create your own audio CDs or make a backup copy of a CD-ROM. If you're interested in doing these things, then what you need is a CD-R drive. Unlike a CD-ROM, a CD-R disc can accept new data (the "R" stands for "recordable"). Since this process is called *burning* data to the disc, these drives are also called *CD burners*.

The problem with a CD-R disc is that you can only write to it once. So even though the disc is capable of holding about 600MB of data, if you write just 1MB and stop, that's all you'll be able to write to the disc. A better system is the newer CD-RW drive. The "RW" is short for "ReWritable" and it means that you can write to a CD-RW disc, stop, and then come back later and write some more. This makes CD-RW drives great for making backups of your work. Note, however, that most CD-ROM and CD-R drives can't understand CD-RW discs.

The fun news is that Windows XP now supports burning files and folders to both CD-R and CD-RW discs right out of the box. If you have a CD burner attached to your computer, Windows XP should recognize it and be ready to burn at will. To try this out, follow these steps:

1. Insert a CD-R or CD-RW disc in your CD burner.

2. In My Computer, highlight the files or folders you want to burn to the disc.

3. Select **File, Send To, CD Drive (*D:*)** (where *D* is the drive letter of your CD burner). Windows XP "copies" the file, but nothing is being burned to the disc just yet. Windows XP is just storing the files in a temporary location.

4. Repeat steps 3 and 4 until you've finished copying the files and folders you want to burn. (Remember: you only get one chance to burn data to a CD-R disc.)

5. Use My Computer to open the CD burner drive. You'll see a section titled **Files Ready to Be Written to the CD**. Feel free to delete or rename these files.

6. In the **CD Writing Tasks** section, click **Write these files to CD**. Windows XP asks the CD Writing Wizard to take over from here.

7. The first thing the wizard does is ask you to name the CD and it suggests today's date. If you can think of something more useful (there's a no-brainer), enter it in the box and click **Next**. The wizard then busies itself writing the data to the disc.

8. When the wizard's work is done, it spits out the disc and asks if you want to copy the selected files to another disc. If you do, activate the **Yes, write these files to another CD** check box and click **Next**. Otherwise, click **Finish**.

Finding a File in That Mess You Call a Hard Disk

Bill Gates, Microsoft's Big Cheese, used to summarize his company's mission of easy access to data as "information at your fingertips." We're still a long way off from that laudable goal, but there are a few things you can do to ensure that the info you need is never far away:

➤ **Use the My Documents folder**   The most inefficient way to store your documents is to scatter them hither and yon around your hard disk. A much better approach is to plop everything in a single place so that you always know where to look for things. The perfect place for this is the My Documents folder that Windows XP provides for you.

➤ **Use subfolders to organize your documents**   Using My Documents is a good idea (if I do say so myself), but you shouldn't just cram all your stuff into that one folder. Instead, create subfolders to hold related items. Windows XP starts you off with subfolders named My Pictures and My Music, which are the ideal places for your graphics and music files. Feel free to add other subfolders for things such as letters, memos, projects, presentations, spreadsheets, and whatever other categories you can think of.

➤ **Give your files meaningful names**   Take advantage of Windows XP's long file names to give your documents useful names that tell you exactly what's inside each file. A document named "Letter" doesn't tell you much, but "Letter to A. Gore Re: Inventing the Internet" surely does.

➤ **Dejunk your folders**   Keep your folders clean by deleting any junk files that you'll never use again.

If you're like most people, then you'll probably end up with hundreds of documents, but if you follow these suggestions, finding the one you need shouldn't be a problem. Even so, there will be times when you don't remember exactly which document you need, or you might want to find all those documents that contain a particular word or phrase. For these situations, Windows XP offers a Search feature that can help you track down what you need.

To get started, you have two choices:

➤ To search within the current folder in My Computer, either select the **View, Explorer Bar, Search** command, or click the **Search** toolbar button. (Pressing **Ctrl+E** also works.)

➤ To search all of My Computer (that is, all your hard disk drives), select **Start, Search.**

Figure 6.5 shows the window that appears if you use the former technique.

Figure 6.5

*Windows XP's Search
Companion helps you
find AWOL files.*

What happens from here depends on which link you click in the WebView panel.

If you want to search for multimedia files, click the **Pictures, music, or video** link and then follow these steps:

1. The WebView panel now displays three check boxes: **Pictures and Photos, Music and Sound,** and **Video.** Activate the check boxes that correspond to the type of file (or files) you want to find.

2. Use the **Find files named** text box to type in the name of the file you want. Note that you don't have to enter the entire name of the file; just a word or even a few letters will do.

3. If you want to use some fancier search options (explained a bit later), click the **Use advanced search options** link.

4. Click **Search.**

If you want to search through all the documents you've created, click the **Documents (Word, Excel, etc.)** link and then follow these steps:

1. The WebView panel now displays four **Last time it was modified** option buttons. Select the option that best represents the last time you made changes to the file (or select **Don't remember** if you have no idea).

2. Use the **Find documents named** text box to type in the name of the file you want. (Again, you can enter just a word or even a few letters from the name.)

3. If you want to use some fancier search options (explained a bit later), click the **Use advanced search options** link.

4. Click **Search.**

If you want to search through all the files on your system, click the **All Files and Folders** link and then follow these steps:

1. Use the **Part of all of the name** text box to enter some or all of the file name.

2. Use the **A word or phrase in the file** text box to search for a file by content. Enter a word or part of a word that the desired file contains.

3. Use the **Look in** list to select the folder or disk drive in which you want to search (if the displayed folder isn't the one you want).

4. Use the **When was it modified?** options to refine the search according to the date the file was last edited.

5. If you click **What size is it?** the Search Companion provides a few controls that enable you to locate a file according to its size.

6. If you want to use the advanced search features, click the **More advanced options** link.

7. Click **Search.**

You can refine each of these search techniques even further by using the following advanced options:

➤ **Search system folders**   Activating this check box extends the search to include the Windows XP folders. You probably won't ever need to include these subfolders in your search.

➤ **Search hidden files and folders**   Activating this check box extends the search to include those files and folders that have been hidden by Windows XP. Again, you shouldn't ever need to search these files.

➤ **Search subfolders**   Activating this check box tells the Search Companion to examine not only the current folder, but also all of its subfolders.

➤ **Case sensitive**   Activating this check box tells the Search Companion to match the exact uppercase and lowercase letters you entered for the file name.

➤ **Search tape backup**   Activating this check box forces the Search Companion to extend its search to a tape drive on your system. If you have a tape drive, activating this feature can seriously slow down your searches.

Launching a Program with the Run Command

Now that you're well versed in the arcane arts of files and folders, let's put all that to good use. This section shows you how to use Windows XP's Run command, which offers an alternative to the Start menu for launching programs.

In rare cases, the program you want to run might not appear on any of the Start menus. This is particularly true of older DOS programs that don't do Windows. For the time being, you can use the Run command to get these old geezer programs under way.

This isn't for the faint of heart, however, because it requires a bit more work, as the following steps show:

1. Select **Start, Run.** Windows XP displays the Run dialog box.

2. In the **Open** text box, type the name of the disk drive where the program resides (for example, **d:**), its folder (such as **\install**), and then the name of the file that starts the program (for example, **setup.exe**). With these examples used, you'd enter **d:\install\setup.exe**.

3. Click **OK** to run the program.

Whew! Compared to the Start menu, that's true, calluses-on-the-fingertips manual labor. Bear these points in mind when you're working with the Run dialog box:

➤ Instead of typing the command, you can click the **Browse** button and choose the program from the Browse dialog box that appears.

➤ If any part of the file name or folder name contains spaces or is longer than eight characters, you have to surround the whole thing with quotation marks. If you're not sure about this, go ahead and add the quotation marks anyway.

➤ Although you normally use Run to enter program files, you can also use Run to enter the name and location of documents, folders, and even World Wide Web addresses. In each case, Windows XP launches the appropriate program and loads the item you specified.

➤ Windows XP "remembers" the last few commands you entered in the Run dialog box. If you need to repeat a recent command, drop down the **Open** list and select the command.

➤ If you have a keyboard with the Windows logo key on it, press ⊞+**R** to display the Run dialog box.

The Least You Need to Know

➤ **What *not* to do**   Don't muck about with anything inside the drives and folders that Windows XP hides from you (unless someone, like me, has given you very explicit instructions) and don't move, rename, delete, fold, spindle, or mutilate any files that you didn't create yourself.

➤ **Selecting a file or folder**   You select a file or folder by clicking it. To select multiple files or folders, hold down **Ctrl** and click each one.

➤ **Drag 'til you drop**   To drag and drop a file or folder, move the mouse pointer over the item, hold down the right mouse button, move the mouse pointer over the destination, and then release the button. In the shortcut menu that pops up, click either **Copy Here** or **Move Here.**

➤ **Rename restrictions**   When renaming a file (or naming a new file), don't use the following characters: * , \ : " < > ? / .

➤ To burn data to a CD, select the files and folders and then select **File, Send To, CD Drive (D:)** (where **D** is the drive letter of your CD burner). Then open the CD drive and click **Write these files to CD.**

➤ To search for a file in My Computer's current folder, either select the **View, Explorer Bar, Search** command, or click the **Search** toolbar button. To search all of My Computer (that is, all your disk drives), select **Start, Search.**

Chapter 7

Installing and Uninstalling Programs and Devices

In This Chapter

➤ Installing and uninstalling chunks of Windows XP

➤ Installing and uninstalling software programs

➤ Step-by-step procedures for installing all kinds of devices

➤ Installing specific devices such as printers, modems, joysticks, and scanners

➤ Saying *adios* to devices you no longer need

It's one thing to understand that the PC is a versatile beast that can handle all kinds of different programs and devices, but it's quite another to actually install the stuff. This chapter will help by showing you exactly how to install Windows XP components, software programs, and devices on your machine. For good measure, you also learn how to uninstall all those things, just in case they don't get along with your computer.

The Welcome Wagon: Installing a Program

As ou work through this book, you'll see that Windows XP comes stocked with a decent collection of programs, some of which are first-rate (such as Internet Explorer and Outlook Express) and some of which are merely okay (such as Paint and Word-Pad). Also, most PC manufacturers are kind enough to stock their machines with a few extra programs.

However, it's a rare computer owner who's satisfied with just these freebies (or even wants them in the first place). Most of us want something better, faster, *cooler*. If you decide to take the plunge on a new program, this section shows you how to install it in Windows XP. To get you started, the next section shows you how to install new Windows XP components.

Installing a Windows XP Component

Like a hostess who refuses to put out the good china for just anybody, Windows XP may not have installed all of its components automatically. Don't feel insulted; Windows is just trying to go easy on your hard disk. The problem, you see, is that some of the components that come with Windows XP are software behemoths that will happily usurp acres of your precious hard disk land. In a rare act of digital politeness, Windows bypasses these programs (as well as a few other nonessential tidbits) during a typical installation. If you want any of these knickknacks on your system, you have to tell Windows XP to install them for you.

The good news is that Windows XP comes with a handy Windows Component Wizard that enables you to add any of Windows XP's missing pieces to your system without having to trudge through the entire Windows installation routine. Here are the steps to follow:

1. Select **Start**, **Settings**, **Control Panel** to rustle up the Control Panel window.

2. Click the **Add or Remove Programs** icon. Windows XP tosses the Add or Remove Programs window onto your screen.

3. Click the **Add/Remove Windows Components** link to launch the Windows Components Wizard shown in Figure 7.1. (Note that Windows XP takes inventory of the currently installed components, so the wizard takes a few seconds to appear.)

Figure 7.1

The Windows Components Wizard helps you add the bits and pieces that come with Windows XP.

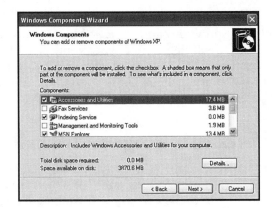

4. The **Components** box lists the various chunks of Windows XP that are already installed as well as those you can add.

   Here's a translation of what the various check box states mean in the Components list: **Unchecked** means the component is not installed. If the component comes in several pieces, none of those pieces is installed. **Checked with a gray background** means the component is partially installed. That is, the component has multiple chunks, but only some of those chunks reside on your system. **Checked with a white background** means the component is installed. If the component comes in several pieces, all of those pieces are installed.

   You have two ways to proceed:

   ➤ To add an entire component, activate its check box.

   ➤ To add only part of a component (assuming that it has multiple parts), click the component name to highlight it and then click **Details.** In the new dialog box that appears, activate the check boxes for the subcomponents you want to install, and click **OK.**

5. Click **Next.** The wizard takes a few moments to gather its thoughts before moving on to the next step.

6. It's likely that the wizard will prompt you to insert your Windows XP CD-ROM. If so, insert the CD-ROM, wait about five seconds, and then click **OK.** The wizard installs the necessary files to your computer.

7. Click **Finish.** The wizard drops you off back at the Add or Remove Programs window.

8. Click **Close.**

9. Depending on the components you add, Windows XP might ask you to restart your computer. If it does, remove the Windows XP CD and then click **Yes** to let Windows XP handle this for you. When the restart is complete, the new components are ready to roll.

Bringing a New Program into Your Computer Home

The built-in Windows XP programs do the job as long as your needs aren't too lofty. However, what if your needs *are* lofty, or if you're looking to fill in a software niche that Windows XP doesn't cover (such as a spreadsheet program, a database, or an action game)? In that case, you need to go outside the Windows box and purchase the appropriate program.

After you have the program, your next chore is to install it. This means you run a "setup" routine that makes the program ready for use on your computer. Most setup procedures perform the following tasks:

➤ Create a new folder for the program.

➤ Copy any files that the program needs to run to the new folder and to other strategic folders on your hard disk.

➤ Adjust Windows XP as needed to ensure that the program runs properly.

How you launch this setup routine depends on how the program is distributed:

Jargon Jar

AutoRun is a feature that automatically launches a program's setup routine (or, later, the program itself) after you insert its CD-ROM or DVD-ROM disc.

➤ **If the program is on a CD** In this case, you might not have to do much of anything. Most computer CDs support a feature called *AutoRun*. This means when you insert the disc into your CD-ROM (or DVD-ROM) drive for the first time, the setup routine gets launched automatically.

➤ **If you downloaded the program from the Internet** In this case, you end up with the downloaded file on your hard disk. Be sure this file resides in an otherwise-empty folder and then double-click the file. This either launches the setup routine or it "extracts" a bunch of files into the folder. If the latter happens, look for an application file named **Setup** (or, more rarely, **Install**), and then double-click that file.

For all other cases—a CD-based program that doesn't start automatically or a program distributed on floppy disks—your best bet is to get Windows XP to launch the setup routine for you. Here's how:

Windows Wisdom

I recommend that you accept the default values offered by the install program (unless you *really* know what you're doing). In particular, if the program gives you a choice of a "typical" or a "custom" installation, go the "typical" route to save yourself time and hassle. You can always go back and install additional components for the specific program later.

1. Select **Start, Settings, Control Panel** to fire up the Control Panel window.

2. Click the **Add or Remove Programs** icon to get to the Add or Remove Programs window.

3. Click the **Add New Programs** link.

4. Click the **CD or Floppy** button. The dialog box that appears asks you to insert the first installation disk or the program's CD-ROM.

5. Insert the CD (or DVD) disc or the floppy disk that came with the program. (Some older programs ship with multiple floppy disks. In this case, look for the disk labeled "Disk 1" or "Setup.")

6. Click **Next.** Windows XP checks your floppy drive and CD (or DVD) drives, searching desperately for any installation program it can find:

   ➤ If the wizard locates a likely candidate, it displays it in the **Open** text box, as you can see in Figure 7.2.

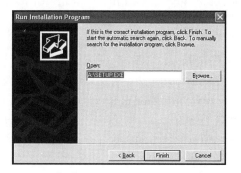

Figure 7.2

Windows XP can hunt down your software's installation program automatically.

   ➤ If it doesn't find an installation program, the wizard asks you to enter the appropriate command in the **Open** text box. If you know where the installation program is located, type the drive, folder, and file name (for example, e:\install\setup). You can also click **Browse** to use a dialog box to pick out the program.

7. Click **Finish.** Windows XP launches the installation program.

From here, follow the instructions and prompts that the setup routine sends your way. (This procedure varies from program to program.)

The Bum's Rush: Uninstalling a Program

Most programs seem like good ideas at the time you install them. Unless you're an outright pessimist, you probably figured that a program you installed was going to help you work harder, be more efficient, or have more fun. Sadly, many programs don't live up to expectations. The good news is that you don't have to put up with a loser program after you realize it's not up to snuff. You can *uninstall* it (completely remove a program from your computer) so that it doesn't clutter up your Start menu, desktop, hard disk, or any other location where it might have inserted itself.

Uninstalling a Windows XP Component

You've seen how the Windows Component Wizard makes it easy to bring Windows XP components in from the cold of the CD-ROM to the warmth of your hard drive. What happens, however, if you grow tired of a particular component's company? For example, the artistically challenged might want to get rid of that Paint program they never use, or the hopelessly unwired might be itching to expunge HyperTerminal from their systems.

Happily, showing these and other Windows XP components to the door is even easier than installing them. And as an added bonus, lopping off some of Windows' limbs serves to free up precious hard disk space, giving you more room for *really* important games—uh, I mean, applications. As you might expect, removing Windows XP components is the opposite of adding them:

1. Select **Start, Settings, Control Panel.**

2. Click the **Add or Remove Programs** icon.

3. Click the **Add/Remove Windows Components** link to once again meet up with the Windows Components Wizard.

4. Deactivate the check boxes for the components you want to blow away. For multiprogram components, click **Details** to see the individual programs, deactivate the check boxes for those you want to nuke, and then click **OK** to return the Windows Setup tab.

5. Click **Next.** Windows XP removes the components you specified without further delay.

6. Click **Finish.**

7. Depending on the components you removed, Windows XP may ask to restart your computer. If so, click **Yes** to make it happen.

Giving a Program the Heave-Ho

If you have a Windows application that has worn out its welcome, this section shows you a couple of methods for uninstalling the darn thing so that it's out of your life forever. The good news is that Windows XP has a feature that enables you to vaporize any application with a simple click of the mouse. The bad news is that this feature is only available for some programs.

To check whether it's available for your program, follow these steps:

1. Display the Control Panel by selecting **Start, Control Panel,** and then click the **Add or Remove Programs** icon.

2. Make sure that the **Change or Remove Programs** link is active.

3. As shown in Figure 7.3, the **Currently installed programs** list shows the programs that have been installed on your computer and that Windows XP knows how to remove automatically. If the program you want to blow to kingdom come is on this list, highlight it and then click its **Change/Remove** button. (Note that some programs have separate Change and Remove buttons. In this case, you need to click the **Remove** button.)

4. What happens next depends on the program. You may see a dialog box asking you to confirm the uninstall, or you may be asked whether you want to run an "Automatic" or "Custom" uninstall. For the latter, be sure to select the **Automatic** option. Whatever happens, follow the instructions on the screen until you return to the Add or Remove Programs window.

5. Click **Close** to wrap things up.

![Add or Remove Programs window showing currently installed programs: Adobe Acrobat 4.0 (8.76MB), CaptureEze97 (2.95MB, Used occasionally, Last Used On 5/18/2001), CuteFTP (2.11MB), MSN Explorer (13.77MB), Netscape Communicator 4.7, Smart tags support for Microsoft Internet Explorer (1.30MB)]

Figure 7.3

The Change or Remove Programs link maintains a list of programs that you can annihilate automatically.

Didn't see the program in the **Currently installed programs** list? All is not lost because there's still one more place to check: the program's home base on the Start menu. Select **Start**, **All Programs** and then open the program's menu (if it has one). Look for a command that includes the word "Uninstall" (or, less likely, "Remove"). If you see one, great: Click it to launch the uninstall procedure.

For those applications that can't be uninstalled automatically, you need to roll up your sleeves and do the whole thing by hand. Here's what to do:

1. Use My Computer to display the program's folder. (Hint: Most programs store their files in a subfolder of the **Program Files** folder on drive C.)

2. Check to see whether the folder contains any data files you want to preserve. If you spent any time at all creating documents (or whatever) in the application, it's a wise precaution to save them for posterity. For one thing, you might want to use them in another application; for another, you might change your mind six months from now and decide to reinstall the application. If you want to save your data, highlight the files and then *move* (not copy) them to another folder (that you can use for storage), or to a floppy disk.

Windows Wisdom

Don't be surprised if the uninstall routine doesn't wipe out absolutely everything for a program. If you created any documents, customized the program, or moved its Start menu items to a new location, the uninstall program leaves behind a few scraps.

3. With that out of the way, go ahead and delete the application's folder.

4. Erase any traces of the program from your Start menu.

5. If the program added any shortcuts to the desktop, delete them, too.

6. To be safe, exit and then restart Windows XP.

Device Advice I: Installing Hardware

Software installation is usually a painless operation that often requires just a few mouse clicks on your part. Hardware, however, is another story altogether. Not only must you attach the device to your machine (which might even require that you remove the cover to get inside the computer), but you also have to hope that the new device doesn't conflict with an existing one.

The latter is less of a problem thanks to Windows XP's support for something called Plug and Play. This enables Windows XP to immediately recognize a new device and to configure that device automatically. It's a kind of hardware nirvana that makes it easy for the average bear to upgrade the physical side of their computers. To make it work, however, you need two things:

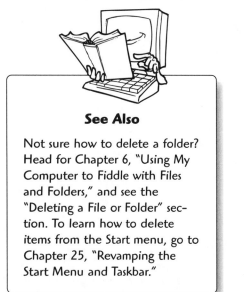

See Also

Not sure how to delete a folder? Head for Chapter 6, "Using My Computer to Fiddle with Files and Folders," and see the "Deleting a File or Folder" section. To learn how to delete items from the Start menu, go to Chapter 25, "Revamping the Start Menu and Taskbar."

➤ **Devices that support Plug and Play** Most new hardware doodads are Plug and Play friendly. However, to be safe, check the box to be sure it says "Plug and Play" before buying anything. Note that the newfangled USB (Universal Serial Bus) devices support Plug and Play. However, your computer needs to have one or more USB ports to use them.

➤ **Devices that are compatible with Windows XP** Windows XP, finicky beast that it is, won't work with just any old device. Again, before buying a device, check the box to see whether it says anything about being compatible with Windows XP. (Devices that are compatible with Windows 98, Me, or 2000 ought to work fine, as well.)

Understanding Hardware Types

Although thousands of devices are available, and dozens of device categories, I like to organize devices according to how you attach them to the computer. From this point of view, there are four types to worry about:

➤ **External plug-in devices**   These are devices that use some kind of cable to plug into a *port* in the back of the PC. These devices include keyboards, mice, joysticks, modems, printers, speakers, and monitors. These kinds of devices are easy to install if you remember one thing: The computer's ports each have a unique shape, and the cable's plug has a shape that matches one of those ports. So, there's usually only one possible place into which any cable can plug. The exception to this is if the back of the computer has two ports with identical configurations. That just means your machine offers two of the same port type, so you can plug your device into either one.

➤ **PC Card (PCMCIA) devices**   These types of devices are the easiest to install because they simply slip into any one of the computer's PC card slots (or *sockets,* as they're called). Note, however, that these slots are almost always found only on notebook computers.

➤ **Internal disk drives**   These are the toughest devices to install not only because you have to get inside your computer, but also because there are many steps involved. Your best bet here is to take the machine to a computer service center or cajole a nearby computer geek into doing the job for you.

➤ **Internal circuit boards**   These are cards that plug into slots inside your computer. There are circuit boards for all kinds of things, including sound cards, graphics cards, network cards, and video decoder cards (which usually come with DVD-ROM drives nowadays). Again, you should get someone who knows what they're doing to install these kinds of devices for you.

Running the Add Hardware Wizard

Your device and your computer are now shacked up, but they're not married yet. To get a full relationship going, Windows XP has to install a tiny bit of software called a *device driver*. This miniprogram has the code that operates (drives) the device, so it acts as a kind of middleman between the device and Windows XP.

In the best of all possible worlds, after you've attached the device (and, if necessary, restarted your computer), Windows XP recognizes the new limb and displays the New Hardware Found dialog box. (This is my favorite dialog box because it means I have little if any work to do from here. An under-your-breath "Yes!" is the appropriate reaction to seeing this dialog box.) Windows XP then proceeds to install the device driver and any other software required to make the device go. This is automatic, for the most part, but you may occasionally be asked a few simple questions to complete the setup. In particular, you might see the Found New Hardware Wizard, which leads you through the installation of a device driver. (The process is similar to upgrading a driver.)

If, for some reason, Windows XP doesn't automatically recognize your new device, all is not lost. That's because Windows XP comes with a hardware helper called the Add

New Hardware Wizard, which scours every nook and cranny of your system to look for new stuff. Here's how it works:

1. Select **Start, Control Panel** to crack open the Control Panel window.

2. Click **Printers and Other Hardware**, and then click the **Add Hardware** link in the WebView panel's **See Also** section. The Add Hardware Wizard wipes the grease from its hands and comes out to meet you.

3. The initial dialog box just tells you some things you already know, so click **Next**. The wizard then checks for new Plug and Play devices that you've connected recently but that haven't been installed. If it finds any, you'll see the Found New Hardware message and the wizard will install the necessary device driver. In this case, skip to step 8.

4. If the wizard didn't find any new Plug and Play devices, it asks if the hardware is connected. Make sure the **Yes, I have already connected the hardware** option is activated and then click **Next**.

5. Now the wizard displays the **Installed hardware** list with all of your computer's devices. Click **Add a new hardware device** at the bottom of the list and then click **Next**.

6. The next wizard dialog box asks whether you want Windows to detect your new hardware automatically. This is the best way to go; make sure to activate the **Search for and install the hardware automatically (Recommended)** option, and then click **Next**. (I tell you a bit later how to specify hardware yourself.)

7. If the Add New Hardware Wizard doesn't find any new hardware, it tells you so. If that happens, click **Cancel**, shut down your computer (make sure that you use the **Start, Turn Off Computer** or **Start, Shut Down** command), check to see whether you attached the new device correctly, and then try again. If it's still a no-go, try installing the hardware by using the instructions given later in this section.

8. More likely, however, the wizard will tell you that it's finished detecting and is ready to install the support files for the device. It will then display a list of the installed devices. Click **Finish**.

If the wizard failed in its quest to find your device, you can stick Windows XP's nose in it, so to speak, by specifying exactly which device you added. To get started, you have two choices:

➤ If you're starting the Add Hardware Wizard from scratch, follow the preceding steps 1 through 4.

➤ If you're still in the wizard at the dialog box that tells you Windows didn't find any new devices, click **Back**.

You now follow these steps:

1. Activate the **Install the hardware that I manually select from a list (Advanced)** option, and click **Next.**

2. The wizard displays a whack of device categories in the **Common hardware types** list. Highlight the category that applies to your device. If you don't see the appropriate category, click **Show All Devices.** When you're ready to proceed, click **Next.**

3. The wizard takes a few seconds to gather its thoughts, and then it displays a list of device manufacturers and devices. For example, Figure 7.4 shows the dialog box that appears for the Display adapters category. You have two ways to proceed from here:

   ➤ Highlight the device maker in the **Manufacturers** list, then highlight the name of your device in the **Models** list.

   ➤ If your device is nowhere to be found, it's likely that you received a disk inside the device package. Insert the disk and then click **Have Disk.** In the Install from Disk dialog box, enter the location of the disk (type the drive letter followed by a colon [:] and a backward slash [\], such as **A:**) and click **OK.** (If Windows XP complains about not being able to find anything on the disk, click **Browse** and look for a subfolder on the disk, usually with some form of "windows" label.) You'll eventually see a list of models that can be installed. Highlight your model.

   ➤ If you don't have a disk from the manufacturer, you can still download the specific device driver for your hardware from the manufacturer's Web site. (See Chapter 29, "When Windows Won't Work: Troubleshooting Common Problems," for more on this.) Once you've done that, you'd then click **Have Disk** and enter the location of the downloaded device driver file.

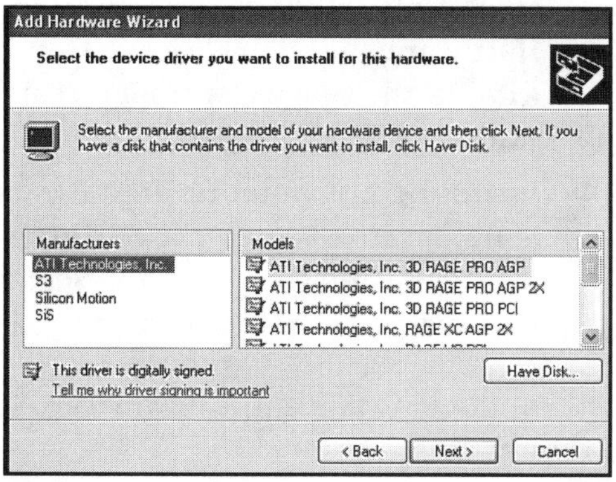

Figure 7.4

Use this dialog box to pick out the device manufacturer and model.

4. Click **Next.** The wizard tells you that it will now install the drivers for the device.

5. Click **Next**. The wizard, true to its word, installs the device drivers. Note that you might need to insert your Windows XP CD at this point.

6. When all is said and done, click **Finish** to close the wizard. If Windows XP asks if you want to restart your computer, click **Yes**.

Installing Specific Devices

Just to keep everyone thoroughly confused (which a cynic might describe as Windows' *real* job), Windows XP offers different installation routes for certain types of devices. These include perennially popular items such as printers, modems, joysticks, scanners, and digital cameras. Here's a quick look at what you have to do to install these types of devices:

➤ **Installing a printer** Select **Start, Control Panel**, click **Printers and Other Hardware** and then click the **Add a printer** icon. This conjures up the Add Printer Wizard to take you through the process. Along the way, you get asked how your printer is attached (choose **Local printer**), the manufacturer and model, and the printer port (this is almost always **LPT1**).

➤ **Installing a modem** Select **Start, Control Panel**, click **Printers and Other Hardware**, and then click **Phone and Modem Options.** This unleashes the Install New Modem Wizard. (If, instead, you see the Phone and Modem Option dialog box, it means your modem is already installed and should be shown in the Modems tab. If it's not, or if you want to install a different modem, click **Add.**) This wizard scours your computer's ports to see if a modem is attached to one of them.

➤ **Installing a game controller** To Windows XP, a joystick or other device you use for gaming is called a *game controller*. To install one, Select **Start, Control Panel**, click **Printers and Other Hardware** and then click the **Game Controllers** icon. In the Game Controllers dialog box, click **Add.**

➤ **Installing a scanner or digital camera** Select **Start, Control Panel**, click **Printers and Other Hardware** and then click the **Scanners and Cameras** icon. In the Scanners and Cameras window, click the **Add an imaging device** link to send in the Scanner and Camera Installation Wizard.

See Also

If you need to install a network printer, instead, see Chapter 31, "Using Windows XP's Networking Features."

Device Advice II: Removing Hardware

If a device suddenly becomes tiresome and boring, or if you get a better device for your birthday, you need to remove the old device from your computer and then let Windows XP know that it's gone. The exception to this is if the device supports Plug and Play. If it does, then Windows XP recognizes that the device is gone and it adjusts itself accordingly. Otherwise, you need to do it by hand:

1. Select **Start, Control Panel,** click **Printers and Other Hardware** and then click the **System** link. Windows XP arranges a meeting with the System Properties dialog box.

2. Display the **Hardware** tab and then click **Device Manager.**

3. Click the plus sign (+) beside the hardware category you want to work with. For example, if the soon-to-be-toast device is a network adapter, open the **Network adapters** branch.

4. Click the device and then select the **Action, Uninstall** command. Windows XP states the obvious and tells you that you're about to remove the device.

5. Say "Duh!" and click **OK.** Windows XP wastes no more of your time and removes the device from the list.

6. Click **Close.**

7. If the device is an internal component, shut down your computer (use **Start, Turn Off Computer** or **Start, Shut Down**) and then remove the device. Otherwise, just unplug the device.

Windows Wisdom

An easier way to get to the System Properties dialog box is to click **Start,** right-click the **My Computer** icon, and then click **Properties** in the shortcut menu.

The Least You Need to Know

➤ **Automatic CDs**   Most computer CD-ROM (and DVD-ROM) discs support AutoRun, so the installation program runs automatically after you insert the disc.

➤ **Installing and uninstalling made easy**   Use Control Panel's **Add or Remove Programs** icon to help you install and uninstall Windows XP components and third-party programs.

➤ **Best hardware bets**   To ensure the easiest hardware configuration, buy only devices that are both Plug and Play–compatible and Windows XP–compatible.

➤ **Peruse the ports**   When installing an external device, remember that its cable can plug into only a single, complementary port on the back of the computer.

➤ **Hardware helper**   If Plug and Play doesn't work, launch Control Panel, click **Printers and Other Hardware,** and then click the **Add Hardware** link to help you install and uninstall devices.

➤ **If you have hardware woes**   See Chapter 29, "When Windows Won't Work: Troubleshooting Common Problems" for some advice.

Part 2

Windows XP at Home

It wasn't all that long ago when computers were viewed as "business only" beasts, and only the most geeklike among us actually had a PC at home. Now, this being the twenty-first century and all, the digital domicile is a reality and computers in the home are as common as the weeds in your neighbor's yard. Just think: All that cursing and fuming you direct toward your work computer can now be continued in the privacy of your own home. But that's not the only advantage to having a home machine. Now you can perform many personal tasks that aren't appropriate at the office: making drawings, manipulating photos, playing and copying music, and making digital movies. And the best news is that Windows XP is set up to handle all of those leisure time activities right out of the box. The chapters here in Part 2 show you how to perform these and other home-sweet-home tasks.

Chapter 8

Playing with Pictures

In This Chapter

➤ GIF, JPEG, and other image format acronyms

➤ Working with image thumbnails, filmstrips, and slide shows

➤ Converting an image from one format to another

➤ Printing images

➤ Ordering prints online

Windows has enabled us to go beyond the workaday world of letters and memos to documents that positively cry out for image enhancement: business presentations, flyers, newsletters, and Web pages, to name only a few. Again, Windows has various tools that let you create images from scratch, mess around with existing images, and capture digital images from an outside source (such as a scanner). None of these tools are good enough for professional artists, but they're more than adequate for amateur dabblers whose needs aren't so grandiose. This chapter shows you how to create and modify images using the Paint program, and how to capture and manipulate digital images from a scanner or digital camera.

The Alphabet Soup of Picture File Formats

There's certainly no shortage of ways that the world's computer geeks have come up with over the years to confuse users and other mere mortals. But few things get the man-or-woman-on-the-street more thoroughly bamboozled than the bewildering array of file formats (also known as file types) that exist in the digital world. And perhaps the worst culprit is the picture file category, which boasts an unseemly large number of formats. My goal in this section is to help you get through the thicket of acronyms and minutiae that characterize picture file formats, and to show you how to simplify things so that they actually make sense.

Before you go any further into this file format business, you might enjoy taking a step or two in reverse to consider the bigger picture: What is a file format and why do we need so many of them? I like to look at file formats as the underlying structure of a file that's akin to a car's underlying structure. The latter is a collection of metal and plastic bits that form the frame, axles, suspension, engine, and other innards that determine how the car performs. A file format is similar in that it consists of a collection of bits and bytes that determines how the picture is viewed. As you'll see, some formats are better suited for displaying photos, while others have a better time with line drawings.

Windows Wisdom

Throughout this chapter and in other parts of the book I'll use the terms *picture, image,* and *graphic* interchangeably.

The sigh-of-relief-inducing news is that even though the computing world is on speaking terms with dozens of different image formats, Windows XP is conversant with only five:

➤ **Bitmap**   This is the standard image file format used by Windows XP. It's good for color drawings, although its files tend to be on the large side. Bitmap image files use the .bmp extension, so these files are also referred to sometimes as BMP files.

➤ **GIF**   This is one of the standard graphics file formats used on the Internet's World Wide Web. It's only capable of storing 256 colors, so it's only suitable for relatively simple line drawings or for images that use only a few colors. The resulting files are compressed, so they end up quite a bit smaller than bitmap files.

➤ **JPEG**   This is the other standard graphics file format that you see on the World Wide Web. This format can reproduce millions of colors, so it's suitable for photographs and other high-quality images. JPEG stores images in a compressed format, so it can knock high-quality images down to a manageable size while still retaining some picture fidelity. (However, the more you compress the image, the poorer the image quality becomes.)

➤ **PNG**   This is a relatively new file format that's becoming more popular on the Internet (although it's still not supported by all browsers). It's a versatile format that can be used with both simple drawings and photos. For the latter, PNG supports compression to keep images relatively small. (And, unlike JPEG, the PNG compression doesn't reduce the quality of the image.)

➤ **TIF** This format is often used with image scanners and digital cameras because it does a great job of rendering photos and other scanned images. The downside is that this format doesn't usually compress the images in any way, so it creates *huge* files. (Note that this file format sometimes goes by the name of TIFF instead of just TIF.)

So which one should you use when creating your own image files? That depends:

➤ If you're creating a drawing that you'll print out or work with only on your computer, use the bitmap format.

➤ If you're creating a simple drawing that you'll be publishing to the World Wide Web, use GIF.

➤ If you're creating a more complex drawing that you'll be publishing to the Web, use PNG.

➤ If you're scanning in an image or downloading a photo from a digital camera for printing or for editing only on your computer, use TIF.

➤ If you're scanning in an image or downloading a photo from a digital camera for e-mailing or publishing to the Web, use JPEG.

A Tour of the My Pictures Folder

Back in Chapter 5, "Saving, Opening, Printing, and Other Document Lore," I told you about the My Documents folder and mentioned that it's the perfect spot to store the documents you create. If you've been doing that, then you no doubt have noticed that My Documents includes a subfolder named My Pictures, and you probably guessed that this subfolder is where you ought to be hoarding your picture files. That's certainly true, but not just because of the folder's name. No, My Pictures is the place to squirrel away your images because it's a special folder that "understands" picture files and so offers you some extra features that are designed specifically for messing around with images:

➤ It has a "thumbnail" view that shows you not only the name of each file, but also gives you a miniature preview of what each image looks like.

➤ It enables you to see a "preview" of any image, from which you can then rotate the image, print it, and perform a few other tasks.

➤ It enables you to view all your images one-by-one in a kind of "slide show."

See Also

The features available with the My Pictures folder can also be applied to other folders where you store images. I'll show you how in Chapter 26, "Renovating My Computer."

➤ It enables you to set up a particular image as your Windows XP desktop background.

➤ It enables you to order prints of your digital photos from an Internet-based printing service.

The rest of this chapter takes you through the specifics of these features. Before getting to that, however, it's probably a good idea to review just how you get to the My Pictures folder. Windows XP offers two methods:

➤ Select **Start, My Pictures**.

➤ If you're currently in the **My Documents** folder, double-click the icon for the **My Pictures** subfolder.

All Thumbs: Using the Thumbnail View

When you arrive at the My Pictures folder, you'll probably see the files arranged something like those shown in Figure 8.1. That is, instead of a boring (and only marginally useful) icon, each file shows a mini-preview of the image contained in the file.

Figure 8.1

By default, Windows XP displays a small preview of each graphics file in the My Pictures folder.

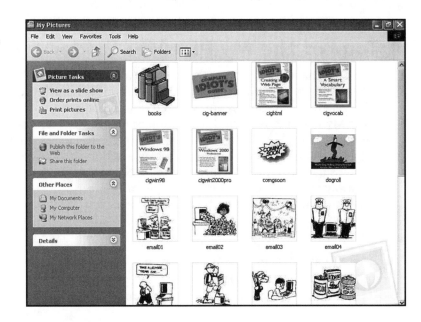

This handy way of looking at things is called the Thumbnail view, and it's the default view used by the My Pictures folder. If you just see filenames instead of thumbnails, you can turn on the latter by activating the **View, Thumbnails** command.

If you want to know details about an image—such as its height and width in pixels, its file type, and its size—move your mouse pointer over the file. After a second or two, a banner appears with that image info written on it.

You should also note at this point that when you click an image file to highlight it, the WebView panel's **Picture Tasks** section offers several image-related links, including **View as slide show** and **Order prints online.** I'll talk about these links as you work through this chapter.

If you have a slow computer, you may find that Windows XP takes quite a bit of time to display each of the thumbnails. In that case, a faster alternative would be to switch to one of the regular views (such as Icons, List, or Details) and then click an image file to highlight it. Then, in the WebView area, click the downward-pointing arrow in the Details section to open it up. This shows you not only a thumbnail of the selected image, but also its type, dimensions, size, and then date it was created or last modified.

Attending a Strip Show: Using the Filmstrip View

NEW!   The thumbnail view is a great way to find the image you're looking for, but it isn't a great way to view that image once you've picked it out from the herd. To see the bigger picture (literally), Windows XP gives you two choices: the Filmstrip view (which I discuss in this section) and the image preview (which I discuss in the next section).

The Filmstrip view is a new Windows XP feature, and you start it up by selecting the **View, Filmstrip** command. When you do that, the My Pictures window converts itself into the configuration shown in Figure 8.2. The bulk of the window displays the currently highlighted picture file, which is shown full-size or as big as possible. At the bottom of the window you see all your picture files arranged in a strip from left to right. In between, you see four icons:

Windows Wisdom

You can also activate the Previous Image icon by pressing the left arrow key on your keyboard. For the Next Image icon, press the right arrow key. Note, too, that you can also rotate the image by pulling down the **File** menu and selecting the **Rotate Clockwise** or **Rotate Counterclockwise** commands.

➤ **Previous Image**   Click this icon to display the previous image in the strip (that is, the image to the left of the current image).

➤ **Next Image**   Click this icon to display the next image in the strip (that is, the image to the right of the current image).

➤ **Rotate Clockwise**   Click this icon to rotate the image clockwise by 90 degrees. Note that this rotation doesn't apply only to the Filmstrip view; Windows XP applies it to the file itself.

103

➤ **Rotate Counterclockwise**   Click this icon to rotate the image counterclockwise by 90 degrees. Again, this change is applied to the file itself.

Figure 8.2

Select View, Filmstrip to see your picture files one-by-one in a kind of film-strip.

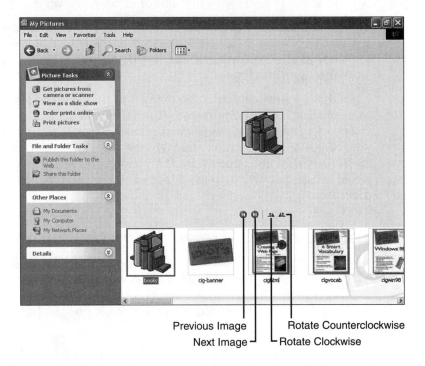

Previous Image
Next Image
Rotate Counterclockwise
Rotate Clockwise

A Closer Look: Previewing a Picture

If you prefer to work with one image at a time, the image preview feature might be just what you're looking for. To activate it, highlight the image you want to work with and then select **File, Preview** (an alternative method is to right-click the image and then click **Preview** in the shortcut menu that shows up). This loads the picture into the Image Preview window, shown in Figure 8.3.

This new window shows you a larger version of the image and is also festooned with a few icons at the bottom. You'll recognize our old friends Previous Image, Next Image, Rotate Clockwise, and Rotate Counterclockwise from the Filmstrip view. Here's what the other icons do:

➤ **Best Fit**   Click this icon (or press Ctrl+B) to display the image in the largest possible size that will still fit entirely within the Image Preview window.

➤ **Actual Size**   Click this icon (or press Ctrl+A) to see a life-sized version of the image.

➤ **Start Slide Show**   Click this icon (or press F11) to start a slide show of the files in the My Pictures folder (more on this later in the chapter).

➤ **Zoom In**   Click this icon (or press + on the numeric keypad only) to get a closer look at the picture.

➤ **Zoom Out**   Click this icon (or press – on the numeric keypad only) to pull back from the picture.

➤ **Delete**   Click this icon (or press Delete) to send the image to the Recycle Bin.

➤ **Print**   Click this icon (or press Ctrl+P) to start the Photo Printing Wizard (which I discuss in the section "Printing Pictures" later in this chapter).

➤ **Copy To**   Click this icon (or press Ctrl+S) to make a copy of the image in another folder.

Note that if you cue up a TIF file in the Image Preview window, you see a lot of other icons besides the ones shown in Figure 8.3. These extra icons are for *annotating* the image, which means adding your own notes and comments. This feature is used most often with faxes (which are often saved in TIF format), so I discuss annotation when I discuss faxing in Chapter 15, "Fax-It-Yourself: Using Windows XP's Faxing Features."

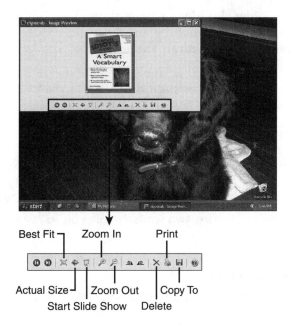

Figure 8.3

Select File, Preview to display the highlighted file in the Image Preview window.

Converting an Image to Another Format

One of the most common image chores is converting a file from one format to a different format. For example, I mentioned earlier that the GIF and JPEG formats are the ones most commonly used on the World Wide Web. If you've scanned in an image or digital photo to the TIF format (see Chapter 9, "Graphics Gadgetry: Working with Scanners and Digital Cameras") and you want to place it on a Web site, then you need to convert the image to JPEG. Similarly, if you've created a drawing in Paint (see Chapter 10, "Giving Your Right Brain a Workout with Paint") and saved it in the bitmap (BMP) format, then you need to convert it to GIF.

Here are the steps to trudge through to perform these and other image format conversions:

1. Display the picture in the Image Preview window.

2. Click the **Copy To** icon.

3. In the Copy To dialog box that comes by, use the **Save as type** list to choose the new file format you want.

4. (Optional) Select a new destination folder and change the **File name.**

5. Click **Save.**

Setting Up an Image Slide Show

For its next trick, the My Pictures folder also offers a "slide show" view. This means that Windows XP displays a full-screen version of the first file, waits about five seconds, displays the second file, and so on. To activate the slide show, you have two choices:

➤ In the My Pictures folder, click the **View as slide show** link in the WebView panel's **Picture Tasks** section.

➤ In the Image Preview window, click the **Start Slide Show** icon.

Note that you can also control the slide show by hand by using the following techniques:

➤ **To display the slide show controls**   Press **Tab.** This displays five icons in the upper-right corner of the screen. The first two icons enable you to restart and pause the slide show.

➤ **To show the next slide**   Click the mouse, press the right arrow key, or click **Next Picture** in the slide show controls.

➤ **To show the previous slide**   Press the left arrow key or click **Previous Picture** in the slide show controls.

➤ **To stop the slide show**   Press **Esc** or click **Close the window** in the slide show controls.

No Film? No Problem: Ordering Prints Online

NEW!   If you have a digital camera, getting your photos from pixels to prints is often a challenge. It's not so bad if you have a fancy printer, but they tend to be expensive beasts (both to buy and to maintain). Recently, however, a far less expensive solution has been developed (take that as a pun, if you dare): the online printing service. The basic idea is straightforward: you send your digital photo to the online printing service, which then uses its fancy-schmancy printing equipment to convert your digital image into a real-world print. Once that's done, the service then mails the print to your home or business.

Support for this kind of service is a new feature in Windows XP. Here's how it works:

1. Open the My Pictures folder.

2. Select the pictures you want to print online.

3. In the WebView panel's **Picture Tasks** section, click **Order prints online.** Windows XP gets the Online Print Order Wizard on the job.

4. The first wizard dialog box isn't much use, so click **Next.** The Select a Printing Company dialog box appears.

5. Use the **Companies** list to highlight which online printing company you prefer and then click **Next.** The wizard then connects to the Internet and downloads the appropriate data for the company you chose.

6. From here, follow the instructions that come your way for choosing print sizes and quantities, billing information, and so on. (The specific instructions vary depending on which printing company you use.)

Printing Pictures

NEW!   Printing a picture—particularly a digital photo—is a bit different than printing a text document because in most cases you want to choose a different print layout depending on the size of the image and the size of the print you want. For that reason, Windows XP includes a new Photo Printing Wizard that takes you step-by-step through the photo printing process. Here's how it works:

1. You can choose the files you want to print in advance or via the wizard:

   ➤ If you don't want to select any files now, go ahead and click the WebView panel's **Print pictures** link.

   ➤ If you want to print only a single file, select it and then click the WebView panel's **Print this picture** link. Note that if you change your mind about which picture or pictures to print, you can modify your selection using the wizard.

   ➤ If you want to print two or more files, select them and then click the WebView panel's **Print the selected pictures** link. The wizard assumes these are the files you want to print, so it won't give you any opportunity to add to your selections. (However, it does allow you to deselect one or more of the files.)

107

2. In the initial wizard dialog box, click **Next**. The Photo Selection dialog box appears.

3. For each image you want to print, activate the check box in the upper-right corner of the image. (Click **Select All** to activate the check box for every image; click **Clear All** to deactivate the check box for every image.) When you've made your choices, click **Next**. The Printing Options dialog box appears.

4. If you have more than one printer, use the **What printer do you want to use?** list to select a printer. You should also click the **Printing Preferences** button to adjust the settings on your printer. These settings depend on the printer, but they generally include selecting the type of paper you'll be using and whether you want to print in color or black and white. When you're ready to move on, click **Next**. The Layout Selection dialog box appears.

5. Use the **Available layouts** list to select the print size you want. When you select a different layout, the **Print preview** box shows you what your printed image will look like. When you've made your choice, click **Next**. The wizard sends your image (or images) to the printer.

6. Click **Finish**.

Setting a Picture as the Desktop Background

Windows XP's desktop comes with a fairly spiffy background image. However, you may find that you get bored with it after a while or that you have a picture of your own that you'd prefer to use. Either way, it's no problem to change the desktop background to any picture in your My Pictures folder. In fact, it takes just two measly steps:

1. In the My Pictures folder, select the file that contains the image you want to use.

2. In the WebView panel's **Picture Tasks** section, click the **Set as desktop background** link.

Capturing a Picture of the Screen

In the next chapter you'll learn how to get images into your computer by using a scanner or digital camera. Another way to get an image without having to draw anything is to "capture" what's on your screen. You have two ways to go about this:

➤ To capture the entire screen, lock, stock, and taskbar, press your keyboard's **Print Screen** key. (Depending on your keyboard, this key may be labeled Print Scrn, PrtScn, PrtSc, or some other variation on this theme.)

➤ If you want to capture only whatever is in the active window, press **Alt+Print Screen.**

Either way, you can then toss the captured image onto your hard disk by launching Paint (select **Start, All Programs, Accessories, Paint**) and selecting **Edit, Paste.** If Paint complains that the image you're pasting is too large, click **Yes** to enlarge your drawing to fit the image.

The Least You Need to Know

➤ **If you're working only on your computer** In this case, the best formats to use are bitmap for drawings and TIF for photos.

➤ **If you're going to e-mail pictures or publish them on the Web** In this case, use GIF for drawing and JPEG for photos.

➤ **Picture views you can use** In the My Pictures folder, use the **View** menu's **Thumbnails** command to view the images as thumbnails, and use the **Filmstrip** command to view your images sequentially, sort of like a filmstrip.

➤ **Converting an image** Display the picture in the Image Preview window, click **Copy To,** and then use the **Save as type** list to choose the new format.

➤ **Grabbing screen shots** Press **Print Screen** to capture an image of the full screen, or **Alt+Print Screen** to capture an image of just the active window.

109

Chapter 9

Graphics Gadgetry: Working with Scanners and Digital Cameras

In This Chapter

➤ Telling Windows XP about your scanner or digital camera

➤ Making sure your scanner or camera works properly

➤ Getting images from the scanner or camera to your computer

➤ Working directly with the photos stored in a digital camera

It used to be that the only way to get an image onto your computer was either to create it yourself or to grab a prefab pic from a clip art collection or photo library. If you lacked artistic flair, or if you couldn't find a suitable image, you were out of luck.

Now, however, getting images into digital form is easier than ever, thanks to two graphics gadgets that have become more affordable. A *document scanner* acts much like a photocopier in that it creates an image of a flat surface, such as a photograph or a sheet of paper. The difference is that the scanner saves the image to a graphics file on your hard disk instead of on paper. A *digital camera* acts much like a regular camera in that it captures and stores an image of the outside world. The difference is that the digital camera stores the image internally in its memory instead of on exposed film. It's then possible to connect the digital camera to your computer and save the image as a graphics file on your hard disk.

The big news is that Windows XP understands both types of doohickeys and often identifies them by a single generic name: *imaging devices* (since both produce image files). Windows XP comes with support for a variety of scanners and cameras, so getting your digital images from out here to in there has never been easier, as you'll see in this chapter.

Installing a Scanner or Digital Camera

Windows XP offers a number of options for installing scanners and digital cameras. Make sure the device is turned on and connected to your computer and then try the following:

➤ **Rely on Plug and Play**   Most of today's crop of scanners and cameras are Plug-and-Play compatible. This means that as soon as you turn on and connect the device to your computer, Windows XP should recognize it and set it up for you automatically. Do you have one or more USB ports on your computer? If so, then if you're looking to buy a new scanner or digital camera, you'll save yourself a lot of grief if you make sure that the device supports USB. The advantages to this are twofold: First, it means that Windows XP will almost certainly recognize and install the device as soon as you plug it in to the computer; second, it will take far less time to transfer images from the device to your computer.

➤ **Use the Scanners and Cameras icon**   If Windows XP doesn't recognize your scanner or camera, it may just need a bit of convincing. To do that, select **Start, Control Panel**, click **Printers and Other Hardware**, and then click **Scanners and Cameras.** When the Scanners and Cameras window shows up, click **Add an imaging device** to get the Scanner and Camera Installation Wizard on the job. Click **Next** to see a list of scanner and digital camera manufacturers and models. Find your camera or scanner in this list, click **Next,** and follow the instructions on the screen.

➤ **Install the device software**   Any scanner or digital camera worth its salt will come with software for setting up the device. If the first two options don't work, try installing the software.

Look Out!

Only someone logged on as an Administrator can add imaging devices using the Scanners and Cameras method.

When your scanner or camera is installed, you'll see an icon for it in the Scanners and Cameras window, as shown in Figure 9.1. (Remember: To get to this window, select **Start, Control Panel**, click **Printers and Other Hardware**, and then click **Scanners and Cameras.**) Note, however, that if you turn off or disconnect the device, then it no longer appears in this window.

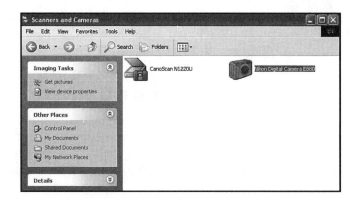

Figure 9.1

The Scanners and Cameras window contains icons for each imaging device installed on your system.

You should also know that Windows XP considers a digital camera to be a type of file storage device. This makes sense because a digital camera uses some kind of memory module or disk to store the digital photos you've taken. The kicker is that since the camera stores files, Windows XP treats it as a folder attached to your computer, so it appears in My Computer, as shown in Figure 9.2. Later in this chapter I'll show you how to use My Computer to get at the images stored in your camera.

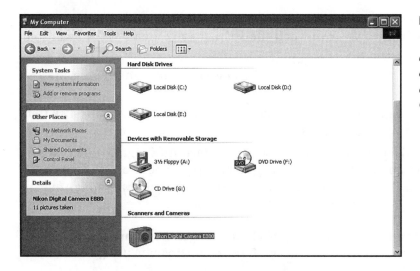

Figure 9.2

Windows XP considers a digital camera just another folder, so the camera shows up in My Computer.

Before you use your scanner or camera, it's a good idea to test it to make sure Windows XP can communicate with it.

1. With the device still connected and turned on, click it in the Scanners and Cameras window to highlight it.

2. In the WebView panel's **Imaging Tasks** section, click **View device properties**.

3. This displays a dialog box that's specific to the device. In all cases, however, the General tab has a button named **Test Scanner** or **Test Camera** (or even **Test Scanner or Camera**). Whatever the name, click the button.

113

If all is well, you'll see a dialog box named Test Successful that tells you the device completed the diagnostic test. If you see the Test Failed dialog box, instead, make sure the scanner is connected and turned on and then try again.

Getting Images from Your Scanner or Camera

The whole point of a scanner or digital camera is to transfer an image of something from the device to your computer hard drive. From there you can edit the image, e-mail it to a friend or colleague, publish it to the World Wide Web, or simply store it for safekeeping. This section shows you how to make a hard (disk) copy of an image.

Using the Scanner and Camera Wizard with Newer Scanners

If you have a newer scanner or camera, Windows XP installs its own Scanner and Camera Wizard to give you a step-by-step method for capturing images. Let's see how it works. First, launch the Scanner and Camera Wizard using one of the following methods:

➤ Connect the device to your computer. After you've installed your scanner or camera, the next time you connect it the Scanner and Camera Wizard will come out to play automatically.

➤ If your device is a scanner and it has some kind of "scan" button, press that button.

➤ In the Scanners and Cameras window, click the device icon and then click **Get pictures** in the WebView panel's **Imaging Tasks** section.

➤ Give the wizard a poke in the ribs by selecting **Start, All Programs, Accessories, Scanner and Camera Wizard.** If you have more than one imaging device, you'll see the Select Device dialog box. Click the device you want to use and then click **OK.**

When the initial wizard window appears, click **Next** to get the wizard to connect to the scanner. What happens from here depends on whether you're using a scanner or a digital camera.

How the Wizard Deals with a Scanner

For a scanner, you'll see the Choose Scanning Preferences dialog box shown in Figure 9.3.

The **Picture type** section offers four options:

➤ **Color picture**   Choose this option if the document you're scanning is a color photograph or drawing.

➤ **Grayscale picture** Choose this option if your document is a picture that renders colors using different shades of gray.

➤ **Black and white picture or text** Choose this option if your document uses only black and white (for example, if it's a page of text).

➤ **Custom** This option doesn't seem to do much of anything, so you may as well ignore it.

If you know what you're doing, click the **Custom Settings** button to adjust properties such as the brightness, contrast, and *resolution* of the scanned image.

If you want to see what your image will look like before committing yourself to the scan, click the **Preview** button.

Jargon Jar

The **resolution** determines the overall quality of the scanned image. The higher the resolution, the higher the quality and (on the downside) the bigger the resulting file. Resolution is measured in dots per inch (DPI).

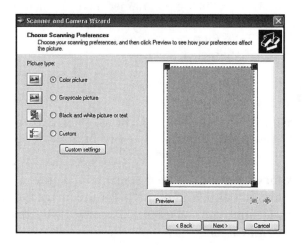

Figure 9.3

If you're working with a scanner, the wizard displays this dialog box.

How the Wizard Deals with a Digital Camera

For a digital camera, you'll see the Choose Pictures to Copy dialog box shown in Figure 9.4. This dialog box offers up a thumbnail image for each digital photo stored in the camera, and each thumbnail sports a check box in the upper-right corner:

➤ Leave the check box activated for each image you want to copy to your hard disk.

➤ Deactivate the check box for each image that you don't want to copy.

Note, too, that you can rotate an image and see information about an image (such as its size) by highlighting it and then clicking the icons pointed out in Figure 9.4.

115

Figure 9.4

If you're working with a digital camera, the wizard displays this dialog box.

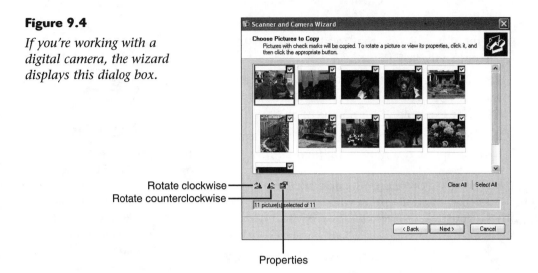

Rotate clockwise
Rotate counterclockwise

Properties

If you have a webcam or other desktop video camera that supports still images, the Scanner and Camera Wizard will display a dialog box named Take and Select Pictures to Copy. This dialog shows the live video feed in the **Preview** box. When the feed displays the image you want, click the **Take Picture** icon to store the still image in the **Pictures** box. Repeat as necessary and then click **Next**.

Completing the Scan

With either type of device, when you've made your selections, click **Next** to get to the Picture Name and Destination dialog box. Here you'll see two or three of the following controls:

➤ **Type a name for this group of pictures**   Use this text box to enter a name for the saved pictures. This name acts as a kind of prefix for the image file names. For example, if you enter Vacation, your pictures will be saved with the names Vacation 001, Vacation 002, and so on.

➤ **Select a file format** (scanners only)   Use this list to choose the file format for the scanned image: BMP, JPEG, TIF, or PNG.

➤ **This group of pictures will be saved in the following folder**   Use this list to choose the folder where you want the images stored. The default is My Pictures\ *Name*, where *Name* is the title of the new folder you entered into the text box. Note that you can also pick out an existing folder by clicking the **Browse** button.

When you click **Next**, the wizard gets together with the scanner or camera and arranges to have the image (or images) copied to the folder you specified. When that's done, you come face-to-face with the Uploading Pictures dialog box, which wants to know if you'd like to publish the picture on a Web site (see Chapter 17, "Getting on the Internet") or have them printed online (see Chapter 8, "Playing with Pictures"). If you don't want to bother with any of this, make sure the **No thanks** option is activated and then click **Next.**

In the final wizard dialog box, you see a link that displays the name of the folder you used to store the image. If you want to see the image in its new hard disk home, click the link. Don't forget to also click **Finish** to unload the wizard.

How the Wizard Deals with a CompactFlash Disk

Many digital cameras store images using a special kind of memory doohickey called a CompactFlash card. They're handy little devils because after you transfer your images to your computer, you can wipe out the card and start all over again. Although you usually get at the card's images by connecting the camera directly to your computer as described in the previous section, some cameras come with separate units into which you insert the CompactFlash card and then connect the unit to the computer.

Windows Wisdom

Windows XP gives you another way to scan pictures: In Paint, select the **File, From Scanner or Camera** command, click the image you want in the dialog box, and click **Get Picture.** Note that any decent graphics program also comes with support for scanning stuff. So if you have a better program than Paint, check to see if you can use it to scan pictures.

Windows XP treats these card holders as disk drives, and they show up in My Computer as either a CompactFlash Drive or as a Removable Disk. You're then free to insert a CompactFlash card and browse its images directly, as described in the next section. In some cases, however, inserting the CompactFlash card prompts Windows XP into displaying the dialog box shown in Figure 9.5. Windows wants to know just what the heck you'd like to do with the images on the card, so click the action you prefer. If you want to make this the default action, activate the **Always do the selected action** check box. Click **OK** to make it so.

Figure 9.5

When you insert a CompactFlash card, Windows XP may toss this dialog box your way.

Browsing Digital Camera Images

One of Windows XP's nicer features is the capability to parley directly with a digital camera using My Computer (or Windows Explorer). This is possible because, as I mentioned earlier, Windows XP treats whatever the camera uses to store the digital photos as an honest-to-goodness folder. This means you can open the folder and get your hands dirty by working with the images yourself.

To do this, Windows XP gives you a few different ways to proceed (all of which assume that your camera is plugged in and ready for action):

➤ In My Computer, double-click the camera icon in the **Scanners and Cameras** section (see Figure 9.2 earlier in this chapter).

➤ If you're displaying My Computer's Folders Explorer bar, click the **camera** in the **Folders** list.

➤ When you start the Scanner and Camera Wizard, the first dialog box has a link that says **advanced users only.** Click that link.

In each case, Windows XP connects to the camera, grabs the waiting images (this may take a while), and displays them thumbnail-style, as shown in Figure 9.6. To copy an image from the camera to your hard disk, you have two choices:

➤ Click the picture you want to copy and then click the WebView panel's **Copy this item** link (it's in the **Folder Tasks** section). In the Copy Items dialog box that pops up, select the folder you want to use and then click **Copy.**

➤ Click **Folders** to display the Folder bar and then drag the picture from the camera to the folder you want to use for storage (such as My Pictures).

Note, too, that you can also clear out the camera's photos by clicking **Delete all pictures on camera** in the WebView panel's **Camera Tasks** section.

Figure 9.6

Windows XP is happy to show your camera's digital photos in a folder window.

The Least You Need to Know

➤ **Go for Plug and Play**   For the easiest installation, go with a scanner or camera that supports Plug and Play, particularly one that connects via a USB cable (provided your computer has a USB port).

➤ **Checking out your installed devices**   To see your installed imaging devices, open the Scanners and Cameras window by selecting **Start, Control Panel,** clicking **Printers and Other Hardware,** and then clicking **Scanners and Cameras.**

➤ **Testing your device**   To make sure Windows XP and your device are getting along, open the Scanners and Cameras window, click the device's icon, click **View device properties,** and then click the button named **Test Scanner** or **Test Camera** (or even **Test Scanner or Camera**).

➤ **Getting pictures**   To get pictures from a scanner or camera, you usually just need to connect the device to launch the Scanner and Camera Wizard. You can also get to this wizard by pressing the device's "scan" button, clicking **Get pictures** in the Scanners and Cameras window, or by selecting **Start, All Programs, Accessories, Scanner and Camera Wizard.**

➤ **Exploring a digital camera**   To access your digital camera's stored images via My Computer, double-click the camera's icon. Alternatively, start the Scanner and Camera Wizard and, in the initial dialog box, click **advanced users only.**

Chapter 10

Giving Your Right Brain a Workout with Paint

Scientists tell us that, for most people, the left side of the brain is verbal, analytic, abstract, rational, and linear, while the right side of the brain is nonverbal, synthetic, analogical, intuitive, and holistic. The left brain enjoys words, but the right brain revels in images, so it's the latter that will get a kick out of Paint, Windows XP's main graphics program.

Even if you're a nonartist (that is, someone who hears "Leonardo" and thinks *Titanic*), Paint has plenty of easy-to-use tools that can help you get the job done. This chapter gives you a brief explanation of Paint's basic drawing techniques, and then sends you to the master class so that you can play with Paint's *really* fun features.

A Tour of the Paint Studio

To open your Paint studio, select **Start, All Programs, Accessories, Paint**. Figure 10.1 shows the Paint window that materializes.

Tool Box   Drawing area

Figure 10.1

A few key facts about the Paint window.

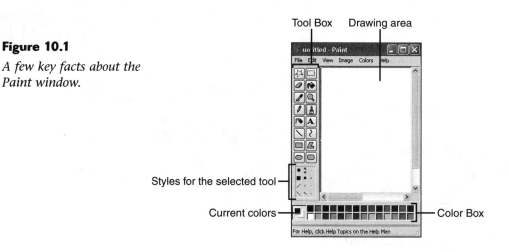

Styles for the selected tool —

Current colors —

— Color Box

The Paint window is loaded with interesting-looking buttons and lots of color. Here's a rundown of the major features:

➤ **Tool Box**   This box holds the various tools you use to create or edit your art-work. There's a "pencil," a "brush," an "eraser," and all sorts of utensils for drawing lines and shapes. I describe the individual Tool Box tools in more detail in the next section.

➤ **Tool styles**   This box shows the styles that are available with the currently se-lected tool. You use these styles to add some variety to your drawings. For exam-ple, the Brush tool offers a selection of brush sizes and shapes.

➤ **Color Box**   This box holds all the colors and patterns you can use for drawing or filling shapes. It's just like having your own personal 28-box of Crayola crayons, except these never need sharpening.

➤ **Current colors**   This area contains two boxes that display the currently se-lected foreground color (the top box) and background color (the bottom box). Selecting a new foreground color is a simple matter of clicking one of the color rectangles in the Color Box. If it's a new background color you're after, right-click a color swatch. (Confusingly, the definition of "foreground color" and "background color" varies depending on which tool you're using. I'll give you the details when I discuss each tool.)

➤ **Drawing area**   This white expanse is your Paint canvas. It's where you perform the mouse moves that lead to the creation of your digital drawings. It is, in other words, the place where all the fun happens.

Tool Time: How to Use the Paint Tools

The best way to tackle Paint is simply to enjoy yourself by experimenting with various tools, styles, and colors. Just let yourself go, toss off those inhibitions, and free yourself from the shackles of adult responsibilities. Give yourself permission to regress to an immature, to-heck-with-it-I'm-going-to-be-at-one-with-my-inner-child state. (It might be a good idea to close the door for this.)

When you're ready to go, roll up your sleeves, pick out a tool, and just start playing. However, just so you know, there *is* a basic four-step method you use for each tool:

1. In the Tool Box, click the tool you want to play with.
2. Click a tool style (if the tool has any).
3. In the Color Box, left-click a foreground color and right-click a background color.
4. Move the mouse pointer into the drawing area and then draw the shape you want. (The specifics of the drawing process vary from tool to tool, as you'll see in a second.)

Paint's Drawing Tools

Here's a review of the drawing-related tools you can grab from the Tool Box:

 Pencil   You use this tool to draw freehand lines. After selecting this tool, move the mouse pointer into the drawing area, hold down the left mouse button, and then wiggle the mouse around. Paint draws a freehand line that follows your every twitch and shimmy.

Brush   This is another tool for drawing freehand lines. It differs from the Pencil tool in that it gives you a selection of brush shapes and sizes (in the tool styles area).

Line   You use this tool to draw straight lines (the tool styles offer five different widths for your line-drawing pleasure). To create a line, drag the mouse pointer within the drawing area. You can make Paint draw a perfect horizontal or vertical line, or a line pitched at a 45-degree angle, by holding down the **Shift** key while you drag the mouse.

Rectangle   This tool draws rectangles. The point where you hold down the mouse button defines one corner of the rectangle, and

Windows Wisdom

For most of the Paint tools, a left-drag or a left-click draws a shape using the current foreground color. If you'd prefer to use the current background color, right-drag or right-click instead.

123

you create the rest of it by dragging the mouse. Need to draw a perfect square? No problem: just hold down the **Shift** key while dragging. The Rectangle tool offers three styles: a "border only" style that draws only the border of the shape; a "border and fill" style that draws a border (using the foreground color) and fills it with a color (the background color); and a "no border" style that leaves off the shape's border and draws only the fill.

 Ellipse   You use this tool for drawing ovals. Again, you do this by dragging the mouse inside the drawing area. If what you really need is a perfect circle, hold down the **Shift** key while doing the dragging thing.

 Rounded Rectangle   This tool combines the Rectangle and Ellipse tools to produce a rectangle that has rounded corners.

Curve   Use this tool when you need a wavy line. This one works a little differently than the others you've seen so far. You begin by dragging the mouse pointer until the line is the length you want, and you then release the button. To curve the line, drag the mouse again and then release the button. If you're feeling spunky, you can add a second curve to the line by dragging the mouse once again and then releasing the button when you're done.

Polygon   You use this tool to create a polygon. (In case you can't remember back to high school geometry, a *polygon* is a succession of straight lines that forms an enclosed object. A triangle and a rectangle are examples of polygons.) To wield this tool, begin by dragging the mouse pointer until the first side is the length and angle you want, and then release the mouse button. To create the next side, move the pointer to where you want the side to end, and then click. Paint dutifully draws a line from the end of the previous line to the spot where you clicked. Repeat this move-and-click procedure to add more sides. To complete the polygon, click the start of the first side to enclose the shape.

 Fill with Color   This tool looks like a can of paint being poured, and that's more or less what it does. That is, it fills an enclosed shape with a specified color. To use it, just click anywhere inside the shape (make sure it's completely closed!) and Paint fills it up with the current foreground color.

 Airbrush   This tool resembles (and works like) a can of spray paint, so I'm not sure why it's called an Airbrush. No matter, it's loads of fun to use because as you drag the mouse, Paint "sprays" the current foreground color. (Drag the mouse quickly to get a light spray; drag the mouse slowly to get a heavy spray.)

Text   If your left brain is feeling thoroughly ignored by now, you can toss it a bone by using the Text tool to add text to your drawing. The first step is to drag the mouse inside the drawing area to create a box to hold your text. When you release the mouse button, Paint places a cursor inside the box, so you can just start typing. Paint also displays the Fonts toolbar (see Figure 10.2). To change the font of the text, select the typeface, size, and other font options. Note, too, that this tool offers two styles: opaque (the text is the foreground color and the text box is filled with the background color) and transparent (the text is the foreground color and the text box background is transparent).

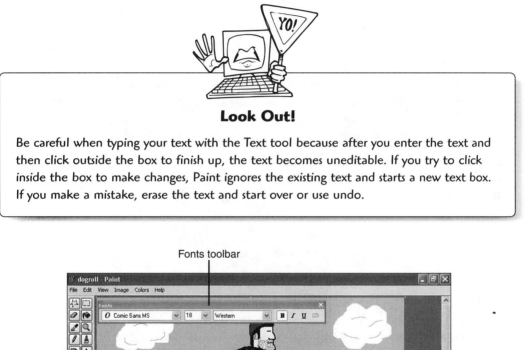

Look Out!

Be careful when typing your text with the Text tool because after you enter the text and then click outside the box to finish up, the text becomes uneditable. If you try to click inside the box to make changes, Paint ignores the existing text and starts a new text box. If you make a mistake, erase the text and start over or use undo.

Figure 10.2

A Paint file demonstrating the opaque and transparent text styles.

125

Paint's Nondrawing Tools

The Paint Tool Box also offers a few other nondrawing tools to enhance your creative powers:

 Pick Color   You use this tool to select an existing color from the currently open image. This is handy, for example, if the image has a color that doesn't appear in the Color Box. You select the color by clicking (for the foreground color) or right-clicking (for the background color) an example of the color within the image.

Eraser   This not-to-be-wielded-lightly tool enables you to erase parts of your image. The tool styles offer various widths, and dragging the mouse in the drawing area wipes out everything in the mouse pointer's path. Also refer to the section "Erasing Paint Mistakes" later in this chapter for more tips.

Windows Wisdom

If you prefer to erase only a particularly ill-chosen color and replace it with something else, use the Color Eraser tool. First, set the foreground color to the color you want to wipe out, and set the background color to the color you want to use in its stead. Now select the Eraser tool and then right-drag the mouse inside the drawing area.

Magnifier   You use this tool to zoom in on your drawing and get a closer look at things, which is handy for doing detail work. When you select this tool, use the tool styles box to choose a magnification: 1× (normal size), 2×, 6×, or 8×. The latter gets you so close that you can see the individual pixels, which are the individual pinpoints of light that make up a Paint drawing (and, for that matter, everything you see on your screen). Then click the section of the drawing that you want to magnify. Figure 10.3 shows this tool in action. Also refer to the section "Other Ways to Zoom" later in this chapter for more tips.

Select This tool lets you select a rectangular chunk—called a cutout—of the drawing, which you can then copy or cut out (hence the name). As you might expect, you use the Select tool much like you do the Rectangle tool. That is, you move the mouse pointer to the corner of the area you want to select, and then drag the mouse until the box encloses the area. Refer to the section "'I've Got a Cutout. Now What?'" later in this chapter for more tips on using cutouts.

Free-Form Select This tool is similar to Select, but it lets you mark an area using a free-form line. Click the tool, move the pointer into the drawing area, and then drag the mouse pointer around the area you want to select.

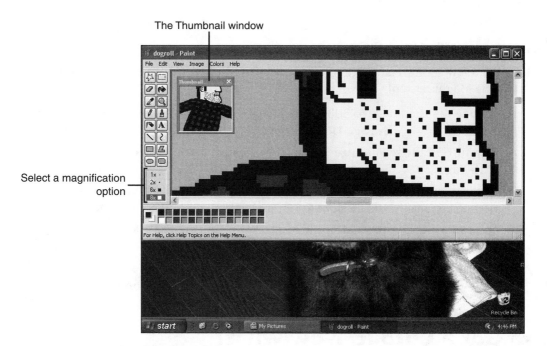

Figure 10.3

The Magnifier tool in action.

Erasing Paint Mistakes

While you're on the steep part of the Paint learning curve, you'll end up with lots of botched lines and mutinous shapes that you won't want in your final drawing. Here's how to get rid of these things (see also the Eraser tool, discussed in the previous section):

➤ Most of the Paint tools operate by holding down a mouse button and then dragging the mouse. If you make a mess during the drawing, you can start again by clicking the other mouse button *before* you release the button you're drawing with.

➤ If you've already completed the shape, select **Edit, Undo** (pressing **Ctrl+Z** will also get you there). Note that Paint allows you to undo the last three things you did.

➤ If the drawing is a complete write-off, you can start over by selecting **Image, Clear Image** (or by pressing **Ctrl+Shift+N**).

Other Ways to Zoom

Here are a few zoom-related techniques that you can use with Paint, in addition to using the Magnifier tool:

➤ To magnify the image to 400 percent, select the **View, Zoom, Large Size** command (or press **Ctrl+Page Down**).

➤ To return to the regular size, select **View, Zoom, Normal Size** (or press **Ctrl+Page Up**).

➤ You can also select the **View, Zoom, Custom** command, activate a magnification percentage in the Custom Zoom dialog box, and then click **OK**.

➤ You can see the individual pixels easier if you activate the grid (shown in Figure 10.4) by selecting **View, Zoom, Show Grid** (hitting **Ctrl+G** also works).

➤ You can display a separate "thumbnail image" that shows the drawing at regular size (see Figure 10.4) by selecting **View, Zoom, Show Thumbnail**.

"I've Got a Cutout. Now What?"

Paint gives you all kinds of cutout maneuvers that range from the mundane to the marvelous. Here's a rundown:

➤ **Cut the cutout**   Select **Edit, Cut** (or press **Ctrl+X**) to pluck the cutout from the drawing. Tip: To avoid unsightly gaps in your drawing, make sure the background color box is set to the same color as the background of whatever part of the drawing you're cutting out.

➤ **Copy the cutout**   Select **Edit, Copy** (or press **Ctrl+C**) to copy the cutout to the Windows XP Clipboard.

➤ **Paste the cutout**   Once you've cut or copied the cutout, you can paste it into the same drawing or a different drawing by selecting **Edit, Paste** (or by pressing **Ctrl+V**). The cutout appears in the upper-left corner of the drawing. Use the next technique to drag the cutout to the spot you want.

➤ **Move the cutout**   Position the mouse pointer inside the cutout; the pointer changes to a four-headed arrow. This means that you can drag the cutout to another part of the drawing.

➤ **Move a copy of the cutout**   If you hold down **Ctrl** while dragging a cutout, Paint leaves the original intact and moves a copy.

➤ **Save the cutout to a file**   Select the **Edit, Copy To** command to save the cutout in its own file. In the Copy To dialog box that appears, select a location, enter a **File name**, and then click **Save**. (If you want to use the saved cutout in another drawing, open the drawing and select the **Edit, Paste From** command. In the Paste From dialog box, highlight the cutout file and then click **Open**.)

➤ **Flip the cutout**   To flip a cutout, select **Image, Flip/Rotate** (or press **Ctrl+R**) to display the Flip and Rotate dialog box. Activate either the **Flip horizontal** option (left becomes right, and vice versa) or the **Flip vertical** option (up becomes down, and vice versa). Alternatively, activate **Rotate by angle** and then choose an angle option.

➤ **Invert the cutout colors**   Select **Image, Invert Colors** (or tap **Ctrl+I**). This technique tells Paint to change black to white and white to black, and the other colors change to their complementary colors.

➤ **Stretch the cutout**   To scale the cutout to either a smaller or larger size, use the **Stretch/Skew** command (or press **Ctrl+W**). Paint displays the Stretch and Skew dialog box. In the **Stretch** group, use the **Horizontal** and **Vertical** text boxes to enter the percentage value that you want to use to stretch the cutout. Values over 100 percent get you a larger image, while values less than 100 percent get you a smaller image.

➤ **Skew the cutout**   To tilt the cutout at an angle, run the **Stretch/Skew** command to display the Stretch and Skew dialog box. In the **Skew** group, use the **Horizontal** and **Vertical** text boxes to enter the number of degrees by which you want the cutout tilted. Enter values between –89 and 89.

The Paint window shown in Figure 10.4 demonstrates a few of these cutout techniques.

➤ **Use the cutout to create a sweep**   This is one of Paint's best effects. Choose the Transparent style, hold down the **Shift** key, and then drag the cutout around the drawing area. As you do this, Paint leaves behind copies of the cutout.

Figure 10.4

Examples of Paint's cutout special effects.

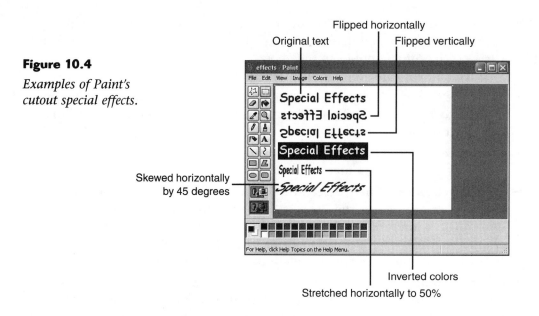

Setting the Image Attributes

If you find yourself running out of room in the drawing area, you can expand the canvas by increasing the size of the drawing. The size of the image as well as a few other options are part of the image attributes. To work with these attributes, follow these steps:

1. Select the **Image, Attributes** command (or press **Ctrl+E**). Paint fires up the Attributes dialog box.

2. Use the options in the **Units** group to select the measurement unit you want to work with.

3. Use the **Width** and **Height** text boxes to enter the new dimensions of the image.

4. While you're here, you may also need to convert the image between black and white and colors. You'll use the **Colors** option most of the time, but you should choose **Black and white** if your image uses only black, white, and shades of gray. This means your image will take up far less disk space.

5. When you're done, click **OK**.

Another way to change the size of the image is to use the *sizing handles*. If you look very carefully at the edges of the drawing area, you'll see eight tiny squares: one on each corner and one in the middle of each side. These sizing handles enable you to change the size of the drawing without bothering with the Attributes dialog box. You do this by dragging a handle with your mouse.

The Least You Need to Know

➤ **The basic Paint method** Click a tool, select a style (if applicable), choose the foreground and background colors, and then draw the shape. Most Paint tools operate by clicking and dragging within the drawing area.

➤ **Selecting stuff** Use the Select or Free-Form Select tools to select pieces of your drawing for cutting or copying. When you paste a cutout into a drawing, you need to drag the image to its proper location.

➤ **To erase stuff from a drawing** Use the Eraser tool to erase everything and the Color Eraser (right-drag the Eraser) to replace the foreground color with the background color.

➤ **Shift for accuracy** Holding down **Shift** gets you a horizontal, vertical, or 45-degree angle line with the Line tool, a square with the Rectangle tool, or a circle with the Ellipse tool.

Chapter 11

Sights and Sounds: Music and Other Multimedia

In This Chapter

➤ Understanding multimedia files and hardware

➤ Playing multimedia files

➤ Listening to audio CDs and watching DVD movies

➤ Copying music tracks to and from a CD

The graphics you gawked at in the previous few chapters represent only a selection of Windows XP's visual treats. There are actually quite a few more goodies that fall into the "sights for sore eyes" category, and even a few that could be called "sounds for sore ears." In this chapter, you see that Windows XP turns your lowly computer into a multimedia powerhouse capable of showing videos, playing audio CDs, making realistic burping noises, watching slick DVD movies, and even creating your own sound recordings.

Notes About Multimedia Files

Most of the multimedia your eyes will see and ears will hear resides in files on your hard disk, on a CD-ROM or DVD disc, or on the Internet. Just to keep us all thoroughly confused, the world's multimedia mavens have invented dozens of different file formats, each of which has its own incomprehensible two- or three-letter acronym. To help you make some sense of all this, I've grouped all the various formats into a mere five categories for easier consumption:

Jargon Jar

MIDI stands for **Musical Instrument Digital Interface.** It's a sound file that plays music generated by electronic synthesizers.

➤ **Sound files**   Files that contain sounds or music only. The two main types are audio files and *MIDI* sequence files. You'll deal with audio files mostly, and you'll also hear them referred to using their specific formats, including WAV, AU, AIFF, WMA (Windows Media Audio), and MP3. (The latter is a format that's used to play songs with near- or full-CD quality. MP3 is an extremely popular and growing format on the Internet.)

➤ **Animation files**   Files that contain animated movies or shorts, and they might include sound. The three most popular formats are video files (also called AVI files), MPEG files, and QuickTime files.

➤ **Movie files**   Files that contain live action movies or shorts, and they usually have a soundtrack. These files use the same formats as animation files.

➤ **Audio CD tracks**   Files that Windows XP uses to represent individual tracks on an audio CD; however, you rarely deal with them that way yourself. Instead, you can have Windows XP play some or all of a CD's tracks from your CD-ROM or DVD-ROM drive. You can even talk Windows XP into copying audio CD tracks to your hard drive or to a portable player.

➤ **DVD movies**   Files that contain high-quality versions of feature films, documentaries, and other big-screen entertainment. Again, you never have to deal with these files directly.

How can you recognize these files in My Computer? If you're dealing with sound or music files or audio CD tracks that have been copied to your computer (more on this later), then Windows XP displays the files with the icon shown in Figure 11.1. For animation or movie files, you see the first frame of the flick, again as pointed out in Figure 11.1. (Note, however, that you only see the first frame if My Computer is in Thumbnails view, which you get by activating the **View, Thumbnails** command.)

These are music or sound files

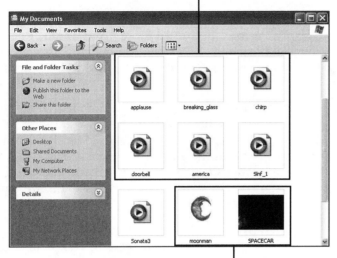

Figure 11.1

How Windows XP displays media files.

These are animation or movie files

Notes About Multimedia Hardware

More than most other computer features, multimedia is strongly tied to specialized hardware. In many (but not all) cases, your multimedia will be multimediocre if your computer isn't loaded down with the requisite devices. To help you get your computer multimedia-ready, this section takes a quick look at the hardware side of things.

Audio Hardware

If you're sick of carrying on a one-way conversation with your computer, you can get into the sound thing by using a *sound card*. This is an internal circuit board that's standard equipment on almost all new PCs. How can you tell if your system has a sound card? The easiest way is just to listen: If Windows XP plays a snippet of music at startup, then you've got sound.

Audio CD Hardware

If you want to listen to the soothing sounds of the Beastie Boys or Rage Against the Machine on your machine, you could just plop the appropriate CD into a nearby stereo. However, it may also be possible to play the CD directly from your computer. All you need is a sound card, some speakers, and either a CD drive or a DVD drive.

DVD Hardware

In the currency of computing power, the bells and whistles that comprise the Windows DVD experience don't come cheaply. Pushing around all those pixels and belting out all those notes puts quite a strain on a machine. So, as you can imagine, specialized hardware for DVD is a must. Unfortunately, how Windows XP reacts to DVD hardware is weird and confusing.

Windows Wisdom

If Windows XP doesn't recognize your hardware decoder, you may need to get updated *device driver* files from the manufacturer. (A device driver is a little program that lets a device talk to Windows XP—and vice versa.) The latest driver will either be on a disk that comes with the decoder or on the manufacturer's Web site.

Let's start with the easy part: the basic requirements. The basic needs are a DVD drive and a sound card/speakers combo. Not too bad, so far. Where things get twisted is in the add-on—called a *decoder*—that your system requires to process the video and audio torrent that the DVD drive sends its way. There are two kinds of these decoders:

➤ **Hardware decoder**   This is a device—usually a circuit board—that attaches to your computer. This is the kind Windows XP prefers. In fact, the DVD Player only plays DVD movies if your system has a hardware decoder *and* if it's a decoder that Windows XP recognizes.

➤ **Software decoder**   This is a program that performs the translation from DVD to video and audio output. This requires a reasonably powerful computer: at least a Pentium II machine running at 266 MHz or better. If your machine qualifies, your DVD drive should have a disc that includes a setup program for installing the decoder.

Making Multimedia Whoopee with Media Player

You saw earlier that Windows supports all kinds of multimedia formats. In previous versions of Windows, the bad news was that to play those formats you had to master a passel of player programs. In Windows XP, the good news is that you now need to wrestle with only a single program: Media Player. This clever chunk of software is a true one-stop multimedia shop that's capable of playing sound files, music files, audio CDs, animations, movie files, and even DVDs. It can even copy audio CD tracks to your computer, burn music files to a CD, tune in to Internet radio stations, and more.

To try Media Player, you have a bunch of ways to proceed:

➤ Select **Start, Windows Media Player.** If you don't see the Windows Media Player icon in the main Start menu, you can convince it to come out to play by selecting **Start, All Programs, Windows Media Player.**

➤ Insert an audio CD in your CD drive, or insert a DVD disc in your DVD drive. (Note that most DVD drives are also happy to play audio CDs for you.)

➤ If you have a CompactFlash drive, insert a CompactFlash card. If Windows XP asks what you want to do with this disk, highlight **Play the music files.** If you don't want to be pestered with this dialog box each time, activate the **Always do the selected action** check box. Click **OK** to proceed.

➤ Use My Computer to find a media file and then double-click the file. Remember that My Documents has a subfolder named My Music, which is the default folder that Windows XP uses when you save music files.

➤ Download media from the Internet. In most cases, Media Player will launch right away and start playing the sound or movie or whatever. (This is called *streaming* the media.) Sometimes, however, you may have to wait for the entire file to download before Media Player will spring into action.

Figure 11.2 shows the Media Player window that shows up.

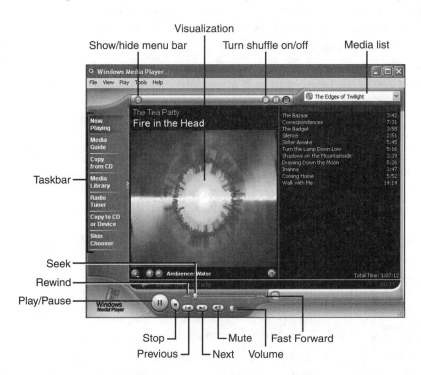

Figure 11.2

This is the window you see when you launch Media Player.

As you can see, the Media Player window with its wavy lines and roundish buttons is quite a bit different than what you're probably used to seeing. The first thing I'll point out is that if you don't see the menu bar in your version of Media Player, you can get it out of hiding by clicking the **Show menu bar** (pointed out in Figure 11.2) or by pressing **Ctrl+M**.

The second thing I'll point out is the taskbar that runs down the left side of the window. The idea here is that when you click an item in the taskbar, the Media Player switches to a different part of the program. You'll use this feature quite a bit, so let's take a second to run through each item so you know what you'll be getting yourself into:

➤ **Now Playing**   This section shows information about the currently playing media (see Figure 11.2). For an audio CD, the left side of the window shows a *visualization* (a psychedelic pattern that moves in time with the music) and the right side shows the *playlist,* the list of tracks on the disc. For a DVD, the left side shows the movie and the right side shows the various chapters that comprise the movie. You can jump directly to a track or chapter by double-clicking it.

➤ **Media Guide**   This section displays the WindowsMedia.com Web page, assuming your computer is connected to the Internet. This page gives you access to all kind of media marvels, including songs, videos, movie trailers, news clips, live feeds, and more.

➤ **Copy from CD**   This section enables you to copy one or more tracks from an audio CD to your computer's hard disk. See the "Hard Disk Rock: Copying Tracks from a CD" section later in this chapter.

➤ **Media Library**   This section organizes the media that you've played and that's on your computer into various categories. It also enables you to create your own playlists of songs. See the "Becoming a Program Director: Creating a Custom Playlist" section later in this chapter.

➤ **Radio Tuner**   This section enables you to listen to radio stations that broadcast over the Internet. I tell you how it works later in this chapter in the "Web Waves: Listening to Internet Radio" section.

➤ **Copy to CD or Device**   This section enables you to copy music from your computer to a recordable CD or to a device that can play digital music (such as a portable MP3 player). The scoop on this is in the "Rollin' Your Own Music: Copying Tracks to a CD or Device" section.

➤ **Skin Chooser**   This section offers a number of wild and wacky looks for when you put Media Player into *skin mode.* This means that the program shrinks to a smaller version of itself that features just the basic buttons for playback.

Windows Wisdom

The first time you enter the Media Library section, you may see a dialog box that asks if you want Media Player to search your computer—click **Yes.** This will add all your computer's media files to the library for easy access—a very convenient thing. If you don't see this dialog box, select the **Tools, Search for Media Files** command (or press **F3**).

138

To choose a new skin, highlight it and then click **Apply Skin.** To switch to skin mode, select **View, Skin Mode,** or press **Ctrl+2.** (Press **Ctrl+1** to return to full mode.)

Giving Media Player Some Media to Play

I mentioned earlier that Media Player will launch and start playing automatically if you double-click or download a media file or insert an audio CD or DVD disc. If you opened Media Player directly or if you want to get it to play something else, then you need to learn how to load media from within the program.

To open a media file, you have two possibilities:

➤ **To open a file on your computer** Select the **File, Open** command (or press **Ctrl+O**), use the Open dialog box to highlight the file, and then click **Open.**

➤ **To open a file from the Internet** Select **File, Open URL** (or press **Ctrl+U**), use the Open text box to enter the Internet address of the file, and then click **OK.**

If it's an audio CD that you want to start, first click **Copy from CD** in the taskbar.

Let's Make Some Noise: Playing Media

To control the playback of your media, the Media Player program offers the following buttons:

➤ **Play/Pause** Starts the media file; pauses the file while it's playing. Alternatives: Select **Play, Play/Pause** or press **Ctrl+P.**

➤ **Stop** Stops the media file and returns to the beginning of the file (or to the beginning of the current audio CD track). Alternatives: Select **Play, Stop** or press **Ctrl+S.**

➤ **Rewind** Rewinds continuously through a media file (such as a streaming video file). Click Play/Pause to continue playing. Alternatives: Select **Play, Rewind,** or press **Ctrl+Shift+B.**

➤ **Previous** Returns you to the beginning of the file or track. Alternatives: Select **Play, Previous** or press **Ctrl+B.**

➤ **Seek** Drag this slider left to rewind or right to fast forward.

➤ **Next** Sends you to the next file or track. Alternatives: Select **Play, Next,** or press **Ctrl+F.**

➤ **Mute** Turns off the sound playback. Alternatives: Select **Play, Volume, Mute** or press **F8.**

➤ **Volume**   Controls the playback volume. Drag the slider to the left to reduce the volume, or to the right to increase the volume. Alternatives: Select **Play, Volume, Up** or press **F10** to increase the volume; select **Play, Volume, Down** or press **F9** to decrease the volume.

➤ **Fast Forward**   Fast forwards continuously through a media file (such as a streaming video file). Click Play/Pause to continue playing. Alternatives: Select **Play, Fast Forward,** or press **Ctrl+Shift+F**.

➤ **Turn shuffle on/off**   Toggles shuffle mode on and off. Shuffle mode means that an audio CD's tracks play in random order. Alternatives: Select **Play, Shuffle,** or press **Ctrl+H**.

And here are a few juicy tidbits you might want to keep in mind:

➤ To get a DVD up and running, either select it from the media list (refer to Figure 11.2) or select **Play, DVD or CD Audio**. (If you have multiple drives in your system, select the DVD drive from the menu that appears.)

➤ If you want to control the volume of the other sounds that Windows XP makes (such as its opening theme music), first select **Start, Control Panel**. Click **Sounds, Speech, and Audio Devices** and then click **Adjust the system volume**. In the dialog box that appears, use the **Device volume** slider to raise or lower Windows' voice.

➤ If you want a media file to play over and over, activate the **Play, Repeat** command (or press **Ctrl+T**).

Windows Wisdom

Some audio CDs do double-duty as data CDs and come with programs you can run. In some cases, the program will run automatically when you insert the CD. So be forewarned that after you insert an audio CD, you may see something other than (or in addition to) CD Player on the screen.

Messing with Media Player's Audio CD Features

If you like to listen to music while you use your computer, the typical MIDI file isn't likely to set your toes a-tapping. No, if it's *real* music you're after, you need to convince Media Player to crank up an audio CD. Audio CDs use the same dimensions as CD-ROM discs, so any audio CD will fit snugly inside your CD drive (or your DVD drive, if you have one). From there, you use Media Player to play the CD's tracks.

Let's run through a few notes to bear in mind when playing audio CDs in Media Player. First, Media Player can access information about a CD over the Internet:

➤ If your computer is connected to the Internet when you insert the disc, Media Player will automatically reach out and grab various bits of data about the CD: its title, the name of the performer or group, the name and length of each track, and more.

➤ If you connect to the Internet after the disc is already playing, you can get the disc info by clicking **Copy from CD** in the taskbar and then clicking **Get Names.** When Media Player shows the disc data, check it out to make sure it's the right CD. If it is, click **Confirm** to save the data. If you want to make changes to the information, click **Edit,** make your changes in the text boxes that appear, and then click **Finish.** In most cases you need to eject and then re-insert the disc for the changes to take effect.

➤ If Media Player doesn't recognize your disc at all, it will start up a wizard that will ask you for information about the disc and then attempt to locate the disc info on the Internet. If the wizard finds the data, great: just follow the wizard to the end. Otherwise, click **Not Found** and then enter the disc data by hand.

As an added and slightly surprising bonus, the list of tracks that appears in both the **Now Playing** section and the **Copy from CD** section is customizable:

➤ If Media Player can't get the name of a track, or if you want to change the existing name, right-click the track and then click **Edit.** Type in the new name and then press **Enter.**

➤ If you have a track that you particularly dislike, you can ask Media Player to bypass it during playback by right-clicking the track and then clicking **Disable Select Tracks.**

➤ To change the order in which Media Player spins the tracks, right-click any track and then click either **Move Up** or **Move Down.** You can also change the order of the tracks by using your mouse to track them up and down in the playlist.

Hard Disk Rock: Copying Tracks from a CD

Media Player's audio CD playback is flexible, for sure, but playing audio CDs suffers from two important drawbacks:

➤ Shuffling discs in and out of the drive can be a hassle.

➤ There isn't any way to mix tunes from two or more CDs into a single playlist, even if your system has multiple CD and/or DVD drives.

NEW!   To solve these dilemmas, the Windows XP version of Media Player enables you to copy individual tracks from one or more CDs and store them on your computer's hard disk. From there, you can create a custom playlist that combines the tracks in any order you like.

Before I show you how you go about copying tracks from an audio CD, let's take a second to set a few options related to track copying. In the Media Player window, select the **Tools, Options** command to display the Options dialog box, and then select the **Copy Music** tab.

Here's what you can do in this tab:

➤ **Change the location of the copied tracks**   The default location is your My Music folder. Note that Media Player creates a new subfolder for the artist and then uses that to create another subfolder for the CD. Your best bet is to leave this as is, but if you want to change the location, click the **Change** button.

➤ **Set the file name format for the tracks**   By default, Media Player stores the tracks using file names of the form *nn Song Name*, where *nn* is the two-digit track number and *Song Name* is the title of the song. To change that, click **Advanced** to open the File Name Options dialog box. Activate the check box beside each item you want to include in the filename (such as the **Artist** name and the **Album** name).

➤ **Changing the file format**   The default format for the copied tracks is Windows Media Audio. If your computer supports other formats (such as MP3), you'll be able to use the **File format** list to select a different format. If you want to use MP3 but you can't select it in the list, click the **MP3 Information** button to get data from Microsoft on how to enable the MP3 format.

➤ **Changing the audio quality**   The quality of the copied files is proportional to the acreage they consume on your hard disk. That is, the higher the quality, the fatter the file. Use the **Copy music at this quality** slider to choose which quality level you want. Each level is measured in kilobits per second (Kbps), where there are 8 bits in a byte and 1,024 bytes in a kilobyte (KB). To help you decide, here's a summary of each quality level for the WMA format and how much disk space it will usurp in kilobytes per minute and megabytes (MB; 1,025 kilobytes) per hour:

Kbps	KB/Minute	MB/Hour
48	360	21
64	480	28
96	720	42
128	960	56
160	1,200	70
192	1,440	84

Click **OK** when you've made your choices.

To do the actual copying, follow these steps:

1. Insert the audio CD from which you want to copy.

2. Display the **Copy from CD** section.

3. For each track that you want to copy, activate the check box to the left of the track number.

4. Click **Copy Music.** Media Player starts the copy process, which you can monitor by watching the **Copy Status** column (see Figure 11.3).

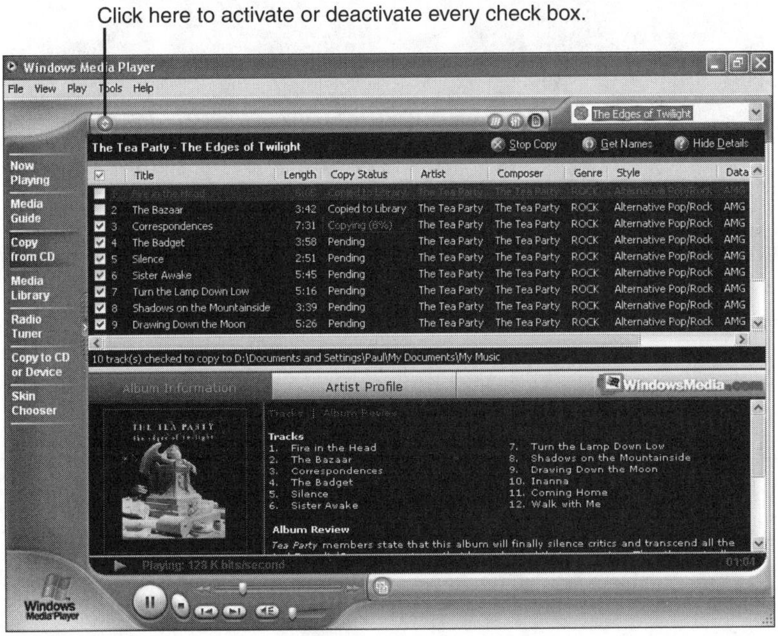

Click here to activate or deactivate every check box.

Figure 11.3

Use the Copy from CD section to copy audio CD tracks to your hard disk.

Becoming a Program Director: Creating a Custom Playlist

Once you've copied a mess of CD tracks to your hard disk, you're free to combine these tracks and play them in any order. If you just want to play an individual track, here's the easiest way to go about it:

1. Display the **Media Library** section.

2. Open the **Audio** branch.

3. Open one of the sub-branches: Album, Artist, or Genre.

4. Click the album, artist, or genre that contains the track you want (see Figure 11.4).

5. Double-click the track.

143

Figure 11.4

Use the Copy from CD section to copy audio CD tracks to your hard disk.

Rather than playing single tracks using this method, you might prefer to combine multiple tracks into a *playlist*. You can then select the playlist and Media Player will play all the tunes for you automatically.

The first thing you need to do is create a new playlist:

1. Click **New Playlist** to display the New Playlist dialog box.

2. Type a descriptive name in the **Enter the new playlist name** text box.

3. Click **OK**. Media Player creates the playlist and displays it in the Media Library's **My Playlists** branch.

With that done, use the following techniques to work with the playlist:

Windows Wisdom

The techniques in this section apply equally to MP3 files and other music files that you download from the Internet.

➤ **Adding a song to the playlist** Find the file in the Audio branch and highlight it. Click **Add to Playlist** and then click the name of the playlist you want to use.

➤ **Removing a song from the playlist** Open the **My Playlists** branch and highlight the playlist. Right-click the song and then click **Delete from Playlist**.

➤ **Changing the playlist order** Open the **My Playlists** branch and highlight the playlist. Then use your mouse to drag the songs up or down in the list.

➤ **Playing a playlist** Open the **My Playlists** branch, highlight the playlist, and then click the **Play** button.

➤ **Renaming a playlist** Open the **My Playlists** branch, right-click the playlist, and then click **Rename.** Type in the new name and then press **Enter.**

➤ **Deleting a playlist** Open the **My Playlists** branch, right-click the playlist, and then click **Delete.**

Rollin' Your Own Music: Copying Tracks to a CD or Device

NEW! Listening to music while working on your computer is loads of fun, but I certainly hope you don't spend every waking minute in front of your PC. When it's time to get away, why not take some of your digital music with you? Sure you can. Windows XP's version of Media Player can perform the neat trick of copying music files from your computer to a CD-R disc or to a portable digital music player. Here's how it works:

1. Select the **Copy to CD or Device** section.

2. The **Music to Copy** list holds the music selections from your Media Library. Select the item (playlist, genre, album, or artist) that contains the music you want to copy.

3. Activate the check boxes beside the tracks that you want to copy. Make sure that the total number of megabytes (or minutes, if you're recording to a CD-R disc) that you select isn't greater than the total number of megabytes (or minutes) available on the recording device (see Figure 11.5).

4. Use the **Music on Device** list to select the drive or device that you want to use to store the tracks.

5. Click **Copy to Music.**

Windows Wisdom

You can create a quick playlist from the My Music folder by opening it and clicking the WebView panel's **Play all** link. For a more specific list, create a new subfolder and then copy or move all the music files that you want in your playlist to that folder. Open the folder and click the **Play all** link.

Look Out!

Remember that once Media Player finishes writing to a CD-R disc, it "closes" the disc, which means that you can never write anything else to the disc. Therefore, make sure you have enough music available to fill up the CD-R (about 70 minutes) so as not to waste space on the disc.

Figure 11.5

In the Media Library, open the Audio branches until you get to the song you want to play or work with.

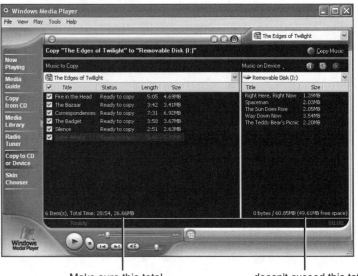

Make sure this total ...   ... doesn't exceed this total.

Web Waves: Listening to Internet Radio

Hundreds of radio stations are sending their signals over the Net, and Media Player can tune in to many of them. First, click **Radio Tuner** in the taskbar. The **PRESETS** list shows some stations defined by Media Player. To hear a station, highlight it and then click **Play**.

Media Player also enables you to create a custom list. To add your own stations, first select **My Presets** in the **PRESETS** list. Now move over to the **STATION FINDER** side of the window and use the **Find By** list to choose how you want to search for a station (such as by format or location). Use the controls that appear to enter your search criteria and run the search. Click the station you want and then click the <<< button to put the station in your presets list.

Assigning Sounds to Things Windows XP Does

As you work with Windows XP, you'll hear various beeps and boops in response to certain events, such as when some dialog boxes appear and when a new e-mail message arrives. Although you might think all these sounds are set in stone, it turns out that you can control not only which sounds play in response to which events, but whether Windows XP plays *any* sounds at all.

To change the sound that plays for a Windows event, follow these steps:

1. Select **Start**, **Control Panel**, click **Sounds, Speech, and Audio Devices** and then click **Change the sound scheme.** You eventually end up at the Speech and Audio Devices Properties dialog box.

2. Use the **Program events** list to highlight the event you want to work with. (If an event has a volume icon beside it, it means a sound is associated with that event.)

3. Use the **Sounds** list to select the sound you want played when the event occurs. If you'd prefer blissful silence, select **(None).** If the sound you want doesn't appear in the list, click **Browse** to pick out the sound file using a dialog box.

Besides changing the sounds for individual events, you can also work with entire *sound schemes* that control many events at once. Windows XP offers two methods for dealing with sound schemes:

➤ **To select a predefined sound scheme**   Use the **Sound scheme** list. If you want to put a gag on Windows XP, select the **No Sounds** scheme.

➤ **To create your own custom sound scheme** Begin by associating sounds to the various events you want to hear. After that's done, click **Save As**, enter a catchy name for the new scheme, and then click **OK**.

When you've completed your sound labors, click **OK** to confirm everything.

Windows Wisdom

Not sure what a particular sound sounds like? No problem: Just click the **Play** button (the right-pointing arrow), and Windows XP will give you a preview of the sound.

The Least You Need to Know

➤ **Multiple multimedia formats**   Multimedia files come in five generic flavors: sound files (such as wave, WMA, and MP3), animation files, movie files, audio CD tracks, and DVD movies.

➤ **Media Player is the workhorse**   The Media Player program can handle almost any kind of multimedia file. To use it, launch the Start menu's **Windows Media Player** icon or double-click a file.

➤ **Automatic CD and DVD playing**   In most cases, your audio CDs and DVDs will start playing automatically after you insert the disc.

➤ **Quality is job one**   Before copying audio CD tracks to your computer, your first task should be to choose the quality setting you want. To do this, select **Tools, Options** and use the **Copy Music** tab's **Copy music at this quality** slider.

Chapter 12

Creating Movies with Windows Movie Maker

In the magical multimedia tour of the past four chapters, you've seen how Windows XP handles images and sounds. In this chapter you'll take all of that to its logical conclusion by learning how to string together multiple images and sounds. You'll learn, in other words, how to record and edit videos on your computer. The tool that will turn you into a veritable videographer is Windows Movie Maker, a scaled-down, but still quite functional, video recording and editing program.

Movie Maker can capture video from a camcorder, VCR, desktop camera, or even a TV, and save it on your computer. From there, you can cut out the bits you don't want, re-arrange the footage, add narration and between-scenes transitions, and perform other Spielbergian tasks. You can then save your creation to a recordable CD, plop it on your Web site, or e-mail it to an unsuspecting friend or co-worker (or even to a suspecting one, for that matter).

This chapter tells you what equipment you need for Movie Maker to do its thing, how to record footage, how to edit it into a crowd-pleasing shape, and how to distribute the final product.

What Hardware Do You Need to Use Movie Maker?

Before I answer the question that forms the title of this section, let me first say that you don't necessarily need *any* extra hardware to use Movie Maker. That's because the program is perfectly happy to work with existing digital video files. As you'll see a bit later, it's possible to import video files into Movie Maker and then play with them as you see fit. In fact, Movie Maker can deal with video files in all of the following formats:

➤ Advanced Streaming Format (also known as ASF)

➤ Motion Picture Experts Group (MPEG or MPG)

➤ Video for Windows (AVI)

➤ Windows Movie File (WMF)

➤ Windows Media Video (WMV; this is the format that Movie Maker uses when it saves your movies)

Besides all that, Movie Maker can also import many of the image file formats discussed in Chapter 8, "Playing with Pictures," the sound file formats I rambled on about in Chapter 11, "Sights and Sounds: Music and Other Multimedia," and also PowerPoint presentations and slides.

However, if it's your own video footage you're after, then you need to attach a video device to your computer. How you do this depends on what type of device you have and what type of attachment (port or jacks) your computer has:

➤ **If you have an analog camcorder, VCR, or TV and your computer has a video capture card** Analog camcorders, VCRs, and TVs usually output *composite* video and audio using three RCA-style jacks, which are almost always color-coded: yellow for the video and red and white for the audio. If your computer has a separate video capture card or a graphics card that's capable of capturing video, then you'll see the corresponding yellow, red, and white jacks on the back of your computer. (Some cards have a separate cable that has the RCA jacks on it; see Figure 12.1.) In this case, you need to use the appropriate cable (usually supplied with the card) to attach the camcorder or VCR to your computer, as shown in Figure 12.1. Some newer camcorders, VCRs, and TVs have an *SVideo* jack that outputs both audio and video, but you need a corresponding SVideo input jack on your computer's video card.

➤ **If you have an analog camcorder or VCR and your computer has a USB port** There are products—known affectionately as *video dongles* in the trade—available that have the yellow, red, and white RCA jacks on one end and a USB connector on the other (see Figure 12.1). In this case, you run an RCA cable from the camcorder or VCR to the dongle and then attach the dongle to your computer's USB port.

➤ **If you have a digital camcorder or desktop video camera (also called a Web camera or webcam) and your computer has a USB port** If your camcorder or camera supports USB, it should come with a USB cable that you attach directly to the computer's USB port.

➤ **If you have a digital camcorder or desktop video camera and your computer has a IEEE 1394 (FireWire) port** IEEE 1394 is a relatively new method for getting digital video (and other kinds of data) into a computer. IEEE 1394 is one of those names that only a geek could love; fortunately, there's a more fun synonym that the likes of us can use: *FireWire*. A few new computers are now shipping with FireWire ports, and there are also FireWire boards and PC Cards that you can install. If your digital camera supports FireWire, it should come with a FireWire cable that you attach directly to the computer's FireWire port.

Windows Wisdom

As I write this, the only video dongle on the market is the USB VideoBus II, made by Belkin (see www.belkin.com). I used this dongle to capture the video examples that I show in this chapter, so I can tell you that it works well (and, no, I didn't get paid to say that).

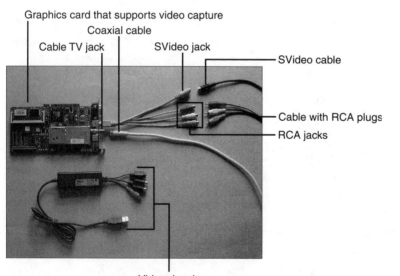

Graphics card that supports video capture
Coaxial cable
Cable TV jack   SVideo jack
SVideo cable
Cable with RCA plugs
RCA jacks
Video dongle

Figure 12.1

Some of the hardware you can use to get digital video into your computer.

A Tour of the Movie Maker Screen

With all that out of the way, it's time to start making some digital movies. To get Movie Maker rolling, first click **Start** to open the Start menu. If you see an icon for

151

Windows Movie Maker, go ahead and click it; if not, select **All Programs, Accessories, Windows Movie Maker.** XP releases the Windows Movie Maker window onto the screen. Figure 12.2 shows the Movie Maker window with a movie project already on the go to help you understand the various parts of the program.

Figure 12.2

The Movie Maker window with a movie project in progress.

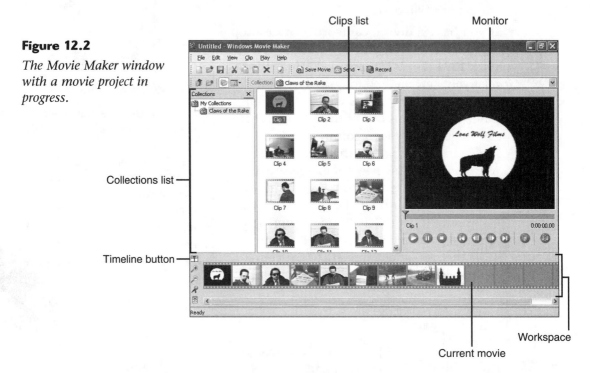

Clips list

Monitor

Collections list

Timeline button

Workspace

Current movie

Let's run through the various Movie Maker actors and the roles they play:

➤ **Collections list**   In Movie Maker, a collection is a file that contains raw video footage captured from a video device. It's called a collection because each one contains one or more clips that represent the different scene changes in your video. (You'll see a bit later that Movie Maker creates these clips automatically when you record the video. You can also create your own clips.) The **Collections** area lists the video files that you've captured.

➤ **Clips list**   This list displays the various clips that are part of the currently highlighted collection. Each clip shows the first *frame* of the video segment.

➤ **Monitor**   You use this area to play a clip or your movie (continuously or frame-by-frame) and to split a single clip into multiple clips.

➤ **Workspace**   This is the area that holds the clips for your current movie project and it's where you edit the movie.

➤ **Current project**   This is the collection of clips that form your movie.

Adding Video to a Project

Movie Maker starts a new movie project for you automatically when you crank it up. However, you can start a fresh project at any time by selecting the **File, New, Project** command (or by pressing **Ctrl+N**).

With your bouncing baby project ready to go, your next step is to get some video "in the can" (as they say in the movie biz). That is, you need to add a collection of clips to the project to use as your editing raw materials. You have two choices:

➤ Record footage from a video device such as a camcorder, VCR, or desktop camera.

➤ Import a video file or other type of media file.

The next two sections show you how to use both techniques.

Jargon Jar

A **frame** is a single image from a movie. All movies simulate motion by playing a rapid sequence of still images. The more images displayed per second, the better the quality of the movie, and this measure is called the frame rate and it's measured in frames per second (fps). Low quality is about 8 fps and high quality is 30 fps.

Recording Footage from a Video Device

Assuming you now have your camcorder, VCR, desktop camera, or TV attached to your computer, you can get right to the action by selecting the **File, Record** command (or, if you feel like shunning the menu, click the toolbar's **Record** button or press **Ctrl+R**). Movie Maker fires up the Record window, shown in Figure 12.3. If your device is set up to show a live feed, you'll see it automatically in the video window. Otherwise, you'll see the image once you press Play on your device.

The video you'll record appears here

Figure 12.3

Use the Record window to capture your raw audio and video footage.

Video size
Frame rate

Maximum amount you can record

153

Before you get to that, you need to understand all the recording bells and whistles that populate the Record window. Here's a rundown:

➤ **Record**   Use this list to tell Movie Maker what you want to record: **Video and audio**, **Video only**, or **Audio only**.

➤ **Change Device**   The **Video device** and **Audio device** lines tell you which device Movie Maker will use to record video and audio. If you have multiple devices installed for one or both and you want to use a different one, click the **Change Device** button and use the Change Device dialog box to choose the devices you prefer. (If you know what you're doing, click **Configure** to adjust settings such as the video standard [NTSC, PAL, or SECAM], brightness, and contrast.)

➤ **Record time limit**   Use this spin box to set the maximum number of hours, minutes, and seconds that you want to record. (The default setting is two hours.) This is useful if you're recording a live feed and want to limit how much footage you capture, just in case you forget to stop the recording. If you don't care (and have lots of disk space; see the Setting item, below), deactivate this check box to disable the limit.

➤ **Create clips**   If you leave this check box activated, Movie Maker will automatically create separate clips for your footage based on scene changes. If you have a long sequence to capture, dividing it into separate clips can make your editing life much easier, so I recommend leaving this check box turned on. (The exception is if your video has a large number of quick scene changes and jump cuts. In this case you might consider deactivating the **Create clips** check box and then creating the clips yourself; see "Splitting a Clip," later in this chapter.)

➤ **Setting**   Use this list to choose the quality level you want to use for your recording. The text below the list tells you four things about what each setting represents: what the movie is suitable for (such as sending over e-mail), the width and height of the movie (in pixels), the frame rate, and the total amount of recording time you have based on the amount of free space you have on your hard disk. Notice that there is a trade-off between the quality and the amount of footage you can record. (That is, the higher the quality, the less you can record.)

➤ **Take Photo**   Click this button to take a still image of the current video frame. This brings

Windows Wisdom

The Change Device dialog box has a **Line** list that determines the type of input source you're using. Depending on how your computer is configured, you can select one of the following: **Video Composite** (the yellow, red, and white RCA jacks), **Video SVideo** (an SVideo jack), or **Video Tuner** (a cable TV jack).

the Save Photo dialog box onto the screen, which you then use to save the image to a file in JPEG format.

Here are the steps to follow to record some footage:

1. Cue up the video (for recorded media) or set up the camera (for live video).

2. Click the **Record** button.

3. When you see the word **Recording** flashing inside the Record window, start playing your tape or whatever. The **Elapsed** line tells you the amount of time that you've recorded.

4. When you've recorded the footage you need, click **Stop.** The Save Windows Media File dialog box appears.

5. Enter a name for the video file (you should probably leave the folder as the default My Videos folder) and then click **Save.** Movie Maker creates the clips (assuming you left the **Create clips** check box activated) and then drops you off back in the Movie Maker window.

Importing Video Files and Other Media

Besides capturing footage from a video device, you can also populate the Collections list with other kinds of media, including video files, graphics, photos, music, and sound files. Here's how it works:

1. Select the **File, Import** command (or press **Ctrl+I**). Movie Maker tosses you the Select the File to Import dialog box.

2. Highlight the media file you want to import. Here's what to expect:

   ➤ **Video file**   If you leave the **Create clips for video files** check box activated, Movie Maker will divide a video file into a sequence of clips.

   ➤ **Image or photo**   The file is imported as a single clip. However, if you add this clip to your project, Movie Maker sets it up to display for five seconds.

   ➤ **Sound or music file**   No clips are created and the length of the clip is the same as the length of the music or sound.

3. Click **Open.** Movie Maker creates the clips (if necessary) and then adds the media to the Collections list.

Hip Clip Tips: Working with Clips

Judging from the previous section, it's safe to say that clips play an important role in Movie Maker's movie-making process. Not only is everything stored as a clip, but as you'll see later when you learn how to build and edit a movie, almost everything you do operates at the clip level. This means that you need to be comfortable with clips if you hope to get anything done in Movie Maker without too much fuss. This section helps you get to that state by running through a few common clip tasks.

Windows Wisdom

To launch a clip quickly, either double-click it or drag it from the Clips list and drop it on the monitor. Movie Maker loads the clip into the monitor and starts playing it immediately.

Playing a Clip

Before plopping a clip into your movie project, you'll probably want to play it so that you're sure what's in the clip and so you can decide whether you want to split the clip into two parts. Here's how you play a clip using the monitor:

1. Use the **Collections** tree to highlight the collection that has the clip you want to view.

2. Use the Clips list to highlight the clip. As shown in Figure 12.4, the first frame of the clip appears in the monitor and the monitor controls become activated. (If you want to see multiple clips, hold down **Ctrl** and click each clip that you want to play.)

Figure 12.4

When you highlight a clip, the first frame appears in the monitor.

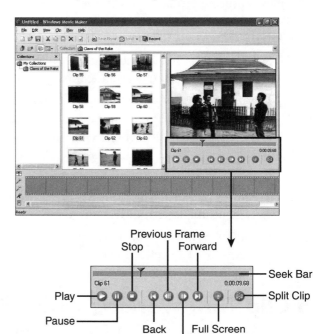

3. Use the following buttons to control the playback of the clip:

   ➤ **Play**   Starts playing the clip.

   ➤ **Pause**   Pauses the clip playback while still maintaining your current position within the clip.

   ➤ **Stop**   Removes the clip from the monitor.

   ➤ **Back**   Returns you to the beginning of the clip.

   ➤ **Previous Frame**   Moves back to the previous frame in the clip.

   ➤ **Next Frame**   Moves ahead to the next frame in the clip.

   ➤ **Forward**   Moves you to the end of the clip.

   ➤ **Seek Bar**   The leftmost portion of this bar represents the beginning of the clip, while the rightmost portion represents the end of the clip. Click anywhere inside this bar to advance the clip to that position. You can also drag the arrow left or right to the appropriate position.

   ➤ **Full Screen**   Click this button to expand the monitor so that it takes up the full height and width of your screen. To get back to the regular view, either click the mouse or press **Escape**.

The following table lists some keyboard shortcuts you can use in place of clicking the monitor controls:

Action	Shortcut
Play/Pause	**Spacebar**
Stop	**Period (.)**
Back	**Ctrl+Alt+Left arrow**
Previous Frame	**Alt+Left arrow**
Next Frame	**Alt+Right arrow**
Forward	**Ctrl+Alt+Right arrow**
Full Screen	**Alt+Enter**

Renaming a Clip

When Movie Maker creates clips for you, it supplies them with dishwater-dull names such as Clip 57 or Clip 101. These prosaic names also appear when you're editing the clips that you've added to your movie, so it's a good idea to give your clips more meaningful names.

To do that, highlight the clip in the Clips list and then select the **Edit, Rename** command, or press **F2**. (You can also right-click a clip and then click **Rename**.) Type in your new name (up to 255 characters) and then press **Enter**.

157

Splitting a Clip

If you have a particularly long clip that's too unwieldy to use as is, you can split the clip into two separate clips at any point you like. This technique is also useful if Movie Maker didn't split your collection or if you elected not to create clips when you captured or imported your footage. Here's what you do:

1. Load the clip into the monitor.

2. Use the monitor controls to play the clip to the exact point where you want it split.

3. Click the **Split Clip** button (see Figure 12.4). Alternatively, select **Clip, Split** or press **Ctrl+Shift+S.** Movie Maker divides the clip in two and gives the second clip (the one with the footage that comes after the split point) the same name as the original clip, except for **(1)** tacked onto the end.

Combining Multiple Clips

I mentioned earlier that Movie Maker has an annoying tendency to create too many clips during the recording process. If Movie Maker has chopped up a scene a little too much to your liking, you can fix things by combining two or more clips into a single clip. Here's the procedure:

1. Highlight the clips you want to combine. Here are the techniques you can use to select multiple clips:

   ➤ Hold down **Ctrl** and click each clip.

   ➤ Click the first clip, hold down **Shift**, and click the last clip.

   ➤ Drag your mouse to create a box that touches or encloses each clip.

   ➤ If you want to highlight every clip in the collection, select the **Edit, Select All** command, or press **Ctrl+A.**

2. Select **Clip, Combine**, or press **Ctrl+Shift+C.**

From Projector to Project: Creating Your Movie Project

Your footage is safely ensconced on your hard disk and you can play with clips until the cows come home. Now what? Now it's nitty-gritty time as you start constructing your movie—which Movie Maker calls a "project"—piece-by-piece.

The first thing you need to know is that you can view your movie in one of two ways:

158

➤ **Storyboard** This view shows the sequence of clips that you've added to the movie, and for each clip it shows the first frame. The storyboard is where you see the big picture of your movie. You get this view by activating the **View, Storyboard** command, or by clicking the **Storyboard** button when the timeline is displayed (see Figure 12.5).

➤ **Timeline** This view displays a *timeline*, which is a kind of ruler that tracks time. You use it to see how much time your clips take and to edit the clips (for example, by shortening them). You get this view by activating the **View, Timeline** command, or by clicking the **Timeline** button when the storyboard is on-screen (see Figure 12.2).

Creating a movie in Movie Maker roughly involves the following steps:

1. Add a clip to the storyboard or timeline.
2. Use the storyboard to move the clip into the section of the movie where you want it to be seen.
3. Use the timeline to cut out unwanted sections of the clip.
4. Add a transition effect between the previous clip and the new clip.
5. Insert narration, music, or sounds.
6. Save the movie.
7. Repeat steps 1 through 6 until you're done.

The rest of this chapter takes you through each of these steps.

Adding a Clip to the Project

To add a clip to the movie, it doesn't matter if you're viewing the storyboard or the timeline. However, clips are easier to insert using the storyboard because you can see at a glance exactly where the clip will be inserted. Movie Maker gives you two techniques to add a clip (or clips) to your movie:

➤ Highlight the clip and select **Clip, Add to Storyboard/Timeline.** This technique always inserts the clip at the end of the movie.

➤ Drag the clip from the Clips list and drop it on the project in the Movie Maker workspace. When you move your mouse into the workspace and over the project, a vertical black bar appears as a marker that shows you where the clip will be inserted when you drop it. Drag the mouse left or right to insert the clip where you want it.

If you **really** want to add only a segment of a clip right now, you can do it by making one or two splits of the clip. First position the Seek Bar at the beginning of the good segment and then split the clip. Load the second half of the clip, move the Seek Bar to the end of the good segment, and split the clip again.

Using the Storyboard to Juggle Clips

When you insert your clips into the project, you don't need to worry too much about the order the clips appear because the order is easy to change. View the storyboard and then use any of the following techniques:

➤ Use your mouse to drag a clip left or right. Again, a black vertical bar tells you where the clip will appear when you drop it.

➤ To move a clip, highlight it and select **Edit, Cut** (or press **Ctrl+X**). Click the clip before which you want the cut clip inserted and then select **Edit, Paste** (or press **Ctrl+V**).

➤ To copy a clip, highlight it and select **Edit, Copy** (or press **Ctrl+C**). Click the clip before which you want the copied clip inserted and then select **Edit, Paste** (or press **Ctrl+V**).

➤ To combine two or more clips, select them and then select **Clip, Combine** (or press **Ctrl+Shift+C**).

➤ To delete a clip, highlight it and select **Edit, Delete** (or press **Delete**).

Remember, too, that you can work with multiple clips in the storyboard. Use the same techniques to select multiple clips in the storyboard as the ones I went through earlier for the Clips list (see the "Combining Multiple Clips" section earlier in this chapter).

Trimming a Clip

Figure 12.5 shows a Movie Maker project displaying the timeline view. Notice that the icons on the left side of the workspace become active when you switch to the timeline. Notice in particular the Zoom In and Zoom Out icons. You use these to change the timeline scale: If you want to see a more precise scale, click **Zoom In;** if you want to see the bigger picture, click **Zoom Out.**

The timeline's most useful feature is the capability it gives you to *trim* a clip, which means lopping off footage from the beginning or end (or both). Movie Maker offers two techniques:

➤ Click the clip in the timeline to select it. The first frame appears in the monitor. Use the monitor controls to move to the position where you want the good clip to start, and then select the **Clip, Set Start Trim Point** command (or press **Ctrl+Shift+Left arrow**). Use the monitor controls to move to the position where you want the good clip to end, and then select the **Clip, Set End Trim Point** command (or press **Ctrl+Shift+Right arrow**).

➤ In the timeline, drag the Start Trim triangle to the right to set the starting point of the good clip. Drag the End Trim triangle to the left to set the end point of the good clip.

In either case, you can eliminate the trim points by selecting the **Clip, Clear Trim Points** command (or by pressing **Ctrl+Shift+Delete**).

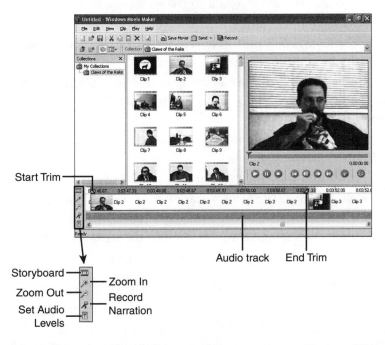

Figure 12.5

A Movie Maker project with the timeline displayed.

Adding a Transition Between Two Clips

In video editing, a *transition* is an effect that accompanies the change from one scene to another. In Movie Maker, the default transition from one clip to another is a *jump cut:* an immediate scene change from the first clip to the next. Movie Maker also supports a second type of transition: the *cross-fade*. In this transition, the first clip fades out while the next clip fades in. It can be quite effective as long as you don't use it for every scene change.

To create the cross-fade transition, first make sure you're viewing the timeline and scroll until you can see the two clips. In particular, you want to see the end of the first clip and the beginning of the second. Then use your mouse to drag the second clip to the left so that it overlaps the first clip. Use the timeline to judge the length of the transition and remember that most cross-fades last only one or two seconds.

161

Adding Narration, Music, and Sound Effects

If you choose to record both video and audio when capturing your footage, your clips will come with a *video track* that represents the audio portion of the video. You can supplement this track with a separate audio track that can play narration, background music, sound effects, or whatever other auditory marvels your project needs.

For the narration, you don't need a separate program to record it because Movie Maker is happy to handle that chore for you. Here's how it works:

1. Click the timeline's **Record Narration** button or select **File, Record Narration.** Movie Maker displays the Record Narration Track dialog box.

2. If you want to use a different device to capture the narration (unlikely, but you never know), click **Change** and use the Configure Audio dialog box to choose your narration weapon.

3. If you don't want to hear the video soundtrack while you're recording, activate the **Mute video soundtrack** check box.

4. Get your microphone ready and then click **Record.**

5. Say your piece and then click **Stop.** The Save Narration Sound Track dialog box shows up.

6. Enter a **File name** and then click **Save.** Movie Maker adds the narration file to the current collection and displays it in the Clips list.

Windows Wisdom

You can change the relative volume of the video track and the audio track by clicking the timeline's **Set Audio Levels** button (or select **Edit, Audio Levels**). In the Audio Levels dialog box, drag the slider to the left to increase the video track volume, or to the right to increase the audio track volume.

To add a narration, music, or sound file to the movie, follow these steps:

1. Import the file as described earlier (unless it's a narration file, which should already be imported into the current collection).

2. Make sure you're in the timeline view.

3. Drag the sound clip from the Clips list and drop it on the audio track section of the workspace.

4. Move the sound clip (by dragging it left or right along the audio track) as needed.

Show Time: Playing the Movie

As you edit the movie, you should play some or all of it back from time to time to make sure the result is what you wanted. Movie Maker offers two different ways to get set to play your movie:

➤ In the storyboard or timeline, click a clip or select multiple clips.

➤ In the timeline, click the timeline at the spot where you want playback to start.

In either case, you then use the monitor's buttons (or the commands on the **Play** menu) to start and control the playback. If you just want to see the whole movie from the first clip to the last, select the **Play, Play Entire Storyboard/Timeline** command.

Saving the Project and Movie

As with any program, you should save your project as often as you can to avoid losing any work. To do that in Movie Maker, select **File, Save Project**, or press **Ctrl+S.** The first time you do this, Movie Maker asks you to enter a name for the project and to select a location (the default My Videos folder is ideal).

Somewhat confusingly, saving your project does *not* create your movie file. To do that, you need to select **File, Save Movie**, or press **Ctrl+M.** In the Save Movie dialog box, use the **Setting** list to select the quality of the movie file. You can also enter other data such as a **Title, Author,** and **Rating.** When you've done that, the Save As dialog box appears so that you can enter a **File name** and choose a location (again, use the My Videos folder). Click **Save** to create the movie. (Note that this process will take a long time, depending on your machine, the length of the movie, and the number of transitions you used.)

Windows Wisdom

If you want to send your movie to another person via e-mail, select the **File, Send Movie To, E-mail** command. Use the Send Movie Via E-mail dialog box to choose the quality you want, enter a **Title,** and so on. When you click **OK,** Movie Maker prompts you for a file name and then asks you to choose your e-mail program.

The Least You Need to Know

➤ **Attaching an analog device**   If you have an analog camcorder, VCR, or TV, you need a video capture card (or a graphics card that supports video capture) and you need the proper composite or SVideo cable to make the attachment. If your device supports USB, attach it to one of your computer's USB ports.

➤ **Attaching a digital camcorder or camera**   These devices attach to either a USB port or to a IEEE 1394 (FireWire) port.

➤ **Recording video footage**   Attach your device and then select **File, Record** (or click **Record** or press **Ctrl+F**). In the Record window, change the settings to taste and then click **Record.**

➤ **Watching video on the monitor**   To watch a clip, click it in the Clips list or in the workspace and then click the **Play** button.

➤ **Selecting multiple clips**   For random clips, hold down **Ctrl** and click each clip; for consecutive clips, click the first clip, hold down **Shift,** and click the last clip.

➤ **Dragging clips**   You add a clip to a project by dragging it from the Clips list and dropping it on your project in the spot you want it to appear; also, you can change the order of the project's clips by dragging them left or right within the Storyboard view.

Chapter 13

Avoiding Fistfights While Sharing Your Computer

In This Chapter

➤ Creating accounts for each person who uses your computer

➤ Understanding the differences between administrators and limited accounts

➤ Setting up accounts with passwords and custom pictures

➤ Sharing and hiding your documents

Do you share your computer with other people either at work or at home? Then you've probably run smack dab into one undeniable fact: People are individuals with minds of their own! One person prefers Windows in a black-and-purple color scheme; another person just loves the far out "Vortec space" wallpaper; yet another person prefers to have a zillion shortcuts on the Windows desktop; and, of course, *everybody* uses a different mix of applications and creates their own documents. How can you possibly satisfy all these diverse tastes and prevent people from coming to blows?

Well, it's a lot easier than you might think. Windows XP enables you to set up a different *user account* for each person who uses the computer. These accounts keep your stuff separate from everyone else's stuff, which includes not only documents and programs, but also the desktop and Start menu configuration, Internet Explorer favorites, and more. This means that each person can customize Windows XP to their heart's content without foisting their tastes on anyone else. This chapter shows you how to set up, maintain, and use Windows XP's user accounts.

Understanding Windows XP's New User Accounts

Previous versions of the "consumer" line of Windows (Windows Me, Windows 98, and so on) tried various methods for letting people share a computer. There was one problem, however: those methods didn't work very well! In Windows XP, Microsoft is giving it another shot with something called *user accounts* and the good news is that this time it looks like they finally got it right.

In a sense, a user account gives each person their own version of Windows XP that they can muck around with as they see fit. This includes the following:

➤ All the customization stuff covered in Part 5, "Windows XP at the Shop: Customizing, Maintaining, and Troubleshooting." This means that each user can set up their own colors, wallpaper, and screen saver, customize their toolbar, and change the icons that appear on the Start menu.

➤ Favorite Web sites defined in Internet Explorer.

➤ E-mail and newsgroup accounts set up in Outlook Express.

Not only that, but Windows XP also supports a new doohickey called *fast user switching*. What this means is that different users can switch in and out of Windows while leaving their programs running. For example, suppose little Alphonse is blowing away some aliens and Dad needs to check his e-mail. In the old days, Alphonse would have to shut down his game so that Dad could log on and run his e-mail program. In Windows XP, Alphonse can leave his game running while Dad switches to his account and does his e-mail duties. Alphonse can then switch back right away and resume doing nasty things to strange creatures.

The last thing you need to know before getting started is that Windows XP offers two different user account types:

Jargon Jar

The **user accounts** feature is part of Windows XP Home, and you also get it if you use Windows XP Pro either on its own or on a small, noncorporate network. If you use Windows XP Pro on a corporate network (technically, a network where your computer is part of a *domain*), then setting up users is part of the network user setup.

➤ **Computer administrator**   This type of account has full access to the computer. The administrator can install any type of program or device, make changes that affect the entire system, access the documents created by all users, and add, change, and delete user accounts.

➤ **Limited**   This type of account has access to only some of the computer's features. It can view its own files, view those files that have been set up to be shared with other users, perform their own customizations, and change their password.

166

The idea here is that you set up only the most trusted or competent users (such as yourself, of course, and maybe, just *maybe,* your spouse) as administrators and you set up everyone else (such as the kids) as limited users.

Creating a New Account

When you or some suitably savvy geek set up Windows XP on your computer, the installation program asked for the name of one or more users. At the very least, a computer administrator account will have been created for the person who has overall responsibility for the machine, and a "Guest" account will have been created for temporary users of the machine.

If there were other accounts created, you'll see the Windows XP Welcome screen each time you start the computer (refer to Figure 2.1). If you don't see that screen, then only the one account was created. In any case, if you're the administrator, then you're free to add more accounts as you see fit.

Here are the steps to follow:

1. Select **Start, Control Panel** to open the Control Panel window and then click **User Accounts.** Windows XP sends the User Accounts window over to you.

2. Click **Create a new account.** This launches a wizard to guide you through the process.

3. In the first wizard window, use the **Type a name for the new account** text box to enter a name for the user and then click **Next.**

4. Choose an account type—**Computer administrator** or **Limited**—and then click **Create Account.**

Changing an Existing Account

If you need to make changes to a user account, what you can do depends on your account type:

➤ **If you're an administrator** You can change anything about any account, including the user's name, password, picture, and account type. You can also delete any account.

➤ **If you're a limited user** You can only change your own account and there are only three tasks you can perform: creating or changing a password, changing your picture, and setting up a .NET passport.

In either case, you get started by selecting **Start, Control Panel** to open the Control Panel window and then clicking **User Accounts** to return to the User Accounts window. If you're an administrator, click the icon for the user you want to work with. The next few sections run through the instructions for all the available tasks.

Changing the User's Name

If a user doesn't like the name you supplied, or if they've changed their name or joined a cult, it's not a problem to supply them with a new name that's more to their liking. If you're one of the poobah administrators, here's what you do to change the user's name:

1. Click **Change user name.**

2. In the **Type a new name for *User*** text box (where *User* is the user's current name), enter the new name for the user.

3. Click **Change Name.**

Creating an Account Password

After you go to all this trouble to set up separate user accounts, you'll likely be shocked and appalled to discover a dismaying fact: Any other user can log on to your account just by selecting it in the Welcome screen. To get around this, you can protect your things with a password.

Look Out!

If you store sensitive data on your computer (or just don't want someone to snoop), then you should think carefully about the password you choose. That is, don't use an obvious word (such as your name), use words that are at least five characters long (the longer the better), and mix uppercase and lowercase letters and toss in a number or two.

Here are the steps to cruise through to set a password for the selected account:

1. Click **Create a password.**

2. Use the **Type a new password** text box to enter the password for the user. (Note that you see a bunch of dots instead of the actual characters you type. This is a security feature to prevent someone from spying the password.)

3. Use the **Type the new password again to confirm** text box to enter the password once again.

4. Use the **Type a word or phrase to use as a password hint** text box to enter a password. This word or phrase is accessible in the Welcome screen and is visible to all and sundry. Therefore, make the hint as vague as possible while still being useful to you if you forget your password.

5. Click **Create password.**

Once you've created a password, the user account window sprouts two new tasks:

➤ **Change the password** (or **Change my password,** if it's your own account)
   Click this link to change the password. Note that you need to enter the old password before Windows XP sets the new one.

➤ **Remove the password** (or **Remove my password,** if it's your own account)
   Click this link to stop using a password. (Again, you need to enter your existing password first.)

Changing the User's Picture

User accounts isn't the most exciting topic in the computing world, so it's a welcome relief that Windows XP includes a feature that lets you have a bit of fun: You can assign a picture to each user. This picture is visible in the Welcome screen and on the top of the Start menu when the user is logged on. Windows XP supplies a random picture when you create an account, but here's how you change it to something else:

1. Click **Change the picture** (or **Change my picture** if this is your account). Windows XP displays a selection of pictures, as shown in Figure 13.1.

Figure 13.1

Use this window to select a picture for the user's account.

2. Click the picture you want and then click **Change Picture.** If you have your own picture, click **Browse for more pictures,** use the Open dialog box to find the image you want, and then click **Open.**

Changing the Account Type

If you want to promote a trusted user to administrator status, or if you want to demote some miscreant to limited status, it's not hard:

1. Click **Change the account type.**

2. Activate either **Computer administrator** or **Limited.**

3. Click **Change Account Type.**

Setting Up Your Account with a .NET Passport

In 2000, Microsoft announced what is by far its most ambitious project yet: Microsoft.NET. The idea behind .NET is both big and bold: to enable you to access your documents, e-mail messages, Web favorites, and other digital essentials no matter where you are and no matter what device you have in front of you. As this book went to press, the Microsoft programmers were busy making this vision a reality, so the specifics of .NET weren't available. However, the one thing we do know is that you're going to need a *passport* from Microsoft as your point of entry into this new system.

To associate a passport with your account, click your icon in the User Accounts window and then click **Set up my account to use a .NET Passport.** This launches the .NET Passport Wizard. I take you through the various screens presented by this wizard in Chapter 23, "Using Windows Messenger to Fire Off Instant Messages."

Deleting an Account

If you no longer need an account, you may as well delete it to reduce clutter in the User Accounts window. Here's how:

1. Click **Delete the account**. Windows XP asks if you want to keep the contents of the account's My Documents folder and desktop.

2. If you want to save these things, click **Keep Files** to store them in a new folder named after the user. Otherwise, click **Delete Files.**

3. Click **Delete Account.**

Logging On to an Account

Once you have two or more user accounts on the go (excluding the Guest account, that is), then each time you crank up Windows XP you'll see the Welcome screen, as shown earlier in the book in Figure 2.1. Click your user icon to log on to Windows. If the account is protected by a password, a text box will appear. In that case, enter the password and press **Enter**. (If you need to see your password hint, click the question mark button.)

Once you're logged on to an account, you can switch to another user by following these steps:

1. Select **Start, Log Off.** The Log Off Windows box appears.

2. Click one of the following buttons:

   ➤ **Switch User**   Click this button if you want to leave the current user's windows and programs open and running. (This is a new Windows XP feature that's called *fast-user switching*.)

➤ **Log Off** Click this button if you prefer to shut down all of the current user's windows and programs.

3. When the Welcome screen reappears, log on as a different user.

Sharing Documents with (and Hiding Them from) Other Users

Although you'll want to keep most of your documents to yourself, it's conceivable that you'll want other users to be able to see and work with some files. For example, you might scan in some family photos that you want everyone to see or you might store some music that you want other folks to hear.

Using the Shared Documents Folder

By far the easiest way to go about this is to take advantage of the special "shared" folders that Windows XP sets up automatically. To get to these folders, select **Start, My Documents** and then click **Shared Documents** in the **Other Places** section. The Shared Documents folder is the shared equivalent of My Documents, and it also includes two subfolders—Shared Music and Shared Pictures—that are the equivalent of My Music and My Pictures. If you move or copy a document into one of these folders, every user will be able to see and work with the file.

Sharing (or Keeping Private) My Documents

Access to a user's My Documents folder is controlled by the account type:

➤ If you're an administrator, you can access My Documents for any limited user.

➤ If you're a limited user, you can't access any other user's My Document folder.

However, it's possible to change this behavior. To see how, follow these steps:

1. Select **Start, My Computer**.
2. Click the toolbar's **Folders** button.
3. In the **Folders** bar, open the drive where Windows XP is installed (this is usually drive C), then open the **Documents and Settings** folder. The subfolders you see are where the user documents and computer settings are stored:

   ➤ The **All Users** subfolder is where the Shared Documents folder exists, along with the stuff everyone sees on the Start menu.

   ➤ There's also a subfolder for each user.

4. Right-click your subfolder and then click **Sharing and Security.** (If you're an administrator, you can do this to any of the user subfolders.) Windows XP launches the Properties dialog box for the folder with the Sharing tab displayed, as shown in Figure 13.2.

Figure 13.2

Use the Sharing tab to make a folder private or share it with others.

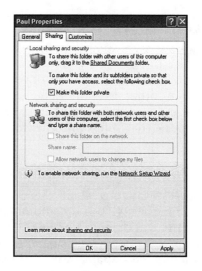

5. You have two choices:

   ➤ If you're a limited user and you don't want an administrator to be able to access your documents, activate the **Make this folder private** check box. If your account doesn't have a password, Windows XP asks if you want to create one. If you do, click **Yes** and then create a password as described earlier.

   ➤ If you're an administrator and you want limited users to be able to access your documents, deactivate the **Make this folder private** check box.

6. Click **OK.**

Making a Program Available Only to Specific Users

By default, if an administrator installs a program, it usually shows up on the Start menu's **All Programs** submenu and anyone can run it from there. That's usually a reasonable setup, but there may be times when you want to hide a program from one or more users. To do that, you need to manipulate the various Start menu icons by hand.

Here are the basic steps to follow:

1. Select **Start, My Computer.**

2. Click the toolbar's **Folders** button.

3. In the **Folders** bar, open the drive where Windows XP is installed (usually drive C), then open the **Documents and Settings** folder.

4. Open **All Users** and then **Start Menu**, then click **Programs**. You should now see a folder icon for the program you're dealing with. Right-click that folder's icon and then click **Cut**.

5. Open the subfolder of whatever user you want to have access to the program, then open **Start Menu** and click **Programs**. Select **Edit**, **Paste** to add the program's folder.

6. Repeat step 5 for any other user that you want to access the program.

See Also

To manipulate the various Start menu icons by hand, see Chapter 25, "Revamping the Start Menu and Taskbar" (the section titled "A Smart Start: Reconstructing the Start Menu").

The Least You Need to Know

➤ **All users are not created equal**   XP supports two types of user: *administrators* who can pretty much do what they want, including install programs and devices, change system settings, access documents for all users, and work with user accounts; and *limited users* who can only view their own files, view shared files, and perform their own Windows customizations.

➤ **Getting to the User Accounts window**   The User Accounts window is where everything happens; you get there by selecting **Start, Control Panel, User Accounts.**

➤ **Forging a new account**   To create a new user account, click **Create a new account** in the User Accounts window.

➤ **Changing a user's account doodads**   Open the User Accounts window and then click the user's icon.

➤ **Password pointers**   If you have important stuff you want to keep secure, add a password to your account and make sure that the password isn't an obvious word, is at least five characters long, and combines uppercase and lowercase letters and numbers.

➤ **Switching to a different user**   Select **Start, Log Off,** click **Switch User,** and then click the user's icon.

Part 3

Windows XP at Work

Playing around with images and videos and music can be a heckuva lot of fun, but one of these days you've gotta get some work done. (Insert groan of disappointment here.) When the time comes for your nose and the grindstone to get reacquainted, Windows XP will be there for you with some competent business tools. The chapters here in Part 3 look at the most commonly used of these tools. Chapter 14, "Prose Programs: Windows XP's Writing Tools," covers Notepad and WordPad; Chapter 15, "Fax-It-Yourself: Using Windows XP's Faxing Features," covers faxing; and Chapter 16, "A Moveable Feast: Windows XP and Your Notebook Computer," covers the Windows XP notebook features. Don't work too hard!

I think that I shall never see, a poem as lovely as XP...

Prose Programs: Windows XP's Writing Tools

In This Chapter

➤ Using Notepad for simple text tasks

➤ Using WordPad for full-bore word processing

➤ Techniques for automatically finding and replacing text

➤ Inserting ã, ö, ¢, ©, and other oddball characters

Windows XP comes with just about all the writing tools you'll ever pine for, whether you just need to dash off a quick to-do list or whether you need to compose a professional-looking letter or resumé. This chapter gives you the goods on these writing tools.

Before getting started, you should know that the written documents you deal with will come in two flavors: plain and formatted. A plain document contains characters that have no special formatting: just plain, unadorned, text. So, unshockingly, these types of documents are called *text files*. In the Windows XP world, you read, edit, and create text files using the Notepad text editor. A formatted document contains characters that have (or can have) formatting such as **bold** or *italics*. These types of documents are called *word processing files*. In Windows XP, you read, edit, and create word processing files using the WordPad word processor.

Notepad is the subject of the first part of this chapter, and I discuss WordPad's eccentricities a bit later (see the section "Using WordPad for Fancier Word Processing Files" later in this chapter). Note also that whether your computer comes stocked with Microsoft Word, Microsoft Works, or some other program, if you write a lot, you'll be better off using the other program rather than WordPad.

Using Notepad for Garden-Variety Text Files

If text files are so plain, why on earth would anyone want to use them? Perhaps you want to send a document to another person and you want to make sure they can open it. Most of the personal computers on the planet can deal with a text file, so that's your safest bet. If you used WordPad, on the other hand, your friend has to have WordPad (or a relatively recent version of Microsoft Word) installed to open the file. Another reason to use a text file is that perhaps you need to create a document that *must* be plain text. For example, if you want to create a Web page from scratch, you have to save it as a text file; a word processing file won't work.

Just about anyone using just about any PC can read a text file. This universality means that you'll get a lot of text files coming your way. For example, if you examine the installation disk of most programs, you'll almost always see at least one text file with a name like "Readme" or "Setup." This file usually contains information about the installation process (such as how to prepare for the install and how the install operates), last-minute changes to the manual, and so on.

You can identify these and other text files by the icon they use in My Computer. Figure 14.1 points out a couple of text files. When you see the text file icon, double-click the file to open it in Notepad.

Figure 14.1

Windows XP shows text files using a special icon.

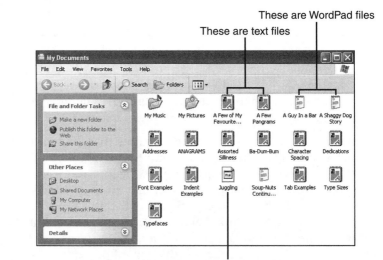

These are WordPad files

These are text files

This icon means Windows XP has no idea what the file is

If you need to create a text file, begin by opening Notepad: **Start, All Programs, Accessories, Notepad.** Figure 14.2 shows the window that materializes on your screen.

Figure 14.2

Notepad: a simple window for a simple type of file.

As you can see, Notepad sports a plain, no-frills, look that perfectly matches the plain, no-frills, text files you work with. There's nary a bell or whistle in sight, and even the menus contain, for the most part, just a bare-bones collection of commands: New, Open, Save, Cut, Copy, Paste, and so on. Dullsville. That's okay, though, because that's the nature of the Notepad beast. You just fire it up and then read, type, and edit as necessary. However, Notepad is not without its small quirks and one-of-a-kind features. Here's a summary:

➤ **Inserting the date and time** To plop the current date and time into your text file, select the **Edit, Time/Date** command (or press **F5**).

➤ **Wrapping text** When you type in most normal programs and the cursor hits the right edge of the window, the cursor automatically jumps down one line and starts again on the left edge of the window (this feature is known as *word wrap*). But not Notepad, no. It just blithely continues along the same line for exactly 1,024 characters, and only *then* will it wrap onto the next line. Dumb! To avoid this annoyance, activate the **Format, Word Wrap** command.

➤ **Opening other files** I mentioned earlier that some text files don't have the Notepad icon. Unfortunately, if you select Notepad's **File, Open** command, the Open dialog box only shows files with that icon. To see other text files, go to the **Files of type** drop-down list at the bottom of the dialog box and select the **All Files** option.

Windows Wisdom

If you come across a text file that doesn't have the proper icon, you can talk Notepad into attempting to open the file by highlighting the file and then selecting **File, Open With** to get to the Open With dialog box. Highlight **Notepad** in the list, and then click **OK.** If you see gobbledygook instead of words and phrases, then it wasn't a text file.

179

➤ **Tweaking the page** The **File, Page Setup** command displays the dialog box shown in Figure 14.3. You can use this dialog box to set various page layout and printing options, including the paper size and orientation, the size of each margin, and text that you want printed in each page's Header and Footer. (The **&f** thingy tells Notepad to print the name of the file, and the **&p** combo tells it to print each page number. You can also enter **&d** to print the current date, **&t** to print the current time, and **&l**, **&c**, or **&r** to align the header or footer text on the left, center, or right, respectively.)

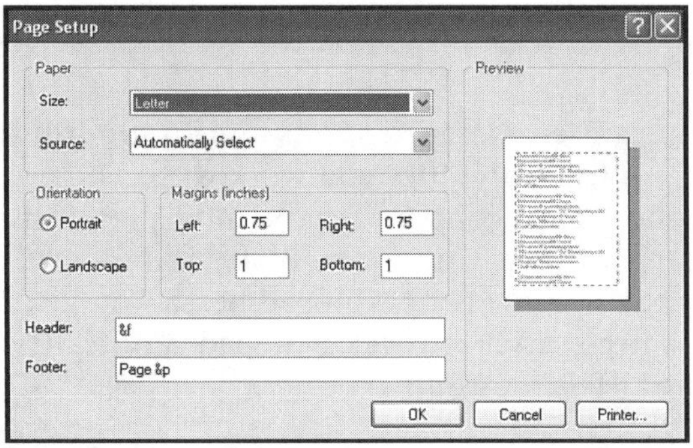

Figure 14.3

Use the Page Setup dialog box to spell out various page layout and printing options for Notepad.

➤ **What's up with the Font command?** Despite what I said about text files not using formatting, Notepad sports a Font command on its Format menu. What gives? I assure you I wasn't lying: that command can and should be ignored because regular text files *don't* use fonts. However, Windows XP does support a special type of text file that can use fonts. So if (and only if) you'll be sending your text file to another Windows XP (or Windows 2000) user, you can select a font (it applies to the entire document). When you go to save the file, make sure you open the **Encoding** list and select **Unicode.**

Using WordPad for Fancier Word Processing Files

Like Dorothy getting whisked from the black-and-white world of Kansas into the Technicolor world of Oz, we turn now to WordPad, Windows XP's word processor. To get this program down the electronic yellow brick road, select **Start, All Programs, Accessories, WordPad.** Figure 14.4 shows the WordPad window. Unlike the Spartan expanse of Notepad, the WordPad window offers a well-appointed interior with lots of word processing amenities.

Toolbar   Format bar

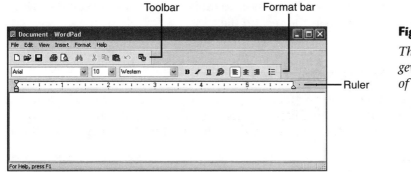

Figure 14.4

The WordPad window gewgaws include a couple of toolbars and a ruler.

—— Ruler

WordPad and Word Processing Files

Here are a few notes to bear in mind when working with WordPad and its word processing files:

➤ **The WordPad file icon**   Like text files, WordPad files also have their own unique icon, as shown earlier in Figure 14.1. When you see a file with this icon, double-click it to load the file in WordPad.

➤ **What type of document do you want?**   When you select the **File, New** command, WordPad winds up and delivers the New dialog box to you. WordPad is wondering what type of document you want to create. You have three choices:

> **Rich Text Document**   This produces a file in the Rich Text Format (RTF, for short), which accepts all kinds of formatting. It's a standard format in computing circles, so it's readable by many other word processing programs. This is a good choice if you'll be sending the document to someone and you're not sure what program they'll be using.

> **Text Document**   This gets you a plain text file.

> **Unicode Text Document**   This is a relatively obscure type of text file that in all likelihood you'll never have to worry about.

➤ **Opening documents: Are you my file type?**   As you've seen, there are several different types of files that fall under the aegis of WordPad. Unfortunately, when you select the **File, Open** command, the Open dialog box only shows RTF files. If you're trying to open a different type (such as Word or text), you need to drop down the **Files of type** list and select either the type you need (such as **Word for Windows** or **Text Documents**) or **All Documents.**

➤ **Working on two files at once**   WordPad's one-track mind means that it can only have one file open at a time. However, there will be plenty of times when you need to work with *two* files at once. For example, you might want to compare text in the two files, or you might want to copy or move text from one file

181

to the other. No problemo! All you have to do is open up a second copy of WordPad and use it to open the second file.

Tip Sheet: Text-Selection Tricks

Before you can format, cut, or copy text, you first have to select it. I showed you the basic text-selection maneuvers in Chapter 5, "Saving, Opening, Printing, and Other Document Lore," but WordPad has a few extra techniques that can make your life a teensy bit easier:

➤ **To select a word**   Double-click it.

➤ **To select a line**   Click inside the narrow strip of white space to the left of the line (that is, between the line and the WordPad window's left border). In word processing circles, this strip is called the *selection area*.

➤ **To select a paragraph**   Double-click the selection area beside the paragraph. (Those with energy to burn also can select a paragraph by *triple*-clicking inside the paragraph.)

➤ **To select the whole document**   Hold down **Ctrl** and click anywhere inside the selection area. (You can also choose **Edit, Select All** or press **Ctrl+A**.)

Fancy-Schmancy Formatting I: Fonts

The whole point of using a word processor (as opposed to a text editor, such as our pal Notepad) is to turn dull-as-dishwater text into beautifully formatted prose that other people will be clamoring to read. Happily, WordPad offers quite a few formatting features that can turn even the plainest file into a document with text appeal.

In this section, you begin with the most common formatting makeover: the font. A *font* is a style of text in which a unique design and other effects have been applied to all the characters. To begin, you need to decide whether you want to format existing text or text that you're about to type:

➤ **To format existing text**   Select the text to which you want to apply the font.

➤ **To format new text**   Position the cursor at the spot where the new typing will appear.

With that done, here are the steps to follow to apply the font:

1. Select WordPad's **Format, Font** command. The Font dialog box puts in an appearance.

2. Use the **Font** list to choose a typeface. The *typeface* is what most people think of when they use the word "font." It represents the distinctive design applied to all the characters. See Figure 14.5 for some examples. (Wondering what's up with

all those typefaces that have the stylized "O" beside them? Those are *OpenType* typefaces and they generally display better that the other typefaces.)

3. Use the **Font style** list to select a style for the text (see Figure 14.5).

4. Use the **Size** list to choose the font height you want to use. The various values are measured in *points*, where 72 points equals an inch (again, see Figure 14.5 for an example or two).

5. The **Effects** group is populated with three controls: activate the **Strikeout** check box to get ~~strikeout~~ characters; activate the **Underline** check box to format characters with an underline; and use the **Color** text box to change the color of the text.

6. The **Script** list tells you which language scripts are available for the selected typeface. You use these scripts to create multilingual documents. If you plan on using only English, leave this list set to **Western.**

7. Click **OK** to put the new font into effect.

Note, too, that WordPad offers a few toolbar shortcuts for many of these font tricks. Figure 14.5 points out the relevant lists and buttons and shows a few fonts in action.

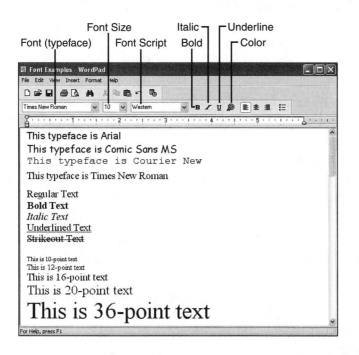

Figure 14.5

Some examples of the various font features.

Speaking of shortcuts, you'll be pleased to hear that WordPad also offers a small collection of keyboard combos for easier font fiddling. For example, to format text as **Bold**, press **Ctrl+B**; *Italic,* press **Ctrl+I**; and Underline, press **Ctrl+U**.

183

Installing New Fonts

Windows XP brings a few dozen fonts to the formatting table, which isn't bad. (Many programs install their own fonts, so your system may have more than that depending on what software you have installed.) However, there are plenty of font collections available on the market, and they generally cost only pennies a font. If you purchase one of these collections, you have to install it. To do that, follow these steps:

1. Select **Start, Control Panel,** click **Appearance and Themes,** and then click the **Fonts** link.

2. When the Fonts window appears, select **File, Install New Font** to open the Add Fonts dialog box.

3. Insert the font disc and select the appropriate drive in the **Drives** list.

4. After a few seconds, the available fonts on the disc will appear in the **List of fonts.**

5. Highlight the ones you want to install, and then click **OK.**

Fancy-Schmancy Formatting II: Paragraphs

Few things are as uninviting to read as a document that's nothing but wall-to-wall text. To give your readers a break (literally), divide up your text into separate paragraphs. (Press **Enter** once to start a new paragraph; press **Enter** twice to give yourself a bit of breathing room between each paragraph.)

As a further measure, consider formatting your paragraphs. WordPad enables you to indent entire paragraphs, indent only the first line of a paragraph, and align your paragraphs with the margins. Here's how it works:

1. Place the cursor within the paragraph that you want to format.

2. Either select the **Format, Paragraph** command, or right-click the paragraph and then click **Paragraph.** WordPad coaxes the Paragraph dialog box onto the screen.

3. Use the **Left** text box to set how far (in inches) the text is indented from the left margin.

4. Use the **Right** text box to set how far (in inches) the text is indented from the right margin.

5. Use the **First line** text box to set how far (in inches) the first line of the paragraph is indented from the left margin.

6. Use the **Alignment** list to align the paragraph relative to either the Left margin or the Right margin. You can also select Center, which centers the paragraph evenly between both margins.

7. Click **OK.**

Figure 14.6 demonstrates a few of WordPad's paragraph formatting options.

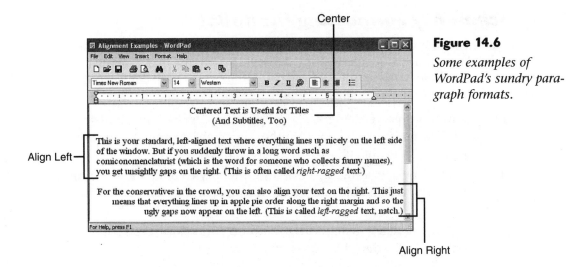

Center

Figure 14.6

Some examples of WordPad's sundry paragraph formats.

Align Left

Align Right

Rather than messing around with inches for the various paragraph indents, try WordPad's ruler. The ruler has various markers that set the paragraph indents (see Figure 14.7). Here's a rundown of what they do:

➤ **Left indent for the first line**   Indents the paragraph's first line from the left margin.

➤ **Left indent for the rest of the paragraph**   Indents the rest of the paragraph from the left margin.

➤ **Left indent for the entire paragraph**   Indents the entire paragraph from the left margin.

➤ **Right indent for the entire paragraph**   Indents the entire paragraph from the right margin.

To use these markers to format a paragraph, place the cursor inside the paragraph and then use your mouse to drag the appropriate marker left or right.

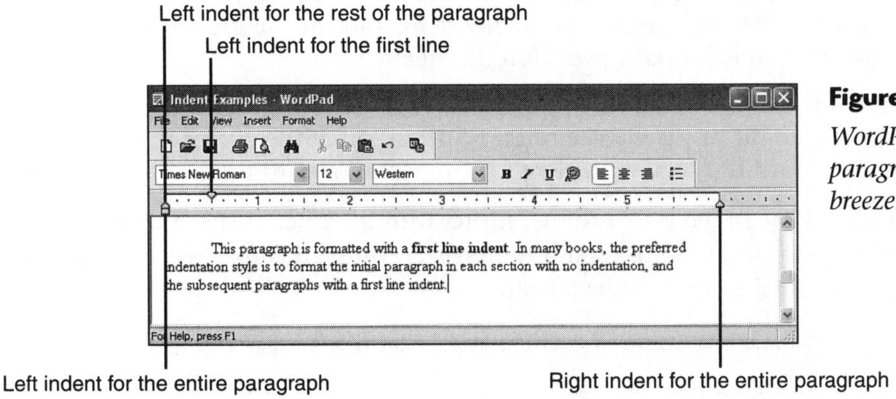

Left indent for the rest of the paragraph

Left indent for the first line

Figure 14.7

WordPad's ruler can make paragraph formatting a breeze.

Left indent for the entire paragraph

Right indent for the entire paragraph

185

Fancy-Schmancy Formatting III: Bullets

When you need to include a list of points or items in your document, it's best to separate those items from the regular text by displaying each one in a separate paragraph. To make these items even easier to read, format them with a *bullet* out front, as shown in Figure 14.8. To use bullets, follow these steps:

1. If you want to turn an existing paragraph into the first item in a bulleted list, first place the cursor anywhere within the paragraph. If you want to convert several paragraphs to bullets, select the paragraphs.

2. Turn on bullets by activating the **Format, Bullet Style** command. (You can also click the **Bullets** toolbar button or right-click the paragraph and then click **Bullet Style.**)

3. To create a new bulleted item, move to the end of the last bulleted item and press **Enter.** WordPad dutifully creates another bullet.

4. Enter the text for the new bullet.

5. Repeat Steps 3 and 4 until you've entered all your bulleted items.

6. Press **Enter** twice to tell WordPad to knock off the bulleted style.

Figure 14.8

An example of a bulleted list.

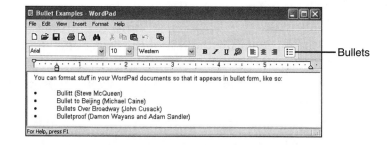

Fancy-Schmancy Formatting IV: Tabs

If you place the cursor on a blank line and press **Tab**, you'll notice that the cursor leaps ahead by exactly half an inch. Press **Tab** again, and you get another half-inch jump. These half-inch intervals are known as *tab stops*, and they're great for making columns or tables that line up like a precision drill team.

WordPad goes one better by enabling you to set your own tab stops anywhere you like. The easiest way to do this is via the ruler. To begin, place the cursor inside the paragraph that you want to mess with. Here are the techniques to use:

➤ **To set a tab stop**   Move your mouse pointer into the ruler at the spot where you want the tab stop to appear, and then click. WordPad adds what looks like a small "L" to the ruler; that's your tab stop.

186

➤ **To move a tab stop**   Use your mouse to drag the tab stop marker left or right.

➤ **To delete a tab stop**   Use your mouse to drag the tab stop marker off the ruler.

Just for the record, there *is* a hard way to set the tabs: select the **Format, Tabs** command to display the Tabs dialog box. In this case, you enter the position (in inches) where you want the tab to appear, and then click **Set**. In addition, clicking the **Clear All** button removes all the tabs from the current paragraph or selection.

Finding and Replacing Text

Back in Chapter 6, "Using My Computer to Fiddle with Files and Folders," I showed you how to use Windows XP's Search feature to find a file needle in a hard disk haystack. However, what if the haystack is a huge, multipage document and the needle is a word or phrase? Not to worry: Windows XP has a solution. It's called the Find feature, and it's part of both Notepad and WordPad.

Here's how it works:

1. In Notepad or WordPad, open the document you want to search, if it isn't open already.

2. Select the **Edit, Find** command (or press **Ctrl+F**). The Find dialog box punches in.

3. Use the **Find what** text box to enter the word or phrase you want to find.

4. (WordPad only) Activate the **Match whole word only** check box to force Find to match only the exact word or phrase you entered in step 3. If you leave this option deactivated, Find looks for text that *includes* the word or phrase. For example, if your search text is waldo and this check box is deactivated, Find will match not only the name *Waldo,* but also words such as *Waldorf* and *Oswaldo.*

5. Activate the **Match case** check box to run a *case-sensitive* search. This means that Find matches only those words or phrases that exactly match the uppercase and lowercase letters you used in your search text. For example, if your search text is Bill and you activate this check box, Find will match the name *Bill* and will ignore the word *bill.*

6. Click the **Find Next** button to let Find loose. If it finds a match, it highlights the text. If that's not what you wanted, click **Find Next** again to resume the search; otherwise, click **Cancel** to shut down the dialog box. If Find fails to ferret out a match, it will display a dialog box to let you know the bad news.

7. If you end up back in the document and realize that the found text was not the instance you needed after all, you don't have to fire up the Find dialog box all over again. Instead, either select the **Edit, Find Next** command, or press **F3**. Find simply repeats your last search from the current position.

187

Instead of merely finding some text, a more common editing chore is to find some text and then replace it with something else. For example, you may have written "St." throughout a document and you want to change each instance to "Street." The Replace feature makes these kinds of adjustments a snap:

1. In Notepad or WordPad, open the document you want to work with, if necessary.

2. Select the **Edit, Replace** command. (Alternatively, you can press **Ctrl+H.**) This gets you face-to-face with the Replace dialog box.

Look Out!

The Replace All feature can save you oodles of time, but use it with care. For example, you might think it's safe to replace all instances of "St." with "Street," but the sentence "He went last." might end up as "He went last-treet." (This is a good example of when the Match case option would come in handy.)

3. The Replace dialog box is pretty much the same as the Find dialog box, except that it has an extra **Replace with** text box. You use this text box to enter the word or phrase with which you want to replace whatever's in the **Find what** text box.

4. Enter the other searching options, as needed.

5. You now have two choices:

   ➤ If you want to replace only selected matches, click **Find Next**. Again, Find highlights the text if it zeroes in on a match. To replace the highlighted text with what's in the Replace with box, click **Replace**. Repeat this until you've finished all the replacements.

   ➤ If you prefer to replace every instance of the Find what text with the Replace with text, click **Replace All**.

Using Character Map for Foreign Characters and Other Symbols

If you need to use a symbol such as © or £ in a document, or if you want to spell a word such as resumé with the requisite accent, don't go hunting around your keyboard because you won't find what you need. Instead, spread open the Character Map program and use it to copy all the strange and exotic symbols and characters you require. Here's how it works:

1. Select **Start, More Programs, Accessories, System Tools, Character Map**. This opens the Character Map window shown in Figure 14.9.

2. Use the **Font** list to pick out a typeface to work with. (Hint: For foreign characters and some common symbols, select any regular typeface; for other symbols, try the Webdings, Wingdings, or Symbol typefaces.)

3. Select the symbol you want by clicking it and then clicking **Select** (you can also double-click the symbol). The symbol appears in the Characters to copy box.

4. Click the **Copy** button to copy the character.

5. Return to WordPad or Notepad, position the cursor where you want the character to appear, and select the **Edit, Paste** command (or press **Ctrl+V**).

When you click a symbol to highlight it, you may see a **Keystroke** listed in the lower-right corner of the window (see Figure 14.9). This means that you can bypass Character Map and enter the symbol directly by pressing the keystroke in your application. Note, however, that you must enter the numbers using your keyboard's numeric keypad.

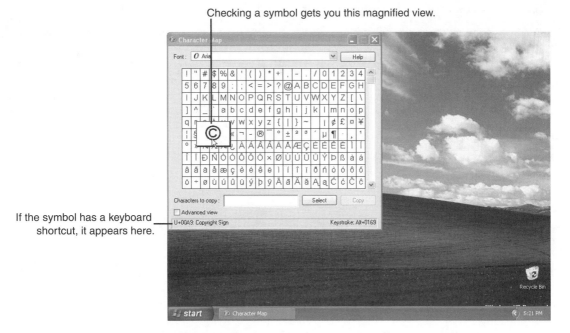

Checking a symbol gets you this magnified view.

If the symbol has a keyboard shortcut, it appears here.

Figure 14.9

Use Character Map to get foreign characters, currency signs, zodiac signs, and lots more silly symbols.

189

The Least You Need to Know

➤ **Smooth versus crunchy** Use Notepad (**Start, All Programs, Accessories, Notepad**) for plain text files, and use WordPad (**Start, All Programs, Accessories, WordPad**) for formatted word processing files.

➤ **Wrap Notepad text** To avoid frustration in Notepad, always activate the **Format, Word Wrap** command to ensure that text wraps inside the Notepad window.

➤ **The ruler rules** Don't forget to use WordPad's ruler when setting indents and tabs. It's much easier to drag the indent markers or click and drag tab stops than to do everything via the dialog boxes.

➤ **Map those characters** Use the Character Map program (**Start, All Programs, Accessories, System Tools, Character Map**) whenever you need foreign characters or symbols that aren't on your keyboard.

Chapter 15

Fax-It-Yourself: Using Windows XP's Faxing Features

In This Chapter

➤ Getting Windows XP ready for faxing

➤ Sending a fax message

➤ Creating custom fax cover pages

➤ Receiving incoming faxes

➤ Annotating received faxes

Nowadays, faxing is just another humdrum part of the workaday world, and any business worth its salt has a fax machine on standby. Increasingly, however, dedicated fax machines are giving way to *fax/modems*—modems that have the capability to send and receive faxes in addition to their regular communications duties. Not only does this make faxing affordable for small businesses and individuals, but it also adds a new level of convenience to the whole fax experience.

You can send faxes right from your computer without having to print the document. Because faxes sent via computer aren't scanned (as they are with a fax machine), the document that the recipient gets is sharper and easier to read. And, you can use your printer to get a hard copy of a fax on regular paper, thus avoiding fax paper (which, besides being inherently slimy, has an annoying tendency to curl; fortunately, most newer fax machines can handle regular paper).

If you want to enjoy the fax fast lane from the comfort of your computer, look no further than Windows XP's fax service. This chapter shows you how to install and configure the fax service, and how to use it to send and receive faxes.

Setting Up Windows XP to Do the Faxing Thing

Windows XP isn't fax-ready right out of the box. To convince XP that, yes, you *really* want to send and receive faxes, you need to set up and configure the fax service.

The first step is to install the fax service:

1. Select **Start**, **Control Panel** to open the Control Panel window.
2. Click **Printers and Other Hardware.**

Look Out!

Only a user who is set up as an administrator can install the fax service in Windows XP.

3. Click **Printers and Faxes.** The Printers and Faxes window shows up.
4. Click **Set up faxing.** The Windows Components Wizard kicks in.
5. If you see the Insert Disk dialog box at this point, insert your Windows XP CD, wait five or ten seconds, and then click **OK.**

The wizard then takes quite a while to install the fax service. When the wizard has completed its labors, it drops you off back at the Printers and Faxes window where a new **Fax** icon appears, as shown in Figure 15.1.

Figure 15.1

After you set up the fax service, a new Fax icon appears in the Printers and Faxes window.

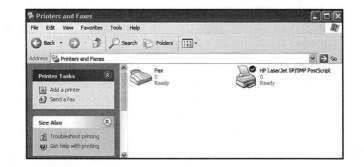

With that out of the way, wipe the digital dirt from your hand and get ready for the next step, configuring the fax service. Here it goes:

1. In the Printers and Faxes window, double-click the **Fax** icon. The first time you do this, the Fax Configuration Wizard leaps onto the desktop.
2. The first wizard dialog box is as useful as a screen door in a submarine, so click **Next.** The wizard displays the Sender Information dialog box.

3. Use this dialog box to enter your name, fax number, address, and so on. Remember that this information will be added automatically to your fax cover pages, so only enter data that you want your fax recipients to eyeball. When you're done, click **Next.** You now see the Select Device for Sending or Receiving Faxes dialog box.

4. This dialog box has the following controls (click **Next** when you've made your choices):

   ➤ **Please select the fax device**   This is a list of the fax modems installed on your computer. If you have more than one, use the list to choose the one you want to perform the faxing chores.

   ➤ **Enable Send**   Leave this check box activated if you want to be able to send faxes from your computer.

   ➤ **Enable Receive**   Activate this check box if you want to be able to receive faxes on your computer. When this check box is activated, the following two controls come into play:

   Manual answer   Activate this option to answer incoming calls manually (as described later in this chapter).

   Automatically answer after *x* rings   Activate this option to have the service answer incoming calls automatically.

5. The wizard now prompts you for your *Transmitting Subscriber Identification,* or *TSID.* Enter the text (such as your name or your company name) and click **Next.**

Jargon Jar

Windows XP assigns a name to your fax machine. This is known in the trade as the **TSID: Transmitting Subscriber Identification** (or sometimes Transmitting Station Identifier). When the other person receives your fax, your TSID is displayed at the top of each page. If the other person is receiving on a computer, the TSID appears in the "TSID" line (or some similar field, depending on the program they're using). Unfortunately, the default TSID in Windows XP is "Fax," which redefines the word "uninspiring." To fix this, edit the TSID as described in step 5. (For example, it's common to change it to your company name, your department name, or your own name.)

6. If you elected to receive faxes, the wizard asks you for your Called Subscriber Identification, or CSID. This identifies your computer to the fax sender. This isn't as important as the TSID, so enter whatever you like and click **Next**.

7. If you'll be receiving faxes, the wizard now wonders what you want to do with incoming faxes (click **Next** when you're done):

   ➤ **Print it on**   Activate this check box to have Windows XP automatically print any received fax. Use the list that becomes activated to choose the printer you want to use.

   ➤ **Store a copy in a folder**   Activate this check box to store a second copy of each fax in the folder that you specify. The original copy of the fax is saved in the Fax Console, which you learn about in the next section.

8. Click **Finish**.

Windows Wisdom

The Fax Console is also the place to go to change any of the fax configuration malarkey that you went through earlier. For example, to change your name, fax number, TSID, or other vital fax stats, select the **Tools, Sender Information** command. If you want to run through the entire Fax Configuration Wizard again, select the **Tools, Configure Fax** command.

Checking Out the Fax Console

When the wizard exits the stage and the smoke clears, you end up with the Fax Console window on-screen, as shown in Figure 15.2. The Fax Console is where you'll do your fax work in Windows XP. It includes four "folders" that store fax-related things:

➤ **Incoming**   This folder displays information about the fax that is currently being received. For example, during fax reception the **Status** column displays **In progress** and the **Extended Status** column displays **Answered** and then **Receiving**.

➤ **Inbox**   This folder stores the incoming faxes that were received successfully. Note that the TSID column shows the name or phone number of the sender.

➤ **Outbox**   This folder stores data about the fax that is currently being sent. For example, during the send the **Status** column displays **In progress**, and the **Extended Status** column displays **Transmitting**.

➤ **Sent Items**   This folder stores a copy of the faxes that were sent successfully.

Figure 15.2

The Fax Console is your home base for Windows XP faxing.

To get the Fax Console perched on your desktop again in the future, Windows XP gives you two methods:

➤ From the Printers and Faxes window, double-click the **Fax** icon.

➤ Select **Start, All Programs, Accessories, Communications, Fax, Fax Console**.

Using "Fax" as a Verb: Sending a Fax

To fax something to a friend or colleague (or, heck, even a total stranger), Windows XP gives you two ways to proceed:

➤ You can fax a simple note by sending just a cover page.

➤ You can fax a more complex document by sending it to Windows XP's fax "printer."

Let's start with the simple cover page route. This is handled by the Send Fax Wizard, which you can call in to work by using any of the following methods:

➤ From the Printers and Faxes window, click the WebView panel's **Send a fax** link. (Alternatively, select the **File, Send Fax** command.)

➤ In the Fax Console, select the **File, Send a Fax** command.

➤ Select **Start, All Programs, Accessories, Communications, Fax, Send a Fax**.

Here's what happens after the Send Fax Wizard arrives on the scene:

1. The initial dialog box isn't much use, so just click **Next** to get on with it. The Send Fax Wizard displays the Recipient Information dialog box, shown in Figure 15.3.

See Also

For more information on dialing rules and locations, see Chapter 17, "Getting on the Internet," particularly the section titled "Locations, Locations, Locations: Setting Up Dialing Rules."

Figure 15.3

The Send Fax Wizard takes you through the steps necessary to send a simple cover page fax.

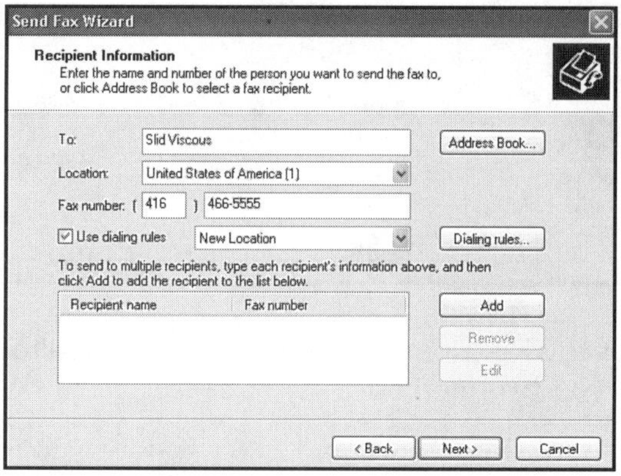

2. Fill in the following fields:

   ➤ **To**   Enter the name of the fax recipient.

   ➤ **Location**   If you're calling long distance and you need to start the dialing with a number other than 1, activate the **Use dialing rules** check box and then use the **Location** list to select the country code for the fax recipient's phone number.

   ➤ **Fax number**   Use these two text boxes to enter the area code (if necessary) and phone number for the fax recipient. (Note that you can't enter the area code unless you activate the **Use dialing rules** check box.)

   ➤ If you need to add details such as the recipient's company name, address, and phone number, click **Address Book**, click **New Contact**, and then use the tabs in the Properties dialog box to fill in all the information about the recipient. (Be sure to fill in the **Fax** field in either the **Business** tab or the **Home** tab.) Click **OK** when you're done. When you return to the Address Book, make sure the contact name is highlighted, click **To**, and then click **OK**.

3. Click **Add.** (This isn't necessary if you're sending the fax to a single recipient or if you inserted the recipient via the Address Book.)

4. If you want to send the fax to several people, repeat steps 2 and 3 as necessary.

5. When you're ready to move on, click **Next**. The Preparing the Cover Page dialog box muscles its way onto the screen.

6. Fill in the following fields (click **Next** when you're done):

   ➤ **Cover page template**   Select the cover page you want to use. (See the "Covering Your Fax: Creating a Fax Cover Page" section later in this chapter to find out about these predefined cover pages.)

   ➤ **Subject line**   Enter the subject of the fax.

   ➤ **Note**   Enter your message.

196

7. The wizard now pesters you for the time you want the fax sent (click **Next** when you're done):

   ➤ **Now** Sends the fax ASAP.

   ➤ **When discount rates apply** Sends the fax between 8:00 P.M. and 7:00 A.M.

   ➤ **Specific time in the next 24 hours** Sends the fax at the specified time. (This is a spin box with a time value. To change the value, click the hour, minute, or seconds and then either type the value you want or click the arrows.)

8. In the final wizard dialog box, click **Preview Fax** to check out the fax in the Windows Picture and Fax Viewer.

9. When you're ready to ship the fax, click **Finish.** The Fax Monitor window replaces the wizard so that you can see what's happening with the fax.

See Also

To learn about the editing buttons in the Windows Picture and Fax Viewer, see the "Annotating a Fax" section later in this chapter. To learn about the other buttons, see Chapter 8, "Playing with Pictures."

Simple notes on a cover page are fine, but if you want to go beyond this, you have to take a different tack. Specifically, you have to use WordPad or some other program to create a document, and you then fax that document to the recipient. Here's how it works:

1. Create the document that you want to ship.

2. Select the program's **File, Print** command to get to the Print dialog box.

3. Select **Fax** as the printer (see Figure 15.4), and then click **Print.** Your old friend, the Send Fax Wizard, reappears.

Figure 15.4

To fax from a program, select Fax as the printer.

197

4. Follow the previously outlined steps to set the fax options. (Note that with this method you don't have to bother with a cover page. If you'd still like to include one, when you get to the Preparing the Cover Page dialog box, activate the **Select a cover page template ...** check box.)

Covering Your Fax: Creating a Fax Cover Page

You saw earlier that the Send Fax Wizard offers four prefab cover pages that you can use:

➤ **confident**   This cover page includes the word **confidential** on it, so it's useful for faxes that you want only the recipient to see.

➤ **fyi**   This cover page includes the phrase **FOR YOUR INFORMATION** on it, so use it for faxes that don't require a response.

➤ **generic**   This cover page has no extra text on it, so use it for basic faxes.

➤ **urgent**   This cover page includes the word **urgent** on it, so it's good for faxes that you want read and responded to as soon as possible.

If you're not exactly thrilled with these default pages, you can create your own pages from scratch.

To edit and create fax cover pages, Windows XP offers the Fax Cover Page Editor. To launch this program, select **Start, All Programs, Accessories, Communications, Fax, Fax Cover Page Editor.** Figure 15.5 shows the Cover Page Editor with a cover page already on the go.

You work with the Fax Cover Page Editor by inserting information, text, and graphics fields. *Information fields* hold data. For example, the {**Sender's Company**} field (these fields always show up surrounded by braces) tells Windows XP to insert the name of the sender's company each time you use this cover page when you send a fax. With the Fax Cover Page Editor, you can insert fields for recipient, sender, and message data:

➤ **Recipient fields**   These are fields related to the recipient of the fax. Select **Insert, Recipient** and then select either **Name** or **Fax Number.**

➤ **Sender fields**   These are the fields you fill in during the Send Fax Wizard (particularly if you use the Address Book method). Select **Insert, Sender** to get a submenu with a whack of choices, including **Name, Fax Number,** and **Company.**

➤ **Message fields**   These are fields related to the fax message. Select **Insert, Message,** and then select one of the following: **Note, Subject, Date/Time Sent,** or **Number of Pages.**

Drawing toolbar   Style toolbar

Text button

Text fields

Information fields

Figure 15.5

Use the Fax Cover Page Editor to create cover pages to use with your faxes.

When you select a field command, the editor plops the field onto the cover page. You then use your mouse to drag the field to the position on the page that you want. You also can format a field by using the buttons on the Style toolbar or by selecting the **Format, Font** or **Format, Align Text** commands.

Text fields are basically just text boxes. They're used to provide captions for the information fields or to jazz up the cover page with titles, subtitles, and headings. Here are some techniques you can use with text fields:

➤ **To insert a text field:** Click the **Text** button on the Drawing toolbar. Now drag the mouse inside the cover page to create a box for the field, and then type in your text.

➤ **To change the text in an existing field:** Double-click the field and then edit the text.

➤ **To format a text field:** Use the Style toolbar or the **Format** menu commands.

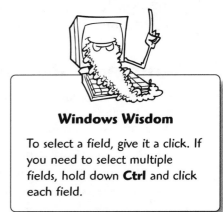

Windows Wisdom

To select a field, give it a click. If you need to select multiple fields, hold down **Ctrl** and click each field.

Graphics fields hold images that you can use for logos, separators, or just to add some style to the cover page. The Cover Page Editor's Drawing toolbar sports several buttons for drawing objects. All these tools work the same way as the corresponding tools in Paint. To refresh your skills with the Paint drawing tools, head back to Chapter 10, "Giving Your Right Brain a Workout with Paint."

The Cover Page Editor also contains quite a few options for mucking around with the layout of the fields. Here's a rundown of the buttons and commands that are available.

Click This	To Do This
	Move the selected field in front of any fields that overlap it. You also can select **Layout, Bring to Front,** or press **Ctrl+F.**
	Move the selected field behind any fields that overlap it. Alternatively, select **Layout, Send to Back,** or tap **Ctrl+B.**
	Space the selected fields evenly across the page. The other way to go about it is to select **Layout, Space Evenly, Across.**
	Space the selected fields evenly down the page. For some variety, select **Layout, Space Evenly, Down.**
	Align the selected fields along their left edges. The other way to go is to select **Layout, Align Objects, Left.**
	Align the selected fields along their right edges. You also can choose the **Layout, Align Objects, Right** command.
	Align the selected fields along their top edges. Selecting **Layout, Align Objects, Top** also works.
	Align the selected fields along their bottom edges. As you've probably guessed by now, you can also select **Layout, Align Objects, Bottom.**

When you're finished with a cover page, save it in the **Personal Cover Pages** folder. Select **File, Save As** and, in the Save As dialog box, open **My Documents,** then **Fax,** then **Personal Cover Pages.**

"Incoming!" Receiving a Fax

The ability to broadcast a fax to the far corners of the planet right from your computer is handy, to say the least. However, my favorite part of computer-based faxing is the opposite chore: receiving incoming faxes. Why? Let me count the ways:

➤ **No more slimy, curly, fax paper** When you receive a fax on your computer, it's stored as a file which you can keep electronically or later print on *real* paper.

➤ **No more wasted paper** If a junk fax comes in, you can delete it from existence without having to ever print it.

➤ **Easier storage** Because received faxes are digital files, you don't need to print them and then file them. Instead, you can use the Fax Console's folders to store them for safekeeping.

➤ **Easier annotation** As you'll see a bit later, Windows XP comes with a program that lets you "write" on a received fax.

When a fax call comes in, what happens next depends on whether you set up the fax service to answer calls automatically or manually. If it's the latter, you hear a ringing tone and the taskbar's notification area pops up a message that says **The line is ringing.** Click that message to receive the fax. (If you happen to have the Fax Monitor open already, click the **Answer now** button.)

When the fax service answers the call, the Fax Monitor dialog box elbows its way to the fore and shows you the progress of receiving the fax (see Figure 15.6). When it's done, you see a **New fax received** message in the notification area. Click that message to open the Fax Console window where you'll see the new fax in the Inbox folder.

Windows Wisdom

If you find the fax service's sounds (such as the ringing associated with an incoming call) annoying, you can disable them. In the Fax Console, select **Tools, Fax Printer Configuration** and then display the **Tracking** tab. Click **Configure Sound Settings** and then deactivate the check boxes for each sound you want to silence.

Figure 15.6

The Fax Monitor appears when the fax service answers the incoming call.

Getting the fax service to answer incoming calls is great if you have a dedicated fax line, but what if you share voice and fax calls on the *same* line? In this case, the first thing you need to do is make sure that the fax service is set up so that you can handle incoming calls manually. Then, the next time the phone rings, pick up the telephone handset. If you hear a series of tones, then you know it's a fax, so click the taskbar's **The line is ringing** message and then hang up the handset. (Don't replace the handset before clicking the message or you'll disconnect the call.)

From the Fax Console window, you can perform the following chores:

➤ **Read the fax** Double-click the fax in the Fax Console's Inbox folder (or highlight the fax and select **File, View**). This launches the Windows Picture and Fax Viewer, which displays your fax (see Figure 15.7) and enables you to annotate it (see the next section).

201

See Also

See Chapter 20, "Sending and Receiving E-Mail Missives," for the Windows XP e-mail details.

➤ **Print the fax** Highlight the fax and then select **File, Print.**

➤ **Save the fax as an image of a file** Highlight the fax and then select **File, Save As.** Use the Save As dialog box to choose a name and location for the file and then click **Save.** Note that the fax is saved as a TIF image.

➤ **E-mail the fax as an attachment** Highlight the fax and then select **File, Mail To.** Use the New Message window to set up the e-mail message and then click **Send.**

➤ **Delete the fax** Highlight the fax and then select **File, Delete** (or just press the **Delete** key).

Figure 15.7

Double-click the received fax in the Fax Console to display the fax in the Windows Picture and Fax Viewer window.

To:	Slid Viscous
Fax number:	416-466-5555
From:	Millicent Peeved
Fax number:	(416) 321-5555
Business phone:	
Home phone:	
Date & Time:	8/23/2001 1:24:31 PM
Pages:	1
Re:	Your junk fax was not appreciated!

Yesterday your company sent a fax advertisement to our fax machine. These "junk" faxes of yours are definitely NOT welcome and I ask that you remove our fax number from your list of callers immediately.

If you do not comply, then the next time we receive a junk fax from you we will retaliate by faxing you one or both of the following:

A "black fax." This is a black piece of paper that should nicely deplete your fax toner.

A "mobius fax." This is a continuous piece of paper that I assure you will tie up your machine and waste your paper for a considerable period of time.

Yours sincerely, but testily,

Millicent Peeved

Annotating a Fax

The Fax Viewer program lets you edit the fax by adding highlights, lines, snarky comments, "sticky notes," or other annotations. This section shows you how it's done.

I told you about most of the buttons along the bottom of the window back in Chapter 8. Here's a rundown of the rest of the buttons, all of which deal with annotating the fax:

Button	Button Name	What It Does
	New Freehand Annotation	Draws a freehand line on the fax.
	New Highlight Annotation	Draws a yellow highlight on the fax.
	New Straight Line Annotation	Draws a straight line on the fax.
	New Frame Annotation	Draws a border-only rectangle on the fax.
	New Solid Rectangle Annotation	Draws a filled rectangle on the fax.
A	New Text Annotation	Draws a text box on the fax. You can then type a note in the text box.
	New Attached Note Annotation	Draws a "sticky note" on the fax. You can then add text to the note.

These buttons work just like those in the Paint toolbox (see Chapter 10). That is, you click the button, move the mouse pointer to the position inside the fax where you want to start, hold down the left mouse button, and then drag the mouse to draw the object.

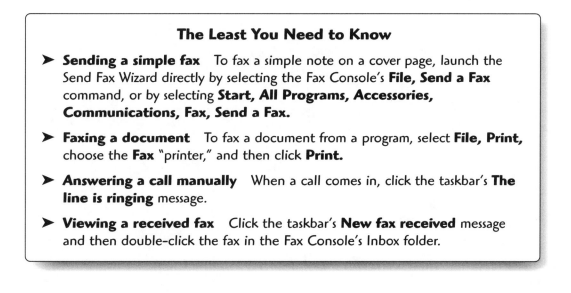

The Least You Need to Know

➤ **Sending a simple fax**   To fax a simple note on a cover page, launch the Send Fax Wizard directly by selecting the Fax Console's **File, Send a Fax** command, or by selecting **Start, All Programs, Accessories, Communications, Fax, Send a Fax.**

➤ **Faxing a document**   To fax a document from a program, select **File, Print,** choose the **Fax** "printer," and then click **Print.**

➤ **Answering a call manually**   When a call comes in, click the taskbar's **The line is ringing** message.

➤ **Viewing a received fax**   Click the taskbar's **New fax received** message and then double-click the fax in the Fax Console's Inbox folder.

Chapter 16

A Movable Feast: Windows XP and Your Notebook Computer

If you have a notebook computer, then you know full well that these machines are fundamentally different from their desktop cousins, and that the difference goes well beyond mere luggability. There are batteries to monitor, weird "PC Card" wafers to slide in and out, and files to exchange with desktop machines.

The Windows XP programmers must have had to wrestle with notebooks a time or two themselves, because they've put together a passel of portable perks. Windows XP offers power management for sensitive notebook batteries and support for those PC Card thingies. It also can help you synchronize files between a notebook and another machine, and even enables you to set up a direct cable connection between them. I discuss all of these capabilities in this chapter.

Better Battery Life Through Power Management

When using batteries to run your notebook computer on an airplane or some other no-power-plug-in-sight location, a worried mind becomes your natural state. That's because the battery can last only so long, so you have a limited amount of time to work or play before your electronic world goes dark. Windows XP can help relieve some of that worry thanks to its *power-management* features. For example, one of these features enables the system to shut down idle components (such as the hard disk and monitor) to prevent them from gobbling up battery power unnecessarily. Another feature lets you keep an eye peeled on how much power is left in the battery. This section takes you on a tour of these and other Windows XP power-management knickknacks.

Using the Power Icon to Monitor Battery Life

The first stop on our tour is the taskbar. When you're running under battery power, you'll see the power icon shown in Figure 16.1. This icon gives you several visual clues about the state of the battery. When the battery is fully charged, the icon is blue from top to bottom; as the battery gradually loses its steam, the level of blue in the icon falls. For example, when there is 50 percent of battery life remaining, the icon shows as half blue and half gray. If you move your mouse pointer over the icon, a small banner shows up with the percentage of power remaining.

Figure 16.1

The power icon tells you how much juice is left in your battery.

The power icon

Displaying the Power Options

If your notebook is running on AC power, Windows XP doesn't display the power icon. If you'd prefer to see the icon full-time, you have to first display Windows XP's Power Options dialog box:

1. Select **Start, Control Panel** to open the Control Panel folder.
2. Click **Printers and Other Hardware.**
3. Click the WebView panel's **Power Options** link. Windows XP opens the Power Options Properties dialog box.

From here, display the **Advanced** tab, activate the **Always show icon on the taskbar** check box, and then click **Apply**. (Don't click **OK** just yet because you'll need the Power Options dialog box in the next section.)

A Word of Warning: Setting Battery Alarms

The power icon is useful, but it's too easy to forget to check it when you're hard at work. To help ensure that you don't power down without warning, Windows XP maintains two different "alarms"—called Low and Critical—that can notify you when your battery's goose is almost cooked. To work with these alarms, follow these steps:

1. Display the Power Options dialog box, as described in the previous section. (Click **Start, Control Panel, Printers and Other Hardware, Power Options.**)

2. Display the **Alarms** tab.

3. The **Low Battery Alarm** group gives you three things to play with:

   ➤ Use the check box to toggle the alarm on and off.

   ➤ Use the slider to set the power level percentage at which the alarm goes off.

   ➤ Click the **Alarm Action** button to display the Low Battery Alarm Actions dialog box. From here, you can request that Windows XP **Sound alarm** or **Display message** when the alarm goes off. You can also activate the **When the alarm goes off, the computer will** check box, and then select **Standby, Hibernate,** or **Shut down** in the list. It's also probably a good idea to activate the **Force stand by or shutdown even if a program stops responding** check box. Click **OK** when you're done.

See Also

I discussed the differences between standby, hibernate, and shut-down in Chapter 2, "A Field Guide to Windows XP."

4. Use **Critical battery alarm** group to set up the critical alarm. Note that you have the same choices as in the Low battery alarm group.

5. Click **OK.**

It's been my experience that when battery power gets low, it tends to go south in a hurry. So although you might think the low battery alarm still gives you a few minutes to keep working, don't believe it! Instead, you should immediately save all your work and either get to an AC outlet as soon as possible, or exit Windows XP until a power source comes your way.

Power to the People: Specifying a Power Scheme

As I mentioned earlier, Windows XP cheerfully shuts down some system components in an effort to keep your battery on its feet longer. Follow these steps to control which components get shut down and when:

1. Display the Power Options dialog box, as described earlier, and activate the **Power Schemes** tab.

2. Use the **Power schemes** list to choose one of Windows XP predefined power schemes (such as **Portable/Laptop**).

3. To adjust the power scheme time intervals, use the following lists in both the **Plugged in** and **Running on batteries** columns:

   Turn off monitor   Sets the number of minutes the notebook must be idle before Windows XP shuts off the monitor.

   Turn off hard disks   Sets the number of minutes the notebook must be idle before Windows XP stops your hard disk (or disks) from spinning.

   System standby   Sets the number of minutes the notebook must be idle before Windows XP puts the notebook into standby mode.

   System hibernates   Sets the number of minutes the notebook must be idle before Windows XP puts the notebook into hibernation mode.

4. If you made changes in step 3 and you want to save those changes under a different scheme name, click **Save As**, enter a new name for the scheme, and then click **OK** to return to the Power Options dialog box.

5. Click **Apply** or **OK**.

Configuring Your Notebook's Power Buttons

Most newer notebooks enable you to configure three "power buttons": closing the lid, the on/off button, and the sleep button. When you activate these buttons, they put your system into standby or hibernate mode, or turn it off altogether. On some notebooks, there isn't a separate sleep button. Instead, you tap the on/off button quickly.

Follow these steps to configure these buttons for power management:

1. Display the Power Options dialog box, as described earlier.

2. Select the **Advanced** tab.

3. In the **Power buttons** group, use the three lists to set a power management option (**Do nothing, Ask me what to do, Stand by, Hibernate,** or **Shut down**) for closing the lid, pressing the on/off (power) button, or pressing the sleep button.

4. Click **Apply** or **OK**.

Using a Briefcase to Synchronize Files

Do you have to deal with both a notebook computer *and* a desktop computer? If so, then I'm sure you know all too well the problems that arise when you try to share files between them. For example, if you transport a few files to the notebook and you end up changing a couple of those files, it's crucial to be sure that the desktop machine gets a copy of the updated files.

In other words, you want to be sure that the notebook and the desktop remain *synchronized*. To help you do this, Windows XP offers a feature called Briefcase. To understand how it works, let's examine how you use a real briefcase to do some work at home. You begin by stuffing your briefcase full of the files and documents you want to work with. You then take the briefcase home, take out the papers, work on them, and put them back in the briefcase. Finally, you take the briefcase back to work and then remove the papers.

Windows XP's Briefcase feature works in much the same way, except that you don't work with the original documents. Instead, you work with special copies called *sync copies*. A Briefcase is really a special type of folder. The basic idea is that you place the documents you want to work with inside a Briefcase, and then lug around the Briefcase using a floppy disk, Zip disk, or some other removable disk. You can then copy the documents from the Briefcase to the notebook and work on them. The key thing is that the Briefcase "remembers" where the documents came from originally, and it automatically tracks which ones have changed. You can update the original files with just a couple of mouse clicks.

Before getting started, you need to create a Briefcase. The best place to create the Briefcase is on the removable disk you'll be using to transport the files. Here are the steps to follow to create a Briefcase:

1. Insert the disk you want to use.

2. Use My Computer to display the disk.

3. To create a new Briefcase on the disk, either select **File, New, Briefcase**, or right-click the folder and then click **New, Briefcase.** Windows XP adds an icon named New Briefcase to the disk.

4. Rename the Briefcase (this is optional).

With the Briefcase created, follow these steps to transfer and synchronize documents between a desktop and a notebook computer:

Look Out!

The Briefcase keeps careful tabs on its files: both where they came from originally on the desktop computer and where you copy them to on the notebook. Therefore, don't move or rename the files after they're safely stowed on the notebook, or you'll break the synchronization.

1. Copy the files you want to work with from the desktop computer to the Briefcase. (If you're using drag-and-drop, you don't have to hold down Ctrl because Windows XP will automatically make sync copies of the files that you drop.)

2. Remove the disk and insert it into the notebook.

3. On the notebook, use My Computer to open the removable disk and then open the Briefcase. (The first time you open the Briefcase you'll see a Welcome dialog box. It's a waste of time, so just click **Finish.**) Copy the files from the Briefcase to the notebook computer.

4. Work with the files on the notebook.

5. When you're done, insert the disk into the notebook and open the Briefcase folder. The Briefcase then checks its files with the copies you sent to the notebook. As you can see in Figure 16.2, the Briefcase's **Status** column tells you which files have been changed. (To get the various columns, activate the **View, Details** command.)

This column tells you which files have been changed
Update All

Figure 16.2

The Briefcase folder keeps track of which files you changed on the notebook.

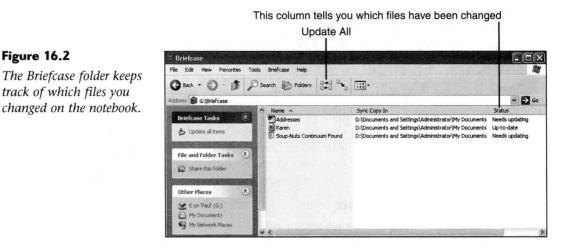

6. To update the Briefcase copies of the changed files, either click **Update all items** in the WebView panel or select **Briefcase, Update All.** (You can also click the **Update All** toolbar button.) Briefcase displays a list of the files to be updated.

7. Click **Update.** Briefcase grabs copies of the changed files.

8. Close the Briefcase window.

9. Insert the disk into the desktop computer and open the Briefcase folder. This time, the Briefcase compares its files with the originals on the desktop machine. Again, the **Status** column tells you which files have been changed.

10. To update the desktop computer's original copies of the changed files, either click **Update all items** in the WebView panel or select **Briefcase, Update All.** (Again, you can also click the **Update All** toolbar button.) Briefcase displays a list of the files to be updated.

11. Click **Update.** Briefcase copies the changed files to the desktop computer.

Working with Those Little PC Card Doodads

Notebook computers are, by definition, small and lightweight to ensure easy luggability. Their relatively Lilliputian size means that there just isn't enough internal room to "expand" a notebook in the same way that you can a desktop machine. That's good news for non-nerds because it means the notebook engineers had to find some other way to enable users to "add on" to their machines. The result was the PC Card: a small, credit card–sized wafer that plugged into a special slot—or *socket*—on the *outside* of the notebook. There are PC Card devices for modems, network adapters, hard disks, and much more. So, now even the digitally maladroit can upgrade their machines with little or no effort.

Windows XP helps by recognizing your notebook's PC Card sockets (most machines have at least two), and by supporting *hot swapping,* which sounds like some sort of swinging singles party, but is really just the capability to insert and remove PC Cards without having to shut down the system.

Windows Wisdom

PC Cards were originally known as PCMCIA cards, where PCM-CIA stood for Personal Computer Memory Card International Association. I use PC Card in this section, but just remember that PC Card and PCMCIA are the same thing. In addition, there's a newer type of PC Card device that is known as a *CardBus* device. Most newer notebooks support both types in the same socket.

Popping In a PC Card Device

To use a PC Card device, insert it gently and as far as it will go into any free PC Card socket. (You should feel a slight "click" at the end.) Windows XP recognizes that a new device is in the socket and beeps the speaker. One of two things now happens. If you've used the device before, it will be ready for use within a few seconds. Or, if you've never used the device before, you'll see the New Hardware Found message and Windows XP will proceed to install the necessary software to make the device run. You might see the New Hardware Found Wizard, which will take you through the appropriate steps.

After the device is up and at 'em, Windows XP displays a special Safely Remove Hardware icon on the right side of the taskbar, as shown in Figure 16.3. (Note, too, that this icon will also appear if you have certain other devices—such as certain USB devices—plugged into the machine.)

Figure 16.3

When you wedge a PC Card device into your notebook, Windows XP displays this icon in the taskbar.

The Safely Remove Hardware icon

If you want to see a list of all your PC Card devices, right-click the Safely Remove Hardware icon. Windows XP displays the Safely Remove Hardware dialog box shown in Figure 16.4.

Figure 16.4

Right-click the Safely Remove Hardware icon to see a list of all your plugged-in devices.

Yanking Out a PC Card Device

This hot-swapping thing should really be called *tepid swapping* because you can't just grab out a PC Card device by the scruff of the neck and drag it out of the slot. Such willy-nillyness is frowned upon. Instead, you need to tell Windows XP which device you're giving the heave-ho. This gives Windows a chance to shut down the device. Here's the easiest way to go about this:

1. Click the Safely Remove Hardware icon. Windows XP displays a list of the devices attached to your system.

2. Click the device you want to remove. Your computer beeps, and Windows XP displays a message telling you it's safe to remove the device.

3. Click the message and then remove the device. (On most notebooks, you do this by pushing a button beside the socket.)

212

If your computer is turned off, you can just go ahead and spit out the device without any danger. Note, too, that another way to go about this is to display the Safely Remove Hardware dialog box (as described in the previous section), highlight the device you want to spit out, and then click **Stop.**

Setting Up a Direct Connection Between Two Computers

Instead of using floppies to transfer files between your notebook and another machine, connect them with a cable and then perform the transfers along that cable. What kind of cable do you need? Windows XP gets along with two kinds:

➤ **A null-modem cable** This is a special cable that attaches to the serial port in the back of both machines. Null-modem cables are common and are available from any decent computer or electronics store. Note, however, that this is *not* the same as the cable you use with your modem.

➤ **A Direct Parallel cable** This cable attaches to the parallel (or printer) port in the back of the computers. This kind is preferred because it can transmit data quite a bit faster than the null-modem variety. Unfortunately, at the time of writing, these cables were available only directly from the manufacturer (see www.lpt.com).

After you've attached the cable to both machines (they don't need to be turned off while you make the attachments), you're ready to begin the setup. This involves setting up the host and guest computers and configuring both machines so that they can converse with each other. The *host computer* is the one that will be sharing its resources, while the guest computer is the one that will be accessing those shared resources.

The next three sections take you through the necessary steps.

See Also

Another way to connect two computers is to network them. See Chapters 30, "Using Windows XP to Set Up a Small Network," and 31, "Using Windows XP's Networking Features."

Step 1: Configure the Host Computer

Here's how to configure the host machine:

1. Select **Start, Control Panel** to display the Control Panel window.

2. Click **Network and Internet Connections** to display the Network and Internet Connections window.

3. Click **Network Connections** to get to the Network Connections window.

4. In the WebView panel, click the **New Connection Wizard** link (or select the **File, New Connection** command) to launch the New Connection Wizard.

5. Click **Next**. The wizard asks what kind of connection you want.

Windows Wisdom

After you've created a connection, selecting **Start, Settings, Network and Dial-Up Connections** displays a submenu of the items in the Network and Dial-Up Connections window (including the Make New Connection icon). If you need to access this window in the future, you have to go the long way: **Start, Programs, Accessories, Communications, Network and Dial-Up Connections.**

6. Activate the **Set up an advanced connection** option, and then click **Next**. The wizard wonders what connection type you want.

7. Activate the **Connect directly to another computer** option and click **Next**. The wizard asks what role you want for the computer.

8. Activate **Host** and click **Next**. The wizard now asks you to choose which communications port you'll be using.

9. Select the port to which your cable is attached, and then click **Next**.

10. Your next chore is to select which users are allowed to make the connection from the other machine. Activate the check box beside each user you want to have access. If the user isn't listed, click **Add** and enter a **User name, Full name**, and **Password** (twice), and click **OK**. Click **Next** when you're done.

11. In the final wizard dialog box, click **Finish**. The wizard creates the new connection and leaves you in the Network Connections dialog box. You'll see a new icon named **Incoming Connections**.

Step 2: Configure the Guest Computer

To set up the guest computer, follow steps 1 through 7 in the previous section, and then do this:

1. When the wizard asks whether this machine is to be the host or the guest, activate **Guest** and click **Next**. The wizard wonders what the name of the other computer is.

2. Type the name and click **Next**. The wizard asks you to choose a port.

3. Select the port to which your cable is attached, and then click **Next**.

4. The wizard next asks whether you want to make this connection available for **Anyone's use** or **My use only.** Make your choice (if in doubt, select the latter) and click **Next.**

5. In the final wizard dialog box, you can put a shortcut to the host on the desktop by activating the **Add a shortcut to this connection to may desktop** check box. To wrap things up, click **Finish.** An icon with the name of the host computer is added to the Network Connections window.

Windows XP will now display the Connect dialog box so that you can connect to the other computer. Continue with the next section and start at step 3.

Step 3: Make the Connection

To establish the connection between the two computers, you need to do the following:

1. On the guest computer, select **Start, Connect To** and then click the name of the connection (the default name is the name of the host computer). Windows XP pastes up a Connect dialog box.

Windows Wisdom

If you're not sure what the host computer's name is, here's a quick way to find out: On the host computer, click **Start,** right-click the **My Computer** icon, and then click **Properties.** In the System Properties dialog box, display the **Computer Name** tab. The text that appears beside **Full computer name** (without the dot [.] at the end) is the name you want to use in step 2.

2. Fill in the **User name** and **Password.** These should be the same as one of the users you specified during the host setup. If you want Windows XP to keep an internal sticky note for the password, be sure the **Save this user name and password for the following users** check box is activated, and then choose **My only** or **Anyone who uses this computer.**

3. Click **Connect.** Windows XP accesses the cable and alerts the host that a guest is knocking on the door. The host authenticates the incoming user and makes the connection. How do you know you're connected? Windows XP offers lots of clues:

   ➤ A connection message appears in the taskbar's notification area.

   ➤ A new icon appears in the notification area on both the host and guest.

   ➤ In the host's Network Connections window, a new icon appears for the guest computer and the **Incoming Connections** icon includes the text `1 client connected.`

➤ In the guest's Network Connections window, the host computer's icon includes the text **Connected.**

From here, you use the usual networking techniques to access data on the host (see Chapter 31).

Direct Connections and the Briefcase

After you have a direct connection established, you might want to use a Briefcase to coordinate the exchange of files. Here's how it works:

1. Be sure that the host folder containing the files you want to work with is either shared directly or resides in a shared folder.
2. Use the guest computer to access the shared folder.
3. Copy the files to the guest computer's Briefcase.
4. Use the guest computer to work on the files directly from the Briefcase folder. (There's no need for a connection at this point.)
5. When you're done, connect again and then open the guest's Briefcase folder.
6. Either click **Update all items** in the WebView panel or select **Briefcase, Update All** to update the host computer's files with the changed files in the guest computer's Briefcase.

Disconnecting from the Host

When you feel you've imposed upon the host computer quite enough, it's time to take your leave. Windows XP gives you the following ways to bid goodnight:

➤ On the host or guest, right-click the connection icon in the taskbar's notification area, and then click **Disconnect.**

➤ On the host, open the Network Connections window, highlight the icon for the connected guest, and then click **Disconnect this connection** in the WebView panel (or select the **File, Disconnect** command).

➤ On the guest, open the Network Connections window, highlight the icon for the direct connection, and then click the WebView panel's **Disconnect this connection** link (or select the **File, Disconnect** command).

The Least You Need to Know

➤ **Use the power icon**   When running your notebook on batteries, be sure you use the power icon to keep a close eye on the battery level.

➤ **Manage your power**   To maximize battery life, create a power scheme that shuts down the monitor and hard disk within a minute or two of idle time.

➤ **Lug the Briefcase**   The easiest way to use a Briefcase is to move it onto a removable disk and keep it there. You can then add files to the Briefcase, copy those files to the other machine, and use the update feature to keep the files synchronized.

➤ **Hot swap PC Cards**   You can insert a PC Card, and Windows XP would recognize it right away (and, if necessary, installs the required files). Before removing a PC Card device, tell Windows XP to stop using it.

➤ **The direct connection**   String a null-modem or Direct Parallel cable between two machines and then set up one as the host and the other as the guest.

Part 4

Windows XP on the Internet

For many years, lots of purse-lipped parents, uptight teachers, and pontificating pundits frowned upon computers because they saw them as noninteractive machines that only served to encourage anti-social behavior. Boy, did they ever get that wrong! As proof, you need look no further than the tens of millions of people who are on the Internet, and the hundreds of millions of people who want to be on the Internet. Believe me, these people aren't clamoring to listen to cheesy MIDI music. No, they want to connect. They want to read what other people have written; they want to exchange e-mail epistles; they want to natter in newsgroups; they want to chinwag in chat rooms. In other words, the opposite has happened: Computers have become interactive machines that encourage socializing. Who'da thunk it? If you want to get in on all this fun, the seven chapters here in Part 4 will tell you everything you need to know.

Getting on the Internet

The Internet's tentacles have insinuated themselves into every nook and cranny of modern life. Businesses from corner-hugging Mom 'n' Pop shops to continent-straddling corporations are online; Web pages are now counted in the billions; and people send far more e-mail messages than postal messages.

It truly is a wired (which, remember, is just "weird" spelled sideways) world, and if you feel like you're the only person left who isn't online, this chapter will help. I'll tell you exactly what you need to make it happen, and then I'll take you through the connection process, step-by-finicky-step.

Modems and Phone Cables

If you're like most people, your telephone and modem will probably share the same line. In this case, you don't have to switch the cable between the phone and the modem all the time. Instead, it's possible to get a permanent, no-hassle setup that'll make everyone happy. The secret is that all modems have two telephone cable jacks in the back:

➤ **Line jack**   This one is usually labeled "Line" or "Telco," or has a picture of a wall jack.

➤ **Telephone jack**   This one is usually labeled "Phone" or has a picture of a telephone.

Follow these directions to set things up:

1. Run a phone cable from the wall jack to the modem's line jack.

2. Run a second phone cable from the telephone to the modem's telephone jack.

This setup lets you use the phone whenever you need it—the signal goes right through the modem (when you're not using it, of course)—and lets you use the modem whenever you need it.

What to Look For in an Internet Service Provider

The route to the Internet isn't a direct one. Instead, you can only get there by engaging the services of a middleman or, more accurately, a middlecompany: an *Internet service provider* (*ISP,* for short).

An ISP is a business that has negotiated a deal with the local telephone company or some other behemoth organization to get a direct connection to the Internet's highways and byways. These kinds of connections cost thousands of dollars a month, so they're out of reach for all but the most well-heeled tycoons. The ISP affords it by signing up subscribers and offering them a piece of the ISP's Internet connection. After you have an account with an ISP, the connection process works as follows:

1. You use your computer's modem to dial up the ISP.

2. The ISP's computer verifies that you're one of their subscribers.

3. The ISP's computer sets up a connection between your computer and the Internet.

4. You go, girl (or boy, as the case may be)!

Jargon Jar

An **Internet service provider** (**ISP**) takes your money in exchange for an Internet account, which you need to get online.

So before you can do anything on the Internet, you have to set up an account with an ISP and then you need to give Windows the details. Before we get to that, let's take a second to run through a few pointers to bear in mind when deciding which ISP to use:

➤ Most ISPs charge a monthly fee, which typically ranges from US$5 to US$30. Decide in advance the maximum that you're willing to shell out each month.

➤ When comparing prices, remember that ISP plans usually trade off between price and the number of hours of connection time. For example, the lower the price, the fewer the hours you get.

➤ It's important to note that most plans charge you by the minute or by the hour if you exceed the number of hours the plan offers. These charges can be exorbitant (a buck or two an hour), so you don't want to get into that. Therefore, you need to give some thought to how much time you plan to spend online. That's hard to do at this stage, I know, but you just need to ballpark it. If in doubt, get a plan with a large number of hours (say, 100 or 150). You can always scale it back later on.

Windows Wisdom

Most people find that they spend a ton of time on the Internet for the first few months as they discover all the wonders and weirdness that's available. After they get used to everything, their connection time drops dramatically.

➤ Most major ISPs offer an "unlimited usage" plan. This means you can connect whenever you want for as long as you want, and you just pay a set fee per month (usually around US$20). This is a good option to take for a few months until you figure out how often you use the Internet.

➤ If you have a newish modem, then it probably supports a faster connection speed called 56K (or sometimes V.90). If so, make sure the ISP you choose also supports 56K.

➤ Make sure the ISP offers a local access number to avoid long-distance charges. If that's not an option, make sure they offer access via a toll-free number. (Note: Watch out for extra charges for the use of the toll-free line.) Even better, some nationwide ISPs offer local access in various cities across the land. This is particularly useful if you do a lot of traveling.

➤ Make sure the ISP offers a local or toll-free number for technical support.

➤ I recommend only dealing with large ISPs. There are still plenty of fly-by-night operations out there, and they're just not worth the hassle of dropped connections, busy signals, lack of support, going belly-up when you most need them, and so on.

➤ If you can't decide between two or more ISPs, see what extra goodies they offer: space for your own Web pages, extra e-mail accounts, Internet software bundles, and so on.

To help you compare major ISPs, Windows XP's Internet Connection Wizard has a feature that can display rates and special offers from the companies that provide Internet access in your area.

Getting Started on Your Road to the Internet

The Windows XP installation program has a section where it offers to set up an Internet connection. This means that there's a good chance your computer is already Net-friendly. To find out, select **Start, Internet.** If Internet Explorer starts and takes you to a Web page, your Internet connection is a going concern. If you see the New Connection Wizard, instead, then you've got a few hoops that you still need to jump through.

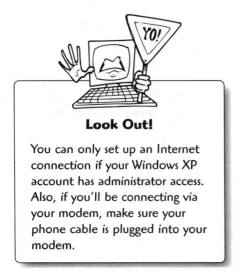

Look Out!

You can only set up an Internet connection if your Windows XP account has administrator access. Also, if you'll be connecting via your modem, make sure your phone cable is plugged into your modem.

Windows XP offers no fewer than three different routes to Internet connection glory. Whichever avenue you pursue, you start things up either by trying to access the Internet (as just described) or by selecting **Start, Control Panel, Network and Internet Connections, Network Connections, Create a new connection.** The New Connection Wizard fades in and requires the following steps off the bat:

1. Click **Next** in the initial dialog box.

2. Activate the **Connect to the Internet** option and click **Next.**

3. Choose one of the following options and then click **Next:**

    ➤ **Choose from a list of Internet service providers** Choose this option to sign up for a new Internet account through Windows XP. When you click **Next,** the wizard downloads a list of ISPs in your area and gives you information about each one. You choose the one you want and then run through a signup process.

    ➤ **Set up my connection manually** If you have an existing Internet account, choose this option to provide the details about it by hand. See the "Setting Up an Existing Account Manually" section that follows.

    ➤ **Use the CD I got from an ISP** This is the easiest road of them all. Insert the ISP's CD and then click **Next** until the installation program begins. Then run through the install and let the ISP handle all the hard stuff for you.

Setting Up an Existing Account Manually

If you need to build the connection to your existing account with your bare hands, this section runs through the data you need and takes you through the rest of the New Connection Wizard's steps.

What You Need to Know Before Getting Started

To successfully set up a connection to your Internet account, you need to have the proper bits of information from your ISP. Here are the basic tidbits you need to *log on:*

➤ The phone number you have to dial to connect to the ISP.

➤ The username (which might also be called your logon name) and password that you use to log on to the ISP.

Some ISPs also require some or all of the following advanced settings:

➤ The type of connection the ISP requires. This is usually PPP, but SLIP is also sometimes used. (Don't worry if you don't understand these terms. Believe me, you'll never have to deal with them face-to-face in the real world.)

➤ Whether you need to log on to the ISP manually.

➤ Whether your ISP provides you with a "script" for the logon procedure. A script is a tiny program that automates the logon so that you don't have to enter your username, password, and whatever other tidbits your ISP requires. Most ISP logons are automatic anyway, these days, so it's unlikely you'll ever need a script.

➤ Whether your ISP assigns you a permanent *IP address*. If so, you need to know the address.

➤ Whether your ISP provides you with IP addresses for their Domain Name Servers (DNS). If so, you need to know the addresses for the primary and alternate servers.

Didn't I tell you this was finicky stuff? Don't worry if you find all this gobbledygook to be completely meaningless. You need to hold it in your brain

Jargon Jar

To **log on** means to provide your ISP with your username and password, and so gain access to the wonder that is the Internet.

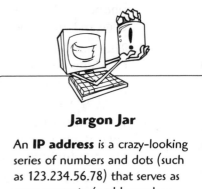

Jargon Jar

An **IP address** is a crazy-looking series of numbers and dots (such as 123.234.56.78) that serves as your computer's address when you're connected to the Internet.

225

only for as long as it takes to set up your connection, and then it can be discarded for all time (or at least until you get your next computer and have to start everything from scratch once again; doh!).

What You Need to Do After Getting Started

With all that info at your side, you're now ready to set up the account. Here are the rest of the steps to trudge through:

1. The next wizard dialog box presents you with some options related to how you connect to your ISP (click **Next** when you've made the appropriate choice):

   ➤ **Connect using a dial-up modem**   Choose this option if you use a regular modem to connect.

   ➤ **Connect using a broadband connection that requires a username and password**   Choose this option if you use a cable modem or a DSL (high-speed) modem and you also have to enter a username and password.

   ➤ **Connect using a broadband connection that is always on**   Choose this option if you use a cable modem or a DSL (high-speed) modem but you don't have to enter a username and password. If you choose this route, the wizard will end because it assumes your connection is already set up. If it's not, click **Back**, activate the **Use the CD I got from an ISP** option, and then follow that path, instead.

2. The wizard asks for the name of your ISP. This is really just the name that XP will assign to your connection, so enter anything you darn well please and click **Next**.

3. If you're configuring a dial-up connection, the wizard now asks you for the phone number of your ISP. Enter the phone number (including the country code and area code, if they're required) and click **Next**.

4. The wizard may now wonder who you want to use this connection. If you want all who use your computer to be able to use the connection, activate **Anyone's use**; if you prefer to keep the connection to yourself, activate **My use only**, instead. Click **Next**.

5. In the next wizard dialog box, enter your username and password. You need to enter the latter twice: in the **Password** text box and in the **Confirm password** text box (in both cases, the password appears only as asterisks, for security).

6. The wizard also foists the following options on you (click **Next** when you're done):

   ➤ **Use this account name and password when anyone connects to the Internet from this computer**   You only see this check box if you activated the **Anyone's use** option in the previous dialog box. If the other users have different usernames and passwords with the ISP, deactivate this check box.

➤ **Make this the default Internet connection**   Leaving this check box activated tells Windows XP to use this connection whenever you attempt to access an Internet resource (such as a Web site or your e-mail account).

➤ **Turn on Internet Connection Firewall for this connection**   Leave this check box activated to protect your computer from crackers and other Net miscreants.

7. In the final wizard dialog box, click **Finish**.

Windows Wisdom

Why on earth does your Internet connection need protection from a fire? Actually, that's just a metaphor: There are no real fires on the Internet. Instead, there are plenty of nefarious types who would like nothing more than to break into your computer system. The problem, you see, is that your computer exposes itself (so to speak) to the Internet while you're connected. (This is particularly true if you have one of those "always on" cable modem or DSL connections.) Crackers (as hackers who have succumbed to the dark side of the Force are usually called) can take advantage of well-known vulnerabilities to look around or even commandeer your machine. To protect yourself, you need to block those vulnerabilities by setting up what's known in the security trade as a *firewall*. To check that your computer is connected, use Internet Explorer to go to grc.com and click the **Shields Up** link (you may have to click **Shields Up** again on the new page that appears).

Configuring Advanced ISP Settings

If your ISP requires you to configure any of the advanced settings that I mentioned earlier, let's see how you do it. Begin by selecting **Start, Connect To, Show all connections.** Click your connection and then click **Change settings of this connection** (or choose the **File, Properties** command). You use the Properties dialog box to put in the advanced settings:

➤ If you need to log on to the ISP manually, display the **Security** tab and activate the **Show terminal window** check box.

➤ If your ISP provides you with a "script" for automating the logon procedure, display the **Security** tab and activate the **Run script** check box. Then click **Browse** to locate the script file on your computer.

➤ For the type of connection, display the **Networking** tab and then use the **Type of dial-up server I am calling** list to choose either **PPP** or **SLIP.**

➤ If your ISP assigns you a permanent IP address, display the **Networking** tab, highlight **Internet Protocol (TCP/IP)** and then click **Properties.** Activate **Use the following IP address** and then enter your IP address in the **IP address** text box.

➤ If your ISP provides you with IP addresses for their Domain Name Servers (DNS), display the **Networking** tab, highlight **Internet Protocol (TCP/IP)** and then click **Properties.** Activate **Use the following DNS server addresses** and then enter the DNS server addresses in the **Preferred DNS Server** and **Alternate DNS Server** text boxes.

Making the Connection

Now that you have your account details down pat, it's time to put that account to good use by connecting to the Internet. There are two ways to go about this:

➤ Crank up any of the Internet programs. For example, you can launch the Internet Explorer Web browser.

➤ Select **Start, Connect To** and then click the Internet connection you created.

At this point, Windows XP might mumble something about **The Web Page You Requested Is Not Available Offline.** Say "Well, duh!" and click **Connect.** This gets you to a Connect dialog box that's similar to the one shown in Figure 17.1.

Figure 17.1

This dialog box is the launch pad for your Internet forays.

This dialog box offers the following toys:

➤ **Username**   This is the username you use to log on to your ISP.

➤ **Password**   This is the password you use to log on to your ISP.

➤ **Save this username and password for the following users**   When this check box is activated, Windows XP is kind enough to enter your password automatically. If you're worried about somebody else monkeying around with your account, you'll sleep better at night if you activate the **Me only** option.

➤ **Dial**   Click this button to get the connection process going.

➤ **Properties**   Click this button to adjust your connection settings.

➤ **Cancel**   Click this button if you change your mind about connecting.

Adjust the data as necessary and, when you're ready, click **Dial.** Windows XP taps your modem on the shoulder and passes it the phone number, and the connection process begins in the usually noisy modem fashion. If your ISP requires you to log on manually, a screen will appear and the ISP's prompts (such as "Username" and "Password") will appear. Type in whatever information you're asked for (press **Enter** after you've entered each item).

After a few more seconds of navel-gazing, Windows XP finally lets you know that you're now up and online by adding a connection icon to the notification area and displaying a message that you're connected. If you need to track how long you've been online, double-click the connection icon. The dialog box that shows up tells you how long you've been connected.

Windows Wisdom

Many ISPs provide you with two or more phone numbers so that you can try other numbers if the main number is busy or down. To add the other numbers, click **Properties** in the Connect dialog box and then click **Alternates.** In the Alternate Phone Numbers dialog box, click **Add,** enter the **Phone number,** and then click **OK.**

Severing the Connection

When you've stood just about all you can stand of the Internet's wiles, you can log off by right-clicking the connection icon in the taskbar's notification area, and then clicking **Disconnect** (see Figure 17.2).

This icon appears while you're on the Internet

Figure 17.2

Right-click the connection icon to disconnect from the Internet.

229

Locations, Locations, Locations: Setting Up Dialing Rules

Do you get your Internet fix using a modem and a dial-up connection? If so, then you probably always use your modem from the same place (such as at the office or at home). In that case, it's fine that Windows XP just dials the modem the same way every time. However, what if your location changes and you need to deal with different dialing options? (I'm assuming here that you're using a notebook computer that can come along for the ride.) Here are some examples:

➤ You travel to another area code, so the call becomes long distance.

➤ You're out of town on business and you need to place all calls through a long-distance provider or a calling card.

➤ You want to connect from some remote location that requires you to first dial 9 to get an outside line.

➤ You bring your computer home and have to disable call waiting before making the connection.

For all these and many similar situations, Windows XP lets you set up separate *locations* in which you change one or more *dialing rules*. This section shows you how to create and work with these locations and rules.

To get things going, follow these steps:

1. Select **Start, Control Panel, Printers and Other Hardware, Phone and Modem Options.**

2. Make sure the **Dialing Rules** tab is displayed.

3. The locations you create will be listed in the **Locations** list. You should see an existing location—called **New Location**—that was set up during the Windows XP installation. Click **New** to drag the New Location dialog box in by the scruff of the neck.

The **General** tab contains the basic options for the new location:

➤ **Location name**   Enter a name for the new location (such as "Calls from the Coast" or "Call Waiting's Outta There!").

➤ **Country/region**   Use this list to specify the country you'll be in when you're dialing.

➤ **Area code**   Use this text box to specify the area code you'll be in when you're dialing.

➤ **To access an outside line for local calls, dial**   Use this text box to type in the number (or numbers) that must be dialed to get an outside line for local calls (such as 9).

230

➤ **To access an outside line for long-distance calls, dial**   Use this text box to type in the number (or numbers) that must be dialed to get an outside line for long-distance calls (such as 8).

➤ **Use this carrier code to make long-distance calls**   Use this text box to type in the number (or numbers) that must be dialed to access your long distance provider.

➤ **Use this carrier code to make international calls**   Use this text box to type in the number (or numbers) that must be dialed to access your international call provider.

➤ **To disable call waiting, dial**   Activate this check box to disable call waiting before initiating the call. Note, too, that you also have to use the list to specify the proper code that the phone system requires to disable call waiting. (If you're not sure about the proper code, ask your phone company. If the code they give you isn't in the list, type it in by hand.)

➤ **Dial using**   Activate the appropriate option for your phone dialing: **Tone** or **Pulse**.

Windows Wisdom

Your modem spends much of its time converting computer data into tones that can be sent across phone lines. Call waiting also uses tones to signal an incoming call. If the modem hears those tones, it will probably get *very* confused and you could lose your connection.

Area Code Rules, Dude!

Area codes are getting increasingly confusing. There are two main things that are causing the weirdness:

➤ **Calling the same area code**   In this situation, you don't usually have to bother with the area code. However, some phone systems insist that you include the area code even if the other number is in the same area code. In some cases, these are long-distance calls, so you even have to dial a 1 (or some other country or region code) to start the call.

➤ **Calling a different area code**   This situation normally requires that you dial a 1 (or whatever), followed by the area code, followed by the number. However, in some larger cities, the phone company has actually run out of numbers in the main area code, so they've created a whole new area code for the city. These aren't usually long-distance calls, however, so even though you have to include the area code, you don't usually have to dial a 1 to get started.

Note that in both cases, the area code may apply only to certain phone number pre-fixes. (The prefix is the first three digits of the seven-digit number.) If you have to make any calls in these situations, you need to define a new *area code rule* to handle it. Here's how it's done:

1. In the New Location dialog box, display the **Area Code Rules** tab.

2. Click **New** to display the New Area Code Rule dialog box.

3. Use the **Area code** text box to enter the area code you'll be calling.

4. If the rule will apply only to certain phone number prefixes, activate the **Include only the prefixes in the list below** option. Then click **Add**, enter the prefix (or prefixes), and click **OK**.

5. If you need to dial a country code (such as 1) before the area code, activate the **Dial** check box and use the text box to enter the number.

6. To force Windows XP to dial this area code, activate the **Include the area code** check box.

7. Click **OK**.

Using Calling Card Dialing

When you're on the road, you'll often find yourself having to make calls that cost money. For example, if you're in a hotel that charges for calls, you might want the charge to go through your calling card.

For this type of situation, Windows XP lets you specify a calling card to use when making the call. To get started, display the **Calling Card** tab in the New Location dialog box.

Here's the simplest route to take:

1. In the **Card Types** list, highlight the type of calling card you have.

2. Enter your **Account number.**

3. Enter your **Personal ID Number** (**PIN**).

If your calling card isn't in the list, click **New** to get to the New Calling Card dialog box. Alternatively, if your card is listed, you might need to adjust its settings. In that case, highlight the card and then click **Edit** to get the Edit Calling Card dialog box (which is identical to the New Calling Card dialog box). This dialog box has four tabs, so let's see what each one holds.

The **General** tab is as good a place as any to start. Here you need to enter three things: the **Calling card name** (this will appear in the Card Types list), your **Account number,** and your **Personal Identification Number** (**PIN**).

You use the **Long Distance** tab to specify the steps that must be followed to make a long distance call. The first thing to do is specify your card's **Access number for long-distance calls.** After that's done, you define the steps by clicking the buttons below the **Calling card dialing steps** box. There are six buttons for your clicking finger to tickle:

➤ **Access Number** Click this button to add the long-distance access number to the steps.

➤ **PIN** Click this button to add your PIN to the steps.

➤ **Wait for Prompt** Click this button to display a dialog box with various things that the system must wait for before continuing the dialing. You can have the system wait for a dial tone, a completed voice message, or a specified number of seconds.

➤ **Account Number** Click this button to add your account number to the steps.

➤ **Destination Number** Click this button to add the number you're calling to the steps. You also get a dialog box in which you can tell Windows XP to also dial the country code and area code.

➤ **Specify Digits** Click this button to add one or more digits (as well as * and #) to the steps.

The idea is that you click these buttons in the order that they must appear in the card's calling sequence. If you make a mistake, use the **Move Up** and **Move Down** buttons to shuffle things around. If your card requires different sequences for international and local calls, follow the same steps using the **International** and **Local Calls** tabs. When you're done, click **OK** to return to the New Location dialog box. Then click **OK** to return to the Phone And Modem Options dialog box.

Using a Different Location When Connecting to the Internet

To put all this to good use when connecting to the Internet, first select **Start, Connect To** and then click your Internet connection. In the Connect dialog box, click **Properties.** In the **General** tab, activate the **Use dialing rules** check box. You now have two choices:

➤ Enter an **Area code** and/or the **Country/region code**

➤ Click **Dialing Rules** to get to the Phone and Modem Options dialog box, use the **Locations** list to highlight the location you prefer to use, and then click **OK**.

The Least You Need to Know

➤ **Manual connection tidbits** If you'll be setting up your connection by hand, your ISP should provide you with the settings and data you need: the access phone number, your username and password, your IP address, and so on.

➤ **Getting connected** Making the leap to the Internet is as easy as starting any Internet program, such as Internet Explorer. When the Connect dialog box wanders in, click **Dial.**

➤ **Getting disconnected** To return to the real world, right-click the connection icon in the taskbar's system tray and then click **Disconnect.**

➤ **Your phone and your modem** To have both your phone and your modem available for use, run a phone cable from the wall jack to the modem's line port, and run a second cable from the phone to the modem's telephone jack.

➤ **Turn off call waiting** If you're using your modem on a line that has call waiting, be sure you tell Windows XP to turn off call waiting before dialing for data dollars.

Chapter 18

It's a Small Web After All: Using Internet Explorer

Whether you're 19 or 90, a world traveler or a channel surfer, I don't think I'm going out on a limb when I say that you've probably never seen anything quite like the World Wide Web. We're talking here about an improbably vast conglomeration of the world's wit, wisdom, and weirdness. Arranged in separate pages of information, the Web is home to just about every conceivable topic under the sun. If someone's thought of it, chances are someone else has a Web page about it.

The great thing about the Web is that it's not just a bunch of corporate marketing hoo-ha (although there's plenty of that, to be sure). No, *anyone* can publish a page, so the Web reflects the different interests, idiosyncrasies, and eccentricities of the general population.

The Web may sound like just some giant encyclopedia, but it boasts something that you won't find in any encyclopedia printed on mere paper: interaction. For example, almost every Web page in existence comes equipped with a few *links*. Links are special sections of the document that, when clicked, immediately whisk you away to some other page on the current site or even to a page on another site (which may be on the other side of town or on the other side of the planet). You can also use the Web to play games, post messages, buy things, sell things, grab files and programs, and much more.

If the Web has a downside, it's that it's *too* big (there's no "index," per se, so finding the info you need can be hard) and that it's *too* easy to publish a page (with no editors in sight, there's no guarantee that the info you find is accurate or even true). Still, there are ways to search for data, and you can usually corroborate something by looking for other pages that have the same data.

So the Web is definitely worth a look or three. This chapter helps you get those looks by showing you how to use Windows XP's Internet Explorer program, which is designed to surf (to use the proper Web verb) Web sites. You'll learn all the standard page navigation techniques, and you'll learn all the features that Internet Explorer offers for making your online journeys more efficient and pleasant.

Internet Explorer Nuts and Bolts

The most straightforward way to get Internet Explorer up and surfing is to select **Start, Internet.** If this doesn't launch Internet Explorer for some reason, you can also select **Start, All Programs, Internet Explorer.**

If you connect to the Internet using a modem, you may now see a dialog box telling you that something or other is "not available offline." If so, click **Connect.**

See Also

If you haven't yet signed up with an Internet service provider, it means you've skipped ahead in this book (and I've caught you!). To learn about signing up with an ISP, check out Chapter 17, "Getting on the Internet."

If you don't have a connection established with your Internet service provider, the Dial-Up Connection dialog box shows up at this point. Go ahead and click **Connect** to reunite Windows XP and the Internet.

There's a good chance that you'll now arrive at the MSN.com Web site, shown in Figure 8.1. (You may end up at a different site if your version of Windows XP comes with custom Internet settings.) Note that this screen changes constantly, so the one you see will almost certainly look different than the one shown in Figure 8.1.

MSN.com is Microsoft's Internet starting point. (This kind of site is known as a *portal* in the Web trade.) Fortunately, not all the sites you see in your travels will be as cramped-looking and as ugly as the MSN.com page.

Address bar
Page title
Links bar

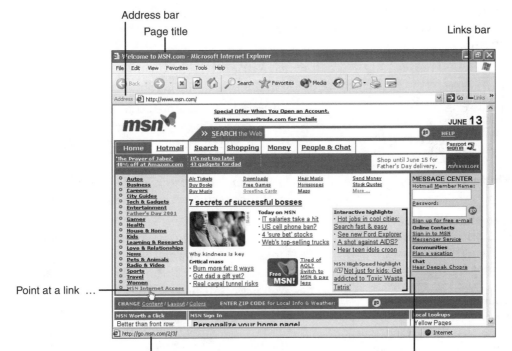

Point at a link …

… and the address of the linked page appears here

Most links are underlined

Figure 18.1

When you launch Internet Explorer, you usually end up at the MSN.com Web site.

Windows Wisdom

If you don't like MSN.com (or whatever you have as Internet Explorer's default start page), it's easy to change it. First, surf to the page that you want to use as the new start page. Then select the **Tools, Internet Options** command to lure the Internet Options dialog box out into the open. In the **General** tab, click **Use Current.** If you decide later on that you prefer Internet Explorer's default home page, click **Use Default.** If you'd rather not see any page at startup, click **Use Blank.**

Before I show you how to use this page to see more of the Web, let's take a minute or two and get our bearings by checking out the main features of the Internet Explorer window:

➤ **Page title**   The top line of the screen shows you the title of the current Web page.

➤ **Address bar**   This area shows you the address of the current page. Web page addresses are strange beasts, indeed. I'll help you figure them out a bit later in this chapter.

➤ **Links bar**   This barely visible toolbar has various buttons that each represent a predefined link.

➤ **Content area**   This area below the Address and Links bars takes up the bulk of the Internet Explorer screen. It's where the body of each Web page is displayed. You can use the vertical scrollbar to see more of the current page.

➤ **Links**   The content area for most Web pages also boasts a link or two (or 10). These links come in two flavors: images and text (the latter are usually underlined or in a different color than the rest of the text). When you put the mouse pointer over a link, Internet Explorer does two things (see Figure 18.1): It changes the pointer into a hand with a pointing finger, and it displays, in the status bar, the address of the linked page.

Web Page Navigation Basics

With that brief introduction out of the way, it's time to start wandering the Web. This section runs through a few techniques for getting from one page to another.

The most straightforward method is to click any link that strikes your fancy. Click the link, and you're immediately (depending on the speed of your Internet connection) whisked to the other page.

How can I tell what's a link and what isn't?

That, unfortunately, is not as easy as it used to be. Originally, link text appeared underlined and in a different color. That's still the usual case for a link these days, but you can also get nonunderlined links, as well as images that are links. The only real way to be sure is to park your mouse pointer over some likely looking text or an image, and then watch what happens to the pointer. If it changes into the hand with a pointing finger, then you know for sure that you've got a link on your hands.

What if I know the address of the page I want to peruse?

Easy money. Here's what you do:

➤ Click inside the Address bar, delete the existing address, type in the address you want to check out, and then either press **Enter** or click **Go** (it's to the right of the Address bar).

➤ If the address is one that you've visited recently, use the Address bar's drop-down list to select it.

Windows Wisdom

Internet Explorer also assumes that most Web addresses are of the form http://www.whatever.com. Therefore, if you simply type the "whatever" part and press **Ctrl+Enter,** Internet Explorer automatically adds the http://www. prefix and the .com suffix. For example, you can get to my home page (http://www.mcfedries.com) by typing `mcfedries` and pressing **Ctrl+Enter.**

Why the heck are Web addresses so, well, weird!

Probably because they were created by geeks who never imagined they'd be used by normal people. Still, they're not so bad after you figure out what's going on. Here's a summary of the various bits and pieces of a typical Web address (or *URL,* which is short for Uniform Resource Locator, another geekism):

http://www.mcfedries.com/cigwinxp/index.html

http://	This strange combination of letters and symbols tells the browser that you're entering a Web address. Note that the browser assumes *every* address is a Web address, so you don't need to include this part if you don't want to.
www.mcfedries.com	This is what's known as the *domain name* of the server computer that hosts the Web page (www.mcfedries.com is my Web server).
/cigwinxp/	This is the Web server directory in which the Web page makes its home.
index.html	This is the Web page's file name.

239

Ugh. Is there any easier way to get somewhere?

If you're not sure where you want to go, the default start page—it's called MSN.com—has lots of choices. For example, click any of the categories on the left (Autos, Business, and so on) to see lots of links related to that topic.

What if I jump to one page and then decide I want to double back to where I was?

That's a pretty common scenario. In fact, you'll often find that you need to leap back several pages, and then leap forward again. Fortunately, Internet Explorer makes this easy thanks to its Back and Forward toolbar buttons. Here's what you can do with them:

➤ Click **Back** to return to the previous page.

➤ Click **Forward** to move ahead to the next page.

➤ To go back several pages at once, drop down the **Back** button's list and click the page you want.

➤ To go forward several pages, drop down the **Forward** button's list and click the page you want.

➤ What if you want to go forward or back to a page but you also want to keep the current page in view? Easy money: Select **File, New, Window** (or press **Ctrl+N**) to open up a copy of the Internet Explorer window. You can then use that copy to leap to whatever page you want.

Techniques for Efficient Web Gallivanting

The paradox of the Web is that even though it doesn't really exist anywhere (after all, where is the amorphous never-never land of cyberspace?), it's still one of the biggest earthly things you can imagine. There aren't hundreds of thousands of pages, or even millions of them for that matter. No, there are *billions* of Web pages. (Of course, if you ignore all the pages that are devoted to Pamela Anderson Lee, then, yes, there *are* only a few hundred thousand pages.)

To have even a faint hope of managing just a tiny fraction of such an inconceivably vast array of data and bad MIDI music, you need to hone your Web browsing skills with a few useful techniques. Fortunately, as you'll see in the next few sections, Internet Explorer has all kinds of features that can help.

Saving Sites for Subsequent Surfs: Managing Your Favorites

One of the most common experiences that folks new to Web browsing go through is to stumble upon a really great site, and then not be able to find it again later. They try to retrace their steps, but usually just end up clicking links furiously and winding up in strange Net neighborhoods.

240

If this has happened to you, the solution is to get Internet Explorer to do all the grunt work of remembering sites for you. This is the job of the Favorites feature, which holds "shortcuts" to Web pages and even lets you organize those shortcuts into separate folders.

Here's how you tell Internet Explorer to remember a Web page as a favorite:

1. Use Internet Explorer to display the page.

2. Select **Favorites, Add to Favorites** to get the Add Favorite dialog box on-screen. (I'm going to ignore the **Make Available Offline** check box for now. I'll tackle it later on in Chapter 19, "The Savvy Surfer: More Internet Explorer Fun.")

3. The **Name** text box shows the name of the page, which is what you'll select from a menu later on when you want to view this page again. If you can think of a better name, don't hesitate to edit this text.

Windows Wisdom

You can add the current page to your list of favorites lickety-split by pressing **Ctrl+D.**

4. Most people end up with dozens or even hundreds of favorites, so it's a good idea to organize them into folders. To save this favorite in a folder, click **Create In.** (If you don't want to bother with this, skip to step 7.)

5. The Favorites feature has only one folder at the start: Links, which you shouldn't use for this. Instead, click **New Folder,** enter a name for the new folder in the dialog box that comes up, and then click **OK.**

6. Click the folder in which you want to store your favorite.

7. Click **OK** to finish.

After you have some pages lined up as favorites, you can return to any one of them at any time by pulling down the **Favorites** menu and clicking the page title. (If the favorite is stored in a folder, click that folder to open its submenu, and then click the page.)

If you need to make changes to your favorites, you can do a couple of things right from the Favorites menu. Pull down the menu and then right-click the item you want to work with. In the shortcut menu that slinks in, click **Rename** to change the item's name, or click **Delete** to blow it away. If your list is jumbled, you can put things in alphabetical order by clicking **Sort by Name.**

For more heavy-duty adjustments, select the **Favorites, Organize Favorites** command. Not surprisingly, this pushes the Organize Favorites dialog box into view. You get four buttons to play with:

Windows Wisdom

If you find yourself constantly pulling down the Favorites menu to get at your favorite pages, you might prefer to have the Favorites list displayed full-time. You can do that by clicking the **Favorites** button in the toolbar. Internet Explorer then sets aside a chunk of real estate on the left side of the window to display the Favorites list.

➤ **Create Folder** Click this button to create a new folder. (Tip: If you click an existing folder and then click this button, Internet Explorer creates a subfolder.) Internet Explorer adds the folder and displays **New Folder** inside a text box. Edit the text and then press **Enter.**

➤ **Move to Folder** Click this button to move the currently highlighted favorite into another folder. In the Browse for Folder dialog box that saunters by, highlight the destination folder, and then click **OK.**

➤ **Rename** Click this button to rename the currently highlighted favorite. Edit the name accordingly, and then press **Enter.**

➤ **Delete** Click this button to nuke the currently highlighted favorite. When Windows XP asks whether you're sure about this, click **Yes.**

When you're done, click **Close** to return to Internet Explorer.

Order Out of Chaos: Searching for Sites

Clicking willy-nilly in the hope of finding something interesting can be fun if you've got a few hours to kill. But if you need a specific tidbit of information *now,* then a click click here and click click there just won't cut the research mustard. To save time, you need to knock the Web down to a more manageable size, and Internet Explorer's Search feature can help you do just that.

The idea is straightforward: You supply a search "engine" (as they're called) with a word or two that describes the topic you want to find. The search engine then scours the Web for pages that contain those words, and presents you with a list of matches. Does it work? Well, it depends on which search engine you use. There are quite a few available, and some are better than others at certain kinds of searches. The biggest problem is that, depending on the topic you're looking for, the search engine might still return hundreds or even thousands of matching sites! You can usually get a more targeted search by adding more search terms and by avoiding common words.

Here's the basic procedure to follow to use the Search feature:

1. Click the **Search** button in the toolbar. Internet Explorer responds by shoehorning the Search Companion into the left side of the content area.
2. Use the text box to enter the word or phrase you want to find.

3. Click **Search.** Internet Explorer runs the search and then displays the results a few seconds later. As you can see in Figure 18.2, you get a series of links and descriptions. (Generally speaking, the higher the link is in the list, the better the page it points to matches your search text.) Clicking a link displays the page.

4. To get to more links, scroll down to the bottom of the Search bar. Here you'll see a **Next >>** link, which displays the next 10 matches.

5. When you've finished searching, click the **Search** toolbar button again to close the Search bar.

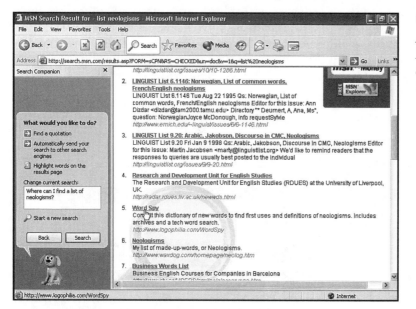

Figure 18.2

After the search is done, Internet Explorer displays a list of links to matching pages.

Here are a few notes to bear in mind when using the Search bar:

➤ **Putting the pup in the pound** The animated puppy that accompanies the Search Companion is cute, for sure, but not all that useful. To search without him, click **Change preferences,** and then click **Without an animated screen character.** If you're not a dog person, you can change the animated character, instead. Click **Change preferences,** click **With a different character,** and then click **Next** until you see the character you prefer; click **OK.**

➤ The Search Companion submits your search text to several search engines. If you have a preferred search site, you can set it as the default engine. To do that, click **Change preferences,** and then click **Change Internet search behavior.** Activate the **With Classic Internet search** option and then click the search engine you want. (Click **OK** to make it so.)

➤ **Address bar searching** If you don't like the Search Companion usurping a big chunk of the Internet Explorer window, you can also run searches from the Address bar. Just type in a word or phrase, press the down arrow key, and then press **Enter**.

Bread Crumbs in Cyberspace: Using the History List

You've seen so far how Internet Explorer keeps track of the pages you've visited in the current session. You can then use the Back and Forward buttons for to-and-fro surfing. That works well for the sites you've seen in the current Internet Explorer session, but what if you want to go back to a nonfavorite site you saw yesterday or even last week? That might seem like a tall order, but it turns out that Internet Explorer has a tall memory. In fact, the program offers a History feature that remembers pretty much everywhere you've gone for the past 20 days! Here's how it works:

1. Click the **History** button in the toolbar. By this time, you won't be surprised to see a History bar show up on the left side of the window, as shown in Figure 18.3.

Figure 18.3

Use the History bar to see a list of the places you've seen over the past 20 days.

The History button

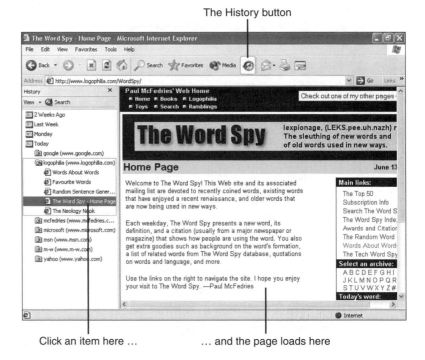

Click an item here …   … and the page loads here

2. You now do one of the following:

   ➤ If the date you want to work with was this week, click the day (such as **Monday**).

   ➤ If the date you want is in a previous week, click the week (such as **2 Weeks Ago**) and then click the day.

3. Internet Explorer displays a list of the sites you visited that day. Click the site you want. This gives you a list of the pages you visited on that site.

4. Click the page you want to see. Internet Explorer displays the page in the rest of the content area.

Internet Explorer also offers a couple of methods for dealing with the History bar's links:

➤ **Sorting the list**   Click the History bar's **View** button and then click a sort option (such as **By Most Visited**).

➤ **Searching the list**   If you do a lot of surfing, your History bar will be crammed to the gills with links. To find the one you want, click the History bar's **Search** button, enter a word or phrase in the **Search for** text box, and then click **Search Now**.

When you're done with the History bar, you can hide it by clicking the **History** toolbar button once again.

"What If I Want to Use Netscape?"

Internet Explorer comes free with Windows XP, and it's built right into the fabric of the operating system. However, that doesn't mean you can't use an alternative Web browser such as Netscape Navigator. Just download the browser from Netscape (go to home.netscape.com) and then install it.

You should note, however, that Netscape will probably set itself up to be Windows XP's default browser. (Some versions of Netscape are polite enough to ask you whether this is what you want.) This means that if you launch a shortcut to a Web page, it's Netscape that displays the page, not Internet Explorer.

Windows Wisdom

If you use both Internet Explorer and Netscape, a big problem you'll run into is that they don't share a common list of favorites—which are called *bookmarks* in the Netscape world. However, Internet Explorer is happy to either export the Favorites look to Netscape's bookmarks list or import the bookmarks as favorites. Select the **File, Import and Export** command.

What do you do if you'd prefer to use Internet Explorer as the default browser? This isn't a problem, but you first have to tell Internet Explorer to check to see whether it's the default. You do this by following these steps:

1. Select **Tools, Internet Options** to open the Internet Options dialog box.

2. Display the **Programs** tab.

3. Make sure the **Internet Explorer should check to see whether it is the default browser** check box is activated.

4. Click **OK.**

Now shut down Internet Explorer and then start it back up again. This time, you'll see a dialog box telling you that Internet Explorer isn't your default browser and asking if you want to make it the default. If you want to restore Internet Explorer's position as the default browser, click **Yes**; otherwise, click **No.**

The Least You Need to Know

➤ **Going Internet Exploring**   To start Internet Explorer, select **Start, Internet.** (Alternatively, select **Start, All Programs, Internet Explorer.**)

➤ **Navigation for novices**   To light out for another page, either click a link or type an address in the Address bar and then press **Enter.** Use the toolbar's Back button to return to the previous page, and use the Forward button to head the other way.

➤ **Site searching**   To scour the Web for a particular topic, click the **Search** button to get the Search Companion on-screen, enter a word or two, and then click **Search.**

➤ **Playing favorites**   Run the **Favorites, Add Favorites** command (or press **Ctrl+D**) to save a page on the Favorites menu.

➤ **Studying history**   To return to any site you visited in the last 20 days, open the History bar by clicking the **History** toolbar button.

Chapter 19

The Savvy Surfer: More Internet Explorer Fun

In This Chapter

➤ Working with Web pages offline

➤ Taking advantage of the Links bar

➤ Understanding Internet Explorer security

➤ Controlling your privacy by controlling cookies

Like electrons passing in the night, Web users never see each other as they surf sites. If they could, however, there might be a mutual flash of recognition between them because most Web users seem to fall into one of three categories:

➤ **Clickstreamers** Users who spend their online time wandering aimlessly from site to site, hoping for serendipitous finds (a new word: surfendipity!). By the way, *clickstream* is Web jargon for the "path" a person takes as he navigates through the Web by clicking links.

➤ **Nooksurfers** People who keep going to the same sites over and over and rarely check out new sites.

➤ **Researchers** People who use the Web exclusively for gathering information.

Whatever kind of Web user you are, your online time will be vastly more fun and productive if you can play your browser like a virtuoso. To that end, this chapter presents a master class for Internet Explorer. You learn how to read pages while you're offline, how to customize the Links bar, how to set up security, how to work with Internet Explorer's options, and much more.

Offline Surfing: Reading Pages When You're Not Connected

Many Web fans have a few pages that they check out regularly because the content is always changing. Let's say you have 12 such pages and it takes you an average of five minutes to read each one. That's an hour of online time you've used up. Wouldn't it be better if Internet Explorer could somehow grab those pages while you weren't around (at night, for example), and then let you read them while you're not connected?

Well, *sure* it would! That's probably why the Windows XP programmers added the Synchronize feature to Internet Explorer. This feature lets you designate Web pages to be available offline (that is, when you're not connected to the Internet). Then, when you run the Synchronize command, Internet Explorer absconds with the latest version of those pages and stores them on your hard disk. Internet Explorer also is happy to set up an automatic synchronization that can be scheduled to run any time you like.

To make a page available offline, begin by using either of the following techniques:

➤ **If the page is set up as a favorite** Pull down the **Favorites** menu and display the shortcut for the page. Then right-click that shortcut and click **Make available offline.**

➤ **If the page isn't yet set up as a favorite** Display the page and then select **Favorites, Add to Favorites** to meet up with the Add Favorite dialog box. Activate the **Make available offline** check box and then click **Customize.**

Whichever route you take, you end up with the Offline Favorite Wizard staring you in the face. Here's how it works:

1. The first wizard dialog box just offers an introduction, so click **Next.** (You can save yourself this step down the road by activating the **In the future, do not show this introduction screen** check box.) You end up at the Offline Favorite Wizard dialog box.

2. This wizard dialog box wonders whether you want any pages that are linked to the favorite to be downloaded, as well. If you don't care about the linked pages, activate **No**; otherwise, activate **Yes** and then use the **Download pages *x* links deep from this page** spin box to specify how many levels of links you want grabbed. Click **Next** when you're ready to proceed.

3. The wizard asks how you want the page *synchronized:*

   ➤ **Only when I choose Synchronize from the Tools menu**   Select this option if you want to control when the synchronization occurs. If you choose this option, click **Next** and then skip to step 5.

   ➤ **I would like to create a new schedule**   Activate this option if you want Internet Explorer to perform the synchronization automatically on a preset schedule. If you select this option, click **Next** and then continue with step 4.

Jargon Jar

Synchronize means to download a copy of a Web page so that the version you have stored on your computer is the same as (that is, is synchronized with) the version on the Web.

4. If you elected to set up a synchronization schedule, you'll see a dialog box with scheduling options. Here's a rundown of the controls you get to mess with (click **Next** when you're ready to move on):

   ➤ **Every *x* days**   Specify the number of days between synchronizations.

   ➤ **at**   Specify the time you want the synchronization to happen.

   ➤ **Name**   Enter a name for this synchronization schedule.

   ➤ **If my computer is not connected …**   Activate this check box to have Internet Explorer connect your computer to the Internet to download the page (or pages). Note that this option works only if you don't have to type in any logon information (such as your user name and password) to connect to your ISP.

5. The final wizard dialog box wants to know whether the Web page requires you to log on. If not (most sites don't), activate **No;** if so, activate **Yes** and then fill in your **User name** and **Password** (twice). Click **Finish** to complete the synchronization setup.

6. If you're adding a new favorite, you'll end up back in the Add Favorite dialog box. Select a folder for the favorite (if necessary) and then click **OK**.

At this point, Internet Explorer performs the initial synchronization: It connects to the page and hauls in a copy that it stores on your system.

If you elected to go the manual synchronization route, you can download the pages for offline perusing at any time by selecting the **Tools, Synchronize** command. In the Items to Synchronize dialog box (see Figure 19.1), deactivate the check boxes for any items you don't want to synchronize, and then click **Synchronize**.

Figure 19.1

Deactivate the check box beside any page you don't want synchronized.

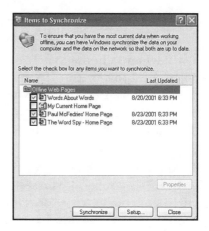

Customizing the Handy Links Bar

Internet Explorer's Links bar contains a few prefab sites that you can try out to get your Web feet wet. To see the buttons, you have two choices:

➤ Click the right-pointing double-arrow.

➤ View the entire toolbar by moving the mouse pointer over the **Links** label and then dragging it below the Address bar. (If the bar won't budge, right-click any toolbar and then deactivate the **Lock the Toolbars** command.)

Here's a summary of each link:

➤ **Customize Links** This link takes you to a page that tells you how to customize the Links bar.

➤ **Free Hotmail** This button takes you to a page where you can sign up for a free e-mail account with Microsoft's Hotmail service.

➤ **Windows** This link takes you to the Windows home page.

➤ **Windows Media** This link takes you to the Windows Media page where you can access music, videos, and other media.

I have two words I use to describe the default Links bar buttons: bo-ring! However, I really like the Links bar itself because, in my never-ending quest to minimize mouse clicks and keystrokes, it offers me one-click access to sites. To get the most out of it,

Windows Wisdom

Internet Explorer's toolbar is a mish-mash of text and nontext buttons. Who's the genius who came up that *that*? The buttons would be much easier to decipher if they all displayed text. Fortunately, that's not a problem. Select **View, Toolbars, Customize** to request the presence of the Customize Toolbar dialog box. Use the **Text options** list to select **Show text labels,** and then click **Close.**

however, I give the default links the heave-ho and replace them with my most frequently accessed sites. Here's a rundown of some of the things you can do to remake the Links bar:

➤ **Sizing the Links bar**   After you drag the Links bar to where it can be seen, you're free to change its size. To give this a whirl, position the mouse pointer over the left edge of the bar and then drag your mouse left or right.

➤ **Changing button positions**   The positions of the Links bar buttons aren't set in stone. To move any button, use your mouse to drag the button left or right along the Links bar.

➤ **Changing a button's address**   If you right-click a button and then click **Properties,** Internet Explorer displays the Properties dialog box for an Internet shortcut. Use the **URL** text box to edit the button's address.

➤ **Creating a button for the current page**   To add a new Links bar button for the current page, drag the page icon from the Address bar and drop it on the Links bar.

➤ **Creating a button from a hypertext link**   If a page has a hypertext link, you can create a button for that link by dragging the link text into the Links bar.

➤ **Renaming a button**   Right-click the button and then click **Rename** in the menu. In the Rename dialog box that barges in, enter the new name and then click **OK.**

➤ **Deleting a button**   To blow away a button from the Links bar, drag the button and then drop it in the Windows XP Recycle Bin. (You can also right-click the button and then click **Delete.**)

Dealing with Files in Internet Explorer

As you click your way around the Web, you find that some links don't take you to other pages but are, instead, tied directly to a file. In this case, Internet Explorer throws the File Download dialog box at you, as shown in Figure 19.2. You need to decide what you want to do with the file:

➤ **Open**   Click this button to run the file right away after it has been downloaded. Only go this route if you're absolutely sure that the file is safe to run.

➤ **Save**   Click this button to save the file to a location on your computer's hard disk. In the Save As dialog box that shows up next, choose a location for the file, and then click **Save.**

➤ **Cancel**   Click this button to bypass downloading the file.

Figure 19.2

When you click a link to a file, Internet Explorer uses this dialog box to find out how you want it to handle the file.

If you elected to save the file, you'll eventually see the Download Complete dialog box, which offers three buttons:

➤ **Open**   Click this button to launch the downloaded file.

➤ **Open Folder**   Click this button to open a window that displays the contents of the folder into which you saved the file. This is a good choice if you want to do something other than launch the file (such as rename it).

➤ **Close**   Click this button to put off dealing with the file until later.

Sometimes Web pages contain things that Internet Explorer can't display properly without installing the appropriate component. This happens with things like Java applets and foreign character sets. In this case, Internet Explorer will pester you with an Install On Demand dialog box similar to the one shown in Figure 19.3. You have two choices:

➤ To update Internet Explorer with the required component, click **Download.**

➤ If you don't want to bother with the component, click **Cancel.** (If you never want Internet Explorer to bug you about this component again, be sure to activate the **Never download any of these components** check box before you click Cancel.)

Look Out!

You need to be careful about downloading files because they can contain viruses that wreck your system. To be safe, you should only download from reputable sites, or from sites that you trust explicitly. If you plan on living dangerously and downloading files willy-nilly, at least get yourself a good antivirus program such as McAfee (www.mcafee.com) or Norton (www.symantec.com).

Figure 19.3

Internet Explorer displays this dialog box if it needs to install a component to render a page properly.

Caveat Surfer: Internet Explorer and Security

Tons of people are flocking to the Web, and tons of content providers are waiting for them there. Still, the Web is by no means in the mainstream. That is, although millions of people surf the Web, that's still only a small percentage of the hundreds of millions of potential Web denizens that remain resolutely unwired. There are many reasons for this, but one of the biggest is the security issue. There are two issues, actually:

➤ **Protecting the data that you send to the Web**   Many Web page forms ask you to supply sensitive data, such as your credit card number. You wouldn't leave credit card receipts lying in the street, but that's more or less what you're doing if you submit a normal Web form that has your Visa number on it. The solution here is to only enter sensitive data on Web pages that are secure (more on this in a sec).

➤ **Being protected from the data that the Web sends to you**   The nature of the Web means that all kinds of items—text, graphics, sounds, Java applets (a kind of mini-program), ActiveX controls (another mini-program), and more—get deposited on your computer, at least temporarily. How do you know all that stuff is safe? And if you're not sure about something, how do you refuse delivery?

Internet Explorer offers quite a number of features that tackle these issues directly. For example, the Internet Explorer window gives you visual cues that tell you whether a particular document is secure. For example, Figure 19.4 shows Internet Explorer displaying a secure Web page. Notice how a lock icon appears in the lower-right corner, and that the address of a secure page uses **https** up front rather than **http**. Both of these features tell you that the Web page has a security certificate that passed muster with Internet Explorer.

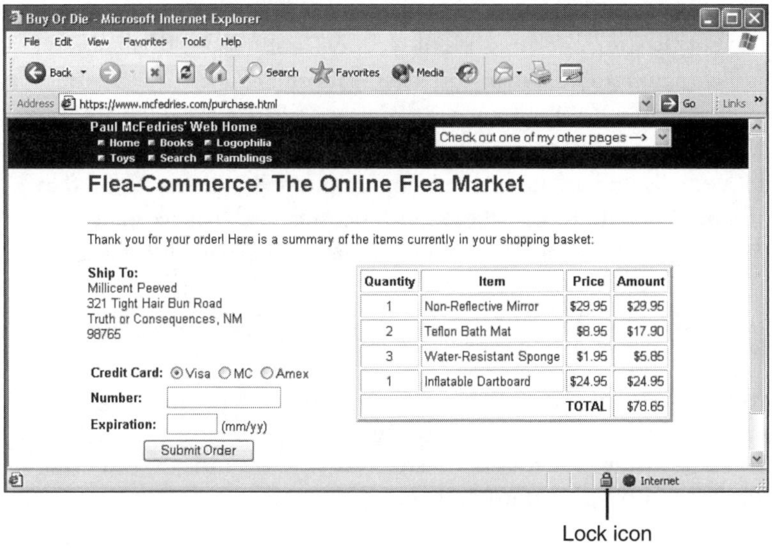

Lock icon

Figure 19.4

An example of a secure Web document.

Internet Explorer also displays security warning dialog boxes. These seemingly paranoid notes are actually quite useful most of the time. They warn you about all kinds of security-related activities:

➤ Entering a secure Web site.

➤ Browsing allegedly secure Web sites that don't have a valid security certificate.

➤ Leaving a secure Web site (see Figure 19.5).

➤ Being redirected to a page other than the one you specified.

➤ Downloading and running objects, including files, ActiveX controls, Java applets, and scripts.

➤ Submitting a form unsecurely.

Figure 19.5

Internet Explorer warns you when you're about to leave a secure page.

Windows Wisdom

Many folks want to try out these newfangled e-commerce and online banking sites that everyone's talking about, but they're concerned about security. That's smart, because financial data *must* be as secure as possible. When you investigate these kinds of sites, you often see them yammering on about "128-bit encryption" and similar-sounding gobbledygook. The gist is that any Web browser that boasts 128-bit encryption can scramble your financial data to make it virtually uncrackable by nefarious nogoodniks. It used to be that you had to download a special update to get this super-duper security. That's a thing of the past now because Windows XP's version of Internet Explorer comes with 128-bit security built right in.

Note that these dialog boxes contain a check box that enables you to turn the warning off. You can also use the Security tab in the Internet Options dialog box (select **Tools, Internet Options** to get there) to toggle these warnings on and off and customize the level of security used by Internet Explorer.

The way Internet Explorer handles security is to classify Web pages according to different security *zones*. Each zone is a collection of Web pages that implements a common security level. There are four zones:

➤ **Internet zone** This is a catch-all zone that includes all Web pages that aren't in any of the other zones. The default security level is medium.

➤ **Local intranet zone** This zone covers Web pages on your local hard drives and on your local area network (intranet). The default security level is medium-low.

➤ **Trusted sites zone** You use this zone to specify Web sites that you trust. That is, these are sites for which you're certain that any objects you download and run are safe. The default security level is low.

➤ **Restricted sites zone** You use this zone to specify Web sites that you don't trust, and so want to implement the tightest possible security. The default security level is high.

You can add sites to three of Internet Explorer's security zones: Local intranet, Trusted sites, and Restricted sites. Here's how you do it:

1. In the Security tab, click the icon of the zone you want to work with.

2. Click the **Sites** button.

3. If you're working with the Local intranet zone, you see a dialog box with three check boxes that determine the sites that are part of the default settings for this zone. Leave these as is and click **Advanced.**

4. To add a site, enter the address in the **Add this Web site to the zone** text box, and then click **Add.**

5. To remove a site from the zone, highlight it in the **Web sites** list, and then click **Remove.**

6. If you want Internet Explorer to make sure each site's Web server is using the HTTPS security protocol (a good idea), activate the **Require server verification (https:) for all sites in this zone** check box.

7. Click **OK.**

Look Out!

Why not just select the High setting to get the most security? Because this setting blocks certain common Web site activities such as file downloads and scripting, and without these many sites won't work properly.

Internet Explorer has four predefined security levels: **High** (most secure), **Low** (least secure), **Medium-low,** and **Medium.** You can assign any of these levels within the Security tab by first using the **Zone** list to choose the security zone, and then dragging the slider to the security level you want. Note that Internet Explorer displays the types of security each setting provides next to the slider.

Restricting Your Cookie Diet: Internet Explorer's Privacy Features

As you weave your way around the Web, you'll occasionally come across sites that offer to "remember" bits of data that you enter. For example, the site shown in Figure 19.6 offers to store the user name and password for a game, which means this data will be entered into the text boxes automatically the next time the person visits the same page. Similarly, if you do any online shopping, your selections get stored in a "shopping cart" that remembers what and how much you ordered. Still other sites (such as MSN.com) enable you to create "customized" pages that display your local news and weather as well as info tidbits of your choosing (such as sports headlines).

Figure 19.6

Some Web sites have the seemingly miraculous ability to remember things about you.

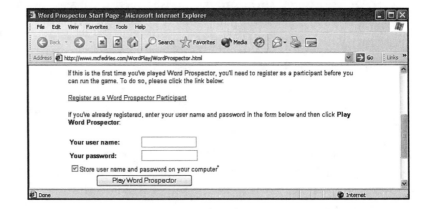

The source of a Web site's "memory" is actually a teensy file that gets stored automatically on your computer. This file is called, somewhat bizarrely, a *cookie*. Web sites use these cookies to store data (such as the user name and password you use to access the site), shopping cart particulars, customization settings, and much more.

If a site can store a file on my computer, what's to stop them from sending me a virus or some other nasty electronic bug?

That's not possible with cookies because Internet Explorer will only allow the site to store the data in a particular location and in a plain text format that can do no harm to your machine.

Okay, but isn't it dangerous to have user names and passwords and stuff like that sitting around in text files?

Good point, but it's not dangerous because only the site that created the cookie can read it. No other site can access anybody else's cookie, so your data can't get spread around.

So cookies are totally benign creatures and we have nothing to worry about?

Actually, that's not quite true. To understand why, you have to understand about the different cookie types:

➤ **Temporary cookie** This type of cookie lives just as long as you have Internet Explorer running. When you shut down the program, all the temporary cookies are given the heave-ho.

➤ **Persistent cookie** This type of cookie remains on your hard disk even after you exit Internet Explorer. The cookie's length of stay depends on how it's set up, but it can be anything from a few seconds to a few years.

➤ **First-party cookie** This is a cookie that's set by the Web site that you're viewing.

➤ **Third-party cookie** This is a cookie that's set by a site other than the one you're viewing. Most third-party cookies are created and stored by advertisers who have placed an ad on the site you're viewing.

> **Jargon Jar**
>
> The term **cookie** is based on the old programming term *magic cookie,* which the Jargon File (the definitive dictionary of geekspeak; see tuxedo.org/jargon/) defines as "something passed between routines or programs that enables the receiver to perform some operation." It's this idea of passing data from one thing to another (in this case, from a page to your computer) that inspired the original cookie creators.

Given these cookie flavors, there are two types of cookie problems that civil libertarians and other privacy advocates fret about:

➤ A site might store *personally identifiable information*—your name, e-mail address, home address, phone number, and so on—in a persistent first- or third-party cookie and then use that information in some way (such as filling in a form) without your consent.

➤ A site might store information about you in a persistent third-party cookie and then use that cookie to track your online movements and activities. They can do this because they might have (for example) an ad on dozens or hundreds of Web sites and that ad is the mechanism that enables the site to set and read their cookies. Such sites are supposed to come up with *privacy policies* stating that they won't engage in surreptitious monitoring of users, they won't sell user data, and so on.

To help you handle these scenarios, the Windows XP version of Internet Explorer implements a new privacy feature that gives you extra control over whether sites can store cookies on your machine. To check out this feature, select the **Tool, Internet Options** command, and then display the **Privacy** tab.

You set your cookie privacy level by using the slider in the **Settings** group. There are two settings that fall into the all-or-nothing category:

➤ **Accept All Cookies** This setting (it's at the bottom of the slider) tells Internet Explorer to accept any and all cookie comers.

➤ **Block All Cookies** This setting (it's at the top of the slider) tells Internet Explorer to turn back all requests to set and read cookies.

In between there are four settings that offer more detailed control. The following table shows you how each setting affects the three types of privacy issues:

	Third-Party Cookies with No Compact Privacy Policy	Third-Party Cookies Using Personally Identifiable Information Without the Type of Consent	First-Party Cookies Using Personally Identifiable Information Without Consent
Low	Restricted	Restricted (implicit)	OK
Medium (the default)	Blocked	Blocked (implicit)	Restricted (implicit)
Medium High	Blocked	Blocked (explicit)	Blocked (implicit)
High	Blocked	Blocked (explicit)	Blocked (explicit)

Look Out!

Blocking all cookies may sound like the easiest way to handle this privacy rigmarole. However, there are a lot of sites out there that rely on cookies to operate properly, so if you shun all cookies you may find that your Web surfing isn't as convenient or as smooth as it used to be.

Here are some notes about the terminology in this table:

➤ *Restricted* means that Internet Explorer doesn't allow the site to set a persistent cookie, just a temporary one.

➤ A *compact* privacy policy is a shortened form of a privacy policy that can be sent along with the cookie and that can be read by the browser.

➤ *Implicit consent* means that on one or more pages leading up to the cookie, you were warned that your personally identifiable information would be used and you agreed that it was okay.

➤ *Explicit consent* means that on the page that reads the cookie, you were warned that your personally identifiable information would be used and you agreed that it was okay.

If Internet Explorer comes across a Web site that tries to set a blocked or restricted type of cookie, two things happen (see Figure 19.7):

➤ A Privacy Report icon appears in the status bar.

➤ The Privacy dialog box appears with a message letting you know what the privacy icon is all about. If you don't want to be bothered by this dialog box each time, be sure to leave the **Don't show this message again** check box activated. Note, too, that you can also click the **Settings** button to bring up the Internet Properties dialog box with the **Privacy** tab displayed.

To find out what's going on, double-click the Privacy Report icon to get to a Privacy Report dialog box similar to the one shown in Figure 19.8. This dialog box tells you which sites tried to set the cookies and what action Internet Explorer took (such as **Blocked**).

Windows Wisdom

If you change the privacy setting, you should first delete all your cookies because the new setting won't apply to any cookies already on your computer. To delete your cookies, select **Tools, Internet Options,** display the **General** tab, and then click **Delete Cookies.** (If you prefer to delete individual cookies, click **Settings,** click **View Files,** and then look for file names that begin with **"cookie:".**)

Figure 19.7

The Privacy Report icon shows up in the Internet Explorer status bar when you visit a site that uses a type of cookie that you've restricted.

The Privacy Report icon

Figure 19.8

Double-click the Privacy Report icon to see this dialog box.

The Least You Need to Know

➤ **Offline surfing**   To get Internet Explorer to download a page for leisurely offline reading, select **Favorites, Add Favorites** and activate the **Make available offline** check box.

➤ **Links hi-jinks**   Right-click a Links bar button to rename or delete the button or to change the link address. To add a button to the Links bar, either drag the Address bar icon into the Links bar or drag a link into the Links bar.

➤ **Feeling secure**   Only submit sensitive data (such as your credit card number) to a secure site (that is, one that has a lock icon in the status bar).

➤ **Customizing Internet Explorer**   Select the **Tools, Internet Options** command (or launch the Control Panel's **Internet Options** icon) to display the Internet Options dialog box.

Chapter 20

Sending and Receiving E-Mail Missives

The world passed a milestone of sorts a few years ago when it was reported that, in North America at least, more e-mail messages are sent each day than postal messages. Now, e-mail message volume is several times that of "snail mail" (as regular mail is derisively called by the wired set), and the number of e-notes shipped out each day is counted in the *billions*.

The really good news is that e-mail has become extremely easy to use because e-mail programs have become much better over the years. An excellent example of this trend is Outlook Express, Windows XP's Internet e-mail program. As you see in this chapter, shipping out messages and reading incoming messages is a painless affair thanks to the admirable e-mail capabilities of Outlook Express.

Windows XP gives you a couple of ways to launch the program:

➤ Select **Start, E-mail.**

➤ Select **Start, All Programs, Outlook Express.**

Setting Up Your Internet E-Mail Account

Before Outlook Express loads, it calls in the Internet Connection Wizard to handle the various steps required to divulge the details of the e-mail account you have with your ISP. Here's a rundown of the information you should have at your fingertips:

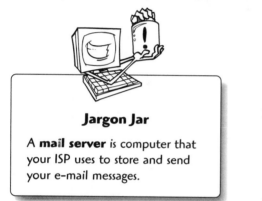

Jargon Jar

A **mail server** is computer that your ISP uses to store and send your e-mail messages.

➤ The username and password for your e-mail account. (These are almost always the same as your Internet logon name and password.)

➤ The type of server the ISP uses for incoming e-mail: POP3, IMAP, or HTTP.

➤ The Internet name used by the ISP's incoming *mail server* (this often takes the form mail. *provider*.com, where *provider* is the name of the ISP). Note that your ISP might call this their *POP3 server.*

➤ The Internet name used by the ISP's outgoing mail server (this is almost always the same as the incoming e-mail server). Some ISPs call this their *SMTP server.*

Here's what happens:

1. The wizard asks for your display name, which is the name other folks see when you send them a message. Enter the name you want to use in the **Display name** text box (most people just use their real name), and click **Next.**

2. Now the wizard pesters you for your e-mail address. Enter your address in the **E-mail address** text box, and click **Next.**

3. Next on the wizard's to-do list is gathering info about your ISP's e-mail server. You have three things to fill in (as usual, click **Next** when you're done):

   ➤ **My incoming mail server is a ...**   Use this list to specify the type of e-mail server your ISP uses; most are **POP3.**

   ➤ **Incoming mail (POP3, IMAP, or HTTP) server**   Enter the name of the server that your ISP uses for incoming mail.

   ➤ **Outgoing mail (SMTP) server**   Enter the name of the server that your ISP uses for outgoing mail.

4. The next items on the agenda are your account details: your **Account name** (this should already be filled in for you) and your **Password.** If you don't want to be pestered for your password each time you connect, leave the **Remember password** check box activated. Click **Next** after that's finished.

5. Click **Finish.**

The Lay of the Outlook Express Land

By default, Outlook Express is set up to go online and grab your waiting messages at startup. We'll get there eventually, so for now just close the Connect dialog box if it shows up.

At long last, the Outlook Express window shows itself, and it looks much like the one in Figure 20.1.

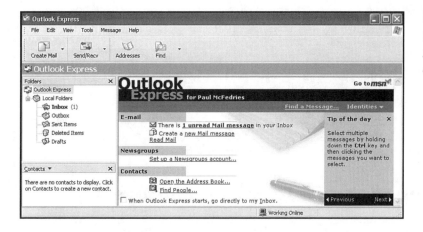

Figure 20.1

Use Outlook Express to ship and receive Internet e-mail messages.

The Folders bar on the left uses a tree-like structure to list the various storage areas that come with Outlook Express. I talk about folders in more detail in Chapter 21, "More E-Mail Bonding: Extending Outlook Express." However, here's a quick summary of what the default folders are all about:

➤ **Inbox**   This folder is where Outlook Express stores the e-mail messages that you receive.

➤ **Outbox**   This folder stores messages that you've composed but haven't sent yet.

➤ **Sent Items**   This folder stores a copy of the messages that you've sent.

➤ **Deleted Items**   This folder stores the messages that you delete.

➤ **Drafts**   This folder stores messages that you're in the middle of composing and have saved.

263

You also see a Contacts list, which gives you quick access to people who are in your address book.

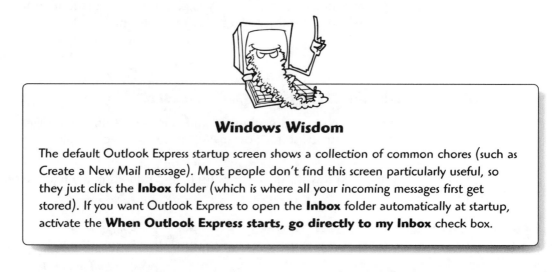

Windows Wisdom

The default Outlook Express startup screen shows a collection of common chores (such as Create a New Mail message). Most people don't find this screen particularly useful, so they just click the **Inbox** folder (which is where all your incoming messages first get stored). If you want Outlook Express to open the **Inbox** folder automatically at startup, activate the **When Outlook Express starts, go directly to my Inbox** check box.

The Outbox: Sending an E-Mail Message

Let's begin the Outlook Express tour with a look at how to foist your e-prose on unsuspecting colleagues, friends, family, and *Brady Bunch* cast members. This section shows you the basic technique to use, and then gets a bit fancier in discussing the Address Book, attachments, and other Outlook Express sending features.

The Basics: Composing and Sending a Message

Without further ado (not that there's been much ado to this point, mind you), here are the basic steps to follow to fire off an e-mail message to some lucky recipient:

1. Click the **Create Mail** button in the toolbar, or select **Message, New Message**. (Keyboard fans will be pleased to note that pressing **Ctrl+N** also works.) You end up with the New Message window on-screen, as shown in Figure 20.2.

2. In the **To** text box, type in the e-mail address of the recipient. (It's perfectly acceptable to enter multiple addresses in this text box. Use a semicolon [;] or a comma [,] to separate each address.)

3. The address you put in the To box is the "main" recipient of the message. However, it's common to shoot a copy of the message off to a "secondary" recipient. To do that, enter their e-mail address in the Cc text box. (Again, you can enter multiple addresses, if you're so inclined.)

    There's also a *blind courtesy* (or *carbon*) *copy* (Bcc), which delivers a copy of the message to a specified recipient. However, none of the other recipients see that person's address anywhere. To enter a Bcc address, activate the **View, All Headers** command to add a **Bcc** field to the New Message window.

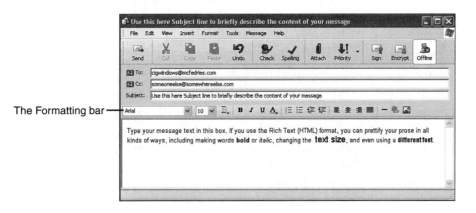

The Formatting bar

Figure 20.2

You cobble together an e-mail message in the New Message window.

4. Use the **Subject** line to enter a subject for the message. (The subject acts as a kind of title for your message. It's the first thing the recipient sees, so it should accurately reflect the content of your message, and it shouldn't be too long. Think *pithy*.)

5. Decide what type of message you want to send. You have two choices, both of which are commands on the Format menu:

   ➤ **Rich Text (HTML)**   Choose this command to include formatting in your message. This enables you to make your message look its best. However, your recipient might have problems if his e-mail program doesn't support this formatting. (Just so you know, HTML stands for Hypertext Markup Language. It's a series of codes used to format characters and things, and it's used to create Web pages. Don't worry, you don't have to know anything about HTML to use this feature.)

   ➤ **Plain Text**   Choose this command to send out the message without any formatting. This makes life easier for your recipient if he doesn't have an e-mail program that supports formatting. If you're not sure what your recipient is using, choose this command anyway.

6. Use the large, empty, area below the Subject line to type in the message text (also known as the *message body*).

7. If you chose the Rich Text (HTML) format, after you're inside the message text area, notice that the buttons on the Formatting bar suddenly come alive, as do more of the Format menu commands. Use these buttons and commands to change the font, format paragraphs, add a background image, apply stationery, and more. (*Stationery* is a prefab set of formatting options.)

8. When your message is fit for human consumption, you have two sending choices:

   ➤ **If you're working online** Click the **Send** toolbar button or select **File, Send Message** (or try **Alt+S** on for size). Outlook Express sends the message, no questions asked.

   ➤ **If you're working offline** Click the **Send** toolbar button or select **File, Send Later.** In this case, Outlook Express coughs up a dialog box that tells you the message will bunk down in the Outbox folder until you're ready to send it. This is good because it means you can compose a few messages before connecting to the Internet. When you're ready to actually ship the messages, select the **Tools, Send and Receive, Send All** command in Outlook Express. (You also can drop down the **Send/Recv** toolbar button, and then click **Send All.**)

Note that after your message is Net-bound, Outlook Express also is kind enough to save a copy of the message in the Sent Items folder. This is handy because it gives you a record of all the missives you launch into cyberspace.

Easier Addressing: Using the Address Book

If you find yourself with a bunch of recipients to whom you send stuff regularly (and it's a rare e-mailer who doesn't), you soon grow tired of entering their addresses by hand. The solution is to toss those regulars into the Windows XP Address Book. That way, you can fire them into the To or Cc lines with just a few mouse clicks.

Here's how you add someone to the Address Book:

1. In Outlook Express, click the **Addresses** button or select the **Tools, Address Book** command. (Keyboard diehards can get their kicks by pressing **Ctrl+Shift+B.** Note, too, that you also can

Windows Wisdom

Outlook Express has a **Spelling** command on the **Tools** menu (as well as a **Spelling** toolbar button). If you can't select it, it's because Outlook Express doesn't actually have its own spell checker. Instead, it rides the spell checking coattails of other programs, such as Microsoft Word. So you can run the Spelling command only if you have a spell-check–equipped program installed.

work on your Address Book when Outlook Express isn't running. In this case, select **Start, All Programs, Accessories, Address Book.**)

2. In the Address Book window that reports for duty, click the **New** toolbar button and then click **New Contact.** (Alternatively, either select **File, New Contact** or slam **Ctrl+N.**) The Address Book conjures up the Properties dialog box shown in Figure 20.3.

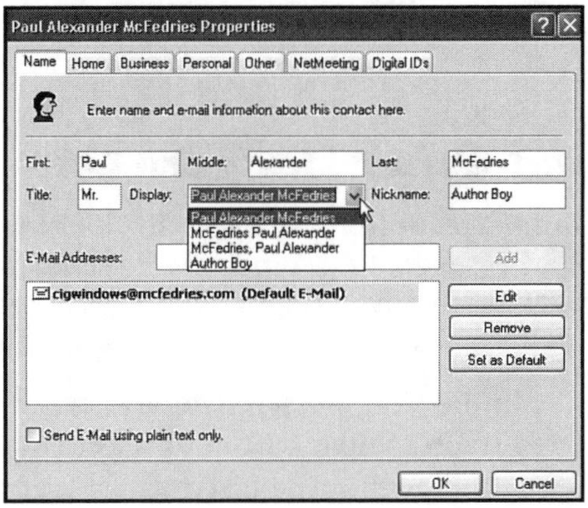

Figure 20.3

Use this dialog box to spell out the particulars of the new recipient.

3. In the **Name** tab, enter at least the person's **First** and **Last** names.

4. Use the **E-Mail Addresses** text box to enter the recipient's address, and then click **Add.** (If this person has multiple e-mail addresses, repeat this procedure as often as necessary. To set one of these addresses as the default, highlight it and click **Set as Default.**)

5. If you want this person to receive only plain text messages, activate the **Send E-Mail using plain text only** check box.

6. Fill in the fields in the other tabs, if you feel like it.

7. When you're done, click **OK** to add the new recipient.

After you have a contact in your Address Book, Outlook Express gives you a ton of ways to get them a message. Here are my three favorite methods:

➤ In the New Message window, start typing the person's name or nickname (a special name you type in when entering a person in your Address Book). If Outlook Express recognizes the name you're typing, it will fill in the rest of the name for you automatically. When the name is correct, press **Tab** to set it.

➤ In the New Message window, click **To** or **Cc** to get the Select Recipients dialog box. Click the contact name and then click **To** (or **Cc** or **Bcc**). (If the person has multiple addresses, Outlook Express assumes you want to use the default

267

address. To use a different address, right-click the person's name, click **Action,** **Send Mail To,** and then click the address you want to use.)

➤ The Outlook Express window has a Contacts area that lists everyone in the Address Book. Use this area to double-click the name of the recipient you want to use.

One final note. If you set up the recipient to receive only plain text messages, when you send the message, you see a dialog box asking what format you want to use. In this case, you'd click **Send Plain Text.**

Inserting Attachments and Other Hangers-On

Most of your messages will be text-only creations (perhaps with a bit of formatting tossed in to keep things interesting). However, it's also possible to send entire files along for the ride. Such files are called, naturally enough, *attachments*. They're very common in the business world, and it's useful to know how they work. Here it goes:

Windows Wisdom

If you want to send a message to a particular set of recipients, you can organize them into a *group* and then specify the group name in the To line. To create a group, open the Address Book, click the **New** button and then click **New Group.** Enter a **Group Name** and then click **Select Members** to add recipients to the group.

1. In the New Message window, either click the **Attach** toolbar button or select **Insert, File Attachment.** The Insert Attachment dialog box rears its head.

2. Find the file you want to attach and then highlight it.

3. Click **Attach.** Outlook Express returns you to the New Message window where you see a new **Attach** box that includes the name of the file.

As you can see, adding attachments isn't that hard. However, that doesn't mean you should bolt an attachment or two onto every message you send. Adding attachments can greatly increase the size of your message, so it may take the recipient quite a while to download your message, which won't be appreciated, I can tell you. Some ISP's put an upper limit on the size of a message, so it's also possible that your recipient may never see your note. Use common sense and only attach files when it's absolutely necessary.

The Inbox: Getting and Reading E-Mail Messages

Some people like to think of e-mail as a return to the days of *belles-lettres* and *billets-doux* (these people tend to be a bit pretentious). Yes, it's true that e-mail has people writing again, but this isn't like the letter writing of old. The major difference is that e-mail's turnaround time is usually much quicker. Instead of waiting weeks or even months to get a return letter, a return e-mail might take as little as a few minutes or a few hours.

So, if you send out a message with a question or comment, chances are you get a reply coming right back at you before too long. Any messages sent to your e-mail address are stored in your account at your ISP. Your job is to use Outlook Express to access your account and grab any waiting messages. This section shows you how to do that and shows you what to do with those messages after they're safely stowed on your computer.

Getting Your Messages

Here are the steps to stride through to get your e-mail messages:

1. Outlook Express offers two different postal routes:

    ➤ **To only receive messages** Either drop down the **Send/Recv** toolbar button and then click **Receive All**, or select **Tools, Send and Receive, Receive All**.

    ➤ **To send and receive messages** If you have outgoing messages waiting in your Outbox folder, either drop down the **Send/Recv** toolbar button and then click **Send and Receive All**, or select **Tools, Send and Receive, Send and Receive All**. (Keyboardists can get away with pressing **Ctrl+M**.)

2. Outlook Express connects to the Internet (if necessary), accesses your mail account, absconds with any waiting messages, and then stuffs them into the Outlook Express Inbox folder. If you were working offline previously, disconnect from the Internet if you no longer need the connection.

3. If it's not already displayed, click the **Inbox** folder so you can see what the e-postman delivered.

When you're working online, Outlook Express automatically checks for new messages every 30 minutes. You can change that by selecting **Tools, Options**. In the **General** tab, use the spin box that's part of the **Check for new messages every *x* minute(s)** option to set the checking interval.

Reading Your Messages

Figure 20.4 shows the Inbox folder with a few messages. The first thing to notice is that Outlook Express uses a bold font for all messages that you haven't read yet. You also get info about each message organized with the following half-dozen columns:

➤ **Priority** This column tells you whether the sender set up the message with a priority ranking. If you see a red exclamation mark, it means the message was sent with high priority (this is the "handle this pronto, buster!" symbol); if you see a blue, downward-pointing arrow, it means the note was sent with low priority (this is the "handle this whenever, man" symbol).

➤ **Attachment** If you see a paper clip icon in this column, it means the message is accompanied by a file attachment. See the "Attending to Attachments" section later in this chapter.

➤ **Flag** If you want to remind yourself to deal with a message, you can "flag" it for a future follow-up (a sort of digital string-tied-to-the-finger thing). You do this by highlighting the message and then selecting the **Message, Flag Message** command. This adds a flag icon in this column.

➤ **From** This column tells you the name (or occasionally, just the e-mail address) of the person or company that sent you the message.

➤ **Subject** This column shows you the subject line of the message which will, hopefully, give you a brief description of the contents of the message.

➤ **Received** This column tells you the date and time the message was received.

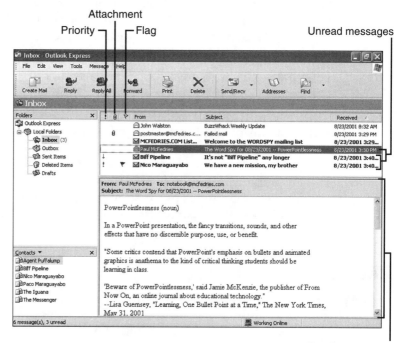

Figure 20.4

After you've pilfered your incoming messages from your ISP, they get stored in your Inbox folder.

Outlook Express offers two methods for seeing what a message has to say:

➤ Highlight the message in the Inbox folder. Outlook Express displays the text of the note in the Preview pane. After about five seconds, Outlook Express removes the bolding from the message to indicate that it has been read.

➤ Highlight the message in the Inbox folder and then double-click it or select **File, Open.** (For the heck of it, you also can press **Ctrl+O** or just **Enter.**) This method opens the message in its own window.

To read other messages, either repeat these procedures or use any of the following Outlook Express techniques:

➤ **To read the previous message in the list**   Select **View, Previous Message.** (**Ctrl+<** works, as well; if you have the message window open, click the **Previous** toolbar button.)

➤ **To read the next message in the list**   Select **View, Next, Next Message.** (**Ctrl+>** also does the job; if you have the message window open, click the **Next** toolbar button.)

➤ **To read the next *unread* message**   Select **View, Next, Next Unread Message** (or press **Ctrl+U**).

➤ **To read the next unread *conversation*** Select **View, Next, Next Unread Conversation** (or press **Ctrl+Shift+U**).

Jargon Jar

A **conversation** is a series of messages with the same subject line. It's also known as a *thread* in e-mail circles.

If you plan on using the Next Unread Conversation command, you first have to group all the messages from the same conversation. To do that, activate the **View, Current View, Group Messages by Conversation** command.

Attending to Attachments

As I mentioned earlier, if you get a message that has one or more files tied to it, you see a paper clip icon in the Inbox folder's Attachment column. You also see a larger paper clip icon in the upper-right corner of the preview pane. Outlook Express gives you a few ways to handle any attachments in the current message:

➤ **Saving the file**   Select **File, Save Attachments** to convince the Save Attachments dialog box to drop by. If there are multiple files, use the **Attachments To Be Saved** list to highlight the ones you want to save. Use the **Save To** text box to specify where you want the files to be stored (click **Browse** to choose the folder from a dialog box). Then click **Save** to dump the file (or files) onto your hard disk.

➤ **Saving the file from the preview pane**   Click the paper clip icon in the upper-right corner of the preview pane to see a list that includes the file name of the attachment. Click **Save Attachments** and follow the steps I just took you through.

➤ **Opening the file**   If you just want to see what's in the file, you can open it. To do that, click the paper clip icon in the upper-right corner of the preview pane, and then click the file name. This gets you to the Open Attachment Warning dialog box. From here, be sure the **Open it** option is activated, and then click **OK**.

Look Out!

Although Outlook Express makes it easy to deal with attachments, you should never just blithely open an attached file. The reason is that the Internet is inundated with rogue messages that carry virus-infected programs as attachments. If you run such a program, it infects your system and then (usually) ships out more copies of itself to people in your Address Book! This is how the famous Melissa virus works. The rule of thumb with attachments is to only open those you receive from people you know and trust. Even then, if a friend unexpectedly sends you a program as an attachment, drop them a quick note to confirm that they really sent it. To be sure that you never accidentally infect your system by opening a virus-laden attachment, select **Tools, Options** and then display the **Security** tab. Activate the **Do not allow attachments to be saved or opened ...** check box. While you're here, you can make your system extra safe by making sure the **Restricted sites zone** option is activated.

What to Do with a Message After You've Read It

This section gives you a rundown of all the things you can do with a message after you've read it. In each case, you either need to have a message highlighted in the Inbox folder, or you need to have the message open. Here's the list:

➤ **Ship out a reply**   If you think of a witty retort, you can e-mail it back to the sender either by selecting **Message, Reply to Sender,** or by clicking the **Reply** toolbar button. (The keyboard route is **Ctrl+R.**)

➤ **Ship out a reply to every recipient** If the note was foisted on several people, you might prefer to send your response to everyone who received the original. To do that, either select **Message, Reply to All,** or click the **Reply All** button. (The keyboard shortcut is **Ctrl+Shift+R.**)

➤ **Forward the message to someone else** To have someone else take a gander at a message you received, you can forward it to her either by selecting **Message, Forward,** or by clicking the **Forward** button. (Keyboard dudes and dudettes can press **Ctrl+F.**)

➤ **Move the message to some other folder** If you find your Inbox folder is getting seriously overcrowded, you should think about moving some messages to other folders. The easiest way to go about this is to drag the message from its current folder and drop it on the other folder in the Folders list. If that's too easy, select **Edit, Move to Folder** (or press **Ctrl+Shift+V**). In the Move dialog box that shows up, highlight the destination folder and then click **OK.** (You can create a new folder by clicking the **New Folder** button, entering a name for the folder in the New Folder dialog box, and then clicking **OK.**)

➤ **Delete the message** If you don't think you have cause to read a message again, you might as well delete it to keep the Inbox clutter to a minimum. To delete a message, either select **Edit, Delete,** or click the **Delete** button. (A message also can be vaporized by pressing **Ctrl+D** or by dragging it to the Deleted Items folder.) Note that Outlook Express doesn't get rid of a deleted message completely. Instead, it just dumps it in the Deleted Items folder. If you later realize that you deleted the message accidentally (insert forehead slap here), you can head for Deleted Items and then move it back into the Inbox.

Windows Wisdom

A forwarded message contains the original message text, which is preceded by an "Original Message" header and some of the message particulars (who sent it, when they sent it, and so on). If you want your recipient to see the message exactly as you received it, use the **Message, Forward As Attachment** command instead.

The Least You Need to Know

➤ **Outlook Express takeoff**   Either select **Start, E-mail** or select **Start, All Programs, Outlook Express.**

➤ **Go to the Inbox**   It's best to launch Outlook Express and go directly to the Inbox folder. To do that, activate the **When Outlook Express starts, go directly to my Inbox folder** check box.

➤ **Composing a message**   Click the **Create Mail** button (or select **Message, New Message**), enter the address and a Subject line, fill in the message body, and then either select **File, Send Message** (if you're online) or **File, Send Later** (if you're offline).

➤ **Receiving messages**   Click the **Send/Recv** button and then click **Receive All** (or select **Tools, Send and Receive, Receive All**).

Chapter 21

More E-Mail Bonding: Extending Outlook Express

In This Chapter

➤ Basic message folder maintenance

➤ Fonts, stationery, signatures, filtering, and other message techniques

➤ Sharing Outlook Express with others by creating separate e-mail identities

If all you're doing is pecking out your missives and then slamming the Send button, you're missing out on some of the most useful and fun features of Outlook Express. In this chapter, you go beyond the previous chapter's basics and learn many of the program's more interesting features and options. I show you how to manage message folders, work with stationery and signatures, create identities, filter incoming messages, and customize all kinds of Outlook Express options, including some crucial security settings.

Taking Charge of Your Message Folders

Right out of the box, Outlook Express comes with five prefab folders: Inbox (incoming messages), Outbox (messages waiting to be sent), Sent Items (messages that you've sent), Deleted Items (messages that you've blown away), and Drafts (saved messages that you're still working on). Surely that's enough folders for anyone, right?

Maybe not. Even if you're good at deleting the detritus from your Inbox folder, it still won't take long before it becomes bloated with messages and finding the note you need becomes a real needle-in-a-haystack exercise. What you really need is a way to organize your mail. For example, suppose you and your boss exchange a lot of e-mail. Rather than storing all her messages in your Inbox folder, you could create a separate folder just for her messages. You could also create folders for each of the Internet mailing lists you subscribe to, for current projects on the go, or for each of your regular e-mail correspondents. There are, in short, 1,001 uses for folders and this section tells you everything you need to know.

To create a new folder, follow these steps:

1. Select the **File, Folder, New** command to display the Create Folder dialog box. (Attention keyboardists: Pressing **Ctrl+Shift+E** also gets you where you want to go.) If the Folder command is unavailable, it means you have the Outlook Express "folder" selected in the Folders list. To unlock this command, first click any other folder (such as Local Folders or Inbox).

2. In the **Select the folder ...** list, highlight the folder within which you want the new folder to appear. For example, if you want your new folder to be inside your inbox, click the Inbox folder.

3. Use the **Folder name** text box to enter the name of the new folder.

4. Click **OK**.

Here's a quick look at a few other folder maintenance chores you may need from time to time:

➤ **Renaming a folder**   The names of the five predefined Outlook Express folders are written in stone, but it's easy to rename any folder that you created yourself. To do so, highlight the folder and then select **File, Folder, Rename**. (Alternatively, press **F2** or click the folder twice, with a pause of a couple of seconds between each click.) In the Rename Folder dialog box, enter the new name and then click **OK**.

Windows Wisdom

You can save yourself a step or two by heading for the Folders list and right-clicking the folder in which you want the new folder to appear. Then click **New Folder,** enter the folder name, and click **OK**.

➤ **Compacting a folder**   To help minimize the size of the files that Outlook Express uses to store messages, you should *compact* the files regularly. To do this, select **File, Folder** and then select either **Compact** (to compact just the currently highlighted folder) or **Compact All Folders** (to compact the whole shooting match). You don't have to worry about this one too much because Outlook Express keeps an eye peeled on your folders and offers to compact them automatically every once in a while.

➤ **Moving a folder**   If you want to move a folder to a different location, the easiest method is to use your mouse to drag the folder and drop it on the new location. (The harder method is to highlight the folder and select **File, Folder, Move.** In the Move dialog box, use the folder tree to highlight the new location for the folder, and then click **OK.**)

➤ **Deleting a folder**   To get rid of a folder you no longer need (and all the messages it contains), highlight the folder and then either drag it to the Deleted Items folder or select **File, Folder, Delete.** (If your mouse is tired, the keyboard alternative is to press the **Delete** key.) Outlook Express then wonders if you're sure about this (note that it doesn't do this if you dragged the folder to Deleted Items). Ponder your next move carefully and, if you still want to go ahead, click **Yes** to delete the folder. (Click **No** if you get cold feet and decide not to nuke the folder.) As with messages, folders that you delete are stuffed into the Deleted Items folder. If you made a horrible mistake by deleting the folder, you can get it back by moving it out of Deleted Items.

Windows Wisdom

You need to compact your folders because when you permanently delete messages, Outlook Express lazily leaves gaps in its files where the messages used to be. Compacting scrunches the files together so that the gaps are eliminated, which makes the files smaller, which saves you disk space. The good news is that this has absolutely no effect on your remaining messages and folders.

Some Handy Message Maneuvers

You spend the bulk of your Outlook Express time shipping out messages to far-flung folks, and reading messages that those folks fire back at you. To help you get the most out of these sending and reading tasks, this section looks at the wide range of message options offered by Outlook Express.

Better E-Letters: Setting the Default Message Font

In Chapter 20, "Sending and Receiving E-Mail Missives," you learned about the difference between plain text messages and rich text (HTML) messages. For the latter, you can use the Formatting toolbar to mess with, among other things, the font in which your typed characters appear. The font controls the typeface, the type style (bold or italic, for example), the type size, and the color.

If you have a particular font combo that you're particularly fond of, you can tell Outlook Express to use it automatically. Here's how:

1. Select **Tools, Options** to invite in the Options dialog box.

2. Click the **Compose** tab.

3. In the **Compose Font** group, click the **Font Settings** button that appears beside the **Mail** heading. This lands you smack dab in the middle of the Font dialog box, which looks suspiciously like the WordPad Font dialog box I showed you back in Chapter 14, "Prose Programs: Windows XP's Writing Tools" (see Figure 14.5).

4. Use the various controls to pick the font options you want, and then click **OK** to get back to the Options dialog box.

5. Click **OK** to put the new settings into effect.

Working with Stationery

In the real world, stationery is paper that includes predefined text, colors, and images. Outlook Express lets you set up the electronic equivalent. That is, you can define e-mail stationery that includes a background image and predefined text. This is essentially a Web page to which you can also add your own text. Outlook Express gives you three choices:

➤ Use any of the Outlook Express predefined stationery designs on an individual message.

➤ Set up a stationery as the default that gets applied to all your outgoing messages.

➤ Create your own stationery.

Let's begin with using one of the built-in stationery patterns on a single message. Outlook Express gives you two ways to do this:

➤ To start a new message using a specific stationery, select **Message, New Message Using** (you can also click the downward-pointing arrow in the **Create Mail** toolbar button). When Outlook Express displays its menu of stationery options (such as Clear Day and Nature), click the one you want to use.

➤ If you've already started a message, you can choose a stationery by selecting the **Format, Apply Stationery** command, and then picking out the stationery you want from the submenu that appears.

Windows Wisdom

Keep in mind that your recipients may not have an e-mail program that understands stationery. In fact, some e-mail programs have been known to choke on messages that are festooned with stationery and other nontext frippery. So if a correspondent complains that he couldn't read your message, resend it without the stationery.

If you find yourself using the same stationery over and over, perhaps it's time to set up that stationery so that Outlook Express applies it automatically whenever you start a new message. Here's what you have to do:

1. In Outlook Express, select **Tools, Options** to request the presence of the Options dialog box.

2. Click the **Compose** tab.

3. In the **Stationery** group, activate the **Mail** check box, and then click the **Select** button to the right of it. Outlook Express reaches into its bag of tricks and pulls out the Select Stationery dialog box.

4. Highlight the stationery file you want to use. (If you're not sure, make certain the **Show preview** check box is activated. This displays a preview of the highlighted stationery in the **Preview** box.)

5. When you've settled on a stationery, click **OK** to return to the Options dialog box.

6. Click **OK.**

Finally, Outlook Express is happy to use a stationery that you create yourself. It even provides a cheerful little wizard to take you through the steps. Here's what happens:

1. In Outlook Express, select **Tools, Options** to request the presence of the Options dialog box.

2. Click the **Compose** tab.

3. In the **Stationery** group, click **Create New.** The Stationery Setup Wizard comes bursting through the door.

4. The initial wizard dialog box just has some not-very-useful introductory material, so click **Next.** The wizard proffers its Background dialog box, shown in Figure 21.1.

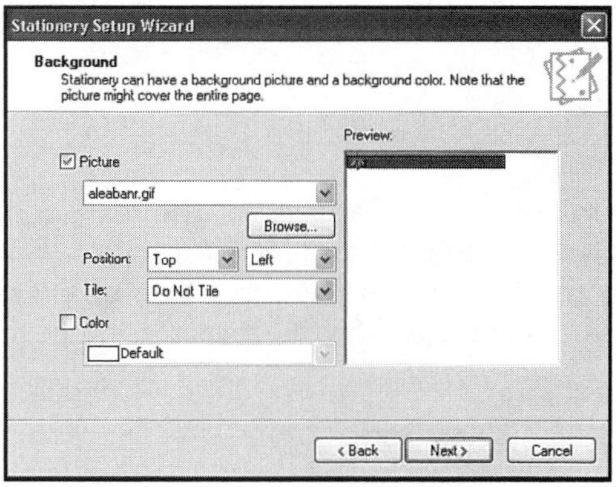

Figure 21.1

Use this wizard dialog box to pick out a background picture or color for your stationery.

5. You have two ways to set the stationery background (when you're done, click **Next**):

   ➤ If you want to use a picture as the background, leave the **Picture** check box activated and use the list box below it to select the picture file you want (or click **Browse** to pick out the picture using a dialog box). Use the two **Position** lists to choose where the picture appears in the stationery, and use the **Tile** list to determine whether the picture appears just once (**Do Not Tile**) or is repeated until it covers the stationery.

   ➤ If you prefer (or also want) to use a solid color as the background, activate the **Color** check box and then use the list below it to choose a color that suits your fancy.

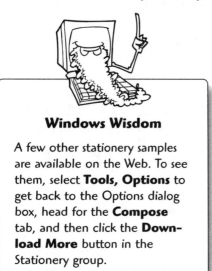

Windows Wisdom

A few other stationery samples are available on the Web. To see them, select **Tools, Options** to get back to the Options dialog box, head for the **Compose** tab, and then click the **Download More** button in the Stationery group.

6. Next up are the stationery fonts. Choose the **Font** (typeface), **Size, Color,** and whether the text is **Bold** and/or **Italic.** Click **Next** to keep things moving.

7. The wizard's to-do list continues with setting the stationery margin widths. The margins determine where in the stationery your typing starts. Use the **Left Margin** spin box to set the distance from the left edge, and use the **Top Margin** spin box to set the distance from the top edge. Click **Next** to continue.

8. In the last of the wizard's dialog boxes, enter a **Name** for your funky new stationery (such as **Funky New Stationery**), and click **Finish** to send the wizard home.

After you've completed your stationery creation, you can use it in your messages just like any other stationery.

Setting Up a Signature

In e-mail lingo, a *signature* is a chunk of text that appears at the bottom of all your messages. Most people use their signature to give contact information, and you often see sigs (that's the hip short form) adorned with witty quotations or sayings. Outlook Express even lets you create multiple signatures, so you can tailor them to various audiences.

Here are the steps to plow through to create a signature or two:

1. Select the **Tools, Options** command.

2. In the Options dialog box that climbs into the ring, display the **Signatures** tab.

3. Click **New.** Outlook Express adds a new item to the Signatures list.

4. Use the **Text** box to compose the signature.

5. Annoyingly, Outlook Express gives each signature a boring name such as Signature #1 (see Figure 21.2). A more meaningful name would be nice, so click the signature in the **Signatures** list, click **Rename,** enter a snappier name, and then press **Enter.**

6. Repeat steps 3 through 5 to create more signatures, if you so desire.

7. If you want Outlook Express to tack on the default signature to all your messages, activate the **Add signatures to all outgoing messages** check box. If you don't want the signature to show up when you reply to a message or forward a message to someone, leave the **Don't add signatures to Replies and Forwards** check box activated.

8. When you're done, click **OK** to return to Outlook Express.

Windows Wisdom

The "default signature" is the first signature you create. To set up some other signature as the default, highlight it in the **Signatures** list, and then click **Set As Default.**

Figure 21.2

Use the Signatures tab to enter one or more signatures.

If you elected not to add your signature automatically, it's easy enough to toss it into a message that you're composing. In the New Message window, move the cursor to where you want the text to appear, and then select **Insert, Signature.** (If you have multiple signatures defined, a submenu with a list of the sigs slides out. Select the one you want to use.)

281

Seven Useful Sending Settings

Let's spend a little more time hanging out in the handy Options dialog box. In this section, I'll take you through a few settings related to sending messages. To see these options, select the **Tools, Options** command and then display the **Send** tab.

Here's a once-over of what's available (click **OK** when you're done):

➤ **Save copy of sent messages in the "Sent Items" folder**   Deactivate this check box to tell Outlook Express not to bother putting copies of your messages in Sent Items. I don't recommend doing this because you'll probably refer to previously sent notes on many an occasion.

➤ **Send messages immediately**   When this option is activated and you're working online, Outlook Express transmits your messages as soon as you send them (unless, of course, you select the Send Later command). If you want Outlook Express to hold its sending horses, deactivate this check box.

➤ **Automatically put people I reply to in my Address Book**   This option is on by default, which is downright silly because it means that every last person to whom you send a reply will get stuffed into your Address Book. That's dumb, so you may want to consider deactivating this one.

➤ **Automatically complete e-mail addresses when composing**   As I mentioned in the previous chapter, after you have some names in your Address Book, you can start typing a name and Outlook Express will "guess" the rest of the name based on the Address Book entries. If you don't like this feature, deactivate this check box to turn it off.

➤ **Include message in reply**   When this option is activated and you reply to a message, Outlook Express adds the original message to your reply message. This is a good idea because it reminds the recipient of what they said, so you should leave this option on.

➤ **Reply to messages using the format in which they were sent**   When this check box is activated, Outlook Express sets up your replies using the same format that the sender used. For example, if you get a plain text message and you reply to it, the reply will automatically be set up as plain text, as well. Again, I recommend leaving this one on.

➤ **Mail Sending Format**   These options determine the default format that Outlook Express uses for your messages. Select either **HTML** or **Plain Text.**

Dealing with the Onslaught: Filtering Messages

It's an unfortunate fact of online life that the e-mail system is the source of many unwanted messages. Whether it's the scourge of unsolicited commercial e-mail (also know whimsically as spam), or someone you've had a falling out with, you inevitably end up getting some messages that you instantly delete.

You can save yourself the bother by setting up Outlook Express to delete these annoyances for you. You can also go beyond this by having Outlook Express look for certain messages and then automatically move them to another folder, send out a reply, flag the messages, and much more.

Let's begin with the most straightforward case: blocking incoming messages from a particular e-mail address. *Blocking* means that any message that comes in from that address is automatically relegated to the Deleted Items folder, so you never see the message. There are two ways to set up the block:

➤ **Block the sender of a message** If you already have a message from the address that you want to block, highlight the message and then select **Message, Block Sender.** Outlook Express displays a dialog box that tells you the address has been added to the "blocked senders list." It also asks whether you want to expunge any other messages from this address that are in the current folder (click **Yes** if you do).

➤ **Block a specified e-mail address** If you don't have an e-mail specimen from the address you want to block, select **Tools, Message Rules, Blocked Senders List.** This displays the Message Rules window with the **Blocked Senders** tab displayed. Click **Add,** enter the **Address** you want to block, and then click **OK.**

If you have a change of heart down the road, you can remove the block by selecting **Tools, Message Rules, Blocked Senders List**, highlighting the address in the **Blocked Senders** tab, and then clicking **Remove.** Click **Yes** when Outlook Express asks you to confirm.

If you need to filter messages based on conditions other than (or in addition to) the e-mail address, or if you want to do something other than just delete a message, then you need to set up *message rules*. These rules tell Outlook Express exactly what to look for (such as specific words in the subject line or message body) and exactly what to do with any messages that meet those conditions (move them to a folder, forward them, and so on).

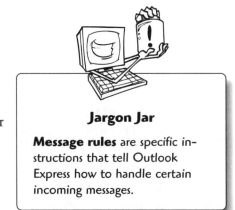

Jargon Jar

Message rules are specific instructions that tell Outlook Express how to handle certain incoming messages.

Here are the steps to follow to set up a message rule:

1. Select the **Tools, Message Rules, Mail** command. Outlook Express relinquishes the New Mail Rule dialog box.

2. In the **Select the Conditions for your rule** list, activate the check box beside a condition that you want to use to single out an incoming message. Outlook Express adds the condition to the Rule Description box.

3. In most cases, the condition includes some underlined text. For example, if you activate the **Where the Subject line contains specific words** condition, the "contains specific words" portion will be underlined, as shown in Figure 21.3. The idea here is that you click the underlined text to specify the exact condition (in this case, a word or two that specifies which subject lines are to be filtered).

Figure 21.3

Most conditions require you to add specific words or addresses.

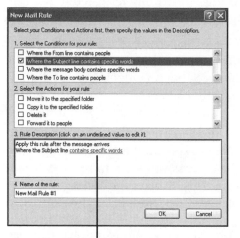

Click the underlined text
to complete the condition

4. Repeat steps 2 and 3 to set up other conditions, if necessary.

5. In the **Select the Actions for your rule** list, activate the check box beside an action you want Outlook Express to perform on the selected messages. Again, Outlook Express adds the action to the Rule Description box.

6. Many actions also have the underlined text, so be sure to click the text to enter a specific value.

7. Repeat steps 5 and 6 to set up other actions, if necessary.

8. Use the **Name of the rule** text box to enter a descriptive name for the rule.

9. Click **OK**. Outlook Express displays the Message Rules dialog box with your new rule shown in the **Mail Rules** tab.

If you're creating a rule based on the address of an existing message, you can save yourself a bit of time by highlighting the message and then selecting **Message, Create Rule from Message.** This displays the New Mail Rule dialog box with the Where the From line contains people condition activated and filled in with the address of the sender.

Sharing Outlook Express with Others: Setting Up Identities

Internet e-mail is such a useful tool that *everyone* wants to get in on the act. That's fine because most ISPs let you set up multiple e-mail accounts, so it's usually not a problem to set up an account for each person in your family or your small office. Sounds good, but what happens if two or more people have to share a single computer? *Nobody* likes having someone else snooping around in their e-mail, so how do you avoid clashes?

There are actually two ways you can go about it:

➤ If you have Windows XP Home, give each person their own user account, which includes the ability to set up Outlook Express with just their own e-mail account. (See Chapter 13, "Avoiding Fistfights While Sharing Your Computer.")

➤ For Windows XP Home or Professional, take advantage of an Outlook Express feature called *identities*. The idea is simple: Each person who uses the computer sets up a distinct identity in Outlook Express. This gives each person his or her own set of folders and settings, and no one sees anyone else's. Each person's identity can be protected with a password to make extra sure that no one pokes around in their stuff.

Creating a New Identity

When you set up your Internet e-mail account, Outlook Express created an identity called, boringly, Main Identity. Here are the steps to follow to set up another identity:

1. Select the **File, Identities, Add New Identity** command. Outlook Express whips out the New Identity dialog box.

2. Use the **Type your name** text box to enter a name for the new identity.

3. If you want the identity protected by a password, activate the **Require a password** check box. In the Enter Password dialog box that materializes, type in the password in both the **New Password** and **Confirm New Password** text boxes, and then click **OK** to return to the New Identity dialog box.

4. Click **OK**.

See Also

Refer to Chapter 20 to go back through the Internet Connection Wizard's mail account setup duties.

5. When Outlook Express asks whether you want to switch to this new identity now, click **Yes.** Outlook Express shuts down and then restarts. Because no account info has been defined for this identity, the Internet Connection Wizard is called in to take down the details.

6. Run through the wizard to define the Internet e-mail account data for the new identity.

Switching From One Identity to Another

After you've set up two or more identities, Outlook Express will always be "logged in" to one of those identities. How do you know which one? Check out the title bar. As shown in Figure 21.4, the name of the current identity appears to the right of "Outlook Express."

Current identity

Figure 21.4

The Outlook Express title bar tells you the name of the currently logged in identity.

To switch to a different identity, follow these steps:

1. Select **File, Switch Identity.** Outlook Express delivers the Switch Identities dialog box.

2. In the list of defined identities, highlight the one you want to use.

3. If the identity is protected by a password, enter it in the **Password** text box.

4. Click **OK.** Outlook Express shuts down and then restarts with the selected identity logged on.

Windows Wisdom

To make changes to your identity, select the **File, Identities, Manage Identities** command. In the Manage Identities dialog box, highlight your identity and click **Properties.**

Logging Off Your Identity

If you exit Outlook Express by selecting the usual **File, Exit** command (or by pressing **Alt+F4** or clicking the window's Close button), the current identity remains logged in. Therefore, the next time you crank up Outlook Express, that identity remains the current one.

Chances are that this isn't what you want. After all, it means that if someone else launches Outlook Express, they start off in your identity. To prevent that from happening, be sure to exit Outlook Express by choosing the **File, Exit and Log Off Identity** command.

Having done that, the next time you or anyone else tries to start Outlook Express, the first thing that shows up is the Identity Login dialog box. From there, you choose your identity, enter a password, if necessary, and then click **OK** to get Outlook Express on-screen.

The Least You Need to Know

➤ **Folder folderol**   Make liberal use of folders to organize your messages. You create new folders by selecting the **File, Folder, New** command (or by pressing **Ctrl+Shift+E**).

➤ **Default fonts and stationery**   If you have fonts or stationery that you use all the time, set them up as the default by selecting **Tools, Options** and displaying the **Compose** tab.

➤ **Blocking boneheads and bores**   To have Outlook Express automatically delete messages from a particular address, highlight one of that person's messages and select **Message, Block Sender.**

➤ **Keeping the e-mail peace**   If you share your computer with other people, set up separate identities for everyone by selecting the **File, Identities, Add New Identity** command.

➤ **Avoiding an identity crisis**   To make sure that no one else accidentally logs in to Outlook Express with your identity, always exit by using the **File, Exit and Log Off Identity** command.

Chapter 22

Spreadin' the News: Participating in Newsgroup Conversations

YAK YAK YAK YAK YAK YAK

In This Chapter

➤ Using Outlook Express to set up your news account

➤ Subscribing to newsgroups

➤ Reading and posting newsgroup messages

If you enjoy the thrust-and-parry of a good conversation, then you'll likely get a kick out of an Internet service called Usenet news (Windows XP just calls it "news") and its associated newsgroups. To understand what newsgroups are all about, think of a newspaper's "Letters to the Editor" section. The newspaper publishes an article or an editorial, and then someone writes to the editor to convey just how shocked and appalled they are. Yet another reader might write to rebut that letter, others might rebut the rebutter, and so on.

That's pretty much a newsgroup in a nutshell. Each one is devoted to a particular topic. People send messages to the newsgroup (this is called *posting* to the group), other people respond to those messages with posts of their own, and so on.

That's not to say, however, that a newsgroup is just one big argument. There's plenty of debating that goes on, to be sure, but a newsgroup also is about sharing information, asking and answering questions, and generally just yakking about whatever topic interests you. And there are *thousands* of these newsgroup things, so there's bound to be *something* that interests you.

However, I don't want to leave you with the impression that newsgroups are so much sweetness and light. Unlike a "Letters to the Editor" section, there's usually no newsgroup "editor" to ensure that messages pass muster. As a result, many newsgroups are a chaotic mass of spam (unsolicited commercial messages), flames (spiteful and insulting posts), and off-topic messages.

Whatever you find out there in newsgroup land, the important thing right now is that you need to know how to access and work with these groups. Besides handling e-mail, Outlook Express doubles as a pretty good *newsreader,* as a program that works with newsgroups is called. This chapter tells you all about the Outlook Express newsreader features.

To get your newsgroups education off on the right foot, I have a newsgroup primer on my Web site that introduces you to some basic concepts and terms. To see it, give the following address a whirl: www.mcfedries.com/Ramblings/usenet-primer.html.

Setting Up a News Account

Your first order of business is to start Outlook Express. (Remember that the quickest route is usually to select **Start, E-mail.**)

After you've done that, follow these steps to set up the news account supplied by your ISP:

1. Select **Tools, Accounts.** Outlook Express slips the Internet Accounts dialog box under the door.

2. Display the **News** tab. If you already see an account listed here, pump your fist and say "Yes!" because it looks like your ISP set one up for you automatically. You have my permission to skip the rest of these steps.

3. Click **Add** and then click **News.** Outlook Express asks the Internet Connection Wizard to make a return engagement. The first wizard dialog box asks you for your display name.

4. Enter your name (you don't have to use your real name if you don't want to), and then click **Next.** The wizard asks for your e-mail address.

5. Enter your e-mail address (again, this is optional) and click **Next.** The wizard mumbles something about an "NNTP" server. This is the name of the computer that your ISP uses to handle newsgroup traffic.

6. Enter the name of the server in the **News (NNTP) Server** text box (your ISP has this information). If you have to sign in to the server, activate the **My news server requires me to log on** check box. Click **Next.**

7. If you told the wizard that you have to log on, use the next dialog box to enter your **Account name** and **Password,** and then click **Next.**

8. In the final wizard dialog box, click **Finish** to return to the Internet Accounts dialog box.

9. Click **Close** to shut down the Internet Accounts dialog box and return to Outlook Express. You're now asked whether you want to download a list of the account's news-groups.

10. Click **Yes** to connect to the Internet and download the newsgroups from the server. Note that, because there are so many groups, this might take quite a while.

When the newsgroup download is done, you're dropped off at the Newsgroup Subscriptions dialog box. You learn more about this dialog box a bit later, so click **Cancel** for now. After you're back in Outlook Express, notice that the Folders tree has grown a new branch, the name of which will be the name of your ISP's news server. Click that "folder" to highlight it. If Outlook Express asks whether you want to view a list of newsgroups, click **No** (you get there in a sec).

Windows Wisdom

I suggest that you don't enter your real e-mail address in step 5. The most popular method that companies use to gather e-mail addresses for spam purposes is to grab them from newsgroup posts. If you still want to give folks the capability to respond to you directly, "munge" your address by adding "NOSPAM" or some other text (for example, *you@yourisp*.com-NOSPAM).

Newsgroup Subscribing and Unsubscribing

The first thing you need to do is subscribe to a newsgroup or two. *Subscribing* means that you add a particular newsgroup to your news account. After you do that, the newsgroup shows up in the Outlook Express Folders list as a subfolder of the news ac-count.

Subscribing to a Newsgroup

Follow these steps to subscribe to a newsgroup:

1. In the Outlook Express Folders list, click the news account name to highlight it.

2. Either select the **Tools, Newsgroups** command, or click the **Newsgroups** toolbar button. (Pressing **Ctrl+W** also works.) You end up at the Newsgroup Subscriptions dialog box.

3. Click the name of the newsgroup you want to subscribe to. To find one you like, the best thing to do is use the **Display newsgroups which contain** text box to enter a word or part of a word that describes the subject you're interested in. In

Windows Wisdom

In the Newsgroup Subscriptions dialog box, two different icons appear beside the newsgroups. An icon that looks like a piece of paper tacked to a folder with a pushpin indicates a subscribed group, whereas an asterisk icon appears beside groups that are new since you last connected. (You can also see the new groups by displaying the **New** tab.)

this case, Outlook Express filters the list to show only those groups that contain the text you entered.

4. With the newsgroup highlighted, you now have two ways to proceed:

➤ **Go to**   Click this button if you just want to have a gander at the newsgroup without committing to a subscription. When you click this button, Outlook Express closes the dialog box.

➤ **Subscribe**   Click this button to subscribe to the newsgroup. Outlook Express adds an icon beside the newsgroup name to remind you that you're subscribed.

5. To continue subscribing, repeat steps 3 and 4 ad nauseam.

6. When you're done, click **OK** to get back to Outlook Express.

Unsubscribing from a Newsgroup

If you get sick and tired of a newsgroup's carryings-on, you can unsubscribe at any time by using either of the following techniques:

➤ In the Newsgroups dialog box, display the **Subscribed** tab, highlight the newsgroup, and then click **Unsubscribe.**

➤ In the Outlook Express window, right-click the newsgroup and then click **Unsubscribe** in the shortcut menu. When Outlook Express asks if you're sure about this, say "Way!" and click **OK.**

Downloading Newsgroup Messages

As I mentioned earlier, subscribing to a newsgroup means the group's name appears as a subfolder of your news account in the Outlook Express Folders list. You're now ready to start reading the group's posts. With Outlook Express, this is a two-stage process:

Step 1. Download the newsgroup's current list of message headers. A header contains only the name of the person who sent the post, the subject line, the date the post was sent, and the size of the post.

Step 2. Choose one or more posts that you want to read and then download the message text for each one.

The next two sections take you through these two steps. Before we get to that, however, you need to understand that Outlook Express operates in two distinctly different modes:

➤ **Online**   Working online means you're logged on to your news account. If you have a full-time connection to the Internet, then you can leave Outlook Express in online mode all the time, which makes things much easier.

➤ **Offline**   Working offline means that you're not logged on to your account. If you connect to the Internet using a modem, then you probably want to minimize your connection time. Outlook Express enables you to do that by letting you go online temporarily to grab just what you need.

You toggle Outlook Express between these two styles by selecting the **File, Work Offline** command. When you see a check mark beside this command, it means that Outlook Express is in offline mode.

Step 1: Downloading the Message Headers

To grab the headers, first use the Outlook Express Folders list to click the name of the newsgroup you want to work with. You now have a couple of ways to proceed:

➤ **If you're working online**   Outlook Express kindly reaches out and takes the group's first 300 headers without further prompting.

➤ **If you're working offline**   In this case, you need to select the **Tools, Get Next 300 Headers** command. When Outlook Express asks you if you want to go online, click **Yes**.

The group may have more than 300 headers. If so, the total remaining to be downloaded appears in the status bar (see Figure 22.1). To get those headers, you have two choices:

➤ If there aren't too many more, repeat the **Tools, Get Next 300 Headers** command as often as necessary.

➤ If there are lots of messages still to come, you can tell Outlook Express to go ahead and download all the remaining headers. Select

Windows Wisdom

You can control the number of headers that Outlook Express downloads at one time. Select **Tools, Options** and display the **Read** tab. Use the **Get x headers at a time** spin box to enter the number of headers you want downloaded each time. (The maximum number is 1,000.)

Tools, **Synchronize Newsgroup** to get on stage with the Synchronize Newsgroup dialog box. Activate the **Get the following items** check box, activate the **Headers only** option, and then click **OK**.

Figure 22.1 shows the Outlook Express window with some downloaded headers.

Click a plus sign
(+) to open a thread

Subscribed groups
appear as subfolders

Mark for
Offline column

Figure 22.1

Outlook Express with a few newsgroup headers downloaded.

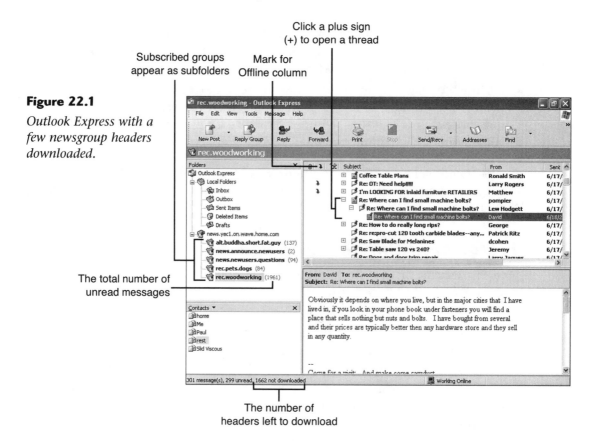

The total number of
unread messages

The number of
headers left to download

Step 2: Downloading the Message Text

As you saw in Figure 22.1, groups such as rec.woodworking often feature a large, intimidating number of messages—in this case, there are nearly 2,000. You can see why Outlook Express downloads only the message headers. If it also took the time to hoist the text of every message onto your system, it could take an hour or two (depending on your connection speed, of course).

So the basic newsgroup modus operandi is to sift through the headers looking for interesting posts and ignoring all the others. (Although, if a group contains only a small number of posts, you may be able to get away with reading everything.) Again, how you do this depends on whether you're working offline or online.

Life is easiest if you're working online. In this case, just click the post you want to read, and Outlook Express dutifully downloads the message text.

If you're working offline, you have to follow these steps:

1. Make sure the newsgroup you want to work with is highlighted in the Folders list.

2. You now need to "mark" which messages you want to download. You have three choices:

   ➤ **To mark a single message** Click beside the header in the Mark for Offline column (pointed out in Figure 22.1). Alternatively, highlight the message and then select **Tools, Mark for Offline, Download Message Later.**

   ➤ **To mark an entire thread** Make sure the thread is closed (that is, it shows a plus sign [+] beside it) and then click beside it in the Mark for Offline column. You can also highlight the first message in the thread and then select **Tools, Mark for Offline, Download Conversation Later.**

   ➤ **To mark every message** Select **Tools, Mark for Offline, Download All Messages Later.**

3. Connect to the Internet.

4. Get Outlook Express online by deactivating the **File, Work Offline** command.

5. To download the marked messages (which are indicated by a downward-pointing blue arrow), select the **Tools, Synchronize Newsgroup** command. The Synchronize Newsgroup dialog box books in.

6. Make sure the **Get messages marked for download** check box is activated, and then click **OK.** Outlook Express displays a dialog box that shows you the progress of the message download.

7. Put Outlook Express offline by activating the **File, Work Offline** command.

8. Disconnect from the Internet.

Windows Wisdom

If you change your mind about a marked message, you can un-mark it by clicking the arrow in the Mark for Offline column, or by highlighting it and then selecting **Tools, Mark for Offline, Do Not Download Message.**

At this point, the newsgroup becomes more or less like the Inbox folder. This means you can read any downloaded message just by highlighting it and viewing the text in the preview pane. (You also can double-click the message to open it.) Note, too, that Outlook Express organizes all the newsgroup messages by thread. That's why you see some messages with plus signs (+) beside them. Clicking the plus sign "opens" the thread so that you can see the other messages.

Posting a Message to a Newsgroup

When you think you're ready to delurk and post something yourself, Outlook Express gives you a few ways to do it:

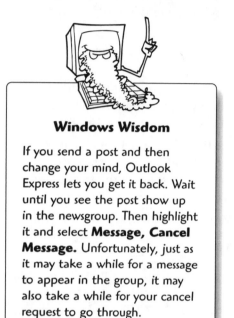

Windows Wisdom

If you send a post and then change your mind, Outlook Express lets you get it back. Wait until you see the post show up in the newsgroup. Then highlight it and select **Message, Cancel Message.** Unfortunately, just as it may take a while for a message to appear in the group, it may also take a while for your cancel request to go through.

➤ **Send a response to the newsgroup**   Click the original message to highlight it, and then either select **Message, Reply to Group** or click the **Reply Group** toolbar button. (Keyboard connoisseurs might prefer to press **Ctrl+G**.)

➤ **Send a response to the message author only**   If you prefer that your response goes only to the author of a message (via e-mail), click the message and then either select **Message, Reply to Sender** or click the **Reply** button. (**Ctrl+R** is the way to go from the keyboard.) Remember that many people monkey with their e-mail address to avoid spam, so double-check the address before sending your response.

➤ **Send a response to the newsgroup and the author**   Click the message and then select **Message, Reply to All.** (Pressing **Ctrl+Shift+R** also gets the job done.)

➤ **Sending a new message**   Either select **Message, New Message** or click the **New Post** button. (You also can press **Ctrl+N**.)

The Least You Need to Know

➤ **Creating a news account**   In Outlook Express, select **Tools, Accounts** and then click **Add, News.**

➤ **Offline/online**   Modem users toggle Outlook Express between offline mode and online mode by selecting the **File, Work Offline** command.

➤ **Subscribing to a newsgroup**   Select **Tools, Newsgroups** (or click the **Newsgroups** button), highlight the group, and then click **Subscribe.**

➤ **Reading a newsgroup**   First download the group's headers and then download the text of the messages you want to read.

Chapter 23

Using Windows Messenger to Fire Off Instant Messages

The last few chapters have focused on conversation, an art that many a parlor-sitting pundit had thought was lost. Of course, the techniques we looked at—e-mail and newsgroups—don't offer the back-and-forth, give-and-take, repartee that you usually associate with the word *conversation*. In both cases, the lag time between message and reply—between post and riposte, if you will—is just too long. Sure, it may be as little as a few minutes, but it doesn't take someone a few minutes to chime in during a *real* conversation.

So if what you're pining for is a good old-fashioned chinwag (and that low-tech bastion of banter, the telephone, isn't available), then the Internet and Windows XP can help. Together, they offer a great way to start up a true conversation with someone: instant messages. I talk about how to send and receive them in this chapter.

What's All This About "Instant Messaging"?

The Internet, once a craze itself, now goes through its own internal crazes. Java applets (mini-programs that run inside Web pages) were big for a while; portals (everything-including-the-kitchen-sink Web sites) were all the rage for a time; and MP3s (music files) continue to generate frenzies among certain copyright-challenged elements of the population.

The big craze nowadays is something called *instant messaging* (usually abbreviated as IM by those in the know). Millions of people use it, and it has been estimated that nearly 200 million Netizens will be doing the instant messaging thing by 2002.

What's the big whoop? It's the real-time conversation hook. If someone sees that you're online (there's special software that lets them know), they compose a quick note, ship it, and it pops up on your screen instantly (well, a few seconds later, anyway). You can then dash off a response, and it gets delivered immediately to your correspondent. Repeat to taste and voilà: an instant conversation.

Who's using instant messaging? At first, it seemed to be mostly those all-time champs of the gabfest world: teenagers. Now, however, many businesses have seen the benefits of instant messages, so they're jumping aboard, as well. And the simple fact that Microsoft chose to include its own instant messaging software—called Windows Messenger—in Windows XP tells you that this thing is getting pretty big. The next few sections show you how to set up and use Windows Messenger.

Windows Wisdom

Just so you know, Windows Messenger is the newfangled replacement for Microsoft's old instant messaging program: MSN Messenger. Also, Windows Messenger isn't the only IM game in town. The most famous service is called ICQ ("I seek you"), and it can be found at www.icq.com. Note, however, that America Online (AOL) now owns ICQ, so its fate has to be considered up in the air. That's because AOL has its own IM service called AOL Instant Messenger (if you're a member, the keyword is AIM). The other major IM service is Yahoo! Messenger, which can be found at www.yahoo.com.

Setting Up Windows Messenger

Getting Windows Messenger fit for active duty doesn't take much effort on your part. Keep in mind, however, that to use Windows Messenger you need to have a *Passport,* which is a Microsoft invention that enables you to quickly log in to Web sites that use the Passport technology. (These Passports sound a bit ominous, I know, but they'll come in handy in a few years when Microsoft owns the planet.) A Passport is tied to an e-mail account, but it has to be an account that's associated with Microsoft, meaning it has to be a hotmail.com, msn.com, or passport.com account.

Here's what you have to do:

1. Select **Start, All Programs, Windows Messenger.** The Windows Messenger window lands on the desktop with an inaudible thud.

2. Click the **Click here to sign in** link. The .NET Passport Wizard flies in.

3. The opening wizard window just offers an overview of what a passport is, so click **Next** to move along. You now come to a fork in the wizard's road, and the path you take depends on whether you have a Microsoft e-mail account (click **Next** when you're done):

   ➤ **Yes, use an existing e-mail account**   Activate this option if you already have an account with Hotmail, MSN, or Passport.com.

   ➤ **No, create a new free e-mail account for my default Windows Passport** Activate this option if you don't have a Microsoft e-mail account. Clicking Next launches Internet Explorer and takes you to the Hotmail site where you can register for an account. Follow the instructions on the page. When you're done, close Internet Explorer, return to the wizard, and click **Next.**

4. Use the **E-mail address or Passport** text box to enter your Microsoft e-mail address and then click **Next.**

5. Now the wizard asks for your **Password.** If you don't want to have to enter this info every time you log on to the Windows Messenger service, be sure to activate the **Sign me in automatically on this computer** check box. Click **Next** to keep on keeping on.

6. In the final wizard dialog box, click **Finish** to put a cap on things.

You might see a message slide up from the taskbar's notification area telling you that you have a "new message in your Hotmail Inbox." This is just a welcome message that's sent out automatically to all new Hotmail users, so don't get too excited. If you want to see the message, click the **1 new e-mail message** link in the Windows Messenger window.

Unfortunately, you can't do anything useful in the Windows Messenger window unless you're signed in to the service. Therefore, you need to connect to the Internet and sign in to perform any of the tasks described in the next few sections.

At this point, the Windows Messenger Service window sets up camp on the desktop and signs you in to the Windows Messenger service. Figure 23.1 shows you the initial window.

Figure 23.1

The Windows Messenger Service window as it looks when it first shows its face.

Friends, Romans, Countrymen: Adding Contacts

The heart and soul of Windows Messenger is the *contacts list,* which is the list of the lucky folks to whom you want to send your instant messages. (And who, of course, will be lobbing instant messages your way.)

So on your metaphorical Windows Messenger to-do list, job number one is add one or more contacts. Here's how:

1. Click the **Add** button or select **File, Add a Contact.** The Add a Contact wizard comes marching by.

Jargon Jar

The **contacts list** is the roster of people with whom you want to exchange instant messages. In some circles (particularly AOL), this is known as a "buddy list."

2. How you proceed from here depends on what you know about the would-be contact:

   ➤ **If you know the person's e-mail address or Passport sign-in name** Activate the **By e-mail address or sign-in name** option and click **Next.** Then enter the contact's e-mail address and click **Next.**

   ➤ **If you know only the person's name** Activate the **Search for a contact** option and click **Next.** Then enter the person's **First Name** and **Last Name** (you can also specify the **City** or **State** if the person is in the United States) and click **Next.** If you get any matches, click the person you want and then click **Next.**

3. In each case, the wizard then offers to send an e-mail message to the potential contact to explain to them how to install Windows Messenger. If you know that the other person already uses the program, click **Next;** otherwise, click **Send Mail.**

4. To add more contacts, click **Next** and then repeat steps 2 and 3 until you're done.

5. Click **Finish** to exit the wizard.

As you can see in Figure 23.2, the Windows Messenger window now lists your contacts, and groups them according to whether each person is online (that is, logged on to the Windows Messenger service) or not. Note, too, that you also see the current status of the online folks.

To get someone off your contacts list, click his name and then select **File, Delete Contact.** (You can also right-click his name and then click **Delete Contact.**)

What happens when someone else adds you to *her* contacts list? If you're logged on to the Windows Messenger service (or the next time you log on), you see a dialog box similar to the one shown in Figure 23.3. If this is okay with you, make sure the **Allow this person ...** option is activated. You probably also want to leave the **Add this person to my contact list** check box activated. If this is just some stranger that you want to shun, activate the **Block this person ...** option, instead (or you can block them later if you're unsure). Click **OK** to get rid of the dialog box.

Windows Wisdom

When you don't want to be bothered with any incoming messages, Windows Messenger offers various "Do Not Disturb" signs that you can "hang." To choose one, select **File, Status** and then choose an item (such as Busy or Out to Lunch). If you really want to make sure you're not disturbed, either log off (select **File, Log off**) or choose the **Appear Offline** status.

Figure 23.2

Windows Messenger segregates contacts into two classes: online and not online.

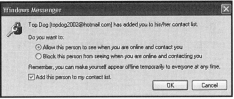

Figure 23.3

This dialog box shows up if someone adds you to her contacts list.

If someone on your contacts list is behaving badly, tell Windows Messenger to prevent them from sending you messages or even seeing your online status. To do that, select **Tools, Options.** In the Options dialog box, display the **Privacy** tab, highlight

Windows Wisdom

Instant messages are meant to be short notes and not story-length essays. To keep things that way, Windows Messenger decrees the maximum message size to be only 400 characters.

Look Out!

When you first open the Instant Message window, it displays a message warning you not to send your password or credit card number in an instant message. Good advice! Messages get shipped out over the cyber air-waves in plain sight, making it relatively easy for someone with the right equipment to monitor traffic looking for telltale words and phrases (such as "password" and "credit card").

the contact's name in the **My Allow List**, and click **Block**. This tosses the boor into the purgatory of the **My Block List**.

Doing the Messaging Thing: Sending an Instant Message

With your contacts list on the go, it's time to do some actual contacting. You have two ways to get started:

➤ Click **Send** and then click the name of the on-line contact you want to converse with, or se-lect **Tools, Send an Instant Message** and then select the contact from the menu that pops out.

➤ In the online contacts list, right-click the person you want to parley with, and then click **Send an Instant Message**.

Either way, Windows Messenger drags the Conver-sation window out into the open. Your instant mes-sage conversation now proceeds as follows:

1. In the message box at the bottom of the win-dow (see Figure 23.4), type in the message you want to ship out.

2. Click **Send** or press **Enter**. The message wings its way to the contact and is also added to the conversation box that takes up the bulk of the window (again, see Figure 23.4).

3. When (or perhaps I should say if) the contact responds, his text appears in the conversation box below your message for your reading pleas-ure.

4. Repeat steps 2 and 3 to get a full-fledged con-versation going. Figure 23.4 shows an example.

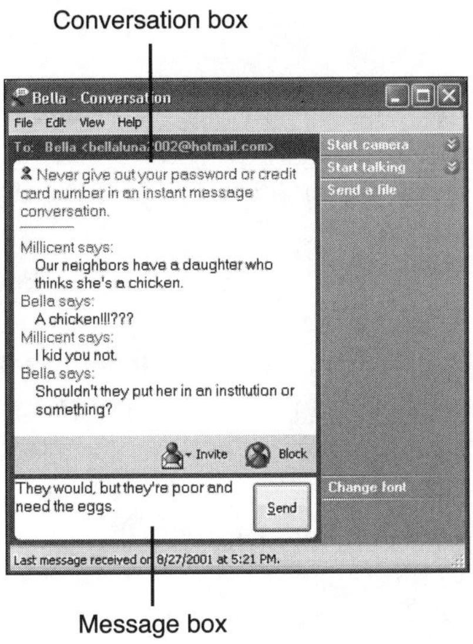

Conversation box

Bella - Conversation
File Edit View Help
To: Bella <bellaluna:002@hotmail.com>
👤 Never give out your password or credit
card number in an instant message
conversation.

Millicent says:
    Our neighbors have a daughter who
    thinks she's a chicken.
Bella says:
    A chicken!!!???
Millicent says:
    I kid you not.
Bella says:
    Shouldn't they put her in an institution or
    something?

👤▾ Invite   🚫 Block

They would, but they're poor and
need the eggs.   Send

Last message received on 8/27/2001 at 5:21 PM.

Start camera
Start talking
Send a file

Change font

Message box

Figure 23.4

An example of a Windows Messenger conversation in progress.

Here are a few notes to bear in mind when playing around in the Conversation window:

➤ If you want someone else to join the fun, click **Invite, To Join This Conversation** and then click the contact name. (Alternatively, select **File, Invite, To Join This Conversation,** and then select the contact.)

➤ If the person turns out to be a goofball, you can prevent him from continuing the conversation by clicking the **Block** button. If you're chatting with two or more people, you're presented with a list of their names, so you need to click the name of the person you want to block.

➤ To change the size of the conversation text, select **View, Text Size** and then select one of the relative sizes from the submenu.

➤ For even more control over the conversation text, click **Change font** and then use the dialog box that comes in to change the typeface, style, size, and the other usual font suspects.

➤ If you end up with some particularly witty repartee, you can save it for posterity by

Look Out!

Heed the virus warning displayed by Windows Messenger. If you don't know the sender of the file, don't accept it; if you do know the sender, don't assume the file is virus-free (it may be infected without the sender knowing it). After the file is transferred to your computer, fire up your anti-virus program and check the file to make sure it doesn't contain anything nasty.

selecting the **File, Save** command. Use the Save As dialog box to save the conversation to a text file.

➤ Windows Messenger can also send entire files instead of simple text blurbs. To send a file, select **File, Send a File.** (If you're talking to two or more folks, select **File, Send a File to,** and then select the contact name. Use the dialog box that shows up to highlight the file, and then click **Open.**)

➤ When a contact sends you a file, Windows Messenger lets you know the file's name, size, and approximate transfer time (for a 28.8Kbps connection), and asks whether you want to proceed. Click **Accept** (or press **Alt+T**) to take delivery of the file, or click **Decline** (or press **Alt+D**) to pass. If you chose to accept the file, Windows Messenger will then warn you that some files contain viruses. Click **OK** to proceed with the transfer.

➤ When you're talked (or typed) out, select **File, Close.** If there are only two of you in the conversation, Windows Messenger shuts down the Conversation window without further ado. However, if there are three or more yakkers, the program presents you with an ambiguous dialog box that tells you that you won't receive future instant messages "from this session." This just means you won't get any more messages from the conversation, so it's okay to click **OK.**

Some Useful Windows Messenger Options

Windows Messenger works pretty good as is, but it comes with a few options that enable you to tweak the program to suit your style. To eyeball these options, select the **Tools, Options** command to get together with the Options dialog box.

The **Personal** tab has four sections:

➤ **My Display Name**   Use this text box to specify the name that your online buddies see when they have you in their contacts list or when you're in conversation with them.

➤ **My Password**   Activate this check box to tell Windows to always prompt you for a password when you're using Hotmail or a Passport service. This is a good idea if other people use your computer and you don't want them signing in to these services automatically.

➤ **My Message Text**   Click **Change Font** to adjust the font particulars for the Conversation window. If you leave the **Show graphics (emoticons) in instant messages** check box activated, you can type certain characters—such as :-)—and Windows Messenger will replace them with a graphic character—such as ☺. Figure 23.5 shows a couple of dozen emoticons on the left and their text equivalents on the right. See the Windows Messenger Help system for the complete list of these graphic dinguses.

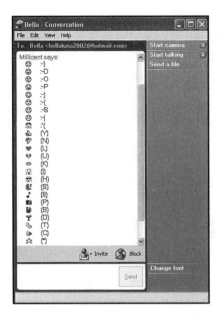

Figure 23.5

This composite image shows you a few of the emoticons, as well as the text you have to type to display them.

The **Preferences** tab offers a bunch of options for you to play with:

➤ **Run this program when Windows starts**   If you leave this check box activated, Windows Messenger runs automatically each time you start Windows XP. (You won't see the Windows Messenger window, however. Instead, you just see the Windows Messenger icon in the taskbar's notification area. To open the window, double-click the icon.) If you have a direct connection to the Internet, you'll also be signed in to the Windows Messenger service.

➤ **Allow this program to run in the background**   If you leave this check box activated, Windows Messenger continues to run behind the scenes after you close the window. This is handy if you want the program to alert you when a contact comes online or when you receive an instant message.

➤ **Show me as "Away" when I'm inactive for *x* minutes**   If you leave this check box activated, you can use the text box to specify the number of minutes after which Windows Messenger will change your status from Online to Away. The default value of 5 minutes seems awfully short to me, so you might consider increasing the value or deactivating this check box altogether.

➤ **Display alerts near the taskbar when contacts come online**   Leave this check box activated to have Windows Messenger display an alert above the notification area when someone in your contacts list comes online.

➤ **Display alerts near the taskbar when an instant message is received**   Leave this check box activated to have Windows Messenger display an alert above the notification area when you get an instant message.

305

➤ **Play sound when contacts sign in or send a message**   Leave this check box activated to have Windows Messenger play a short sound snippet when contacts come online or send you something.

➤ **Files received from other users will be put in this folder**   Use this text box (or the **Browse** button) to specify where the files that are shipped to you via Windows Messenger are stored. The default is My Received Files, which is a sub-folder of My Documents.

Windows Messenger and Outlook Express

It's not obvious at first, but Windows Messenger and Outlook Express are in cahoots and have been cavorting together behind your back. Here are a few things you should know about the relationship between these two conversation cousins:

➤ Your Windows Messenger contacts list also appears in the Outlook Express window. The next time you run Outlook Express, look for the **Contacts** box just below the Folders list.

➤ When you run Outlook Express, it automatically signs you in to the Windows Messenger service. If you prefer to control the sign-in yourself, select the Outlook Express **Tools, Options** command and, in the **General** tab of the Options dialog box, deactivate the **Automatically log on to Windows Messenger** check box.

➤ You can control some Windows Messenger settings from Outlook Express. Select the **Tools, Windows Messenger** command, and a submenu slides out that gives you commands to send an instant message, log on or off the service, change options, or add a contact. You can also change your Windows Messenger status by selecting the **Tools, My Online Status** command.

In other words, after you have your Windows Messenger service particulars set up, you can do almost all your instant messaging chores from the friendly confines of Outlook Express.

The Least You Need to Know

➤ **Passport, please**   To use the Windows Messenger service, you need a Microsoft Passport, which you get by signing up for a Hotmail e-mail account.

➤ **Add some contacts, first**   You can't do much of anything in Windows Messenger until you add a contact or three by clicking the **Add** button or by selecting **File, Add a Contact.**

➤ **Becoming status conscious**   To control your Windows Messenger status, select **File, My Status** and then choose one of the items in the menu that slides out.

➤ **Blocking boobs and rubes**   To block a person in a conversation, click the **Block** button. To shun this person permanently, select **Tools, Options,** display the **Privacy** tab, highlight his name in the **My Allow List,** and then click **Block.**

➤ **Instant safety**   When participating in an instant message conversation, never divulge your credit card number, a password, or any other sensitive data. Also, when you receive a file, run it through your anti-virus program before opening it.

Part 5

Windows XP at the Shop: Customizing, Maintaining, and Troubleshooting

In these media-saturated times, quoting media guru Marshall McCluhan has become the ultimate badge of the so-hip-it-hurts set. Always happy to jump on a passing bandwagon, I hereby offer this book's token McLuhanism: "The mark of our time is its revulsion against imposed patterns." This shameless name- and quote-dropping is meant not to impress, but to introduce the main theme of Part 5: customizing Windows XP. The out-of-the-shrink-wrap look and feel of Windows XP certainly qualifies as an "imposed pattern," and it was designed by Microsoft to be suitable for what they consider to be a typical user. However, if the notion of being "typical" fills you with fear and loathing, then you've come to the right place because the four chapters coming up will show you how to refurbish Windows XP to suit your tastes and the way you work. This part of the book also proffers a few pointers on keeping Windows running smoothly and on fixing problems that crop up.

Chapter 24

Refurbishing the Desktop

In This Chapter

➤ Messing with desktop wallpaper and patterns

➤ Redoing the desktop colors and fonts

➤ Adding icons and Web items to the desktop

➤ Monkeying around with the display's screen resolution and colors

---

For most of its history, the PC has maintained a staid, nay, *dull* exterior. Fortunately, the Nuthin'-But-Beige school has given way in recent years to some almost-stylish machines cavorting in gunmetal gray or shiny black exteriors. And with the Apple iMac available in several different psychedelic shades, it's likely that colorful machines will become the norm before too long.

That's a good thing because lots of people don't like the same old same old. These rugged individualists want to express themselves and that's hard to do with beige. The same goes for the Windows XP desktop. Sure, the standard Windows desktop is pleasant enough, but maybe you prefer a different scene or even a solid color. If so, Windows XP offers plenty of ways to make your mark with a custom desktop color or background.

Yo, Geek Boy! Changing the desktop sounds great and everything, but most of the time I can't even see it. Isn't all this just a waste of time?

Hey, who're you calling a geek? It's actually not a waste of time because many of the changes you make to the desktop apply to Windows XP as a whole. For example, you can change the colors of window titles and borders, alter the font used in the taskbar, and change the overall size of the screen area. You'll learn all about these and many more customization options in this chapter.

Every last one of these customizations take place within the friendly confines of the Display Properties dialog box. To get this dialog box on the desktop, use either of the following techniques:

➤ Right-click an empty section of the desktop and then click **Properties** in the shortcut menu.

➤ Select **Start, Control Panel, Appearance and Themes, Display.**

Changing the Desktop Background

It's true that the desktop is usually hidden, particularly if, like me, you prefer to run your programs maximized. Still, there are plenty of times when the desktop is visible, such as at startup and when you close your programs. If that's enough of an excuse for you to tweak the look of the desktop, then you'll enjoy this section where I show you how to change the desktop background or color.

Windows Wisdom

Windows XP's list of approved images isn't the only wallpaper game in town. There's no problem using some other image if that's what you'd prefer. To do this, click the **Browse** button to promote the Browse dialog box, find and highlight the image file, and then click **Open.**

Wallpapering the Desktop

Wallpaper is an image or design that replaces the desktop's default solid color background. (Before you ask, no, I'm not sure why Microsoft calls it "wallpaper" when you're supposed to be thinking that your screen is like the top of a desk. It's either a mixed metaphor or the Microsoft offices have a *very* strange interior designer.) You can choose one of the prefab wallpapers that come with Windows XP, or you can easily create your own. Let's start with the simplest case of picking out one of the predefined wallpapers:

1. In the Display Properties dialog box, open the **Desktop** tab.

2. Use the **Background** list to click one of the image names. Keep one eye peeled on the fake monitor above the list. This gives you a preview of what the wallpaper will look like. (Some of the images take a second or two to show up, so patience is required.)

3. Use the **Position** list to select one of the following values:

> ➤ **Center**   Displays a single copy of the image in the center of the screen. This is a good choice for large images.

> ➤ **Tile**   Displays multiple copies of the image repeated so they fill the entire desktop. Choose this option for small image.

> ➤ **Stretch**   Displays a single copy of the image extended on all sides so it fills the entire desktop. This is the one to use if the image almost fills the desktop.

4. Click **OK** to put the wallpaper into effect. (You also can click **Apply** if you'd prefer to leave the Display Properties dialog box open and ready for action—for example, if you want to change the wallpaper again after seeing it full-screen.)

Image Is Nothing: Setting the Desktop to a Solid Color

If you find that using an image as the desktop background makes things too "busy," you can tone everything down a few notches by using a solid color instead. Here's how:

1. In the Display Properties dialog box, make sure the **Desktop** tab is displayed.

2. In the **Background** list, select **(None)**.

3. Click the downward-pointing arrow on the right side of the **Color** button. Windows XP spreads out a grid of color boxes, which is known in the trade as a color *palette*.

4. Each of the 20 boxes represents a color. Click the box that represents the color you want to see on the desktop.

You might have noticed that the **Color** palette has a button named Other. You can use this option to pick a different color from those in the standard palette, or you can create your own color. When you click the **Other** button, you see the Color dialog box, shown in Figure 24.1.

The **Basic colors** area boasts 48 colors. To choose one of them, click its box, then click **OK.**

To roll your own color, you can use one of two methods. The first method uses the fact that you can create any color in the spectrum by mixing the three primary colors: red, green, and blue. The Color dialog box lets you enter specific numbers between 0 and 255 for each of these colors, by using the **Red**, **Green**, and **Blue** text boxes. A lower number means the color is less intense, and a higher number means the color is more intense.

To give you some idea of how this works, the following table lists eight common colors and their respective red, green, and blue numbers.

Figure 24.1

Use this dialog box to choose or create a different color.

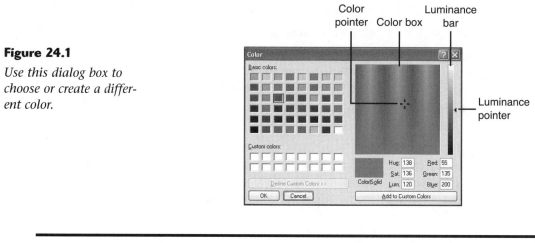

The following labels appear with the figure: Color pointer, Color box, Luminance bar, Luminance pointer.

Color	Red	Green	Blue
Black	0	0	0
White	255	255	255
Red	255	0	0
Green	0	255	0
Blue	0	0	255
Yellow	255	255	0
Magenta	255	0	255
Cyan	0	255	255

The second method for selecting colors involves setting three attributes—hue, saturation, and luminance:

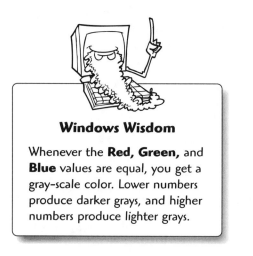

Windows Wisdom

Whenever the **Red, Green,** and **Blue** values are equal, you get a gray-scale color. Lower numbers produce darker grays, and higher numbers produce lighter grays.

➤ **Hue** This number (which is more or less equivalent to the term *color*) measures the position on the color spectrum. Lower numbers indicate a position near the red end, and higher numbers move through the yellow, green, blue, and violet parts of the spectrum. As you increase the hue, the color pointer (refer to Figure 24.1) moves from left to right.

➤ **Sat** This number is a measure of the purity of a given hue. A saturation setting of 240 indicates that the hue is a pure color. Lower numbers indicate that more gray is mixed with the hue until, at 0, the color becomes part of the

314

gray scale. As you increase the saturation, the color pointer moves toward the top of the color box.

➤ **Lum**   This number is a measure of the brightness of a color. Lower numbers are darker, and higher numbers are brighter. The luminance bar to the right of the color box shows the luminance scale for the selected color. As you increase the luminance, the pointer moves toward the top of the bar.

To create a custom color, you can either enter values in the text boxes, as just described, or you can use the mouse to click inside the color box and luminance bar. The **Color|Solid** box shows the selected color on the left and the nearest solid color on the right (these two colors should be identical on your system). If you think you'll want to reuse the color down the road, click the **Add to Custom Colors** button to place the color in one of the boxes in the **Custom colors** area. When you're done, click **OK**.

Adding Desktop Items

If you used any previous version of Windows, probably the first thing you noticed when you first saw Windows XP was the almost total absence of stuff on the desktop. One measly icon—the Recycle Bin—is all the Windows XP desktop has to show for itself. Gone are the old standbys such as the My Computer icon and the Internet Explorer icon. This was a conscious design choice on Microsoft's part because they'd prefer that you make the Start menu your Windows starting point.

However, if you miss having a satisfyingly cluttered desktop, there's nothing to stop you from tossing as many shortcuts on there as you like. Windows XP can even help out by letting you add *desktop items,* which are icons (program or document shortcuts) and *Web items* (Web pages or other Web knickknacks). The next few sections take you through these desktop shenanigans.

Adding and Customizing Desktop Icons

To get started with desktop items, click the **Customize Desktop** button in the **Desktop** tab of the Display Properties dialog box. In the Desktop Items dialog box that jumps aboard, the General tab is where you deal with Windows XP's built-in desktop icons.

Windows Wisdom

Windows XP also enables you to move and sort your desktop icons. Either with your mouse or by right-clicking the desktop, clicking **Arrange Icons By,** and then clicking a sort order: **Name, Type, Size,** or **Modified** (that is, by date). Felix Unger types can keep things in apple-pie order all the time by activating the **Auto Arrange** command and the **Align to Grid** command.

There are two sections to try out:

➤ **Desktop icons**   Use the check boxes to add icons such as **My Documents** and **My Computer** to the desktop. If you want to change the icon displayed by Windows XP, highlight it in the list and then click **Change Icon** (see the following section, "Changing an Icon").

➤ **NEW!**   **Desktop cleanup**   Windows XP has a new feature called the Desktop Cleanup Wizard that can remove desktop icons you haven't used in a while and put them into another folder (called Unused Desktop Shortcuts). This is a good idea, so you should probably leave the **Run Desktop Cleanup Wizard every 60 days** check box activated. Note that you can run the wizard any time you feel like by clicking the **Clean Desktop Now** button.

Changing an Icon

In several places throughout this book (including the previous section), you learn how to customize an object by changing its icon. How you get started depends on the object you're working with. However, in all cases you eventually end up at the Change Icon dialog box shown in Figure 24.2.

Here are some notes about working with this dialog box:

Figure 24.2

The Change Icon dialog box lists the icons that are available in an executable or icon file.

➤ In Windows XP, icons are usually stored in groups within executable files, particularly .exe and .dll files. Files with the .ico extension are pure icon files.

➤ If the icon you want isn't displayed in the Change Icon dialog box, use the **Look for icons in this file** text box to enter the name of an icon file, and then press Tab. Here are a few suggestions (change C:\windows if your version of Windows XP is installed in a different drive or folder):

C:\windows\system32\shell32.dll

C:\windows\system32\Pifmgr.dll

C:\windows\explorer.exe

➤ If you're not sure about which file to try, click the Browse button and choose a file in the dialog box that appears.

➤ Click the icon you want to use, then click **OK.**

Web Items: Your Desktop as a Web Page

The standard desktop backgrounds and colors are fine as far as they go, but they lack that element of interactivity that folks exposed to the World Wide Web have come to expect. If you're one of those folks, then I'm sure you'll get a kick out of Windows XP's Web items. This variation on the desktop theme enables you to populate your desktop with stuff normally seen in Web pages or even with an entire Web page.

To try this out, open the Desktop Items dialog box and display the **Web** tab. The **Web pages** list shows the Web items you can display on your desktop. At first, you have only **My Current Home Page**, which is the home page defined in Internet Explorer. If you activate this item's check box, click **OK,** and then click **Apply,** the desktop suddenly turns into an actual Web page with live links and everything. Note, however, that you can't really "surf" the desktop. If you click a link, Windows XP runs Internet Explorer to fetch the page.

That's pretty slick, but you also can talk Windows XP into displaying a different Web page or other Web page content. Here's how:

1. In the **Web** tab, click **New.** Windows XP coughs up the New Desktop Item dialog box.

2. There are two paths you can take from here:

    ➤ **Visit Gallery** Click this button to launch Internet Explorer and head for Microsoft's Desktop Gallery. This is a Web page that offers quite a few items that you can add to your system. Click the **Add to Active Desktop** button that sits by the item you want. When Internet Explorer asks whether you're sure about all this, click **Yes.**

Windows Wisdom

Rather than making do with Windows XP's built-in icons, you might prefer to use your own, either by editing existing icons or by creating icons from scratch. There are a number of decent icon-creation programs available. The ones I like are IconEdit Pro, IconForge, and Icon Easel (all available from www.zdnet.com/downloads).

➤ **Location** Use this text box to enter the address of a Web page. This can be the full URL of a page on the Web, or the location of an HTML file on your hard disk or your network. (If you're not sure about the location of a non-Web item, click **Browse** to use the Browse dialog box to find it.)

3. Whichever method you use, you eventually end up at the Add item to Active Desktop dialog box. Click **OK**. Windows XP downloads the content and adds the item to the desktop.

4. If you went the Location route, you'll be dropped back in the Web tab. Click **OK** or **Apply.**

The nice thing about Web items is that they can be moved and sized as required. Here's a review of the techniques to use:

➤ **To move an item** First move the mouse pointer over the item. This gets you a border around the item. Now drag any border.

➤ **To resize an item** Move the mouse pointer over the top border. After a couple of seconds, you get a larger bar across the top of the item, as shown in Figure 24.3. Drag this bar to move the item.

➤ **To maximize an item** Click the Cover Desktop button.

➤ **To maximize an item without affecting the desktop icons** Click the Split Desktop with Icons button.

➤ **To close an item** Click the Close button.

Move the mouse pointer over
the top border to get this bar

Cover Desktop
Split Desktop with Icons
Close

Figure 24.3

*Web item doodads can be
moved, resized, and more.*

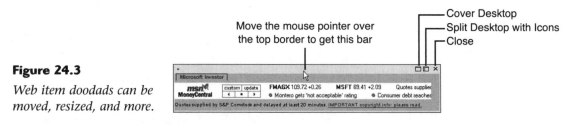

Screen Saver Silliness

In olden times (say, 10 years ago), monitors weren't as good as they are today, and most of us struggled along using ugly DOS screens. One of the problems people faced was leaving their monitors on too long and ending up with some DOS hieroglyphics burned permanently into the screen (this is usually referred to, not surprisingly, as *burn-in*). To prevent this from happening, some genius came up with the idea of a *screen saver:* a program that automatically kicks in after the computer is idle for a few minutes. The screen saver displays some kind of moving pattern on the screen that helps prevent burn-in. However, with a simple touch of a key or jiggle of a mouse, the normal screen returns, unharmed and none the worse for wear.

Nowadays, it's pretty tough to burn an image into your screen. Improvements in monitor quality and the graphical nature of Windows have made such a fate virtually impossible. Curiously, though, screen savers are still around and are, in fact, flourishing. The reason: Most of them are just plain cool. Who cares about preventing burn-in when you can watch wild, psychedelic patterns or your favorite cartoon every few minutes?

There are scads of commercial screen savers on the market, and Windows XP comes equipped with some of its own. To try them out, select the **Screen Saver** tab in the Display Properties dialog box, drop down the **Screen saver** list, and select a screen saver.

You can also choose the following options:

➤ **Wait**   This spin box controls the amount of time your computer must be inactive before the screen saver starts doing its thing. You can enter a number between 1 and 9,999 minutes.

➤ **On resume, display Welcome screen** (Windows XP Home)   Activate this check box to have Windows XP Home display the Welcome screen when you stop the screen saver. This means you have to log on to Windows again.

➤ **On resume, password protect** (Windows XP Pro)   Activate this check box to have Windows XP Professional display the Computer Locked dialog box when you shut off the screen saver. In this case, you have to enter your password to get back to Windows.

➤ **Preview**   Click this button to give the screen saver a trial run. To return to the dialog box, move your mouse or press any key.

➤ **Settings**   Click this button to set various options for the screen saver (note, however, that some screen savers don't have any options). The Settings dialog box that appears depends on which screen saver you chose. Choose the options you want, and then click **OK** to return to the Display Properties dialog box.

Windows Wisdom

Most folks use screen savers for the fun factor, but they have a practical side, as well. For example, if you set up the screen saver to kick in very soon (say, after just one minute), then it's useful for hiding your screen when you're not at your desk. Also, as you'll see in this section, you can secure your computer by adding a password to the screen saver.

Changing the Desktop Colors and Fonts

It's possible to redo much more of the Windows XP interface (as the geeks like to call the stuff you see on your screen) than just the desktop background. Among many other things, you can change the font, color, and size of icon titles; the color of window title bars, scrollbars, and backgrounds; and the fonts and colors used in dialog boxes. This section shows you how to do it.

It all happens in the **Appearance** tab of the Display Properties dialog box. The easiest way to change things is to select one of the ready-made settings from the following lists:

➤ **Windows and buttons**   The styles in this list control the overall look of your windows (including the shape and colors) and the buttons that appear in the windows (including dialog box command buttons and the window buttons: Minimize, Maximize, and Close). If you hanker for the old look of Windows Me, 98, or 2000, choose **Windows Classic** in this list.

Windows Wisdom

If you find you have trouble reading the text on your screen, Windows XP has schemes that can help. Look for scheme names that include either **(large)** or **(extra large)**.

➤ **Color scheme**   This list offers one or more general color schemes for whatever style you select in the **Windows and buttons** list.

➤ **Font size**   This list contains three relative font sizes: **Normal**, **Large Fonts**, and **Extra Large Fonts.** This setting applies not only to the window titles, but also to the desktop icon titles, the taskbar text, and the Start menu text.

Each time you select a setting, take a gander at the fake windows above the lists to get a preview of the havoc the new setting will wreak on your system. When you find a combo that's you, click **OK** or **Apply** to put it into effect.

Making Your Own Appearance Scheme

If you're feeling a bit more ambitious, you can create your own appearance scheme by plowing through these steps:

1. Click **Advanced** to meet up with the Advanced Appearance dialog box.

2. Use the **Item** list to choose which element of the screen you want to play with.

3. Use the following techniques to customize the selected element:

    ➤ If it's possible to change the size of the item, the **Size** spin box beside the Item list will be enabled. Use this spin box to adjust the size to taste.

➤ If it's possible to change the color of the item, the **Color 1** button will be enabled. Use this color palette control (described earlier in this chapter) to choose the color you want.

➤ Some screen elements (such as the Active Title Bar item) can display a color *gradient,* where one color fades into another. In this case, you use the **Color 1** button to pick the first color, and the **Color 2** button to pick the second color.

➤ If the item has text, use the **Font** list to change the typeface. You also can adjust the font using the **Size** list, the **Color** button, and the bold and italic buttons.

4. Repeat steps 1 and 2 until you've customized all the items you want, and then click **OK.**

5. Display the **Themes** tab, click **Save As,** enter a name in the Save As dialog box, and click **OK** to return to the Display Properties dialog box.

6. Click **OK** or **Apply** to put your new scheme into production use.

"Effectations": Changing Desktop Visual Effects

The final bit of appearance wizardry you can wield is found by clicking the **Appearance** tab's **Effects** button. The Effects dialog box that fades in offers the following check boxes:

➤ **Use the following transition effect for menus and tooltips**   With this check box activated, use the list to choose either **Fade effect** (menus and tooltips fade in and fade out) or **Scroll effect** (menus and tooltips scroll in and scroll out). If either of these effects bug you for some reason, deactivate this check box to turn them off.

➤ **Use the following method to smooth edges of screen fonts**   Activating this check box tells Windows XP to smooth the jagged edges (*jaggies,* in the vernacular) that appear when you use large fonts. Most screens will look better using the **Standard** method; if you have an LCD screen (such as found on most notebooks) or a high-resolution monitor, choose the **ClearType** method to get exceptionally sharp text.

➤ **Use large icons**   If you crank up this option, Windows XP inflates the size of the desktop and Start menu icons.

➤ **Show shadows under menus**   When this check box is activated, Windows XP renders menus with a subtle shadow underneath them, which gives the menus a slightly 3-D look.

➤ **Show window contents while dragging**   When you move a window, the entire contents of the window remain visible. If your system takes a long time to

321

display the new window position as you move it, your moves will go much faster if you deactivate this check box. If you do this, then you'll see only the outline of a window as you move it.

➤ **Hide underlined letters for keyboard navigation until I press the Alt Key**
When I told you how to use menus in Chapter 2, "A Field Guide to Windows XP," I told you that you can use the keyboard to pull down a menu by holding down Alt and pressing the underlined letter in the menu name. Unfortunately, Windows XP shows only the underlined letters after you hold down Alt. If you'd prefer that Windows XP show the underlined letters full-time, deactivate this check box.

Changing the Screen Area and Color Depth

The last bit of desktop decoration I'll put you through in this chapter relates to various display settings. Again, these are options that apply not just to the desktop, but to everything you see on your screen. You'll find these settings in the **Settings** tab of the Display Properties dialog box, shown in Figure 24.4.

Figure 24.4

The Settings tab lets you muck around with your display.

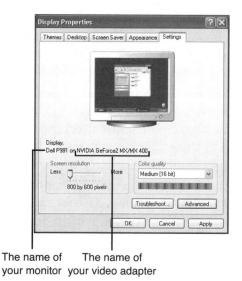

The name of   The name of
your monitor   your video adapter

Let's begin with the **Display** area. This line shows you two things:

➤ **The name of your monitor**   This tells you the name or the type of your monitor.

➤ **The name of your video adapter**   This tells you the name or the type of the *video adapter* that resides inside your system.

These two chunks of hardware determine the values you can select in the **Settings** tab's other two groups: Screen resolution and Color quality.

The **Color quality** group consists of a single list. The items in this list specify how many colors Windows XP can use to display stuff. This is called the *color depth*. Here are some notes:

➤ In general, the more colors you use, the sharper your screen images appear.

➤ If you're working with graphics, you'll want to use as many colors as possible.

➤ On the other hand, if you find that your screen display is sluggish, you should consider reducing the number of colors.

The **Screen resolution** slider determines the number of pixels used to display stuff on the screen. I've mentioned pixels before, but it's worth repeating myself here: A *pixel* is an individual pinpoint of light. All the colors you see are the result of thousands of these pixels getting turned on and set to display a specific hue.

Windows Wisdom

The **Color quality** list gives you a general setting (such as **Medium** or **High**) as well as a bit value (such as **16 bit** or **24 bit**). The deal here is that Windows XP uses a specified number of bits (on/off values) for each screen pixel (see my discussion of the Screen resolution setting that follows). The lowest number of bits is 8, and because 2 to the power of 8 is 256, that's the minimum number of colors you can choose. Other typical bit values are 16 (65,536 colors), and 24 (16,777,216 colors). There's also 32-bit color, but that's the same as 24-bit (the extra 8 bits are used by some applications for "masking" existing colors so that they appear transparent).

The lowest screen area value is 800 by 600. This means that Windows XP uses pixels arranged in a grid that has 800 columns and 600 rows. That's nearly half a million pixels for your viewing pleasure! The number of higher screen area values you can pick depends on your monitor and on your video adapter. Here are some notes:

323

➤ The more pixels you use (that is, the higher you go on the Screen resolution slider), the smaller things will look on the screen.

➤ You might be able to go to a higher screen area value only by using a smaller number of colors. Video adapters have only a certain amount of memory, so you'll often have to trade off one value with the other.

➤ In general, you should tailor the screen area value with the size of your monitor. If you have a standard 14- or 15-inch monitor, try 800 by 600; for 17- or 19-inch monitors, head up to 1,024 by 768; if you're lucky enough to have a 21-inch behemoth, go for 1,600 by 1,200 (if your video adapter will let you).

➤ If you have an older game or other program that has to be run at 640 by 480, it should change the resolution on its own when you start it. If it doesn't, right-click the program's icon in the Start menu and then click **Properties.** In the **Compatibility** tab, activate the **Run in 640 × 480 screen resolution** check box. Note, too, that you can force a program to run with only 256 colors by activating the **Run in 256 colors** check box.

When you've made your changes, click **OK** or **Apply.** If you choose a different resolution, Windows XP changes the setting and then asks whether you want to keep it. Click **Yes.** If things don't look right for some reason, click **No** to return to your normally scheduled display settings.

Look Out!

If your display goes haywire when Windows XP applies the new settings, it probably means that you tried some combo that was beyond the capabilities of your adapter/monitor team. Your screen likely will be unreadable, but don't panic. Windows XP will automatically reset the display after 15 seconds.

Applying Desktop Themes

Earlier I showed you how to select schemes that govern the look of various objects, including menu bars, window borders, title bars, icons, and more. Windows XP takes this idea a step further with desktop *themes.* A theme is also a collection of customizations, but it covers more ground than a simple scheme. Each theme specifies various settings for not only windows and dialog boxes, but also a screen saver, wallpaper, mouse pointers, sounds, desktop icons, and more.

To choose a desktop theme, follow these steps:

1. In the Display Properties dialog box, display the **Themes** tab.

2. Use the **Theme** drop-down list to choose the theme you want to use. The **Sample** area shows you a preview of the theme. You see not only

how the theme will affect the various window objects, but also the wallpaper and desktop icons the theme uses.

3. Click **OK.**

The Least You Need to Know

➤ **Displaying the Display Properties dialog box**   Either right-click the desktop and then click **Properties,** or select **Start, Control Panel, Appearance and Themes, Display.**

➤ **Wallpaper options**   Most wallpaper images are small, so you need to use the **Tile** option to get the fill effect. For larger images, use either **Center** or **Stretch.**

➤ **Screen tradeoff**   Unless your computer has lots of video memory, you'll be faced with a tradeoff when adjusting the screen resolution and color quality. That is, to get the highest resolution, you may need to use a lower color quality, and vice versa.

➤ **Tailor your pixels**   Try to use a screen resolution value that matches your monitor. For most monitors, 800 by 600 is ideal.

➤ **Dare to theme**   To apply a theme that covers colors, desktop settings, pointers, sounds, and more, open the Display Properties dialog box and select a theme from the **Themes** tab.

Chapter 25

Revamping the Start Menu and Taskbar

You probably deal with the Start menu and taskbar dozens of times a day, so you can save yourself lots of time by using these items as efficiently as you can. That's the focus of this chapter as I show you all kinds of ways to customize the Start menu and taskbar.

A Smart Start: Reconstructing the Start Menu

The Start menu is your royal road to Windows XP's riches, as well as to the programs installed on your machine. Because you use this road a lot during the course of a day, you'll probably want to make this road as short and as straight as possible. Fortunately, Windows XP gives you lots of ways to customize the Start menu to do this and to suit the way you work.

Toggling Some Start Menu Settings On and Off

Windows XP's Start menu boasts a number of new settings that you can turn on and off. These settings enable you to, among other things, add the Favorites list as a submenu, display the Control Panel icons as a submenu, and retreat to the "classic" Start menu from older versions of Windows.

To get to these settings, you have a couple of ways to go:

➤ Select **Start, Control Panel, Appearance and Themes, Taskbar and Start Menu.**

➤ Right-click the **Start** button and then click **Properties.**

Either way, the Taskbar and Start Menu Properties dialog box comes off the bench. Now display the **Start Menu** tab. Your first choice involves the Start menu style that you want to use:

➤ **Start Menu**   Choose this option to use the newfangled Start Menu that comes with Windows XP.

➤ **Classic Start Menu**   Choose this option to retreat to the familiar confines of the Start Menu used in Windows Me and Windows 2000.

Personally, I really like the XP incarnation of the Start menu: it's efficient, sensible for the most part, and as you'll see in this section, its not-so-sensible shortcomings are fixable with a couple of tweaks. I digress here in order to justify my decision to cover only the customization settings of the new XP Start menu. Note, however, that if you do decide to revert to the classic menu, many of its customization settings are similar to those I discuss in the rest of this section.

To move on with things, click the **Customize** button that sits next to the **Start menu** option. This gets you a ticket to the Customize Start Menu dialog box. The **General** tab serves up three sections:

➤ **Select an icon size for programs**   This inscrutable semi-sentence is telling you that you use the following option buttons to choose the relative size of the icons that appear in the programs section (the left half) of the Start menu. Choose either **Large icons** (the default) or **Small icons.** (The latter is useful if you up the number of programs Windows XP displays on the Start menu, as described next.)

➤ **Programs**   This section offers a couple of methods to adjust the Start menu's programs section. Recall that this section (excluding the **Internet** and **E-mail** icons at the top) displays icons for the last six programs you fired up. You can use the **Number of programs on Start menu** spin box to set the maximum number of these icons that appear in this section. Enter a number from 0 and

30. If you want to clear out the programs section and get a fresh start, click the **Clear List** button.

➤ **Show on Start menu** When the **Internet** and **E-mail** check boxes are activated, these items appear at the top of the Start menu's programs section. Note, too, that each one offers a list that enables you to choose which Web browser and which e-mail program to associate with these icons.

Windows Wisdom

If you want to give an icon a permanent place in the Start menu's programs section, click **Start** to open the Start menu, right-click the icon, and then click **Pin to Start menu.** Windows XP moves the icon up into the top part of the menu and displays the icon title in bold. (Note that you can do this with any icon on the **All Programs** menus, as well.) If you change your mind about the icon, you can return it to normal by right-clicking it and then clicking **Unpin from Start menu.** If you want to remove a single program icon from the Start menu, click **Start** to open the Start menu, right-click the icon, and then click **Remove from This List.**

The **Advanced** tab of the Customize Start Menu dialog box is shown in Figure 25.1.

Figure 25.1

The Advanced tab is bursting with Start menu settings.

For starters, the **Start menu settings** group has a couple of check boxes:

➤ **Open submenus when I pause on them with my mouse**   When this setting is activated, you can open a submenu just by placing your mouse pointer over the menu item. If you deactivate this check box, you can only open a submenu by clicking the menu item.

➤ **Highlight newly installed programs**   With this setting lit up, Windows XP monitors the Start menu to see if some program adds its own icons or a submenu to the All Programs menu. If it does, XP displays a notice letting you know and it highlights the new icons or submenu.

What you're dealing with in the **Start menu items** group is a long list of check boxes and options that control the structure and behavior of the icons on the right side of the Start menu (the folders and XP features). The items that deal with folders (Control Panel, My Computer, My Documents, My Music, My Pictures, and, in XP Pro only, System Administrative Tools) offer the same set of three option buttons:

➤ **Display as a link**   This option means that when you click the folder icon in the Start menu, Windows XP opens the folder in a window.

➤ **Display as a menu**   This option means that when you click the folder icon in the Start menu, a submenu slides out to display the contents of the folder.

➤ **Don't display this item**   This option means that the folder icon doesn't appear in the Start menu.

Windows Wisdom

Setting up folders such as Control Panel and My Documents as menus is a faster way to work, but what if you need to see those windows in the future? That's no problem. What you need to do is right-click the icon and then click **Open** in the shortcut menu.

(Note that there's also a Network Connections item that offers three similar, but differently worded, options.)

The rest of the list is composed of check boxes. Each one toggles a particular Start menu feature on and off. Here's a quick summary of the features:

➤ **System Administrative Tools**   When this check box is activated, Windows XP adds the Administrative Tools menu to the All Programs menu. (These are geeks-only tools, so it's unlikely that you'll want to bother with this one.)

➤ **Enable dragging and dropping**   When this setting is activated, it enables you to rearrange Start menu stuff by using your mouse to drag the icons here and there. I'll tell you a bit more about this technique later in this chapter; see "Adding Your Own Start Menu Icons."

➤ **Favorites menu** This check box toggles the icon for the Favorites submenu on and off the Start menu.

➤ **Help and Support** This check box toggles the Help and Support icon on and off.

➤ **My Network Places** This check box toggles the icon for the My Network Places folder on and off.

➤ **Printers and Faxes** This check box toggles the icon for the Printers and Faxes folder on and off.

➤ **Run command** This check box toggles the icon for the Run command on and off.

➤ **Scroll Programs** This setting determines what Windows XP does if the All Programs menu contains so many items that the entire menu can't fit into the height of the screen. When this setting is off, Windows XP displays Programs as a two-column menu. When this setting is on, Windows XP displays Programs as a single menu with up and down arrows on the top and bottom, respectively. You click these arrows to scroll through the menu.

➤ **Search** This check box toggles the icon for the Search feature on and off.

Finally, the **Recent documents** group has a check box named **List my most recently opened documents.** If you activate this setting, Windows XP adds an icon named **Recent Documents** to the Start menu. This icon opens a submenu that contains a list of the last 15 documents you worked on in any program. If you display this menu and decide later on that you don't want anyone else to see the list of documents, you can scrub it clean by returning to the **Advanced** tab and clicking the **Clear List** button.

That's all he wrote for the Customize Start Menu dialog box, so click **OK** to return to the Taskbar and Start Menu Properties dialog box, and then click **OK** to put the new settings into effect.

See Also

Remember your Favorites? If you don't, jump back to Chapter 18, "It's a Small Web After All: Using Internet Explorer," and look under "Saving Sites for Subsequent Surfs: Managing Your Favorites."

Adding Your Own Start Menu Icons

Most new users just assume the arrangement of icons on the Start menu is a permanent part of the Windows XP landscape. They're right, to a certain extent. Everything on the main Start menu can only be messed with by using the techniques from the previous section.

What *is* a bit surprising is that the menus that appear when you click **All Programs** are completely open for customization business. You can add icons, move them around, rename them, delete them, and more. I show you how to do all of this in this section.

Let's begin by learning how to add an icon to the Start menu. You usually don't have to worry about this when you install an application. That's because most of today's programs are hip to the Start menu, so they'll add an icon or three during their installation procedure. However, there are two cases when you'll need to add an icon yourself:

➤ If you want easy access to a particular document that you use often.

➤ If you installed an older program that isn't Start-menu savvy.

It's important to bear in mind that the icons you're working with here are *shortcuts* to documents or programs. A shortcut is a teensy file whose sole mission in life is to act as a pointer to some other file. For example, when you launch a shortcut for a document, the shortcut tells Windows XP the location of the *actual* document. XP then finds the document and opens it for you.

Here's how you add an icon to the Start menu:

1. Use My Computer to find the document you want to work with or the file that runs the program you want to add.

2. Drag the document or file from My Computer and hover it over the **Start** button. After a second or two, the Start menu pops up.

3. Drag the file up into the Start menu.

4. Do one of the following:

   ➤ If you want to make the icon a part of the Start menu's permanent program icon section (where the Internet and E-mail icons are), drag it up into that section and then drop it.

   ➤ If you want the icon to appear in the All Programs menu, drag the file over top of **All Programs**, wait a beat until the menu appears, and then drag the file into the All Programs menu. If you want it to appear in one of the All Programs submenus, drag the file up until you see a line just above the submenu, wait until the submenu appears, drag the file into the submenu, and then drop it inside the submenu.

Windows Wisdom

If you drag the document or file from My Computer and then drop it on the **Start** button, Windows XP automatically pins a shortcut to the document or file to the "permanent" part of the Start menu's programs section.

What about the opposite procedure, when you need to get rid of something on the Start menu? I'm glad you asked. What you do is open the Start menu and display the icon you want to remove. Then use your mouse to drag the icon off the menu and drop it on the desktop's **Recycle Bin** icon. (Note that you may need to minimize all your running programs in order to see the Recycle Bin icon.)

Easy Start Menu Maintenance

To close out your look at customizing the Start menu, here are a few tips and techniques that can make this part of your life even easier:

➤ **Right-click convenience**   You can perform many maintenance chores right from the Start menu itself. Right-click a Start menu icon, and you'll get a menu with all kinds of useful commands, including Cut, Copy, Delete, and Rename. (The actual roster of commands depends on the icon. The largest collection is found with the icon on the All Programs menu.)

➤ **Drag-and-drop rearranging**   You can move things around in the All Programs menu by using use your mouse to drag the icons directly. You can drop them higher or lower on the same menu or even drop them onto another menu altogether.

➤ **Sorting an out-of-sorts menu**   If you've been dragging icons hither and yon, you might end up with menus that are no longer in alphabetical order. If that offends your inner neat freak, it's easy enough to fix. Just right-click the offending menu and then click **Sort by Name**.

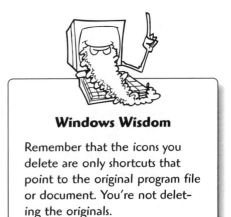

Windows Wisdom

Remember that the icons you delete are only shortcuts that point to the original program file or document. You're not deleting the originals.

Renovating the Taskbar

Like the Start menu, the taskbar also seems to be a nonmalleable feature of the Windows XP landscape. If that were true, however, then this chapter would end right about here. The fact that you still have a few pages left to slog through tells you that, indeed, the taskbar is readily malleable. Not only that, but most of the taskbar customizations you'll see over the next few sections are practical timesavers and not just mere "Hey, Ma, look what I can do!" tricks.

Unlocking the Taskbar

NEW!   When Microsoft was testing Windows with new users, they found that people often ended up with inadvertently customized taskbars that they didn't know how to fix. For example, it's actually quite easy to accidentally resize the taskbar while trying to resize a window (as you'll see a bit later). To prevent this kind of faux customization (and the confusion it creates), Windows XP comes with its taskbar locked so that it can't be moved or sized. Here's how to unlock it so that you can manhandle the taskbar on purpose:

1. Right-click an empty section of the taskbar.
2. In the shortcut that appears, look for the **Lock the Taskbar** command. If there's a checkmark beside it, click the command to remove the checkmark and unlock the taskbar.

Taskbar Travels: Moving and Sizing the Taskbar

The taskbar, recumbent on the bottom of the screen, seems quite comfy. However, that position might not be comfy for *you,* depending on the ergonomics of your desk and chair. Similarly, you might have a program where you need to maximize the available vertical screen space, so you might not appreciate having the taskbar usurp space at the bottom of the screen. These are mere molehills that can be easily leapt by moving the taskbar to a new location:

1. Point the mouse at an empty section of the taskbar.
2. Hold down the left mouse button and move the pointer toward the edge of the screen where you'd rather see the taskbar situated. As you approach an edge, the taskbar suddenly snaps into place.
3. When the taskbar is on the edge you want, release the mouse button.

What if you're not so much interested in moving the taskbar as in resizing it? For example, if you're feeling particularly frisky, you might end up with a whack of programs on the go. However, each of those programs claims a bit of taskbar turf. The more programs you have running, the tinier the taskbar buttons become. Eventually, as you can see in Figure 25.2, the text on the buttons becomes all but indecipherable.

Figure 25.2

Who can tell what each of these taskbar buttons represents?

The way you fix that is by expanding the taskbar from its single-row setup to a setup that has two or more rows. Here's how:

1. Move the mouse pointer so that it rests on the top edge of the taskbar. The pointer changes into a vertical two-headed arrow.

2. Drag the edge of the taskbar up slightly. After you travel a short distance, a second taskbar row springs into view, as shown in Figure 25.3.

3. Keep dragging the taskbar up until the taskbar is the size you want, and then release the mouse button.

If you've moved the taskbar to the left or right side of the screen, dragging the outer edge only increases the width of the taskbar, it doesn't create new rows.

Figure 25.3

To see the button text, stretch the taskbar into this two-row configuration.

Some Useful Taskbar Options

The next round of taskbar touchups involves a small but useful set of properties, which can be displayed by using either of the following techniques:

➤ Select **Start, Control Panel, Appearance and Themes, Taskbar and Start Menu.**

➤ Right-click an empty section of the taskbar and then click **Properties.**

This reunites you with your old friend the Taskbar and Start Menu Properties dialog box. This time, however, you'll be dealing with the **Taskbar** tab.

NEW!   The **Taskbar appearance** group controls the look and feel of the taskbar. As you play with the settings in this group, keep an eye on the fake taskbar that appears just above the Lock taskbar check box. This will give you some idea of how the taskbar will change based on the settings you toggle on and off. Here's a summary of the available check boxes:

➤ **Lock the taskbar**   This check box toggles the taskbar lock on and off.

➤ **Auto-hide the taskbar**   If you activate this check box, Windows XP shrinks the taskbar to a teensy blue strip that's barely visible along the bottom of the screen. This gives a maximized window more room to stretch its legs. When you need the taskbar for something, just move the mouse pointer to the bottom of the screen. Lo and behold, the full taskbar slides into view. When you move the mouse above the taskbar, the taskbar sinks back whence it came.

➤ **Keep the taskbar on top of other windows**   When this option is activated, the taskbar remains in view even if you maximize a window. That's usually a

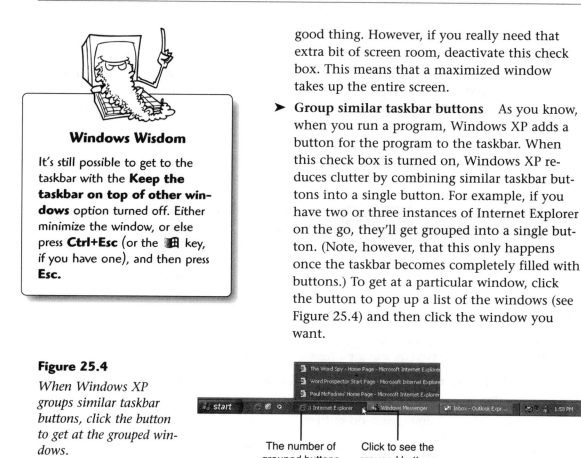

Windows Wisdom

It's still possible to get to the taskbar with the **Keep the taskbar on top of other windows** option turned off. Either minimize the window, or else press **Ctrl+Esc** (or the 🪟 key, if you have one), and then press **Esc.**

good thing. However, if you really need that extra bit of screen room, deactivate this check box. This means that a maximized window takes up the entire screen.

➤ **Group similar taskbar buttons**   As you know, when you run a program, Windows XP adds a button for the program to the taskbar. When this check box is turned on, Windows XP reduces clutter by combining similar taskbar buttons into a single button. For example, if you have two or three instances of Internet Explorer on the go, they'll get grouped into a single button. (Note, however, that this only happens once the taskbar becomes completely filled with buttons.) To get at a particular window, click the button to pop up a list of the windows (see Figure 25.4) and then click the window you want.

Figure 25.4

When Windows XP groups similar taskbar buttons, click the button to get at the grouped windows.

The number of grouped buttons

Click to see the grouped buttons

➤ **Show Quick Launch**   If you activate this check box, Windows XP adds the Quick Launch toolbar beside the Start button, as shown in Figure 25.5. This gives you one-click access to three icons: **Launch Internet Explorer Browser, Show Desktop,** and **Windows Media Player.** The Show Desktop icon minimizes all running programs so that you get a pristine view of the desktop.

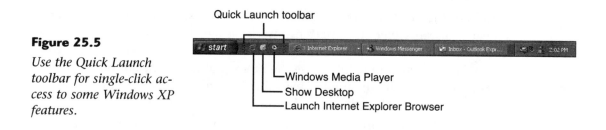

Quick Launch toolbar

Windows Media Player
Show Desktop
Launch Internet Explorer Browser

Figure 25.5

Use the Quick Launch toolbar for single-click access to some Windows XP features.

The **Notification area** group has just two check boxes:

➤ **Show Clock**   Deactivating this check box hides the clock that normally resides in the notification area.

➤ **NEW!   Hide inactive icons**   When this check box is activated, Windows XP will hide notification area icons that you haven't used in a while. In their place, you see a left-pointing arrow, as shown in Figure 25.6. Click that arrow to see the hidden icons. To gain some control over this, click **Customize** to meet up with the Customize Notifications dialog box. In the list of notifications, click one to enable a list of options for that icon. You get three choices: **Hide when inactive, Always hide,** and **Always show.**

Windows Wisdom

To add your own icons to the Quick Launch toolbar, open My Computer, drag the document or program file you want to add, and drop it inside the Quick Launch toolbar. (You can also drag an icon from any Start menu and drop it inside the Quick Launch toolbar.)

start   2:12 PM

Click this button to
see the hidden icons

Figure 25.6

Windows XP can hide notification area icons that you haven't used in a while.

The Least You Need to Know

➤ **Start menu and taskbar options**   These are available by selecting **Start, Control Panel, Appearance and Themes, Taskbar and Start Menu,** or by right-clicking the **Start** button or an empty stretch of the taskbar and then clicking **Properties.**

➤ **Adding Start menu stuff**   Drag a document or program file from My Computer, hover the mouse over the **Start** button, and then drop it on the menu you want.

➤ **Direct Start menu modifications**   Display the Start menu and then right-click any command.

➤ **Unlock the taskbar**   Before embarking on any taskbar modifications, be sure to unlock it first. The quickest route is to right-click an empty part of the taskbar and then deactivate the **Lock the Taskbar** command.

➤ **Moving and sizing the taskbar**   Drag an empty section of the taskbar to move it; drag the top edge of the taskbar to size it.

➤ **Quick Quick Launch customizing**   The easiest way to add icons to the Quick Launch toolbar is to drag program files and drop them onto the toolbar.

Chapter 26

Renovating My Computer

<table>
<tr><td>

In This Chapter

➤ Messing with the My Computer window

➤ Changing the file and folder view

➤ Sorting files and folders

➤ Customizing your folders

</td></tr>
</table>

After the mostly esthetic redecorating you did back in Chapter 24, "Refurbishing the Desktop," things turned decidedly more practical with the customizations outlined in Chapter 25, "Revamping the Start Menu and Taskbar." You'll stay on that practical path in this chapter as I show you a few ways to reconstruct My Computer. You'll learn how to rearrange the My Computer window, change how files and folders are displayed, and sort files and folders. On a slightly more frivolous note, you'll also learn how to create custom folder backgrounds and perform other Web view tweaks.

Points of View: Changing the My Computer View

Let's begin the My Computer renovations with a few methods for changing the view. I'll divide this into four areas: changing the layout of the My Computer window, customizing the toolbar, switching how file and folders are displayed in the content area, and sorting files and folders.

Bar-Gains: Toggling My Computer's Bars On and Off

My Computer is awash in bars. There's the title bar, the menu bar, the toolbar, and the Address bar. And those are just the ones you see by default. There are plenty of other bars lurking beneath the surface. So, to start things off on an easy note, this section shows you how to display the various My Computer bars, as well as how to hide those that you don't use.

The commands you need are on the **View** menu. Let's start with the **Toolbars** command, which shoves out a submenu that contains three commands that correspond to My Computer's three available toolbars. In each case, you display a toolbar by activating its command (so that it has a check mark beside it), and you hide a toolbar by deactivating its command. Here's a summary of the three toolbars:

➤ **Standard Buttons** This toolbar is displayed by default and it's the one that you see under the menu bar. (See the next section, "Customizing the Standard Buttons Toolbar," to learn how to control the look of this all-important toolbar.)

➤ **Address Bar** This toolbar is displayed by default and it appears under the Standard Buttons toolbar. It displays the name of the current folder, and you can use it to navigate to other folders (or even to Web page addresses).

➤ **Links** This is the Links bar that you normally see only in Internet Explorer. If you display it here, clicking any button in the Links bar will display the corresponding Web page within the My Computer window.

NEW! Also on the **View, Toolbars** submenu is the **Lock the Toolbars** command. When this is activated, you can move or resize the toolbars. If you deactivate this command, you can move any toolbar by dragging the left edge of the toolbar up or down. If you end up with two toolbars side-by-side, you can resize either of them by dragging the toolbar's left edge to the right or left.

Windows Wisdom

You also can toggle a toolbar on and off by right-clicking any displayed toolbar and then clicking the toolbar name in the shortcut menu that shows up.

Next up on the **View** menu is the **Status Bar** command. This command toggles the status bar at the bottom of the window on and off. I recommend that you activate the status bar because it offers some semi-useful info:

➤ If you highlight a menu command, a short description of the command appears in the status bar.

➤ Each time you open a folder, the status bar tells you how many files and subfolders ("objects") are in the folder and how much hard disk space the files take up.

➤ If you select one or more files, the status bar tells you how many files you selected and what their total size is.

The **View** menu's **Explorer Bar** command also spits out a submenu. In this case, the submenu offers a number of commands that toggle various bars on and off within the Explorer bar. There are six in all:

➤ **Search**   This toggles the Search bar on and off. You use the Search bar to find files on your hard disk. (See Chapter 6, "Using My Computer to Fiddle with Files and Folders.")

➤ **Favorites**   This toggles the Favorites bar on and off. You use the Favorites bar to display your list of favorites. These are normally Web sites, but you also can define a folder as a favorite. (See Chapter 18, "It's a Small Web After All: Using Internet Explorer.")

➤ **Media**   This toggles the Media bar on and off. The Media bar displays links to WindowsMedia.com and controls whatever media files are found in the current folder.

➤ **History**   This toggles the History bar on and off. The History bar displays a list of the Web sites that you've visited each day for the past 20 days. (See Chapter 18.)

➤ **Folders**   Toggles the Folders bar on and off. The Folders bar gives you a bird's-eye view of your computer's disks and folders, which makes it much easier to navigate your system (as explained in Chapter 6; see the "Taking Advantage of the Handy Folders List" section).

Three of the Explorer bars offer shortcut methods for toggling themselves on and off:

➤ **Search**   Click **Search** in the Standard Buttons toolbar, or press **Ctrl+E**.

➤ **Favorites**   Click **Favorites** in the Standard Buttons toolbar, or press **Ctrl+I**.

➤ **History**   Press **Ctrl+H**.

Customizing the Standard Buttons Toolbar

The Standard Buttons toolbar (which I'll just call "the toolbar" from now on) is a bit of an odd duck. Some buttons have text (such as the Back button) and some don't (such as the Forward button). Also, it doesn't include buttons for three commonly used commands: Cut, Copy, and Paste. You can fix this idiosyncratic behavior by tweaking the toolbar.

To begin, select **View, Toolbars, Customize**. (You also can right-click the toolbar and then click **Customize** in the shortcut menu.) My Computer lobs the Customize Toolbar dialog box your way, as shown in Figure 26.1.

Figure 26.1

Use this dialog box to knock some sense into My Computer's main toolbar.

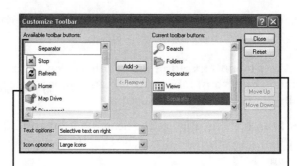

The extra toolbar buttons that you can display

The toolbar buttons that are currently displayed

Here's a summary of the techniques you can use:

➤ **Adding an extra button to the toolbar**   Highlight it in the **Available toolbar buttons** list and then click **Add.** Use the **Separator** item to add a vertical bar to the toolbar. This is used to separate groups of related buttons.

➤ **Removing a button from the toolbar**   Highlight it in the **Current toolbar buttons** list and then click **Remove.**

➤ **Changing the order of the buttons**   Highlight any button in the **Current toolbar buttons** list and click **Move Up** or **Move Down.**

➤ **Controlling the button text**   Use the **Text Options** list:

Show text labels   This option adds text to every button. This makes the buttons much easier to figure out, so I recommend going with this option.

Selective text on right   This is the default option, and it displays text on only some buttons. As I've mentioned, this is a pretty dumb way of doing things.

Windows Wisdom

If you make a mess of the toolbar, you can return it to square one by displaying the Customize Toolbar dialog box again and clicking **Reset.**

No text labels   This option displays every button using just its icon. If you already know what each icon represents, selecting this option will give you a bit more room because the toolbar will be at its narrowest.

➤ **Controlling the size of the icons**   Use the items in the **Icon Options** list. Select either **Small icons** or **Large icons** (this is the default).

Click **Close** to put your new settings into effect.

Views You Can Use: Changing How Folders and Files Are Displayed

In the standard My Computer view, each file and folder is displayed using a big, fat icon. However, there are also several other views you can try on for size. You access these views either by pulling down the **View** menu or by clicking the **Views** button in the toolbar (see Figure 26.2). There are five possibilities:

➤ **Thumbnails** This view displays previews—called *thumbnails*—of all the image files in the current folder. If you have any HTML files in the folder (these are files that contain Web page data), a thumbnail of the Web page is shown. I told you more about this view in Chapter 8, "Playing with Pictures." For an example, see Figure 8.1.

➤ **Tiles** This is the default honkin' icon view that displays the files in columns.

➤ **Icons** This view displays files and folders using smaller, cuter versions of the icons arranged in rows (see Figure 26.2).

➤ **List** This view also displays the files and folders using even smaller icons, and everything is arrayed in multiple columns (see Figure 26.2).

➤ **Details** This view displays the files and folders using a four-column list (see Figure 26.2). For each file and folder, you see its Name, its Size, its Type (such as WordPad Document), and Date Modified (the date and time it was last changed). However, these aren't the only columns available. There's actually a truckload of them, and you can see the complete list by selecting **View, Choose Details.** (This command is around only when you're in Details view.) In the Column Details dialog box, use the check boxes to toggle columns on and off.

Ordering My Computer Around: Sorting Files

To complete your reading of My Computer's views news, let's see how you sort the files and subfolders in the current folder. By default, file and subfolders are sorted alphabetically by name, with the subfolders displayed first, and then the files. You can change this by selecting the **View, Arrange Icons by** command, which reveals a submenu with seven choices:

➤ **Name** This is the default sort order.

➤ **Size** This command sorts the folder numerically by the size of each file.

➤ **Type** This command sorts the folder alphabetically by the type of document.

➤ **Modified** This command sorts the folder according to the date and time when each item was last modified.

Icons view   List view

Figure 26.2

Three separate My Computer windows demonstrating the Icons, List, and Details views.

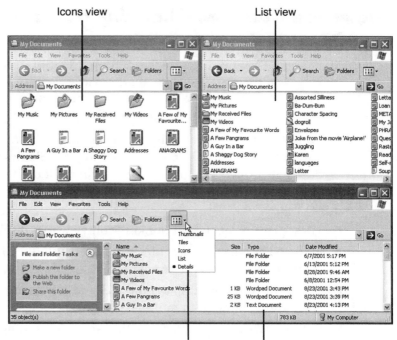

The Views button Details view

Windows Wisdom

Some of Windows XP's special folders have their own sorting options. For example, in the My Music folder you can sort music files by Artist and Album Title. Similarly, in the My Pictures folder you can sort by the Picture Taken On date and by the Dimensions of the image.

➤ **NEW! Show in Groups** When this command is activated (it's not available in the List view), Windows XP arranges the folder contents into categories. The actual categories you see depend on which of the above four sort commands is active:

Name The contents are grouped by the letters of the alphabet (items with names that begin with "A" are in the **A** group, those that begin with "B" are in the **B** group, and so on).

Size The contents are grouped into general size categories: **Tiny, Small, Medium, Large, Gigantic,** and so on.

Type The contents are grouped into file type categories (for example, WordPad Document and Wave Sound).

344

Modified The contents are grouped into general date categories: **Today, Last Week, Last Month, Last Year, A long time ago,** and so on.

➤ **Auto Arrange** Activating this command (it's not available in the List and Details views) toggles the Auto Arrange feature on and off. When it's on, My Computer automatically resorts the folder (using the current sort choice) whenever you add, rename, or delete a file or folder.

➤ **Align to Grid** Activating this command (it's not available in the List and Details views) tells My Computer to herd the files that you move into their proper rows or columns.

Windows Wisdom

If you're in Details view, you can sort a folder by clicking the column headers (**Name, Size,** and so on). For example, clicking the **Size** column header sorts the folder by size. Clicking the header again switches the sort between ascending and descending.

Start Spreading the Views: Applying a View to All Folders

The view options—specifically, the icon view (Tiles, Icons, and so on) and the sort order—you set for one folder are immediately jettisoned when you leap to another folder. If you'd like to use one set of options for *all* your folders, you can tell Windows XP to make it so. Here are the steps to follow:

1. Set up a folder just the way you like it.
2. Select **Tools, Folder Options.** The Folder Options dialog box skids into the screen.
3. Display the **View** tab.
4. Click **Apply to All Folders.** Windows XP asks you to confirm.
5. Click **Yes** to get back to the Folder Options dialog box.
6. Click **OK.**

If you grow tired of these view options and you want to go back to the original look and feel, display the **View** tab once again and click **Reset All Folders.**

A Few More Folder Options

The Folder Options dialog box you visited briefly in the previous section is loaded with settings that change the way My Computer displays folders. Most of the settings in the View tab and all the settings in File Types tab are obscure and can be safely ignored by normal people. However, the options in the **General** tab are relatively useful.

Let's start with the **Tasks** group. Way back in Chapter 6, I told you about Windows XP's new Web view panel that offers links to common tasks related to whatever type of folder or file you're working with. The Tasks group controls the display of this panel:

➤ **Show common tasks in folders**   Activate this option to display the Web view panel.

➤ **Use Windows classic folders**   Activate this option to do away with the Web view panel.

The **Browse folders** groups also gives you two options:

➤ **Open each folder in the same window**   When this option is activated and you double-click a folder icon to open it, My Computer displays that folder in the same window.

➤ **Open each folder in its own window**   When this option is activated and you double-click a folder icon to open it, My Computer displays that folder in a separate window. This option can lead to some serious desktop overcrowding as the folder windows multiply, so I don't recommend using it.

The options in the **Click items as follows** group determine how you launch and select icons:

➤ **Single-click to open an item (point to select)**   Activate this option means that you can launch an icon by single-clicking it instead double-clicking it. It also means that you can select a file just by pointing your mouse at it. Note, too, that the following option buttons also arise from their slumbers:

> **Underline icon titles consistent with my browser**   Activate this option to tell Windows XP to underline all the file names and icon titles using the same style as defined within Internet Explorer. This usually means that file and folder names and icon titles appear in a blue, underlined test. This is a good idea because it gives you a visual reminder that this single-click feature is turned on.

346

Underline icon titles only when I point at them   Activate this option to have Windows XP underline file names and icon titles only when you point at them. This is a bit tidier-looking than having everything underlined.

➤ **Double-click to open an item (single-click to select)**   Activate this option to use the old-fashioned mouse techniques for launching and selecting stuff.

A Folder Face-Lift: Customizing a Folder

NEW!   To close this look at My Computer customization, let's take a peek at some interesting folder tweaks that are new to Windows XP. First, though, I should tell you that these tweaks apply only to folders that you've created with the sweat of your own brow; they don't work with folders created by Windows XP.

With that out of the way, go ahead and open one of your folders and then select the **View, Customize This Folder** command. Windows XP displays a dialog box named *Folder* Properties, where *Folder* is the name of the open folder (see Figure 26.3).

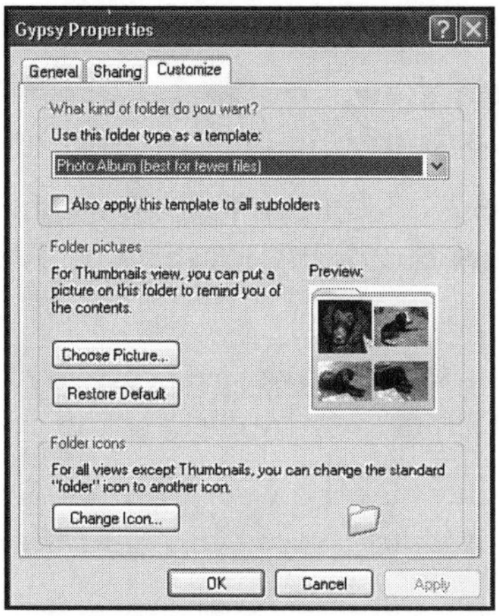

Figure 26.3

Use this dialog box to customize one of your folders.

The **What kind of folder to you want?** group enables you to apply a template to the folder. This means that you can convert your folder into a special folder that uses the same features as My Pictures, My Music, and so on. In the **Use this folder type as a template** list, choose the template type that best suits the content of your folder. For example, if your folder contains mostly images, choose the **Pictures** template or the **Photo Album** template. Note, too, that you can tell Windows XP to use the template with all the folder's subfolders by activating the **Also apply this template to all subfolders** check box.

The **Folder pictures** group enables you to assign one or more pictures that get displayed as part of the folder's icon when you're in Thumbnails view. By default, Windows XP uses the first four images that are in the folder. If you want to use a single picture, instead, click **Choose Picture**, highlight the file you want to use in the Browse dialog box, and then click **Open**. If you prefer the four-picture format, click **Restore Default**.

Finally, the **Folder icons** group enables you to change the icon used to display a folder in all views except Thumbnail. Click **Change Icon** to open the Change Icon dialog box, highlight the icon you prefer to use, and then click **OK**. (I gave you some options for this dialog box in Chapter 25.)

The Least You Need to Know

➤ **Toggling toolbars** Select **View, Toolbars** (or right-click a displayed toolbar) to see a list of toolbars that can be toggled on and off.

➤ **Displaying the Folders bar** Activate the **View, Explorer Bar, Folders** command, or activate the **Folders** button in the toolbar.

➤ **Customizing the toolbar** Select **View, Toolbars, Customize** (or right-click the toolbar and then click **Customize**).

➤ **Changing the icon view** Choose one of the following commands on the **View** menu (or the toolbar's **Views** button): **Thumbnails, Tiles, Icons, List,** or **Details.**

➤ **Sorting files and folders** Select **View, Arrange Icons by** and then select a sort order. You also can sort in Details view by clicking the column headings.

➤ **Getting a global view** Set up a folder the way you want it, select **Tools, Options,** display the **View** tab, and click **Apply to All Folders.**

Chapter 27

Smooth System Sailing: Wielding the System Tools

In Chapter 28, "Getting a Good Night's Sleep: Preparing for Trouble," I'll show you how to back up your system and then recover everything when the inevitable crash occurs. After you've backed up your files, however, that doesn't mean you should just sit around and wait for your computer to start sucking mud. ("Sucking mud" is a colorful phrase used by programmers to refer to a crashed machine. Legend has it that the phrase comes from the oilfield lament "Shut 'er down, Ma, she's a-suckin' mud!")

No, what you *should* be doing is a little proactive system maintenance to help prolong your machine's life and to help propel your system to new heights of efficiency and speed. This chapter takes you through six tools that will help you do just that: Disk Cleanup, Check Disk, Disk Defragmenter, Task Scheduler, the Files and Settings Transfer Wizard, and Automatic Updates.

The Three Hard Disk Musketeers: Some Useful Disk Tools

Let's begin with a look at three programs that tend to that most vital of computer components: your hard disk. The preeminence of the hard disk in the computing pantheon shouldn't be surprising. After all, it's your hard disk that bears the burden of storing your priceless data. To help you keep your hard disk affairs in order and to help preserve your data, the next three sections discuss Windows XP's Disk Cleanup, Check Disk, and Disk Defragmenter programs.

Cleaning House: Using Disk Cleanup to Delete Junk Files

Ever wonder how much free space you have left on your hard disk? It's easy enough to find out. Just select **Start**, **My Computer** and highlight your hard disk. As you can see in Figure 27.1, the information area shows you how much free space you have left to work with.

Figure 27.1

Highlight your hard disk in My Computer to see how much disk real estate is left to be developed.

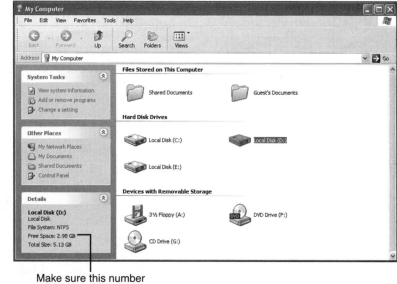

Make sure this number
doesn't get too low

If you find that you're running out of room, Windows XP can help. It has a program called Disk Cleanup that can rid your system of all kinds of unnecessary files, including the following:

➤ **Downloaded Program Files**   These are mini-programs used by some World Wide Web pages and that are downloaded onto your hard disk when you view such pages. After that, they just sit around doing nothing, so they can be safely deleted.

➤ **Temporary Internet files**   These are copies of Web pages that Internet Explorer keeps on hand so that the pages view faster the next time you visit them. Saying goodbye to these files will slow down some of your surfing slightly, but it will also rescue lots of disk space.

➤ **Offline Web pages**   These are Web pages that you've set up as favorites and for which you've activated the "Make available offline" feature. This means that Internet Explorer stores updated copies of these pages on your computer for offline surfing. Deleting them means that you'll have to go online to view them.

➤ **Recycle Bin**   These are the files that you've deleted recently. Windows XP stores them in the Recycle Bin for a while just in case you delete a file accidentally. If you're sure you don't need to recover a file, you can clean out the Recycle Bin and recover the disk space.

➤ **System Restore: Obsolete data stores**   These files are created by the System Restore program (which I discuss in the next chapter) and are used to help you recover from problems. However, some older files can no longer be used (because, for example, you reinstalled Windows XP), so they can be safely deleted.

➤ **Setup Log Files**   These are files that Windows XP created while it was installing itself on your computer. If your computer is running well, then you won't ever need to refer to these logs, so you can toss them.

➤ **Temporary files**   These are "scratch pad" files that some programs use to doodle on while they're up and running. Most programs are courteous enough to toss out these files, but a program or computer crash could prevent that from happening. You can delete these files at will.

➤ **WebClient/Publisher temporary files**   These are copies of existing files that Windows XP stores to improve the performance of the WebClient/Publisher service. It's perfectly okay to delete these copies.

Windows Wisdom

How do you know when your hard disk is getting low on disk space? It depends. If it's the disk where Windows XP is stored, then you should never let that disk get much below 200MB of free space. If it's some other disk that you use to store programs and files, start getting worried when the free space drops to around 100MB.

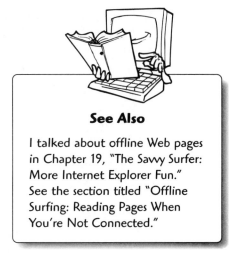

See Also

I talked about offline Web pages in Chapter 19, "The Savvy Surfer: More Internet Explorer Fun." See the section titled "Offline Surfing: Reading Pages When You're Not Connected."

351

➤ **Temporary offline files**   These are copies of network files that Windows XP saves on your hard disk temporarily. It's pretty safe to delete these files.

➤ **Offline files**   These are permanent copies of network files that reside on your hard disk. Having these files enables you to work with them even when you're not connected to the network. If you no longer need these files, delete them to clear some room on your hard disk.

➤ **NEW!   Compress old files**   Windows XP can take files that you haven't messed with in a while (the default is 50 days) and scrunch them down so that they take up less disk space, yet remain accessible to you and your programs.

➤ **Catalog files for the Content Indexer**   These are files that have been left behind by the Windows XP Indexing Service. You don't need these files, so you can delete them with abandon.

Note that you may not have all of these types of files on your system, so if you don't see some of them when you run Disk Cleanup, don't sweat it.

Follow these steps to use Disk Cleanup to trash any or all of these kinds of files:

1. Windows XP offers you three different routes to get started:

    ➤ In My Computer, highlight the hard disk and select **File, Properties.** (Alternatively, right-click the hard disk and then click **Properties.**) In the dialog box that beams up, click the **Disk Cleanup** button.

    ➤ Select **Start, Control Panel, Performance and Maintenance, Free up space on your hard disk.**

    ➤ Select **Start, All Programs, Accessories, System Tools, Disk Cleanup.**

2. If you used either of the last two paths and you have multiple hard disks, the Select Drive dialog box will ask you which one you want to work with. Use the **Drives** list to pick out the drive, and then click **OK.**

3. Either way, you end up at the Disk Cleanup window shown in Figure 27.2. Activate the check box beside each type of file you want to blow to kingdom come.

4. If you activate the **Compress old files** check box, you can determine what "old" means by clicking the **Options** button that appears while **Compress old files** is highlighted. In the Compress Old Files dialog box that puts in an appearance, use the **Compress after *x* days** spin box to set the age, in days, after which Windows XP will compress your files.

5. Click **OK.** Disk Cleanup asks whether you're sure.

6. Click **Yes.**

Keeping Your Hard Disk Humming with Check Disk

You'll see in the next chapter that you should back up your files frequently because all hard disks eventually go to the Great Computer in the Sky. However, it's possible to avoid a premature hard disk death (as well as lost files and otherwise-inexplicable system crashes) by regularly checking your disk for errors. (By "regularly," I mean about once a week or so.) Here's how you do it:

1. Log on to Windows XP with Administrator-level privileges.

2. Shut down any programs that are on the loose.

3. In My Computer, highlight your hard disk and select **File**, **Properties**. (For the heck of it, you also can try right-clicking the hard disk and then clicking **Properties**.)

4. In the dialog box that clears customs, display the **Tools** tab, as shown here.

5. Click the **Check Now** button. This gets you an appointment with the Check Disk dialog box.

6. Check Disk offers two checking options:

   ➤ **Automatically fix file system errors** Activate this check box to have Windows XP handle the dirty work of fixing any file problems that it finds. This gives you one less thing to fret about, so activating this option is a good idea.

Jargon Jar

A **sector** is a tiny piece of a disk and Windows XP uses a disk's sectors as mini storage bins that hold bits of your files. A "bad" sector is one that has gone wonky for some reason, so it can no longer be used to store anything reliably.

➤ **Scan for and attempt recovery of bad sectors**   Activate this option to have Check Disk examine the physical surface of the disk for corruption. This is a good idea because a lot of bad *sectors* means not only that you might not be able to store files reliably, but also that your hard disk might be heading for a crash. Note, however, that this slows down the check considerably, so you should probably use this option only once a month or so.

7. Click **Start** to get the Check Disk show on the road.

8. If any errors are found (and you didn't activate the **Automatically Fix File System Errors** option), you'll see a dialog box alerting you to the bad news. Follow the instructions provided.

9. When the check is done, a dialog box lets you know. Click **OK**.

Remember that Check Disk can take quite a while under some circumstances, so only run the program at the end of the day or when you know you won't be needing your computer for a while.

Tidying Up Your Hard Disk with Disk Defragmenter

With its 3D-ish icons and pastoral desktop, Windows XP surely presents a polished surface to the world. However, when it's just kicking around at home, Windows XP is a bit of a slob. I'm thinking, in particular, about how Windows XP stores files on your hard disk. It's actually remarkably casual about the whole thing, and tosses bits and pieces of each file wherever it can find room. This doesn't matter much at first, but after a while you end up with files that are scattered willy-nilly all over your hard disk. This is a problem because it means that to open a file, Windows XP has to make lots of little, time-consuming trips to the far corners of the hard disk in order to gather up all those disparate chunks.

This is why computers that feel nice and zippy when you first take them out of the box seem to get more sluggish over time. In geek terms, the problem is that the files on your hard disk have become *fragmented*. The solution is to run the Windows XP Disk Defragmenter program, which will rearrange the contents of your hard disk so that each file's hunks are arranged consecutively (or *contiguously,* as the geeks like to say). Don't worry, though: Your documents and programs don't get changed in any way and your disk contents will look exactly the same when you view them in My Computer.

Before getting to the Disk Defragmenter details, here's a bit of prep work you need to do:

Windows Wisdom

It's worth keeping in mind that Disk Defragmenter also works with Zip disks and Jaz disks.

➤ Log on to Windows XP with Administrator-level privileges.

➤ Shut down all running programs.

➤ Run the Check Disk program to be sure there are no errors on your hard disk. In particular, be sure you activate the **Scan for and attempt recovery of bad sectors** check box.

➤ Run Disk Cleanup and get rid of any files you don't need.

Here's how Disk Defragmenter works:

1. You can get underway by using either of the following techniques:

   ➤ In My Computer, highlight your hard disk and select **File, Properties.** (Or right-click the hard disk and then click **Properties.**) In the dialog box that gets piped in, display the **Tools** tab and click the **Defragment Now** button.

   ➤ Select **Start, Control Panel, Performance and Maintenance, Rearrange items on your hard disk to make programs run faster.**

   ➤ Select **Start, All Programs, Accessories, System Tools, Disk Defragmenter.**

2. Figure 27.3 shows the Disk Defragmenter window that results. If you have multiple disk drives, click the one you want to work with.

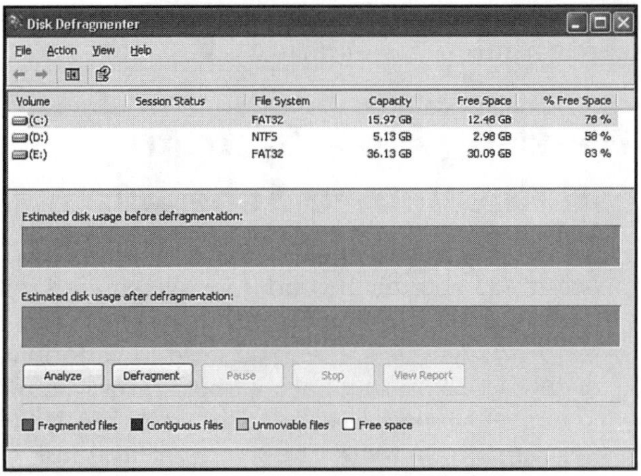

Figure 27.3

Use Disk Defragmenter to put your hard disk affairs in order.

3. Click the **Analyze** button. This tells Disk Defragmenter to have a gander at the chosen disk and see just how defragmented it is.

4. After a few seconds, you'll see the Analysis Complete dialog box, which will display one of the following messages (note that, in both cases, *volume* is XP-speak for a disk drive):

   ➤ **You do not need to defragment this volume** This is the "Woo hoo!" message because it means your disk isn't fragmented too much and you can bypass the defragment for now. Click **Close** and exit Disk Defragmenter.

355

➤ **You should defragment this volume** Disk Defragmenter tends to be a bit reluctant to call for a defragment, so if you see this message, then you *know* that your system needs to be straightened up. In this case, you should click **Defragment** (although you also can click **Close** and start the defragment from the Disk Defragmenter window).

5. If you're back in the Disk Defragmenter window and you want to run the defragment from there, click **Defragment**. Disk Defragmenter reanalyzes the disk and then gets down to work. While this happens, compare the **Estimated disk use before defragmentation** display with the **Estimated disk use after defragmentation** display. Over time, you'll start to see more blue (contiguous files) in the latter and less red (fragmented files).

6. When the job is complete, Disk Defragmenter displays a dialog box to let you know. Click **Close**.

7. If you want to defragment another disk, repeat steps 2 through 6.

8. To exit Disk Defragmenter, select **File, Exit**.

The defragmenting process might take some time, depending on the size of your disk and how severely fragmented it is. Because it's not unusual for a defragment job to take a couple of hours or more, consider running Disk Defragmenter just before you leave the office or go to bed. (Or use the Scheduled Tasks folder—discussed in the next section—to set up Disk Defragmenter to run at night.)

Windows Wisdom

How often you use Disk Defragmenter depends on how much you use your computer. If you give your machine a real workout on most days, run the analysis portion of Disk Defragmenter about once a week. If your computer gets only light use, crank up Disk Defragmenter about once a month.

Setting Up a System Maintenance Schedule

As with backing up, performing system maintenance doesn't do you much good if you get around to it only once in a while. If you want to keep your system firing on all cylinders, then you need to perform regular maintenance. In these hectic times, however, it's hard to remember even to eat, much less to run Disk Cleanup once a week. The solution is the Task Scheduler, which is really a special folder called Scheduled Tasks. Its job is to enable you to set up a particular program to run at a specified time, or to run multiple times on a schedule (such as once a week).

To get started, use either of the following techniques:

➤ Select **Start, Control Panel, Performance and Maintenance, Scheduled Tasks**.

➤ Select **Start, All Programs, Accessories, System Tools, Scheduled Tasks**.

Windows XP donates the Scheduled Tasks folder. You usually just see the Add Scheduled Task icon, but you might see other icons that were created by other programs.

Here are the steps to run through to create a new schedule for a program:

1. Launch the **Add Scheduled Task** icon. The Scheduled Task Wizard arrives in a flurry of electrons.

2. The first dialog box is as useless as all the other wizard openers, so click **Next.**

3. The next wizard dialog box provides you with a list of programs to schedule. Click the program you want to schedule and then click **Next.** If you don't see the program, click **Browse,** use the Select Program to Schedule dialog box to highlight the program, and then click **Open.** Here are some pointers for the system maintenance tools:

   ➤ **Disk Cleanup** If this program doesn't appear in the list, use the Select Program to Schedule dialog box to highlight C:\Windows\system32\cleanmgr.

   ➤ **Check Disk** Unfortunately, this program can't be scheduled. Bummer!

   ➤ **Disk Defragmenter** If this program doesn't appear in the list, use the Select Program to Schedule dialog box to highlight C:\Windows\system32\dfrg.

4. The next wizard dialog box asks you to enter a name for the task. (The wizard suggests the name of the program or the name of its file, but you can use anything you want.)

5. You also use this dialog box to pick out the frequency with which you want the task to run: **Daily, Weekly,** and so on. When you've made your choice, click **Next.**

6. The layout of the dialog box that shows up next depends on the frequency you chose. For example, Figure 27.4 shows the dialog box that lands if you chose the Weekly schedule. Set up the specifics of the schedule, and then click **Next.**

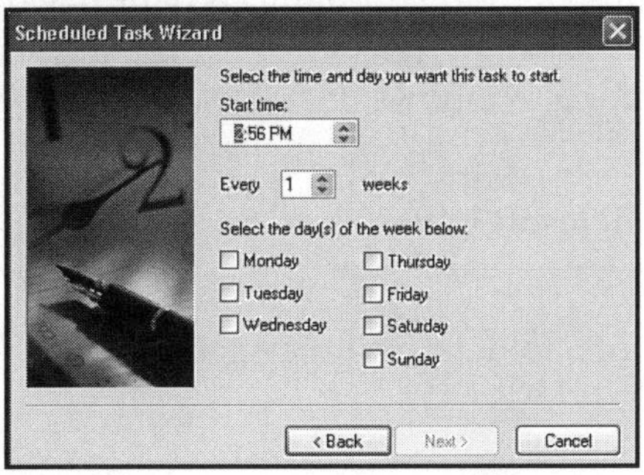

Figure 27.4

This is the dialog box that appears if you chose the Weekly schedule.

Windows Wisdom

You can run a scheduled task at any time by highlighting it in the Scheduled Tasks window and selecting **File, Run.** (It's also permissible to right-click the task and then click **Run.**)

7. Now the wizard pesters you for the username and password of a user. The idea here is that the task will run as though that user were logged on. For example, if you're running Disk Defragmenter, you need to specify a user who has Administrator privileges. Click **Next** when you've entered the info.

8. In the final wizard dialog box, click **Finish**.

If you need to make changes to the scheduled task, highlight it and select **File, Properties**. (You also can double-click the task or right-click the task and then click **Properties**.) The dialog box that elbows its way onto the desktop has three tabs. Use the **Task** tab to change the program command and the user info; use the **Schedule** tab to change the program's schedule; and use the **Settings** tab to adjust some scheduling options.

Using the Files and Settings Transfer Wizard

NEW!   Getting a spiffy new computer should be a time for rejoicing, particularly if the new machine is faster and more powerful than your old clunker. But rejoicing is usually the farthest thing from the mind of most new computer owners. Why? Because it's an annoying pain-in-the-you-know-what to get the computer configured with the same settings as the old machine. Whether it's your e-mail accounts and messages, your Internet Explorer favorites, or your Windows customizations, it's a long and tiresome process to transfer or re-create these things on the new box.

If you've gone through this before, or have been putting off doing it with your current machine, you'll be pleased as punch to know that Windows XP offers a painless way to get your files and settings from your old computer to your new one. It's called, straightforwardly, the Files and Settings Transfer Wizard, and it can grab your things from any computer that's running Windows 95, 98, Me, NT 4, 2000, or XP. It can transfer some or all of the following:

➤ Settings for programs such as Microsoft Office

➤ Internet Explorer options and favorites

➤ Outlook Express options, accounts, folders, and messages

➤ Windows Messenger options

➤ Display settings

➤ Mouse and keyboard settings

➤ Accessibility settings

➤ Mapped network drives and printers

➤ International settings

➤ Taskbar options

➤ Folder options

➤ Windows Media Player options

➤ The following folders: My Documents, My Pictures, Desktop, Fonts, Shared Desktop, and Shared Documents

➤ All the document file types set up on the old system

You have to run the wizard on both your new computer and on your old computer. Here's how it works on the new computer:

1. Establish either a cable or network connection between the two computers.

2. Select **Start**, **All Programs**, **Accessories**, **System Tools**, **Files and Settings Transfer Wizard**. The wizard wanders onto the desktop.

3. Click **Next** to get past the traditionally useless initial dialog box. The wizard wonders which computer it's dealing with.

4. Activate **New computer** and click **Next**. Now the wizard mumbles something about a Wizard Disk. This is a disk that enables you to run the Files and Settings Transfer Wizard on your old computer.

5. If you have a Windows XP CD, activate the **I will use the wizard from the Windows XP CD** option. Otherwise, activate **I want to create a Wizard Disk in the following drive** and then use the list to choose the drive you want to use. (Make sure you have the same type of drive on the old computer.) Click **Next**.

6. If you chose to create a Wizard Disk, put a blank, formatted disk in the drive and click **OK** after the wizard prompts you to insert the disk.

See Also

For cable connections, see Chapter 16, "A Moveable Feast: Windows XP and Your Notebook Computer"; for network connections, see Chapter 30, "Using Windows XP to Set Up a Small Network."

The wizard now instructs you to go to your old computer. That sounds fine to me, so let's switch to the other machine and resume from there. Here are the steps to follow on the old computer:

1. How you get started depends on whether you're using a Wizard Disk:

➤ If you're using a Wizard Disk, insert the disk, open the disk in My Computer, and then double-click the **FASTWiz** file.

➤ If you're using your Windows XP CD, insert the CD and wait until you see the Welcome to Microsoft Windows XP window. Click **Perform other tasks** and then **Transfer files and settings.**

2. When the wizard appears, click **Next.**

3. Activate **Old computer** and click **Next.** The wizard insists that you select the method you'll be using to transfer the files and settings:

➤ **Direct cable**   This method uses a cable connected to the serial port on both computers (the wizard won't work with a parallel port connection). If you choose this option, click **Next** to get to the **Set up your serial connection** dialog box. Return to the new computer and click **Next** until you arrive at the same dialog box. Now click the **Autodetect** button on both computers. When the wizard connects (it takes a few seconds), click **Next** on both machines.

➤ **Home or small network**   This method uses a network connection between the two computers.

➤ **Floppy drive or other removable media**   This method uses a disk in a floppy drive, Zip drive, or some other kind of disk drive that's common to both computers.

➤ **Other**   This method just stores the files and settings on the disk drive or folder that you specify in the **Folder or drive** text box.

4. The wizard next wants to know what you want to transfer. Activate **Settings**, **Files only**, or **Both files and Settings.** If you want to specify your own settings and files, be sure to activate the **Customize** check box. Click **Next.**

5. If you elected to customize the files and settings, you see the dialog box shown in Figure 27.5. Use the **Add Settings**, Add Folder, **Add File**, and **Add File Type** buttons to add your own stuff to the list. To take anything off the list, highlight it and click **Remove.** When you're done, click **Next.** The wizard takes a few minutes to gather up everything it needs.

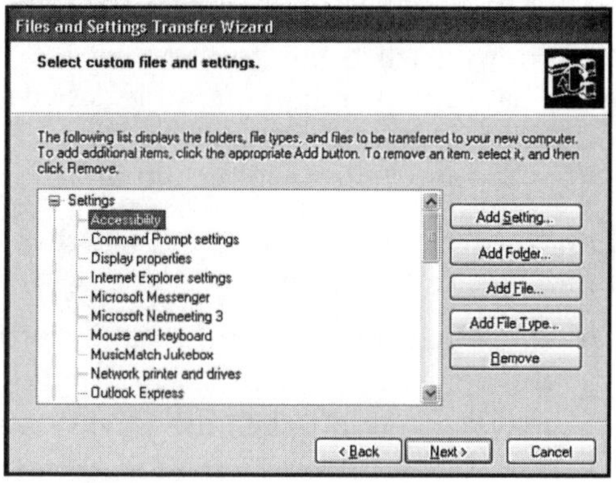

Figure 27.5

Use this wizard dialog box to customize the transfer.

360

6. If you elected to transfer your stuff via a disk, the wizard will prompt you to insert disks until all the files and settings have been stored.

7. When the collection process is complete, click **Finish.**

Now return to the new computer and complete the wizard:

1. Click **Next** until you get to the dialog box where the wizard asks where the older computer's files and settings are located.

2. Activate the appropriate option (**Direct cable, Home or small network**, and so on) and click **Next.**

3. If you're using disks, insert the first disk and click **OK**, and then follow the prompts for any other disks that were needed.

4. When the wizard is done, click **Finish.**

At this point, the wizard might suggest that you log off to put the changes into effect. If so, click **Yes** to make it happen.

Using Automatic Updates to Keeping Up with the Windows Joneses

Windows XP is a moving target. Oh, it might look stationary, but while you're busy learning where things are and how things work, the Microsoft programmers are busy fixing bugs, improving existing features, and adding new features. In previous versions, these changes were packaged into massive *service packs* that you could download from the Web or get on CD. With Windows XP, however, Microsoft is taking a different tack and is going to have individual fixes and improvements available on a special Web site called Windows Update. In fact, you no longer even have to go that far because Windows XP comes with a feature called *automatic updates* that will check for new Windows trinkets and then download and install them automatically.

After Windows XP sees that your computer has Internet access, you eventually see yet another icon in your taskbar's notification area, as well as a message titled **Stay current with automatic updates.** This is the Automatic Updates icon, and its job is to let you know when Windows Update has something new to install.

Before you can use this feature, you have to run through a brief setup procedure:

1. Click the **Automatic Updates** icon or the message. The Automatic Updated Setup Wizard comes by.

2. Click **Next.** The wizard asks you how you want to be notified of updates:

➤ **Download the updates automatically ...** This is the no-brainer option because Windows XP handles all the dirty work behind the scenes. When an update is available, Windows XP downloads it and then displays the Automatic Updates icon with a message telling you that the update is

361

ready to be installed. All you have to do is click the message to make things happen.

➤ **Notify me before downloading ...**   Choose this option to force Windows XP to ask your permission before downloading a component. It's a bit more work, but at least you'll always know what Windows XP is up to.

➤ **Turn off automatic updating ...**   Choose this option if you prefer to go to the Windows Update Web site yourself.

3. Click **Next.**

4. Click **Finish.**

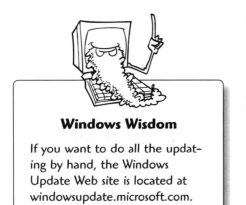

Windows Wisdom

If you want to do all the updating by hand, the Windows Update Web site is located at windowsupdate.microsoft.com.

After that's done, the Automatic Updates feature runs in the background and checks for new components for your computer automatically. If you're connected to the Internet and a new component is available, Automatic Updates either downloads it behind the scenes or lets you know if an update is available (if you chose the **Notify me before downloading ...** option, earlier).

If the latter is the case, click the Automatic Updates icon or the message, and you'll see a list of the updates that are available. Leave the check marks activated beside each update you want downloaded, and click **Start Download.** Note that if you need to disconnect from the Internet while downloading the update, click the Update Reminder icon and then click **Pause.** To continue the download, click the icon again and then click **Resume.**

When the download is done like dinner, the Automatic Updates icon displays a message letting you know that you have a new component to install. To install the component, click the message or the icon, which gets you to the Ready to Install dialog box. You have three choices from here:

➤ **Details**   Click this button to see what the heck was downloaded. Note that each item has a check box beside it. If you prefer not to install an item, deactivate its check box.

➤ **Remind Me Later**   Click this button to bypass the installation for now. The Update Reminder icon will pester you about it again later on.

➤ **Install**   Click this button to install the new component.

To change your Automatic Updates settings, click **Start,** right-click **My Computer,** and then click **Properties.** In the System Properties dialog box that appears, use the **Automatic Updates** tab to adjust your settings. Note, too, that this tab also has a **Previous Updates** section that enables you to be notified again of any earlier updates that you turned down for some reason.

The Least You Need to Know

➤ **The Tools tab**   If you highlight a hard disk in My Computer and then select **File, Properties,** the resulting dialog box has a **Tools** tab with three buttons: **Check Now** (which runs Check Disk), **Backup Now** (which runs Backup; Windows XP Pro only), and **Defragment Now** (which runs Disk Defragmenter).

➤ **Administrator-only tools**   To run Check Disk and Disk Defragmenter, you need to log on to Windows XP with Administrator-level privileges.

➤ **Bad-sector check**   Bad hard disk sectors can cause all kinds of woes. Therefore, you should activate Check Disk's **Scan for and attempt recovery of bad sectors** check box about once a month or so.

➤ **What's the frequency, Kenneth?**   You should run Disk Cleanup every couple of weeks, Check Disk every week (and the bad-sector check every month), and Disk Defragmenter every week (every month if your machine gets only light use).

➤ **XP updating made easy**   If you want your version of Windows XP to always be up-to-date, be sure to turn on XP's new Automatic Updates feature and let it handle everything for you.

Chapter 28

Getting a Good Night's Sleep: Preparing for Trouble

In This Chapter

➤ Using System Restore to return your system to a working configuration

➤ Some pointers for avoiding computer viruses

➤ Using Windows XP Professional to back up your data

➤ Using Automated System Recovery to recover from a major mishap

Hard disks keep your data intact when you switch off your machine. However, hard disks are also mechanical devices that simply wear out over time. Not only that, but a hard disk can succumb to all kinds of other maladies: computer viruses, power surges (not uncommon during lightning storms), program crashes, hard knocks, and more.

In other words, your data is at risk *right now*. Not months or years from now. *Now*. To help prevent the gray hairs, ulcers, and fists through the monitor that would result from losing all your precious documents, you need to start preparing for the in-evitable trouble that comes every computer user's way. This chapter can help by show-ing you the Windows XP tools that can get you in what I like to call "ounce of prevention mode" (and to avoid what I call "pound of cure mode" down the road).

Recovering from a Problem Using System Restore

One of the most frustrating of Windows experiences is to have your system sailing along without so much as an electronic hiccup, and then to have everything crash or become unstable after installing a program or a chunk of hardware. This all-too-common scenario means that some program component or device driver simply doesn't get along with Windows XP, and that the two are now at loggerheads. Uninstalling the program or device can often help, but that's not a foolproof solution.

To help guard against software or hardware installations that bring down the system, Windows XP has a feature called System Restore. Its job is straightforward, yet clever: To take periodic snapshots—called *restore points* or *checkpoints*—of your system, each of which includes the current Windows XP configuration. The idea is that if a program or device installation causes problems on your system, you use System Restore to revert your system to the most recent restore point before the installation.

System Restore creates checkpoints using the following methods:

➤ Automatically every 24 hours if you keep your computer on full-time. If you turn your machine off periodically, Windows XP creates a restore point every 24 hours that the machine is running.

➤ Automatically before installing an update via the Automatic Updates feature (discussed in Chapter 27, "Smooth System Sailing: Wielding the System Tools").

➤ Automatically before installing certain applications. Some newer applications—notably Office 2000—are aware of System Restore and ask it to create a restore point prior to installation.

➤ Automatically when you attempt to install a device driver that is "unsigned" (meaning that it can't be verified that the driver will work properly with Windows XP).

➤ Manually using the System Restore feature.

Creating a Restore Point Manually

To create a restore point manually, follow these steps:

1. Use either of the following methods to launch System Restore:
   ➤ Select **Start, Control Panel, Performance and Maintenance, System Restore.**
   ➤ Select **Start, All Programs, Accessories, System Tools, System Restore.**
2. Activate the **Create a restore point** option and click **Next.**
3. Use the **Restore point description** text box to enter a description for the new restore point, and then click **Create.** System Restore creates the restore point and displays the Restore Point Created window.
4. Click **Close.**

If Things Go South: Using a Restore Point

If you ever need to restore your system to an earlier state, follow these steps:

1. Use either of the following methods to launch System Restore:

   ➤ Select **Start, Control Panel, Performance and Maintenance, System Restore.**

   ➤ Select **Start, All Programs, Accessories, System Tools, System Restore.**

2. Activate the **Restore my computer to an earlier time** option and click **Next.** The Select a Restore Point window appears, as shown in Figure 28.1.

3. Use the calendar to click the date on which the restore point was made. System Restore displays that day's checkpoints in a box to the right of the calendar.

4. Click the restore point you want to restore. (Note that the **System Checkpoint** items are the restore points created automatically by Windows XP every 24 hours.)

5. Click **Next.** System Restore asks you to close all open programs and warns you not to do anything with your computer until the restore is done.

Windows Wisdom

If restoring your system makes things worse or causes additional problems, you have a couple of choices. To undo the restore, launch System Restore, activate the **Undo my last restoration** option, and click **Next.** Alternatively, you can run System Restore and revert the system to an even earlier restore point.

Figure 28.1

Use this window to choose the restore point you want to revert to.

367

6. Click **Next**. System Restore begins restoring the restore point. When it's done, it restarts your computer and displays the Restoration Complete window.

7. Click **OK**.

Protecting Your System from Computer Viruses

Viruses are nasty little programs that live for the sheer thrill of trashing your valuable data. They're crafted in dank basements by repressed, pimple-faced, Jolt Cola–fueled deviants—programming wizards who've succumbed to the dark side of the Force. These amoral hackers like to muddy the waters by describing their wicked offspring as "self-propagating, autonomous computer programs" and giving them innocent-sounding names such as Michelangelo and Christmas. But don't be fooled: these small slices of evil can do irreparable harm to your files. (Just so you know, many viruses have names that more directly reflect their intentions. These include Armageddon, Beast, Black Monday, Dark Avenger, and Darth Vader.)

Although virus infections are, fortunately, still relatively rare, they *do* happen. Note, however, that there is no specific Windows XP feature that can protect your from and eradicate viruses. So the first thing you should do after you finish this section is run out and buy yourself a copy of a good anti-virus program. Utilities such as Norton Anti-Virus and McAfee VirusScan can monitor your system full-time to protect you from viruses. They also include update programs that can keep you protected from the hundreds of new viruses that crawl out of the digital woodwork every year.

Besides getting yourself a top-notch anti-virus program, here are a few other tips to help keep your system disease-free:

➤ These days, most viruses are transmitted via file downloads from the Internet, an online service, or a network connection. Set up a special folder for downloads and always click the **Save** button to save downloaded files to this folder. Then use your anti-virus program to scan this folder every time you download a file.

➤ The second leading cause of viral infections is the lowly floppy disk, so you should always be careful about which used disks you trust in your computer. If you've inherited some old disks, you can make sure there are no viruses lurking in the weeds by formatting all the disks before you use them.

➤ Trust no one when it comes to loading programs on your machine. Whether they come from family, friends, the Internet, or an online bulletin board, use your anti-virus program to scan the files *before* using them on your hard disk.

➤ If you get an e-mail message with a file attachment, delete it immediately if it comes from a stranger. If it comes from someone you know, contact that person and ask her if she sent you a file. (Many viruses propagate by surreptitiously sending copies of themselves to the people in an infected user's address book.)

➤ Make sure you've set up Outlook Express with the maximum protection. Select **Tools, Options,** display the **Security** tab, and activate the **Restricted sites zone** option. Also, activate the **Do not allow attachments to be saved or opened that could potentially be a virus** check box.

➤ Keep your anti-virus program's virus list up to date. As you read this, there are probably dozens, maybe even hundreds, of morally challenged scumnerds designing even nastier viruses. Regular updates will help you keep up.

Backing Up Your Precious Data with Windows XP Professional

Other than a few people who insist on living in It-Can't-Happen-to-Me Land, I think most folks get the "why" part of backing up. They just don't get the "how" part. That is, they'd like to run backups, but it's such a time-consuming chore so it just doesn't seem worth the hassle. "Sorry, I'd like to do a backup, but I have to call the IRS to schedule an audit."

Backing Up: Some Things to Consider

If backing up seems like too much of a bother, there are plenty of things you can do to make it easier:

➤ **Forget floppies**   Yes, it's possible to back up files to floppy disks in Windows XP. However, that's a bad way to go because it requires about 17 floppies to back up just 100MB. If you're like most people, you probably have hundreds of megabytes to protect, so backing up to dozens of floppy disks is no one's idea of fun, I'm sure.

➤ **Use better backup destinations**   For easiest backups, use a medium that has a relatively large capacity. That way, you won't spend your time shuffling disks in and out. Windows XP supports all kinds of backup and storage devices, but here are a few to bear in mind:

    Zip disks   These hold 100MB (the latest ones hold 250MB), which is a heckuva lot better than a floppy disk.

    Jaz disks   These come in 1GB and 2GB flavors, so they have plenty of capacity.

    Tape drives   These typically come in multi-gigabyte capacities and are pretty cheap, so they're the most common choice used by backup aficionados.

Hard disks   This is a great choice if you happen to have a second hard disk in your system. (Be sure it's a second disk, and not just a single disk that's been divided in two.)

Network locales   If you have a small network at home or in a small office, you might consider turning one machine's large hard disk into a backup destination. On larger networks, see whether your system administrator has set aside space for you on a server.

➤ **Back up your documents first**   The only things on your system that are truly irreplaceable are the documents that you've created with the sweat of your own brow. So, if backup space is at a premium, just include your documents in the *backup job.* You can always install your programs again later, if need be.

➤ **Organize your documents**   If you're going to go the documents-only route, you'll make your life immeasurably easier if you store everything in subfolders that all reside within a single folder (such as My Documents). That way, when you're telling Windows XP which files to back up, you need to only select that folder. Another plus for this approach is that any files you add to this folder will be included automatically the next time you run the backup.

➤ **Back up your downloaded programs**   If you've downloaded programs and files from the Internet, it can be a lot of trouble to get new copies of that stuff if your system goes down for the count. So, you should include downloaded files as part of your backup job.

➤ **Take advantage of backup types**   After you've decided on all the files that should be part of the backup, don't waste time by backing up every single one of those files each time you do a backup. Instead, it's possible to use *backup types* To tell Windows XP Pro to back up only those files that have changed. Windows XP Pro supports no fewer than five backup types:

Jargon Jar

A **backup job** is a file that specifies a few particulars about your backup. These particulars include the files you want backed up, the location where the files will be backed up, and any backup options you specify along the way.

Normal   Backs up each and every file, each and every time. (Note that by "each and every file," I mean "each and every file in the backup job.") All files are marked to indicate they've been backed up.

Incremental   Backs up only those files that have changed since the most recent Normal or Incremental backup. This is the fastest type because it includes only the minimum number of files. Again, the files are marked to indicate they've been backed up.

Differential Backs up only those files that have changed since the most recent non-Differential backup. That is, the files are *not* marked to indicate they've been backed up. So, if you run this type of backup again, the same files get backed up (plus any others that have changed in the meantime).

Daily Backs up only those files that were modified on the day you run the backup.

Copy Makes copies of the selected files. This type of backup does not mark the files as having been backed up. This means you can use it for quick backups without interfering with your backup strategy (discussed next).

➤ **Create a backup strategy** Finally, you should come up with a backup strategy that makes sense for you, and then you should stick to that strategy no matter what. A typical strategy might go something like this:

> Run a Daily backup each day.

> Run an Incremental backup once a week. Delete the previous week's Daily and Incremental backups.

> Run a Normal backup once a month. When done, delete the previous month's Incremental and Normal backups.

Windows Wisdom

How does the Backup program mark files as backed up? Each file has what's known in the trade as an archive flag, which gets raised when you make changes to a file. When you include a file in a Normal or an Incremental backup, the flag is lowered to indicate that the file has been backed up. Note that a Differential backup does *not* lower the flag.

Creating and Running a Backup Job

Now that we've knocked the whole backup process down to size, let's whip out the brass tacks and get down to business. To get started, select **Start, All Programs, Accessories, System Tools, Backup.** After a second or two, the Backup or Restore Wizard pulls itself out of a hat. The next two sections take you through the two procedures for backing up: the Backup or Restore Wizard and creating a backup job by hand.

The Backup Wizard's step-by-step approach makes it easy to create and launch a backup job. Here's what happens:

1. In the initial Backup or Restore Wizard dialog box, click **Next.**
2. Activate the **Back up files and settings** option and then click **Next.**

3. The next wizard dialog box gives you four choices (click **Next** when you're done):

   ➤ **My documents and settings**   Choose this option to back up your My Documents folder, your Favorites folders, your desktop, and your cookies.

   ➤ **Everyone's documents and settings**   Choose this option if you have multiple users on the computer and you want to back up their documents and settings as well as your own.

   ➤ **All information on this computer**   Choose this option to be able to completely recover your system in the event of a catastrophe. (See the "Preparing for the Worst: Using Automated System Recovery" section later in this chapter.)

   ➤ **Let me choose what to back up**   Choose this option to pick out exactly which files to back up.

4. If you elected to choose what to back up, you'll see the Items to Back Up dialog box shown in Figure 28.2. The idea here is that you use the items in the **Items to back up** list to choose which drives, folders, or files you want to include in the backup. You do this by activating the check box beside each item you want to back up. (Now you see why I suggested you include all your documents in subfolders within My Documents. To back up all your data files, all you have to do is activate the **My Documents** check box. One click and you're done. What could be easier?) Click **Next** when you're ready to proceed.

Windows Wisdom

Windows XP has a collection of files that store what's known as the *system state*. This is the Windows XP configuration, so these are absolutely crucial files, and you'll be able to recover your system much faster if you back them up. To include the system state stuff in your backup job, open the **My Computer** branch and activate the **System State** check box.

5. Now the wizard wants to know the backup destination. Use the **Select the backup type** list to choose the type of backup medium (such as a file or a tape device) you want to use. Use the **Choose a place to save your backup** list to specify the location of the backup. (You can click **Browse** to choose the location from a dialog box.) You can also enter a name in the **Type a name for this backup** text box. Click **Next** to continue.

6. The wizard displays a summary of the backup job settings. Say "Hold on a minute there, buster!" and click **Advanced**. You'll then run through a series of dialog boxes. Here's a quick summary (click **Next** after each one):

   ➤ **Type of Backup**   Use the **Select the type of backup** list to choose a backup type (Normal, Incremental, and so on).

➤ **How to Back Up** If you have ultra-important data and you don't want anything to go wrong, activate the **Verify data after backup** check box. This ensures that your data was backed up without mishap, but it basically doubles the total backup time.

➤ **Backup Options** You can either append this backup to an existing backup job (this is your best choice in most situations) or have this backup replace an existing backup job.

➤ **When to Back Up** Choose **Now** to start the backup immediately. Alternatively, select **Later** and click **Set Schedule** to run the backup at a future time. (See the "Staying Regular: Scheduling Backup Jobs" section later in this chapter.)

7. Click **Finish.** Backup gathers the files and then starts backing them up. If the backup medium gets full, you'll be prompted to insert another one. When the backup job is complete, you'll see a report. (If the report tells you that errors occurred during the backup, check to see which files were involved and then back them up again.)

8. Click **Close.**

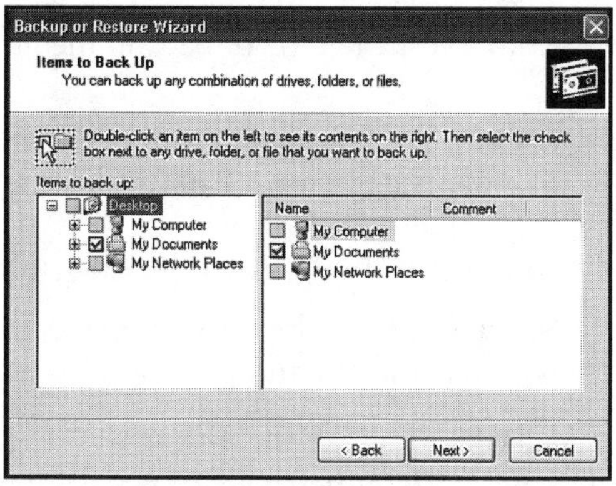

Figure 28.2

If you decided to select the backup job files yourself, you'll get this dialog box coming at you.

From here, you might want to save your backup job for future use. I'll show you how to do that later on (see "Saving and Reusing Backup Jobs").

The Backup or Restore Wizard ensures that you don't forget anything, but it's a bit of a long haul to get from A to Backup. You can usually speed up the entire process by creating a backup job by hand. To give this a whirl, start Backup once again. However, when the Backup or Restore Wizard returns, click the **Advanced Mode** link. (If you find you prefer this method for backing up, you can bypass the wizard in the future by deactivating the **Always start in wizard mode** check box.) Now display the **Backup** tab to get the window shown in Figure 28.3.

Figure 28.3

Use the Backup tab to define a backup job yourself.

To create the backup job, use the following controls:

➤ **Click to select the check box for any drive, folder, or file that you want to back up** As with the Backup or Restore Wizard, you activate the check boxes beside the items you want to include in the backup.

➤ **Backup destination** Use this list to select the type of backup media you're using.

➤ **Backup media or file name** Use this text box to enter the backup location (or click **Browse**).

To choose the backup type, follow these quick steps:

1. Select **Tools, Options** to ask the Options dialog box to come out and play.

2. Display the **Backup Type** tab.

3. Use the **Default Backup Type** list to choose the backup type.

4. Click **OK**.

To launch the backup, click the **Start Backup** button. Again, Backup gathers the files and then performs the backup. When you see the report, click **Close**.

> **Windows Wisdom**
>
> If you want to include Windows XP's configuration data in your backup (which is a darn good idea), be sure to activate the **System State** check box.

Saving and Reusing Backup Jobs

Because you'll be backing up regularly, you'll almost certainly run the same backup job again in the future. To avoid reinventing the backup job wheel, you should save your settings for later use. To do this, be sure the **Backup** tab is displayed and then select **Job, Save Selections.** In the Save As dialog box, enter a **File name** for the job, and then click **Save.**

To reuse a backup job down the road, display the **Backup** tab and select **Job, Load Selections.** If Backup asks whether you want to clear your current sections, click **Yes.** Use the Open dialog box to highlight your backup job, and then click **Open.**

Staying Regular: Scheduling Backup Jobs

Combining my backup tips with the Backup program's ease of use, you see that backing up doesn't have to be drudgery that you avoid at all costs. That's a good thing, to be sure, but it's all for naught if you don't get into the habit of backing up your stuff regularly. We're all busy, I know, so although you might be convinced that backing up is as important as breathing, *remembering* to do it (backing up, that is) can be a problem.

To help out, Backup lets you set up one or more schedules that make everything happen automatically. There are two ways to go about this:

➤ Create a backup job and set up a schedule for it. As described earlier, click **Advanced** in the final wizard dialog box, and then set up the schedule after you see the When to Back Up dialog box. I describe the scheduling details later in this section.

➤ Display the **Schedule Jobs** tab, shown in Figure 28.4. Either double-click the date when you first want to run the backup, or highlight the date and click **Add Job.** This launches the Backup Wizard. Follow the wizard's dialog boxes until you get to the When to Back Up dialog box.

At this point, Backup might ask you to enter a password for the schedule. If so, enter the password you want to use in the two text boxes (this isn't an important step, so I usually just leave them blank), and click **OK.**

Let's run through the specifics of creating a schedule:

1. In the When to Back Up dialog box, enter the name of the backup job in the **Job name** text box.

2. Click **Set Schedule.** The Schedule Job dialog box appears, right on schedule.

3. Use the following controls to set the schedule:

   ➤ **Schedule Task** Specifies the frequency of the schedule (Daily, Weekly, and so on).

   ➤ **Start Time** Specifies when the backup job begins. If the backup job doesn't require you to swap any disks in and out (in other words, if you can run the backup without being there), it's best to choose a time when you won't be using your computer (such as the wee hours of the morning).

➤ **Advanced**   Click this button to set an **End Date** for the schedule (that is, the date after which the schedule is no longer in effect) and whether you want to **Repeat task.**

➤ **Schedule Task** *Whenever*   The group below these options (the name of which depends on what you choose in the Schedule Task list; for example, Schedule Task Once) sets the specifics of the backup frequency. For example, if you selected Weekly in the Schedule Task list, you use this group to specify which day of the week you want the backup to run.

4. The **Settings** tab is chock-full of options for controlling the scheduled backup job. For example, you can have Backup stop the job if it runs beyond a specific length of time, you can have the job run only if your computer has been idle for a while, and much more. I ran through these options when I discussed the Task Scheduler in Chapter 27.

5. When you're done, click **OK.**

Figure 28.4

Use the Schedule Jobs tab to view and create scheduled backup jobs.

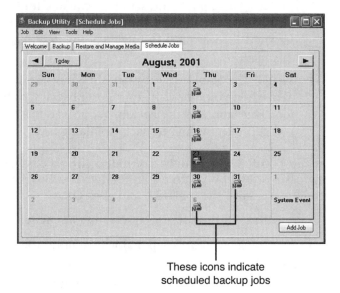

These icons indicate
scheduled backup jobs

Recovering Files from a Backup Job

When disaster strikes (notice I didn't say *if* disaster strikes), you need to first get your system back on its digital feet as described in the previous section. After that's done, you can then restore your files from your backup job (or jobs). Again, you do this either by using a wizard or by hand.

If you use the Backup or Restore Wizard, begin by selecting **Start, All Programs, Accessories, System Tools, Backup** to launch the Backup program. (Alternatively, if the Backup window is open, display the **Welcome** tab and then click **Wizard Mode**.) Here's what happens if you enlist the Backup or Restore Wizard to do the job:

1. In the initial Backup or Restore Wizard dialog box, click **Next**.

2. Activate the **Restore files and settings** option and then click **Next**. The What to Restore dialog box appears.

3. In the **Items to restore** list, open the branch to expose the backup jobs. If you have multiple backup sets in that backup job, open the backup job branch and activate the check box beside the set you want to restore. From there, you can keep opening the branches to expose the drives, folders, and files you included in the backup job. Activate the check boxes for those items you want to restore and then click **Next**.

4. Click **Advanced** to run through the following dialog boxes:

   ➤ **Where to Restore**   Choose where you want Backup to place the restored files. You'll usually select **Original location** for this. You also can choose **Alternate location** to put the files and folders somewhere else (to avoid overwriting newer versions of the files, for example), or **Single folder** to put all the files into one folder. (In both of these cases, a text box appears so that you can enter the new location.)

   ➤ **How to Restore**   Choose whether Backup should replace existing files that have the same name.

   ➤ **Advanced Restore Options**   You can ignore this dialog box.

5. Click **Finish**. Backup recovers the files and displays a report.

6. Click **Close**.

As with backing up, restoring files is a bit faster if you do everything manually. To get started, launch Backup and click the **Advanced Mode** link to get to the Backup window. Then display the **Restore and Manage Media** tab and use the following controls to set up the restore:

➤ **Expand the desired media item ...**   Use this list to open the backup job and backup set you want to use, and then activate the check boxes beside the drives, folders, and files you want to restore (see Figure 28.5).

➤ **Restore files to**   Use this list to specify where you want the files restored.

To determine whether Backup should replace existing files, follow these steps:

1. Select **Tools, Options** to get to the Options dialog box.

2. Display the **Restore** tab.

3. Choose the option you want.

4. Click **OK**.

To get the restore operation underway, click the **Start Restore** button. When Backup says something about advanced options, ignore it and click **OK**. Backup restores the files and then displays a report. Click **Close**.

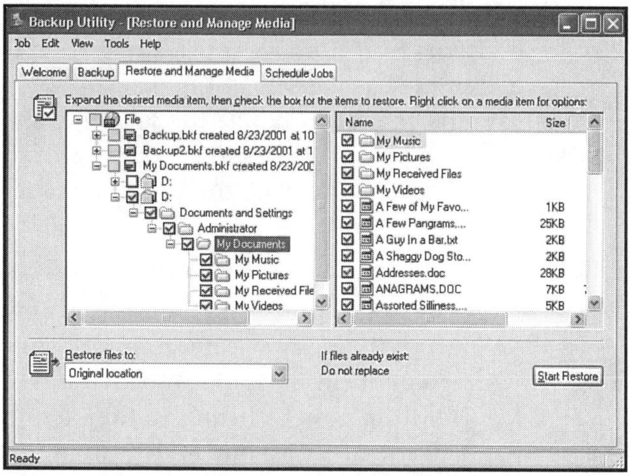

Figure 28.5

Use the Restore and Manage Media tab to restore your backed-up files by hand.

Preparing for the Worst: Using Automated System Recovery

If a system goes kaput, one of the most common reasons is a corrupted system file that Windows XP requires to get itself out of bed in the morning. Therefore, you can often resurrect a seemingly dead system by repairing those mucked-up files. This sounds like it would be hard, but the Backup program has a feature that makes it relatively easy. It's called Automated System Recovery, and I'll show you how to use it in this section.

Backing Up the System and Creating an Emergency Repair Disk

The safety net created by Automated System Recovery is actually composed of two parts:

➤ A full backup of your Windows XP installation (not including your data files; you need to back those up separately).

➤ A special floppy disk called the Automated System Recovery Disk. This disk contains information about your system that can be used to repair a broken Windows XP configuration.

378

Here are the steps to follow to create these things:

1. Launch Backup and, if the Backup or Restore Wizard appears, click the **Advanced Mode** link to get to the Backup window.

2. In the **Welcome** tab, click the **Automated System Recovery Wizard** button. Alternatively, select **Tools, ASR Wizard.** The Automated System Recovery Preparation Wizard (what a mouthful!) slides down the pole.

3. Click **Next.** The Backup Destination dialog box appears.

4. Select your **Backup media type,** choose a **Backup media or file name,** and click **Next.**

5. Click **Finish.** Backup creates a backup of your Windows XP configuration. When it's done, Backup asks for a blank, formatted disk. This will be your ASR disk.

6. Insert the disk in drive A and click **OK.** Backup tosses the repair info onto the disk and then lets you know when it's done.

7. Click **OK** to end up at the Backup Progress dialog box.

8. Click **Close.**

At this point, it would be a good idea to label the disk (use "ASR Disk" or "Emergency Repair Disk" or something equally as dull) and put it in a safe place.

Recovering Your System

Here's the basic procedure to follow if your system has fallen and it can't get up:

1. Insert your Windows XP CD and reboot your computer. If you're prompted to press a key to boot from the CD, go ahead and press whatever key you like. Watch the bottom of the screen for the following message:

   ```
   Press F2 to run Automated System Recovery (ASR)…
   ```

2. Press **F2** while the message is displayed. Setup asks for the ASR disk.

3. Insert the disk into drive A and then press whatever key strikes your fancy. Setup starts the recovery process.

4. When the repair is complete, restart your computer.

The Least You Need to Know

➤ **One last bit of proselytizing** Your hard disk is an accident waiting for a place to happen, so start backing up your files right away.

➤ **Easier backups** To make backups something to look forward to, avoid floppy disks, use a destination with lots of space, keep all your documents in one spot, and use backup types.

➤ **Follow a backup strategy** Run a Daily backup each day, an Incremental backup each week, and a Normal backup each month.

➤ **Stay on schedule** For best results, create a backup schedule so that your backups happen automatically.

Chapter 29

When Windows Won't Work: Troubleshooting Common Problems

In This Chapter

➤ Recovering from startup difficulties

➤ Dealing with those annoying program crashes

➤ Understanding and working with those device driver doodads

➤ Repairing printer, mouse, keyboard, and other hardware problems

---

From time to time, I find myself actually enjoying working in Windows XP. I like the new look, it feels a bit faster than previous versions of Windows, and I love the support for CD burners and other modern gadgetry. But then a program crashes or I lose some settings, and my good mood is gone for the day.

Yes, Windows XP is nice, but it's so darned temperamental. Some days it seems you only have to cough a little too loudly and it gives up the ghost. When faced with such flakiness, one of the keys to remaining a productive (and, so, employed) member of society is to minimize the amount of time you spend hunting down and fixing problems. This chapter is designed to help you do just that. I've broken down Windows' woes into five easy-to-find and easy-to-digest chunks (startup, memory, speed, applications, and hardware), each of which presents real-world problems and offers plain-English solutions.

Ignition Trouble: Solving Startup Snags

Windows startup problems can be quite frustrating. With a deadline looming or an in-basket full of paper, the last thing you need is for your operating system to refuse to run. This section discusses several of the most common Windows XP startup problems and their solutions.

My machine powers up okay, but then it quits before I get to the Windows XP desktop.

This error means that Windows XP is choking on something that it's trying to load during startup. This is most often an older device driver that isn't quite compatible with Windows XP. However, it could also be a Windows XP system file that has gone south for some reason (such as a bad sector on your hard disk).

To solve the problem, you need to gain control over your computer. To do that, restart the machine and then look for one of the following:

➤ If you have two or more operating systems installed on your computer, then at startup you'll see a menu with the following heading:

```
Please select the operating system to start
```

When you get to this menu, press **F8**.

➤ If Windows XP is the only operating system on your machine, then you need to keep a sharp eye out for the following message at the bottom of the screen soon after your computer starts:

```
For advanced startup and troubleshooting options, press F8
```

When you see this message, press **F8**.

Either way, you land smack dab in the middle of the Advanced Options Menu:

```
Microsoft Advanced Options Menu
Please select an option:

  Safe Mode
  Safe Mode with Networking
  Safe Mode with Command Prompt

  Enable Boot Logging
  Enable VGA Mode
  Last Known Good Configuration (your most recent settings that worked)
  Directory Services Restore Mode (Windows domain controllers only)
  Debugging Mode

  Boot Normally
  Reboot
  Return to OS Choices Menu
```

You can use these options to control the rest of the startup procedure. Here's a summary of the options you might need to use:

➤ **Safe Mode** If you're having trouble with Windows XP—for example, if a corrupt or incorrect video driver is mangling your display, or if Windows XP won't start—you can use the safe mode option to run a stripped-down version of Windows XP that includes only the minimal set of device drivers that XP requires to load. You could reinstall or roll back the offending device driver (as described later in this chapter) and then load XP normally. When Windows XP finally loads, the desktop reminds you that you're in safe mode by displaying Safe Mode in each corner.

➤ **Safe Mode with Networking** This option is identical to plain safe mode, except that Windows XP's networking drivers are also loaded at startup. This enables you to log on to your network, which is handy if you need to access the network to load a device driver, run a troubleshooting utility, or send a tech support request.

➤ **Safe Mode with Command Prompt** This option is the same as plain safe mode, except that it doesn't load the Windows XP desktop. Instead, it drops you off at the command prompt where you can enter text commands (assuming you know what you're doing).

➤ **Enable VGA Mode** This option loads Windows XP with the video display set to 640 × 480 and 256 colors. This is a good choice if Windows XP starts but displays a mangled screen. Once Windows XP loads, you can either reinstall or roll back the video driver, or you can adjust the display settings to values that the driver can handle.

➤ **Last Known Good Configuration** This option boots Windows XP using the last configuration that produced a successful startup. This is often your best choice, particularly if Windows XP refused to run after you installed a new device or program.

➤ **Boot Normally** This options loads Windows XP normally.

➤ **Reboot** This option reboots the computer.

➤ **Return to OS Choices Menu** This option displays the operating system menu.

My system won't start even if I choose the Safe Mode thingy.

If Windows XP is so intractable that it won't even start in safe mode, your system is likely afflicted with one of the following problems:

➤ Your system is infected with a virus. You need to run an anti-virus program to cleanse your system.

➤ Your computer's configuration is corrupted. This configuration is sometimes called the *CMOS settings* (or the BIOS settings) and most computers have a setup program that lets you view and change these settings. Watch for a message at startup that says something like `Press F1 for Setup`.

➤ Your system has a hardware conflict. (See the "Handling Hardware Headaches" section later in this chapter.)

I can't get to my previous version of Windows.

If you created a new installation of Windows XP so that you could still use your old version of Windows, then Windows XP should enable you to *dual boot*. That is, at startup you should be able to choose which operating system you want to run by using the menu with the following heading:

`Please select the operating system to start`

If you don't see this menu, here's how to fix it:

1. Select **Start, Control Panel, Performance and Maintenance, System.** The System Properties dialog box rides in.

2. Display the **Advanced** tab.

3. In the **Startup and Recovery** group, click **Settings.** The Startup and Recovery dialog box appears.

4. In the **System startup** group, click **Edit.** This loads the boot (or boot.ini) file into Notepad.

5. Start a new line at the end of the file and enter the following (see Figure 29.1):

   `C:\="Old Windows"`

   Note that you can enter whatever you like instead of **Old Windows** (that is, the text between the quotation marks) because this is the text that will appear in the menu.

Figure 29.1

Enter the text for your old version of Windows at the bottom of the file.

6. Save the file and then select **File, Exit** to shut down Notepad and return to the Startup and Recovery dialog box.

7. Click **OK** to meet up with the System Properties dialog box once again.

8. Click **OK.**

384

Dealing with Applications That Won't Applicate

Let's face facts: most of us use Windows not because of Windows itself, but because it allows us to run some of the best programs on the planet. But no matter how great we think these applications are, it only takes a single inexplicable error or unrecoverable lockup to make us start cursing their very existence. To help you avoid these frustrations, this section looks at some of the most common problems that plague Windows applications and, of course, offers a fistful of solutions.

Handling Program Crashes

My program was running fine, but now it won't do anything.

If you've used Windows for any length of time, you'll be familiar with the fist-poundingly and hair-pullingly frustrating experience of the program crash. You're sailing along, doing whatever it is you do with the program in question, when suddenly it digs in its heels and refuses to go any farther. You press all kinds of keys, click your mouse furiously, hurl uncharitable suggestions at it, but the dumb beast just sits there, frozen in its digital tracks.

Before proceeding, you need to shut down the offending program before it causes system-wide instability or causes your other programs to run slowly. How do you shut down a program that refuses to respond? By using the Windows Task Manager, which you can coax onto the screen by using either of the following methods:

➤ Press **Ctrl+Alt+Delete** (this key combo is known whimsically as both the *three-fingered salute* and the *Vulcan nerve pinch*).

➤ Right-click some empty space on the taskbar and then click **Task Manager.**

If all goes well, you'll see a window similar to the one shown in Figure 29.2. In the **Applications** tab, the **Task** column shows you a list of the programs you have running, and the **Status** column shows one of the following:

➤ **Running**   This means that Windows XP can still communicate with the program. If your seemingly crashed program displays this status, it may mean that it's in the middle of a long or processor-intensive operation. You should wait a few minutes to give the program time to finish the operation.

➤ **Not Responding**   This means that Windows XP can't get the program's attention, so it's official that the program has crashed.

If your program shows the Not Responding status or if it still shows Running after a few minutes, click the program to highlight it and then click **End Task.** Windows XP will then attempt to shut down the program in a civilized manner. If it isn't successful, you'll see the End Program dialog box shown in Figure 29.3. Click **End Now** to tell Windows XP to stop messing around and just blow the darned program out of the water.

385

Figure 29.2

If you see Not Responding beside your program, then you know for sure that the vile thing has collapsed and can't be revived.

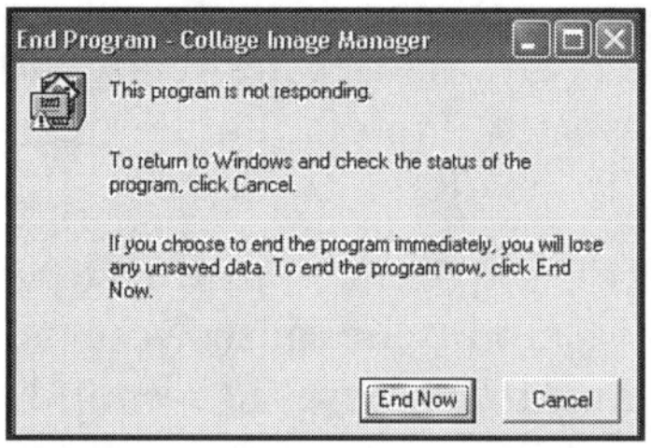

Figure 29.3

You see this dialog box if Windows XP can't shut down the stalled program via the usual channels.

Why do these crashes happen? There are almost as many answers to that question as there are programs. Here are the main causes:

➤ The rogue program wanders into some off-limits area of memory or steps on the toes of another running program. This may be caused by an older program or by a program that's poorly written. Try upgrading to a newer version. Alternatively, contact the manufacturer to see if they're aware of the problem and can provide you with a fix (commonly called a *patch*). If the problem persists or if no newer version is available, consider switching to a different program.

➤ The program is an older version that uses some internal commands that aren't compatible with Windows XP. Again, look into upgrading to a version that's designed to work with Windows XP.

➤ The program uses a device driver that isn't compatible with Windows XP. Visit the vendor's Web site to see if an updated device driver is available (I'll talk about this process in more detail later in this chapter).

➤ One or more of the program's files have become corrupted or deleted. This may be caused by a bad hard disk sector. Run the Check Disk program (see Chapter 27, "Smooth System Sailing: Wielding the System Tools") to fix the problem. If that doesn't help, try uninstalling the program and then reinstalling it.

Perturbing Printing Problems

Windows XP won't print or it reports that "This document failed to print."

Windows printing usually works without a hitch, but when you consider the number of applications that print and the variety of printers they can print to, it's no wonder that Windows printing can sometimes be a real nightmare. This section looks at some solutions you can try if Windows XP refuses to print anything.

Check the printer itself. Before starting any print jobs, check the following:

> ➤ Your printer is powered up.
> ➤ The cable connections are secure.
> ➤ There's paper in the printer.
> ➤ There's no paper jam.

Select a different printer. If you have multiple printers installed, make sure you're printing to the correct one. When you select the **File, Print** command, the Print dialog box will have a list that enables you to select the printer you want to use.

Install a printer driver. Your printer won't work unless the proper printer driver is installed. (See Chapter 7, "Installing and Uninstalling Programs and Devices.") If you do have a driver installed, check with the manufacturer to see if a new driver is available.

Reinstall a corrupted printer driver. Alternatively, your printer driver may have gotten all mangled somehow. You need to remove the driver from your system and then reinstall it. I show you how to reinstall a driver later in this chapter.

Make sure the printer is set up for the correct port. If you can't get Windows to print, it may be trying to print to the wrong port. To check this, select **Start, Printers and Faxes** to open the Printers and Faxes window. Highlight the icon for your printer and then select **File, Properties.** In the **Ports** tab, make sure the check box beside your printer port is activated.

Make sure the printer is online. In the Printers and Faxes window, highlight your printer and then click **Resume printing** in the WebView panel (or select **File, Resume Printing**).

Make sure the printer is available. In the Printers and Faxes window, highlight the printer icon and then select **File, Properties.** In the **Advanced** tab, make sure the **Always Available** option is activated. If the **Available from** option is activated, instead, and you can't change the times that the printer is available, you'll need to print again when the printer is available.

Increase the "timeout" values. Some printer drivers will only wait so long for a job to print before giving up. If you're printing large or complex documents, you may be hitting the wall of these timeout values. To change them, highlight the printer icon in the Printers and Faxes window, and then select **File, Properties.** In the **Device Settings** tab, see if there's a **Job Timeout** setting. If so, and it's not set to **0 seconds**, click the setting and change the value to **0**. If that doesn't solve the problem, return to the Device Settings tab and increase the value of the **Wait Timeout** setting (to, say, **600** seconds), or set it to **0**.

Miscellaneous Program Problems

A program tells me it can't run because it requires an earlier version of Windows.

If a particularly stupid program tells you that it will only run under some older Windows version—such as Windows 95 or Windows 98—you can grant the silly thing its wish by doing the following:

1. Click **Start**, find the program's icon in the Start menu, right-click the icon, and then click **Properties**.
2. Display the **Compatibility** tab.
3. Activate the **Run this program in compatibility mode for** check box.
4. Use the list below the check box to choose the version of Windows that the program has a hankering for.
5. Click **OK**.

A program requires a certain amount of memory, but I don't know how much memory my computer has.

Here's a quick way to find out how much memory is installed on your computer:

1. Select **Start, Control Panel, Performance and Maintenance, System**.
2. In the System Properties dialog box, display the **General** tab.
3. As shown in Figure 29.4, the **Computer** section tells you how much RAM is installed.

Figure 29.4

The General tab tells you how much memory your computer has.

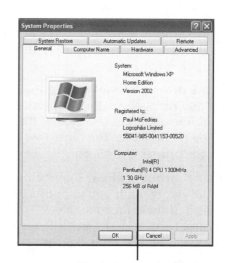

Here's the memory value

A taskbar button has turned orange. What gives?

When you see an orange taskbar button, it means that the program associated with the button has some sort of message for you. It may be reporting on the status of an operation, or it may be an error. Click the button to check out the message.

Overcoming File Failings

I have a file that always opens in a particular program. How do I get it to open in a different program?

When you install some programs, they rudely take over the duties of opening certain types of files (this seems to happen a lot with graphics programs). So when you double-click one of those files, it opens in the new program instead of whatever program it used in the past. Fortunately, it's easy to convince Windows XP to use the old program either whenever you need it or permanently:

1. Use My Computer to find an example of the type of file you want to work with.

2. Select the **File, Open With** command. One of two things will happen:

   ➤ A menu will slide out with a choice of programs to use. If you see the program you want, go ahead and click it to open the file in that program. If you don't see the program, or if you want to change the file type to use a different program permanently, click **Choose Program.** This displays the Open With dialog box (see Figure 29.5).

   ➤ The Open With dialog box appears immediately.

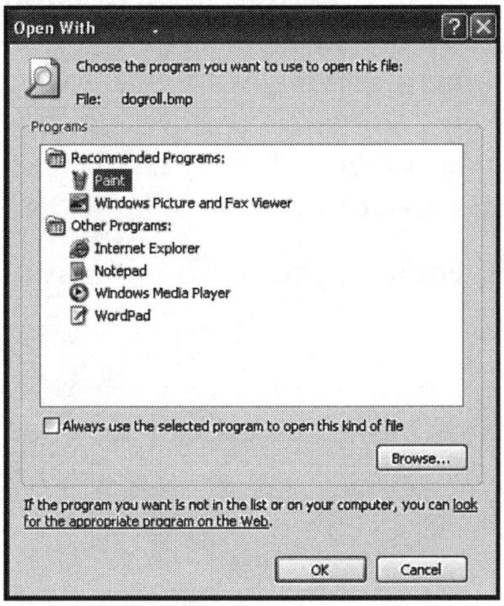

Figure 29.5

Use the Open With dialog box to select the program you want to use to open the file type.

3. Use the **Programs** list to highlight the program you want to use. (If it's not listed for some reason, click **Browse** to pick out the program's file by hand.)

389

4. If you want Windows XP to always use this program for this type of file, activate the **Always use the selected program to open this kind of file** check box.

5. Click **OK.**

I need to change a file's extension, but Windows XP refuses to do it.

When a folder has multiple files with the same name, how does Windows itself keep track of which is which? The answer is that the file name you see isn't the full name of the file. Each file name actually consists of a primary name (the name you see), followed by a period (.), followed by a three-character code (some of these codes are four characters long). The latter is called the *file extension.*

Windows associates each three-character extension with a particular file type. For example, suppose a file's full name is birthday.bmp. The **.bmp** extension is associated with the "Bitmap Image" file type, so that file is a bitmap graphics file.

So why doesn't Windows show the extensions? Well, it's probably because Microsoft doesn't want unwary users to accidentally delete or change an extension when they're renaming a file. Doing so would probably render the file useless, or perhaps associate the file with some other application. Chaos, of course, would ensue.

Can't you change the extension anyway when you rename a file? For example, what if I renamed the birthday.bmp bitmap file to birthday.gif? (The .gif extension signifies a GIF graphics file.) That's a no go, Joe, because Windows is hip to that trick. All this does is change the file's full name to birthday.gif.bmp!

But what if you really do want to change the extension? For example, suppose you want to create a Web page from scratch. Web pages are just text files, so you could start by right-clicking the folder and then clicking **New, Text Document** to create a new text file. However, for Web pages to work, they must use either the .htm or .html extension. Unfortunately, the text document you created will have the .txt extension. Hmmm. There's a head-scratcher. Are you doomed? Nope. The trick is that if you convince Windows to display the file extensions, you can rename extensions at will. Here's how to get Windows to display file extensions:

1. In My Computer, select the **Tools, Folder Options** command to display the Folder Options dialog box.

2. Display the **View** tab.

3. Deactivate the **Hide extensions for known file types** check box.

4. Click **OK.**

I can't copy files to, delete files from, or format a floppy disk.

If you're trying to copy files to a floppy disk, the disk may be full; in this case delete some files from the disk or try another one.

Alternatively, the disk may be *write-protected,* which means you can't copy or move files to the disk, delete or rename files on the disk, or format the disk. On a floppy disk, the write-protection is controlled by a small, movable tab on the back of the disk. If the tab is toward the edge of the disk, the disk is write-protected. To disable the write-protection, slide the tab away from the edge of the disk.

How do I encrypt a file so that no one else can read it?

If you have a file that contains sensitive data and you're paranoid that someone else might read it, it's possible to scramble the contents of the file so that it's only readable when you're logged on to Windows XP with your username and password. This scrambling process is called *encryption.*

Windows Wisdom

You can only encrypt a file if it resides on a hard disk that uses something called the NTFS file system. The specifics of NTFS aren't important, but it's suffice to say that a *file system* determines how file are stored on the hard disk, and NTFS is the most powerful of them all. How do you know whether a hard disk uses NTFS? Select **Start, My Computer** and then highlight the disk drive. In the WebView panel's **Details** section, look at the **File System** value. (You can also see this value by selecting **File, Properties.**) If a disk drive isn't NTFS, you can change that by selecting **Start, All Programs, Accessories, Command Prompt.** At the prompt, type in the following command and press **Enter** (replace d with the letter of the drive you want to convert):

```
convert d: /fs:ntfs
```

When you want to encrypt a file, the safest and easiest method is to encrypt an entire folder and then use that folder to store the file or files that you want encrypted. Here are the steps to follow to encrypt a folder:

1. In My Computer, find and highlight the folder you want to encrypt.

2. Select **File, Properties** to see the folder's Properties dialog box.

3. In the **General** tab, click **Advanced** to catch up with the Advanced Attributes dialog box.

4. Activate the **Encrypt contents to secure data** check box.

5. Click **OK** to return to the Properties dialog box.

6. Click **OK**.

You'll notice at this point that My Computer displays the name of the folder and the names of its files in a green font. This tells you that you're dealing with encrypted stuff.

Windows Wisdom

If you'd rather see your encrypted folder and file names in the regular text color, select My Computer's **Tools, Folder Options** command, display the **View** tab, and then deactivate the **Show encrypted or compressed NTFS files in color** check box.

Handling Hardware Headaches

So far, most of the problems we've looked at have been of the software variety. Unfortunately, our hardware is often just as flaky, and it's usually even trickier to fix. In most cases, you're dealing with a defective part that needs to be replaced, so no amount of fiddling will get you back up and running. Sometimes, though, you can solve a hardware glitch with some simple tweaks. The rest of this chapter takes a look at these more tractable hardware headaches.

First, a Visit with the Device Manager

Windows XP stores everything it knows about your computer's hardware in a special file called the *Registry*. The bad news is that this Registry warehouse is in a hopelessly convoluted and confusing section of town. The good news is that Windows XP offers a way to view the hardware info from a friendlier perch. That perch is called Device Manager, and you get there by following these steps:

1. Select **Start, Control Panel, Performance and Maintenance, System.** The System Properties dialog box jumps up.

2. Display the **Hardware** tab.

3. Click **Device Manager.**

As you can see in Figure 29.6, Device Manager displays a tree-like list that consists of various hardware categories. Opening a branch displays a list of the installed devices within that category.

Device Manager not only provides you with a bit of info about each device, but it also enables you to update device drivers, change settings, enable and disable devices, and more.

Device Manager is also useful as a troubleshooting tool. As pointed out in Figure 29.6, Device Manager displays an icon beside the device name:

➤ A yellow icon with a black exclamation mark means the device has a problem.

➤ A white icon with a blue i means a device's resources have been configured manually.

➤ A red x means the device is missing or disabled.

Open a branch to
see the devices

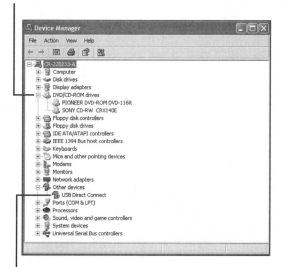

Figure 29.6

Device Manager displays a list of the hardware installed on your system.

An icon appears beside a
device that has a problem

Double-click the device in question, and you'll end up face-to-face with the device's Properties dialog box. In the **General** tab, the **Device status** group gives you a description of the problem.

Each device's Properties dialog box has a number of tabs that enable you to manipulate various device settings. The tabs you see depend on the device, but the following are the most common:

➤ **General** Gives you basic data about the device, such as its name and the manufacturer's name. As I've mentioned, the **Device status** group tells you whether the device is working properly or, if it's not, what the problem is. Also, the **Device usage** list lets you enable (choose **Use this device**) or disable (choose **Do not use this device**) a device. If you're having a problem with a device and you can't figure it out, trying disabling it.

➤ **Properties** Displays one or more controls for working with device settings.

➤ **Driver** Enables you to update or roll back the device's driver (more on this later).

➤ **Resources** Displays a list of the resources used by the device.

393

Handling Device Driver Problems

A *device driver* is a small software program that acts as a kind of digital equivalent to the proverbial one-trick pony: All it does is act as a go-between for a device and other programs (including Windows). The device driver is intimately "familiar" with the instructions and code required to make a device perform a specific task. When a program needs the device to perform that task, it tells the device driver what needs to be done, and the driver handles everything from there.

So if a device isn't working properly (or isn't working at all), there's a good change that a faulty or out-of-date device driver is the culprit. There are three things you can do with a device driver, all of which take place in the **Driver** tab of the device's Properties dialog box:

➤ Update a device driver to a newer version. (I discuss this in more detail later.)

➤ Roll back a device driver to an earlier version. If you replace an existing driver with a new one and the device no longer works or your system becomes flaky, click **Roll Back Driver** to remove the new driver and reinstate the previous driver.

➤ Uninstall a device driver. If a device is not working at all or is causing problems with your system, you might prefer to get it out of your life entirely. In that case, you can usually just physically remove the device and Windows XP will adjust itself accordingly. If it doesn't, or if you can't remove the device, click **Uninstall** and Windows XP will uninstall the driver and remove the device from Device Manager.

Updating a device driver means that you replace the existing device driver with a newer driver. This is probably the most common device troubleshooting technique, and it's the one that has the most likely chance of fixing the problem. Why? Because most manufacturers are constantly tweaking their drivers to fix bugs or to make their devices work better with the latest operating systems.

Windows Wisdom

If you can't find a driver that specifically says it's compatible with Windows XP, you may be able to get away with a driver that works with Windows 2000, instead.

Before you update the driver, you need to get the latest driver from the manufacturer. This is most easily accomplished on the manufacturer's Web site. When you get there, look for a link that says "Support," "Downloads," or "Drivers." Follow the links until you get to the file you need to download. Make sure that the file you get will work with your device *and* is compatible with Windows XP.

When the driver file is downloaded, open the file. You'll probably have to do one of the following:

➤ If the file is a compressed (zipped) archive, double-click it and then extract all the files to some empty folder.

➤ If the file is an executable, it will likely ask you where you want the files to be extracted. Again, be sure to specify an empty folder.

To update the driver, follow these steps:

1. In the device's Properties dialog box, click the **Driver** tab's **Update Driver** button. The Hardware Update Wizard takes a bow.

2. Activate **Install from a list or specific location** and click **Next.**

3. Activate the **Include this location in the search** check box and then use the text box to enter the location of the extracted files (or click **Browse** to find the folder using a dialog box). Click **Next.**

4. If you see a Hardware Installation dialog box warning you that the hardware "has not passed Windows Logo testing," say "whatever" and click **Continue Anyway.**

5. When the wizard lets you know that it has installed the driver, click **Finish.**

When you update to a driver that Windows XP doesn't trust, it creates a restore point to enable you to recover quickly should the driver turn out to be a dud. (See Chapter 27 for info on using System Restore.)

Mending Your Mouse

My mouse pointer moves erratically.

You'll sometimes find that you move your mouse on its pad, and the darn pointer either stays where it is, or it heads off into oblivion or some other equally inconvenient spot. When this happens, try out the following solutions:

Make sure the mouse is attached to your computer. This may seem somewhat obvious, but the number-one rule when troubleshooting any device is to first ask "Is it plugged in?" You'd be surprised how often the answer is a sheepish "No."

Clean the inside of the mouse. If your mouse is behaving erratically, it may simply need to be cleaned inside. A well-used mouse can take in quite a collection of dust, crumbs, and other alien substances, so you should clean yours regularly. Your mouse documentation should tell you the proper cleaning procedure. If your mouse has a roller ball, you can also follow these steps:

1. Remove the cover on the bottom of the mouse.
2. Remove the roller ball.
3. Using a cotton swab dipped lightly in isopropyl alcohol or water, clean the rollers and other contact areas.
4. Wipe off any excess liquid and then replace the ball and cover.

Try a firmer mouse pad. If your mouse pad's too soft, the roller ball sinks down too far when you move the mouse. This can cause the roller to stick and so create erratic pointer movements. Try one of the firmer varieties of mouse pad.

Exit and restart Windows. When you restart Windows, the program reinitializes the mouse; this is often enough to get the thing going again. If this still doesn't work, try exiting Windows and rebooting your computer.

Change the mouse driver. Windows provides you with a list of mouse drivers, each of which is designed to be used with a specific type of mouse. If you're using the wrong driver, then the pointer may not move at all or it may do some crazy things.

Windows doesn't always recognize my double-clicks.

If you find that Windows doesn't recognize some of your double-clicks, the first thing you should check is that you're not moving the mouse ever-so-slightly between (or during) the clicks.

If that's not it, then you may need to set a slower "double-click speed." One of the things that a mouse-aware program must do is distinguish between two consecutive single-clicks and a double-click. For example, if you click once, wait five seconds, and then click again, then that would qualify as two single-clicks in most people's books. But what if there's only a second between clicks? Or half a second? This threshold is called the *double-click speed:* Anything faster is handled as a double-click. Here's how to set a slower double-click speed:

1. Select **Start, Control Panel, Printers and Other Hardware, Mouse.** The Mouse Properties dialog box shows up.

2. In the **Buttons** tab's **Double-click speed** group, move the slider to the left (toward **Slow**).

3. Double-click the **Folder** icon to the right of the slider. The folder will "open" if Windows recognizes your double-click.

4. Repeat steps 2 and 3 until Windows recognizes your double-clicks consistently.

5. Click **OK**.

I'm left-handed and would prefer to use the right button for clicking.

The southpaws of the world have complained for years that mice are "handist" devices that are designed for the right-handed majority. If you think this is unfair, you can get some revenge by switching the mouse buttons. Here's how:

1. Select **Start, Control Panel, Printers and Other Hardware, Mouse** to get to the Mouse Properties dialog box.

2. In the **Buttons** tab, activate the **Switch primary and secondary buttons** check box.

3. Click **OK** (using the right button this time).

My mouse pointer moves too slowly (or too quickly).

When you move the mouse on its pad, Windows translates this movement and tracks the mouse pointer accordingly. If you find your pointer is either leaping across the screen at the merest touch, or crawling across the screen no matter how furiously you shake the mouse, you can adjust the tracking speed by following these steps (once again, see Chapter 2, "A Field Guide to Windows XP," for the new Microsoft Mouse):

1. Select **Start, Control Panel, Printers and Other Hardware, Mouse** to get to the Mouse Properties dialog box.
2. Display the **Pointer Options** tab.
3. In the **Motion** group, move the slider to the left (to get a slower speed) or to the right (to get a faster speed).
4. Click **Apply** and then move your mouse to test the tracking speed.
5. Repeat steps 3 and 4 until you're comfortable with the speed you've set.
6. Click **OK.**

I have trouble seeing or finding the mouse pointer.

If you use a laptop or if your eyesight isn't what it used to be, then you may be having trouble keeping track of the little mouse pointer. There are a number of third-party products on the market that will solve this problem, but before spending your hard-earned money on these utilities, there's an easy solution that comes with Windows: *pointer trails*. This feature leaves a trail of mouse pointers as you move the mouse, which makes it much easier to find the little guy. Try the following steps:

1. Select **Start, Control Panel, Printers and Other Hardware, Mouse** to get to the Mouse Properties dialog box.
2. Display the **Pointer Options** tab.
3. In the **Visibility** group, activate the **Display pointer trails** check box.
4. Use the slider below this check box to set the length of the trail.
5. While you're here, you may also want to activate the **Show location of pointer when I press the CTRL key** check box. This tells Windows to display a series of circles that focus in on the pointer location when you press **Ctrl.**
6. Click **OK.**

Correcting Keyboard Kinks

My keyboard is too slow.

When you press and hold a letter on your keyboard, you notice two things: first, when you press the key, there's a slight *delay* before the second letter appears; second, the subsequent letters appear at a constant rate (called the *repeat rate*). If your keyboard feels slow, then you either have your delay set too long or your repeat rate set too slow (or both). The good news is that Windows allows you to change both of these values. Here's how:

1. Select **Start, Control Panel, Printers and Other Hardware, Keyboard** to display to the Keyboard Properties dialog box.

2. For a shorter delay, move the **Speed** tab's **Repeat delay** slider to the right.

3. For a faster repeat rate, move the **Repeat rate** slider to the right.

4. To check your new settings, click inside the **Click here and hold down a key to test repeat rate** text box, and then press and hold down a key.

5. Repeat steps 2 through 4 until the keyboard speed is set the way you want.

6. Click **OK**.

I'm constantly pressing Caps Lock accidentally. How can I prevent this?

Windows XP doesn't have any way to disable the annoying Caps Lock key. However, it's possible to set things up so that Windows beeps whenever you press that key. This will at least warn you that you've pressed the key and you can press it again before you end up typing an entire paragraph in entirely uppercase letters. Here's what you do:

1. Select **Start, Control Panel, Accessibility Options, Accessibility Options.** This displays—you guessed it—the Accessibility Options dialog box.

2. In the **Keyboard** tab, activate the **Use ToggleKeys** check box.

3. Click **OK**.

Curing Video Ills

Your video display may be the most important component of your system since you're forced to look at it for hours on end every day. Yes, one of Windows XP's most appealing features is its good-looking interface, but the fanciest interface in the world isn't worth a hill of beans if your display is displaying garbage. If your display goes snaky on you, try any of these solutions listed below to bring things back to normal.

However, since your display is distorted, you can't do anything to fix the problem right now, so you have to first exit Windows XP and restart your computer. How do you do that when you can't read the display? Good question. Here's what you do:

➤ In Windows XP Home, press **Ctrl+Esc** (or the Windows logo key—⊞—if you have one), press **u**, and then press **r**.

➤ In Windows XP Pro, press **Ctrl+Esc** (or the Windows logo key—⊞), press **u**, press **r**, and then press **Enter**.

When your computer restarts, display the Advanced Options menu, discussed earlier. Choosing the Safe Mode or Enable VGA Mode option will get you back to Windows XP with a readable screen so that you can perform whatever troubleshooting steps are required.

Reinstall or update the video driver. One of the most common causes of display problems is a corrupt video driver. You can usually fix the problem by reinstalling or updating the driver. (If you just installed a new driver and it has caused the problem, try rolling back the driver instead.)

Change the screen resolution or color quality. All video cards have a limited amount of memory, so they have maximum values for the screen resolution and color quality. If you change either of these values and your screen goes crazy, the best solution is to wait 15 seconds, and Windows XP will restore the screen for you. If that doesn't happen for some reason, restart Windows XP using the Safe Mode or Enable VGA Mode option and then reduce the resolution or color quality (see Chapter 24, "Refurbishing the Desktop").

Exit and restart Windows. Sometimes a display problem is nothing more than a temporary mental lapse on Windows' part. Try exiting Windows and restarting as discussed earlier.

Turn off your screen saver. Some screen savers can cause video problems, so try turning yours off to see if that fixes the problem.

The Least You Need to Know

➤ **A smarter start**   To get to the Windows XP Advanced Options menu, look for either the operating system menu or the For advanced startup and troubleshooting options message, and then press **F8.**

➤ **Unsticking a stuck program**   Press **Ctrl+Alt+Delete** (or right-click some empty space on the taskbar and then click **Task Manager**), highlight the application that says Not Responding, and then click **End Task.**

➤ **Re-programming a file type**   To launch a file with something other than its usual program, highlight it, select **File, Open With,** and then choose the program from the Open With dialog box.

➤ **Arranging a powwow with the Device Manager**   Select **Start, Control Panel, Performance and Maintenance, System,** display the **Hardware** tab, and then click **Device Manager.**

➤ **Device driver defined**   A device driver is a small software program that implements the code necessary for Windows XP to operate a device.

➤ **Modifying your mouse**   Select **Start, Control Panel, Printers and Other Hardware, Mouse** to get to the Mouse Properties dialog box.

➤ **Customizing your keyboard**   Select **Start, Control Panel, Printers and Other Hardware, Keyboard** to display to the Keyboard Properties dialog box.

Part 6
Windows XP on the Network

Windows XP was born to network. In fact, the Setup program assumes your computer is going to be part of a network, and Windows XP almost seems to be disappointed if that turns out not to be the case. So you'll make your operating system very happy indeed if you get your machine connected to a nearby network. Happily for you, the two chapters here in Part 6 will show you how to do exactly that. You'll learn how to get connected to a network, how to make use of network resources (such as printers), how to let other network users access your computer's resources, and how to dial in to your network from a remote locale. You'll even learn how to set up your own small network! Just turn the page and we'll begin …

Chapter 30

Using Windows XP to Set Up a Small Network

In This Chapter

➤ Getting the scoop on the hardware you need for your network

➤ Learning about the two easiest network structures to use

➤ Network configuration and the Windows XP Setup program

➤ Configuring a computer for network duty

Large, company-wide networks have been around for many years, and until recently networking was an exclusive fiefdom ruled by the panjandrums in the IT department. Nobody minded this situation because a big network was (and is) hideously complex to set up and administer. But then people in small offices and home offices (the SOHO crowd) started noticing the numerous benefits of networking computers: easy file sharing, internal e-mail, reduced hardware expenses (because all the computers can share, say, a single printer), and so on. However, they also worried about the costs associated with networking: paying a consultant thousands of dollars to set up the network, the extra time required to administer everything, the charges for technical support calls, and so on.

My goal in this chapter is to show you how to virtually eliminate those costs while still retaining all of the benefits that a network can bestow. Specifically, I'll show you how to take the computers in your small office or home office and turn them into a small network. You'll learn how to install the hardware, connect everything, and configure each machine. The key word here is *small*. Yes, *large* networks are only for those with a Ph.D. in electrical engineering, but a small network is well within the capabilities of most folks, and that includes *you*. Just follow my simple steps in this chapter, and you'll have your network connected before you know it.

Networking Advantages

A *local area network* (LAN) is a group of computers that are relatively close together (for example, in the same office or in the same house) and that are connected via a cable that plugs in to special hardware inside each machine. (For variety, I use the terms *LAN* and *network* interchangeably in this chapter.)

What's the point of such connections? One word: *sharing*. Having your computers lashed together in a network opens up a whole new world for sharing things:

➤ You can send data along the network cables, so it's criminally easy to fire off a file to another machine, or to grab a file you need (assuming, of course, that you have the necessary permission to do so).

➤ Devices—such as a printer or CD-ROM—on one machine can be made visible to the rest of the network. This means the other computers can print to that one printer, for example.

➤ A single Internet connection—whether it's via a regular modem, a cable modem, or a digital subscriber line (DSL)—can be shared with everyone on the network.

➤ If a computer happens to have a lot of empty hard disk space, it can be shared with the network and thus used as a convenient (and fast) location for backups.

A network will make your computing life more convenient, which probably isn't too surprising. However, it will also make your computing life cheaper because you need fewer devices (such as printers and tape drives for backups) and you can share a single Internet account.

Basic Network Know-How

Networks come in two basic flavors:

➤ **Client/server** In this type of network, one machine—called the *server*—acts as kind of "boss" to all the other machines—the *clients*. For example, the server usually won't let you and your client computer on the network unless you enter an approved username and password. For this to work, the server computer must use a special *network operating system* designed for servers. For example, you could use Windows 2002 Server, the big brother of Windows XP. Note, however, that you *can't* use Windows XP as a network operating system.

➤ **Peer-to-peer**   In this type of network constitution, all the machines are created equal. That is, no one machine lords it over any of the others, and each computer has more or less equal access to the network. (I say "more or less" because access depends on the privilege level of the user and on which resources the other machines have shared with the network. I'll give you more details on this in Chapter 31, "Using Windows XP's Networking Features.")

So, which one should you choose? Well, unfortunately, the operating systems required by a server are expensive and relatively difficult to administer. In the end, this means that a client/server setup is overkill for a small network. Conversely, peer-to-peer is a much simpler network style to set up and maintain. Therefore, it's the one I recommend that you adopt and it's the one I discuss in this chapter and the next.

Stuff You Need: Understanding Network Hardware

In a sense, setting up a network is all about setting up the appropriate hardware. This is particularly true of Windows XP, which (as you'll see a bit later) does a great job of installing whatever networking software is required after it detects (or is told about) the presence of networking hardware. Therefore, it's no exaggeration to say that the key to getting your network configured with the least amount of fuss is to research and purchase the correct hardware bric-a-brac up front. The next few sections tell you everything you need to know.

The Connection Point: The Network Interface Card

Networking begins and ends (literally) with a component called the *network interface card,* or NIC, for short. (Depending on the geek you're talking to, a NIC can also be called a *network adapter* or a *network card.*) The network cable (see the next section) that connects all the computers actually plugs into the back of a NIC that resides in each machine. Therefore, the NIC is each machine's connection point to the network.

NICs come in three basic configurations:

➤ **Circuit board**   This is the most common type of NIC, and it plugs into a slot inside the computer. Prices vary widely, but you can get good boards between US$80 and US$130.

➤ **PC Card (PCMCIA)**   This type of NIC comes in the credit card-size PC Card format and it plugs into a PC Card socket on a notebook computer or a docking station. These are handy for notebook users, but they are slightly more expensive (US$100–US$150).

405

➤ **Universal Serial Bus (USB)** This is a relatively new type of NIC and it plugs into a USB connector in the back of the PC. (Most new PCs come with a couple of USB connectors.) These are, obviously, easier to install than the circuit board type, and they're reasonably priced (US$90–US$130).

After you've decided on the basic type (or types) of NIC you want, here's a checklist to run through to help you narrow your search a bit further:

Windows Wisdom

There have been a number of exciting new developments in the home networking field, including the capability to create a network at home by using your existing phone wiring or your existing power lines. To keep up with the latest in this burgeoning area, watch the Home Networking News Web site: www.homenetnews.com.

➤ Be sure the NICs support something called *Ethernet*. (This is a type of network architecture, and it's the one used by the vast majority of networks.) There are two varieties: standard Ethernet (which has a network speed of 10 megabits per second [Mbps] and is less expensive) and Fast Ethernet (which features speeds of 100Mbps but is slightly more expensive). Note, too, that there are "10/100" NICs that support both types.

➤ Be sure the NICs have the appropriate cable ports. As you'll see in the next section, there are two basic types of cable, so you have to be sure that the NICs you choose have a port for the type of cable you decide to use. (Some NICs have ports for both types. Note, too, that a few NICs come with a third type of port—called an AUI port—that's rarely used.)

➤ For easiest installation, get NICs that support Plug and Play.

➤ For fastest performance in a circuit-board NIC, get the type that plugs into a PCI slot inside the computer.

➤ If you want to share a cable modem or DSL Internet connection, then your computer requires two NICs: one to connect to the router that came with your Internet connection and the other to connect to your network.

The Connection: The Network Cable

Although wireless networks have been around for a while, they're still slow and *very* flaky. As a result, the majority of networks still use cables to connect the various machines. As I mentioned earlier, your NICs and cables have to match because the cable connects to a port in the back of the NIC, so the port and cable jack must be compatible. Fortunately, although there are lots of different cable types, you need to consider only two when setting up your small LAN: twisted-pair and coaxial.

Twisted-pair cable is the most common type. (It's called twisted-pair because it consists of two copper wires twisted together.) It has on each end an *RJ-45 jack,* which is similar to (but a bit bigger than) the jacks used on telephone cables. Figure 30.1 points out the RJ-45 jack and shows a twisted-pair cable plugged into a NIC. Here are some other notes:

➤ This type of cable is most commonly used in the "star" network structure. (See the "The Star Structure" section later in this chapter.)

➤ Always ask for "category 5" twisted-pair cable. This is the highest quality and is suitable for all types of Ethernet networks. It costs a bit more, but it's definitely worth it.

➤ Cables come in various lengths, so be sure you buy cables that are long enough to make the proper connections (but not so long that you waste your money on cable you don't use).

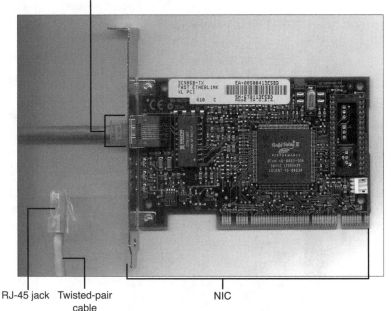

RJ-45 jack   Twisted-pair   NIC
cable

Figure 30.1

The twisted-pair cable's RJ-45 jack plugs into the corresponding RJ-45 port on the NIC.

The other type of cable is *coaxial cable* (some network nerds refer to it as *thinnet cable*). It's somewhat reminiscent of the cables used with cable television connections, but network coaxial cable has "bayonet-style" connectors at each end. (They're called bayonet-style connectors because you plug them into the port and then give them a twist to lock them in place. This is similar, I suppose, to the way you connect a bayonet.) To use this type of cable, your NICs must have a corresponding BNC port

407

in the back. Figure 30.2 shows an example of a coaxial cable, a NIC with a BNC port, and some other hardware you need.

Figure 30.2

The coaxial cable's bayonet-style connector plugs into a T-connector, which then plugs into the corresponding BNC port on the NIC.

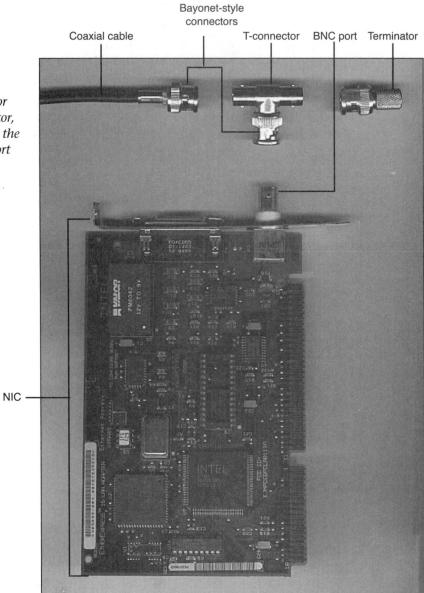

408

Notice in Figure 30.2 that the coaxial cable doesn't plug directly into the NIC. Instead, the cable plugs into a BNC port on the T-connector, and the T-connector plugs into the BNC port on the NIC. The idea is that you'd then plug another coaxial cable into the T-connector's other BNC port (for now, you can ignore the terminator shown in the figure), and then run that cable to another NIC on the network. Here are some notes:

➤ If you're not too clear about how to hook up your network using coaxial cable, I'll discuss this in more detail later on when I discuss the "bus" network structure. (See "The Bus Structure" later in this chapter.)

➤ Coaxial cable can't go any faster than 10MBps, so you can't use it with Fast Ethernet.

➤ Again, be sure you purchase cables that are the correct length.

If you're not sure which cable type to go with, don't sweat it just now. As I said, each type of cable is associated with a different network structure, so you should check out those structures before deciding on the cable.

Deciding How to Structure Your Network

The last thing you have to consider before getting down to the short strokes is the overall network structure. The structure determines how each machine is connected to the network. (Networking jockeys use the highfalutin phrase *network topology*.) There are lots of possible structures, but luckily for you there are only two that are suitable for small LANs: star and bus.

The Star Structure

In the *star* structure, each NIC is connected to a *hub,* which serves as a central connection point for the entire network. A hub is a small box that has several (typically four, six, or eight) RJ-45 ports. Hubs vary widely in price from simple 10Mbps units that cost under US$100 to massive machines costing in the thousands of dollars. For your small network, you shouldn't have to spend more than about US$200.

Windows Wisdom

Your hub must match the type of Ethernet you're using. For example, if you go with Fast Ethernet, then your hub must also support 100Mbps.

For each computer, you run twisted-pair cable from the NIC to a port in the hub, as shown in Figure 30.3.

Figure 30.3

In the star structure, each machine is connected to the network by running twisted-pair cable from the NIC to the hub.

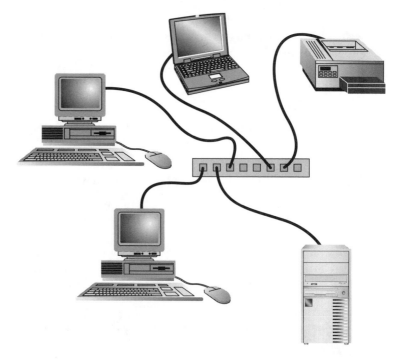

The Bus Structure

In the *bus* structure, each NIC is connected directly to another NIC using coaxial cables, T-connectors, BNC ports, and all that other stuff I mentioned earlier. (Figure 30.4 illustrates how this works.) As you can see, you run the cable from one T-connector to the next. Note that you can't form a "circle" by attaching a cable from the last NIC to the first NIC. Instead, you have to put special connectors called *terminators* on the T-connectors of the first and last NICs.

Figure 30.4

Here's the basic bus structure where you connect NICs using coaxial cable. Note the terminators on the first and last NICs.

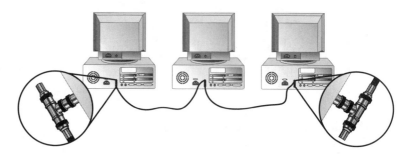

410

Decisions, Decisions: What Route Should You Take?

I've given you lots of choices to mull over so far, so there's a good chance your head is spinning a bit with all the permutations and combinations. Actually, though, you really have to consider only two configurations:

➤ NICs with RJ-45 ports arranged in a star structure that uses twisted-pair cable to connect each computer to a central hub. Here are the pros and cons of this configuration:

Pros It's easy to add and remove computers from the network (just plug them in and out of the hub; the network isn't affected if one of the connections goes down; it can be very speedy if you go with Fast Ethernet; it's the most common configuration, so you have a greater selection of NICs and hubs.

Cons This is more expensive because it requires a hub; it requires more cable because each cable must run from the NIC all the way to the hub.

➤ NICs with BNC ports arranged in a bus structure that uses coaxial cable to connect each computer directly. Some pros and cons to consider:

Pros This is the least expensive option; it requires less cable because each connection has to reach only to the next computer.

Cons It's harder to add and remove computers from the network because each change requires changing the cabling on one or two other machines; the entire network goes down if one connection goes down; it's limited to 10Mbps; there's a lesser selection of NICs.

Of these two configurations, the former is the one I prefer, and it's the one I used to put together the test network that serves as an example throughout the chapters here in Part 6, "Windows XP on the Network."

Getting a Machine Network-Ready

After you've made your decision about what network hardware to purchase, and after you've installed that hardware, your next task is to set up each machine for networking.

Throughout the rest of this chapter (as well as the next chapter), I use the word "workgroup" a lot, so let's take a second here to be sure you know what I'm blathering on about. In network lingo, a *workgroup* is a small collection of related computers on a network. In a large corporate network, for example, there might be one workgroup for the Accounting department and another for the Marketing department. For your small LAN, you have just a single workgroup for all your computers.

411

There are two more points to bear in mind before you get started:

➤ Make sure you've installed and connected all your network hardware.

➤ If you want to share an Internet connection among all the computers, set up that connection on one of the machines. This computer will be known as the *Internet Connection Sharing host*. Also, be sure to run the Network Setup Wizard on that machine first so that Windows XP's Internet Connection Sharing feature is properly set up and ready to go for the other computers.

Some Notes About Networking and the Windows XP Setup

If you're installing Windows XP on one or more of the would-be LAN computers, the Setup program takes you through a brief network setup. Here are some notes to bear in mind:

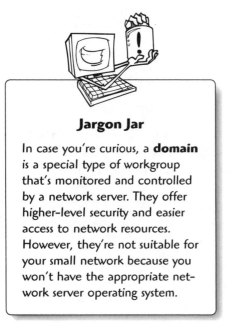

Jargon Jar

In case you're curious, a **domain** is a special type of workgroup that's monitored and controlled by a network server. They offer higher-level security and easier access to network resources. However, they're not suitable for your small network because you won't have the appropriate network server operating system.

➤ Just prior to the network portion of the show, Setup asks you to enter a computer name. This is the name that other people on the LAN will see for the computer, so enter an appropriate (and unique) moniker. It can be as many as 63 characters long and it should use only letters, numbers, and hyphens. It's standard in small networks to use the first or last name of the person who'll be wrestling with the computer.

➤ If Setup asks whether you want to use a typical or custom network setup, be sure to choose the **Typical Settings** option.

➤ For Windows XP Pro, when Setup asks whether your computer will be part of a workgroup or a *domain,* activate the **Workgroup** option and enter the name of your workgroup in the text box below that option. This name can't be longer than 15 characters and can't include any of the following symbols: * = + \ | ; : " , < > ?

For your LAN to work successfully (and simply), all the computers must use the same workgroup name.

Using the Network Setup Wizard to Set Up Your Network

Your companion on the network setup journey is the new Network Setup Wizard, which takes great pains to ensure that your network is properly configured. The rest of this chapter takes you through all the steps required.

In versions of Windows prior to Windows Me, getting your computers configured to handle the burdens of networking was unpleasant, to say the least. It involved wrestling with innumerable dialog boxes, puzzling over esoterica such as "clients" and "protocols," and scratching the hair off your head trying to figure out why things didn't work.

So I'm sure you'll be quite pleased to hear that all that network nincompoopery is a thing of the past thanks to Windows XP Home's Network Setup Wizard. This wizard takes you through the entire network setup process one step at a time, and handles most of the technical stuff behind the scenes where it belongs. Here's how the wizard works:

1. When you install a new NIC, Windows XP should recognize it and then display a message in the taskbar's notification area asking if you want to run the Network Setup Wizard. If so, click the message to start the wizard. If you don't see that message, select **Start, Control Panel, Network and Internet Connections, Set up or change your home or small office network.**

Windows Wisdom

Another way to start the Network Setup Wizard is by selecting **Start, All Programs, Accessories, Communications, Network Setup Wizard.**

2. The initial dialog box is merely an overview, so click **Next.**

3. The wizard then presents a list of things you need to have done at this point. If you're working with the network computer that will host the Internet connection, be sure it's connected to the Internet. Click **Next** to get to something more useful.

4. The wizard asks if this computer connects to the Internet:

   ➤ If so, activate **This computer connects directly to the Internet,** click **Next,** and proceed to step 5.

   ➤ If not, activate **This computer connects to the Internet through another computer on my network ...,** click **Next,** and then fast forward to step 6.

5. If you're configuring the Internet machine, the wizard will likely display a list of the connections that are defined on your computer. Highlight the one that you use to connect to the Internet and click **Next.**

413

6. If the wizard displays a dialog box that rambles on about a "bridge," nod your head knowingly and click **Next**.

7. The next wizard dialog box asks you for two bits of information (click **Next** when you're ready to continue):

   ➤ **Computer description**   This is a brief description that will help other people identify this computer on the network.

   ➤ **Computer name**   This is the name that other people on the LAN will see for the computer, so enter an appropriate (and unique) moniker. It's standard in small networks to use the first or last name of the person who'll be wrestling with the computer, but feel free to be a little creative. The name can be up to 15 characters long (don't use any spaces), and it can include any of the following symbols: ` ! @ # $ % ^ & ( ) - _ { }

8. Now the wizard pesters you for a workgroup name. The wizard suggests MSHOME (dull!), but you can change that by using the **Workgroup name** text box. (As I said earlier, however, make sure that all your computers use the workgroup name.) Click **Next**.

9. The wizard displays a summary of the settings you chose. Click **Next** to get the network configuration show on the road.

10. The wizard now muses about the possibility of there being any computers on your network that aren't running Windows XP. If your network does have such creatures, then you need to create a Network Setup disk. The purpose of this disk is to run a copy of the Network Setup Wizard on those other versions of Windows. This ensures that all your computers will work together with some semblance of harmony. You have four choices (click **Next** after you pick one):

Look Out!

If you're configuring the Internet computer, your ISP may have supplied you with a prefab name for the computer. If so, then you *must* use that name in the **Computer name** text box or your Internet connection won't work.

➤ **Create a Network Setup Disk**   Activate this option to place a copy of the Network Setup Wizard on a disk.

➤ **Use the Network Setup Disk I already have**   Choose this option if you've already created the disk.

➤ **Use my Windows XP CD**   If the other machines have CD-ROM or DVD-ROM drives, choose this option to run the Network Setup Wizard via the Windows XP CD.

➤ **Just finish the wizard; I don't need to run the wizard on other computers**   Activate this option if your workgroup is pure Windows XP. Skip to step 12.

11. If you elected to create the disk, insert a disk (make sure it doesn't contain any data you need) and click **Next**. When the wizard has finished creating the disk, click **Next**.

12. In the final wizard dialog box, click **Finish.**

13. When the wizard asks if you want to restart your computer, click **Yes.**

Changing Your Network Identification

Windows XP makes it fairly easy to change either your computer name or your workgroup name. This is handy if you made a mistake when running through the wizard or if you change your mind about the names you prefer. It's also handy if you have a computer that connects to one network at the office and to your own network at home. The office network is probably set up to use a domain, so you need to switch your network ID from a domain to a workgroup, depending on which network you're connecting to.

Here's how to change your network ID:

1. Select **Start, Control Panel, Printers and Other Hardware, System.** The System Properties dialog box appears.

2. Display the **Computer Name** tab.

3. Click **Change.** The Computer Name Changes dialog box shows up.

4. Use the **Computer name** text box to change the name of the computer.

5. Use the **Member of** group to choose one of the following options (click **OK** when you're done):

   ➤ **Domain**   Activate this option if you're connecting to a network at the office. Use the text box to enter the name of the domain.

   ➤ **Workgroup**   Activate this option if you're connecting to your home or small office network. Use the text box to enter the name of the workgroup.

6. If you see a welcome message first, click **OK** to get rid of it.

7. Windows XP warns you that you must restart your computer. Click **OK** to return to the System Properties dialog box.

8. Click **OK.** Windows XP asks if you want to restart your computer.

9. Click **Yes.**

Dealing with Non-XP Machines

If you want to set up networking on a Windows 98 or Windows Me machine, first follow these steps:

415

1. Grab the Network Setup Disk that you created earlier and slide it into the Windows 98 or Windows Me machine's floppy disk drive.

2. Select **Start, Run** to open the Run dialog box.

3. In the **Open** text box, type `a:\netsetup.exe` and then click **OK**. The Network Setup Wizard gets installed and then makes a guest appearance.

Alternatively, insert the Windows XP CD and, when the Welcome screen appears, click **Perform additional tasks,** and then click **Set up a home or small office network.**

Either way, follow the steps I took you through earlier to let the wizard perform its duties.

The Least You Need to Know

➤ **The nicest NICs**   Get NICs that support Ethernet (Fast Ethernet is best), are compatible with your network cable, and support Plug and Play.

➤ **The cable conundrum**   If you plan on using a star structure, you need twisted-pair cable (I highly recommend category 5 cable); if the bus structure is more your speed, go for coaxial cable.

➤ **The need for network speed**   Networks can travel at two different speeds: 10Mbps and 100Mbps. Equipment designed for the latter costs a bit more, but it's definitely worthwhile if you can afford it. Remember, however, that the coaxial cables can only handle 10Mbps.

➤ **Workgroup names**   Be sure that all the machines in your network use the same workgroup name.

➤ **Ready the host**   If you're looking to share an Internet connection across the network, decide which machine will be the host and then set up that connection on the computer. After that's done, run the Network Setup Wizard on that computer so that Internet Connection Sharing is running for the other network machines.

Chapter 31

Using Windows XP's Networking Features

With your network hardware gadgetry installed, the cables slung, and the workgroup computers configured for working in a group, your network is dressed to the nines and ready to party. Unfortunately, however, there isn't much partying that can be done at this stage.

This chapter shows you how to get your workgroup party into high gear. I'll spend most of the chapter talking about shared resources: disk drives, folders, printers, and even Internet connections that have been set up so that people on the network can access and use them. You'll also learn a few other network techniques that will help you take advantage of this networked beast that you've built.

Your Starting Point: The My Network Places Folder

Most of your network travels will set sail from a special folder called My Network Places. Windows XP offers several ways to get there:

➤ Select **Start, My Network Places.**

➤ Open My Computer and click the **My Network Places** link in the WebView panel.

➤ Display My Computer's Folders bar and highlight **My Network Places** in the tree.

Whichever method you prefer, you end up with the My Network Places window staring back at you, as shown in Figure 31.1.

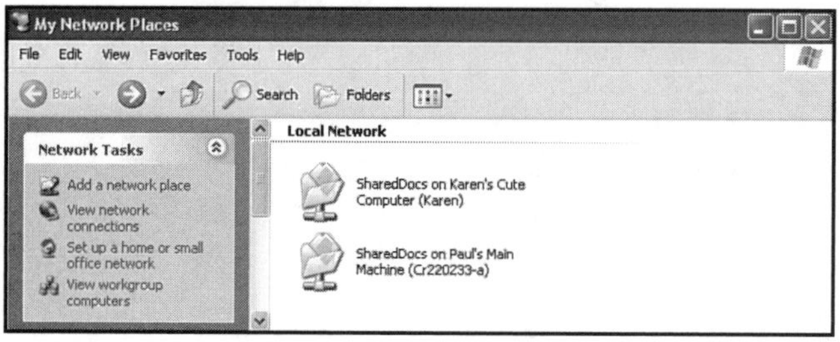

Figure 31.1

The My Network Places folder is the starting point for your network meandering.

If you have other Windows XP Home computers on your network, the **Local Network** section will probably display icons for those computers' Shared Documents folders, which are automatically shared with the network (under the name SharedDocs).

Note, too, that the WebView panel's **Network Tasks** section offers the following links:

➤ **Add a network place** You use this link to set up another computer's shared resource for use from your machine. (See the section "Setting Up Network Places" later in this chapter.)

➤ **View network connections** This link takes you to the Network Connections folder. (See the next section, "Understanding the Network Connections.")

➤ **Set up a home or small office network** This link launches the Network Setup Wizard, which you can use to make changes to your network configuration.

➤ **View workgroup computers** This link represents your workgroup. Clicking this link displays your workgroup window, which will have one icon for each computer in the workgroup (see Figure 31.2). From there, you launch an icon to open another window for the computer and see which resources they've shared. (See the section "Playing with Other Folks' Shared Resources" later in this chapter.)

418

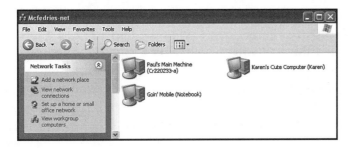

Figure 31.2

The workgroup window has an icon for each computer in your workgroup.

Understanding the Network Connections

The Network Connections window that I mentioned in the previous section is one of those things that you may never need. However, if you have a problem with a connection or want to change some settings, you'll need to be at least familiar with its contents.

No matter what your configuration, you should see an icon named **Local Area Connection** that represents the current computer's network connection (see Figure 31.3).

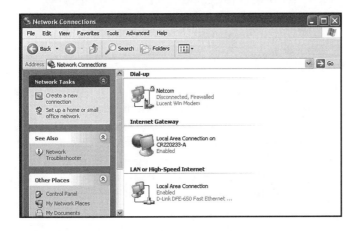

Figure 31.3

The Network Connections window has icons for your various connections.

The other icons you see in the Network Connections window depend on whether your computer or network has Internet access.

➤ **No Internet access** In this case, you probably won't see any other icons in the Network Connections window.

➤ **Direct Internet access (dial-up)** In this case, you also see a **Dial-up** group that has an icon representing your dial-up Internet connection (see Figure 31.3).

419

➤ **Direct Internet access (high-speed)** In this case (and somewhat confusingly), you'll see a second **Local Area Connection** icon in the **LAN or High-Speed Internet** group. Note that this icon's name may have a number, as well (such as Local Area Connection 2).

➤ **Internet access via Internet Connection Sharing** In this case, you'll see an **Internet Gateway** group that has an icon that represents the shared Internet connection on the other network computer (see Figure 31.3).

Here are some notes about working with these icons:

➤ **Checking the status of the connection** Double-click an icon to see its current status, including the current connection speed and the amount of time the connection has been active.

➤ **Disabling a connection** If you no longer need to use a connection, you can disable it by selecting **File, Disable.** (Select **File, Enable** to bring back the connection.)

➤ **Repairing a connection** If the connection seems to be stuck, select **File, Repair** to have Windows XP try to fix the problem.

➤ **Firewalling the connection** If the connection reaches out directly to the Internet, you should protect yourself from malicious hackers by putting up Windows XP's firewall. Highlight the connection, select **File, Properties**, display the **Advanced** tab, and activate the **Protect my computer and network …** check box.

➤ **Controlling Internet Connection Sharing** You can turn off a shared Internet connection by first highlighting the connection, and then selecting **File, Properties.** In the **Advanced** tab, deactivate the **Allow other network users to connect through this computer's Internet connection** check box. If you don't want other users to be able to disable the shared connection or make other changes to it, deactivate the **Allow other network users to control or disable the shared Internet connection** check box.

Sharing Your Resources So Other Folks Can Play with Them

The lifeblood of any peer-to-peer network is the resources that have been shared by the various computers in the workgroup. To see why, just consider the variety of things that can be shared:

➤ **Folders**   You can set up common folders so that some or all of the network users can access files and documents.

➤ **Disk drives**   You can give users access to entire drives, including Zip and Jaz drives.

➤ **CD or DVD drives**   You can set up a shared drive so that another user who doesn't have a CD or DVD drive can still run a program or access data. (Note that not all programs will run from a shared network CD or DVD.)

➤ **Printers**   By sharing a printer, you save either the expense of supplying each user with their own printer, or the hassle of moving a printer from one machine to another.

➤ **Internet connections**   You can set up an Internet connection on one machine, and the other computers in the workgroup can then use that connection to access the Internet.

The next couple of sections take you through the specifics of sharing resources.

Sharing Folders and Disks

The procedure for sharing a folder or a disk drive is the same. Here are the steps to follow:

1. In My Computer, display the folder or disk drive you want to share.

2. Highlight the folder or drive and then select **File, Sharing and Security**. (Another approach is to right-click the folder or drive and then click **Sharing and Security**.) The resource's Properties dialog box appears, and the **Sharing** tab is displayed.

3. If you chose a disk drive, the Sharing tab will recommend that you not share the "root of a drive." If you don't care about this, click the **If you understand the risk ...** link to see the Sharing tab's usual contents.

4. Activate the **Share this folder on the network** option.

5. Enter a **Share name** for the resource. The default here is the name of the folder or the letter of the drive, but feel free to use whatever you like.

6. If you want your network pals to be able to change the files in this folder or drive, activate the **Allow network users to change my files** check box. If you

Windows Wisdom

The *root* of a disk drive is the drive's main folder. Why is there a risk involved when you share this root? Because it gives other networkers full access to the contents of the disk, which may be dangerous. For example, if the disk drive contains your Windows XP system files, then some careless user could damage your system.

deactivate this check box, other users won't be able to rename or delete your files. Also, they'll be able to edit the files, but they won't be able to save those changes. Instead, they can only create a copy by saving the file to their own hard disk.

7. Click **OK**.

After you share a resource, notice that its icon gets tweaked a bit. Specifically, a hand with an open palm gets added underneath the icon, as though to "serve" the resource to the network.

Sharing a Printer

You'll be happy to hear that sharing a printer is a much simpler process than sharing a file or folder. In fact, sharing an existing printer takes just four steps:

1. Select **Start, Control Panel, Printers and Other Hardware, Printers and Faxes** to open the Printers and Faxes folder for business.

2. Highlight the printer you want to share, and then select **File, Sharing.** (On the other hand, you might feel like clicking the WebView panel's **Share this printer** link or right-clicking the printer and then clicking **Sharing.**) The printer's Properties dialog box appears, and the Sharing tab is conveniently picked out from the herd.

3. Activate the **Share this printer** option and then enter a name for the share in the text box beside it.

4. Click **OK**.

Windows Wisdom

I'm assuming in these networking chapters that all your workgroup computers are running Windows XP. However, it's no big whoop to include machines running other networkable flavors of Windows. If you do have a mixed bag of machines, you'll need to install the appropriate printer drivers for each Windows version you have. (There are drivers available for Windows 95, 98, Me, NT 4.0, and 2000.) To do that, click **Additional Drivers** to get a list of drivers, activate the check boxes beside each one you need, and then click **OK**.

If you haven't installed your printer yet, you can set up sharing when you tell Windows XP about the printer. (Just follow the steps that I outlined back in Chapter 7, "Installing and Uninstalling Programs and Devices"; refer to the section "Installing Specific Devices.") When you get to the Add Printer Wizard's Printer Sharing dialog box, activate the **Share name** option and enter a name for the share.

Playing with Other Folks' Shared Resources

With your workgroup machines generously sharing their folders, drives, and printers, it's now time to see just how to get at those resources. There are four ways to go about this:

➤ **Access the resources directly** You do this by opening **My Network Places**, clicking the **View workgroup computers** link, and then opening a computer. As you can see in Figure 31.4, Windows XP then shows the shared resources for that computer. Now just open the shared folders and drives and work with them the same way you would a local folder or drive (depending on whether the sharer has granted permission to change the file, of course).

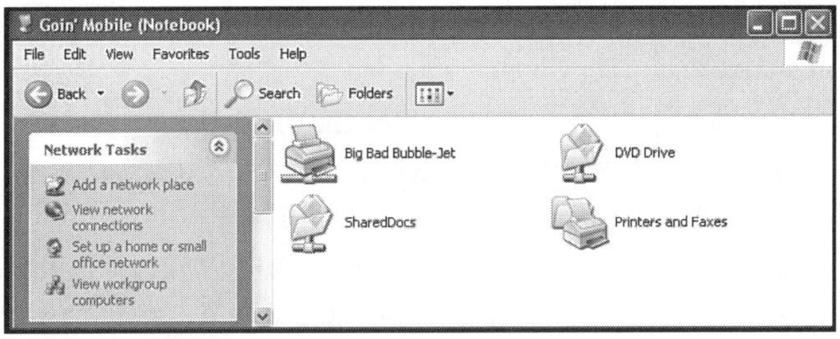

Figure 31.4

Opening a workgroup computer displays that machine's shared resources.

➤ **Define a network place** A *network place* is an icon that resides in the My Network Places folder, and it points to a shared resource. This saves you drilling down to the network computer to get to the resource. (See "Setting Up Network Places" later in this chapter.)

➤ **Map a shared folder or drive** This takes a shared folder or drive and assigns it to an available drive letter on your system. For example, if your hard disk is drive C and your CD-ROM drive is drive D, then you could set up a shared folder or drive as drive E. This gives you even easier access to the shared resource. (See "Making Network Folders Look Like Drives on Your Computer" later in this chapter.)

➤ **Install a network printer** This enables you to print from your machine and have the hard copy appear on the network printer. (You'll have to pick it up yourself, though. Networks are convenient, but they're not *that* convenient.) Check out "Printing Over the Network" a bit later in this chapter.

423

Setting Up Network Places

Windows XP usually does an excellent job of detecting resources as they're shared on the other workgroup computers. This means that your My Network Places folder probably already has an icon for whatever folder or drive some other user has shared.

If it doesn't, for some reason, then here are the steps involved in creating a network place for a shared folder or drive:

1. In the **My Network Places** folder, click the **Add a network place** link. The Add Network Place Wizard takes charge.

2. Click **Next** to skip the introductory hoo-ha. The wizard asks you to "select a service provider."

3. Scratch your head with a perplexed look on your face, highlight the **Choose another network location** item, and click **Next**.

4. Use either of the following methods to specify which shared folder or drive you want to work with (click **Next** when you're done):

   ➤ Use the text box to enter the location of the shared resource. Type two backslashes (\\) followed by the computer name, followed by another backslash (\). The wizard helpfully displays a list of the available shares. Select the one you want.

   ➤ Click **Browse** to arrive at the Browse For Folder dialog box, open the branches of the computer you want to work with until you see the resource you want. Highlight the resource and click **OK**.

5. The wizard suggests a name for the new network place, which takes the form *Share Name* on *Computer Name*. Edit the name, if you feel like it, and then click **Next**.

6. In the final wizard dialog box, if you leave the **Open this network place when I click Finish** check box activated, Windows XP will open a new window that shows the contents of the resource. Deactivate this check box if you don't want to bother with this extra window right now. Click **Finish**.

You end up with a new icon in My Network Places for the shared resource.

Making Network Folders Look Like Drives on Your Computer

You can avoid the My Network Places folder altogether if you map a network folder or drive so that it takes up a drive letter on your system. Here's how:

1. Using **My Network Places** and its **View workgroup computers** link, display the shared resources of the workgroup computer you want to work with.

2. Highlight the shared folder or drive you want to map, and then select **File, Map Network Drive.** (As you might have guessed by now, you also can right-click the folder or drive and then click **Map Network Drive.**) Up pops the Map Network Drive dialog box.

3. Windows XP defaults to the last of the available drive letters (such as Z). If you'd prefer another, use the **Drive** list to choose it.

4. If you want the resource to get mapped again automatically the next time you crank up Windows XP, leave the **Reconnect at Logon** check box activated.

5. Click **Finish.** Windows XP connects to the resource, creates a new drive letter, and then displays a window that shows the contents of the resource.

Look Out!

If you use removable drives such as CompactFlash memory modules, Windows XP assigns the first available drive letter to these drives. This can cause problems if you have a mapped network drive that uses a lower drive letter. Therefore, it's good practice to use higher drive letters (such as X, Y, and Z) for your mapped resources.

Once you've done this, My Computer sprouts a new grouping called **Network Drives** that contains the icons for your mapped folders and drives. If you no longer need a resource mapped to a drive, highlight its icon in My Computer and then select **File, Disconnect** (or right-click the icon and then click **Disconnect**).

Printing Over the Network

After you connect to a network printer, you can use it just like any local printer on your system. Windows XP offers a couple of methods for connecting to a network printer.

The easiest way is to use **My Network Places** to open the computer that has the shared printer, open its **Printers and Faxes** icon, highlight the printer, and then select **File, Connect.** (Right-clicking the printer and then clicking **Connect** also can be done.) Windows XP installs the printer lickety-split using the remote machine's printer driver files.

If you like using a wizard for these kinds of things, you can do it using the Add Printer Wizard:

1. Select **Start, Control Panel, Printers and Other Hardware, Printers and Faxes** and click the **Add a printer** link to get the Add Printer Wizard to the top of the pile.

2. Click **Next** to get past the introductory dialog box.

3. In the next dialog box, activate the **A network printer, or a printer attached to another computer** option and click **Next**.

4. In the next dialog box, make sure the **Browse for a printer** option is activated and click **Next**.

5. In the **Browser for Printer** dialog box, use the **Shared printers** list to highlight the network printer you want to use. (To see a computer's shared printers, double-click the computer name.)

6. Click **Next**. From here, you complete the wizard normally.

Road Scholar: Using Dial-Up Network Connections

Travelers have no shortage of nightmares to fret over (lost luggage, delayed flights, airline food, and so on). For the business traveler, an extra nightmare lurks in the wings: forgetting to pack some crucial network files into your notebook computer. However, it's possible to banish that particular nightmare and always have ready access to whatever you need off the network. The solution is to set up one workgroup computer to accept a "dial-up" network connection. This enables far-flung folks to use their modem to connect to that computer and so gain access to the network. This section shows you not only how to make that connection, but also how to set up the dial-up computer. Now all you have to do is remember to pack your modem!

Setting Up a Network Computer to Accept Incoming Calls

You can't dial up your network unless you have something to dial up *to*. So, your first chore is to convert one of your workgroup computers into a machine that's only too happy to accept incoming calls.

Before getting started on this, you need to be sure of two things:

➤ Any users who might do the dial-up thing are set up with their own user accounts on the computer.

➤ The machine you'll be using has a modem installed and ready to serve.

With all that in place, follow these steps:

1. In the My Network Places window, click **View network connections**, and then click **Create a new connection**. (You can also select **Start, All Programs, Accessories, Communications, New Connection Wizard**.)

2. Click **Next** to sidestep the initial dialog box. The wizard displays a list of connection types.

3. Activate the **Set up an advanced connection** option and click **Next**.

4. Activate **Accept incoming connections** and click **Next**. The wizard sets out a list of connection devices for your selecting pleasure.

5. Activate the check box beside your modem, deactivate any other check boxes, and then click **Next**. Now the wizard muses about "virtual private connections." Say, "Yeah, I wish!" and be sure that the **Do not allow virtual private connections** option is activated. Click **Next** at your earliest convenience. The wizard waves a list of users in your face.

6. Activate the check box beside the name of each user to whom you're willing to grant dial-up access to the computer. (Note, too, that you can click **Add** to set up more users from here.) Feel free to click **Next** when that's done. The wizard's seemingly inexhaustible supply of check box lists continues with a list of networking components.

7. You don't have to worry about any of this, so click **Next** to keep things moving.

8. Mission accomplished! In the last dialog box, click **Finish**. The wizard returns you to the Network Connections window and displays a new icon (usually called Incoming Connections).

That's all you need to do for this machine. Windows XP will now monitor the modem to listen for incoming calls, and will automatically answer any that come in.

Creating a Dial-Up Connection to Your Network

Okay, so that's stage one. Stage two involves setting up the would-be traveling computer to connect to the network using a modem. Again, your first chore is to ensure that this computer has a working modem. After you've done that, follow these steps to run through a few more Network Connection Wizard shenanigans:

1. In the My Network Places window, click **View network connections**, and then click **Create a new connection**. (You can also select **Start, All Programs, Accessories, Communications, New Connection Wizard**.)

2. Click **Next** to get to the list of connection types.

3. Activate the **Connect to the network at my workplace** option and click **Next**.

427

4. Activate **Dial-up connection** and click **Next.** The wizard wonders which name you want to give to the connection.

5. Enter a name and click **Next.** The wizard puzzles over the phone number to use when dialing.

6. Enter the **Phone number** and then click **Next** to forge ahead. The wizard displays its final dialog box.

7. Click **Finish.** (Before doing so, you might consider activating the **Add a shortcut to this connection to my desktop** check box. This tells the wizard to put a connection shortcut on the desktop, which, as you'll see, is a convenience you might like.)

Once again, you're dropped off at the Network Connections window, where you'll see a new icon in the **Dial-up** group. Windows XP will also prompt you to connect to the network. Let's skip this, for now, so just click **Cancel.**

Making the Connection

After all that wizardry, you're now set to make the connection. Assuming your modem is connected and ready for action, here's what you do:

1. Select **Start, Connect To** and then click the name of the connection you created in the previous section. (Alternatively, if you elected to have a shortcut for the connection placed on the desktop, double-click that shortcut.) Windows XP displays a Connect dialog box.

2. Be sure your username is correct and enter your password.

3. If you want Windows XP to include your password automatically in the future, activate the **Save this username and password for the following users** check box and then choose either **Me only** or **Anyone who uses this computer.**

4. Make sure the correct phone number is shown in the **Dial** text box.

5. If you want to use dialing rules or make other changes, click **Properties** and activate **Use dialing rules.**

6. When you're ready, click **Dial** to get on with it. Windows XP dials your modem and connects with the computer you set up to handle incoming calls.

7. When the connection is made, a dialog box pops up to let you know. Click **OK.**

From here, you use the network just like you do when you have a physical connection.

Windows Wisdom

You can also make the connection during the Windows XP startup. When the Log On to Windows dialog box greets you, activate the **Log On Using Dial-Up Connection** check box. When you click **OK,** the Dial-Up Networking dialog box is called in. Use this dialog box to select the connection you want to use (this will be the **Dial-Up Connection** item) and click **Dial.** From here, you follow steps 2 through 7.

When your networking duties are complete, you can disconnect by using either of the following methods:

➤ Select **Start, Connect To,** right-click the connection icon, and then click **Disconnect.**

➤ Right-click the connection icon that Windows XP shoehorned into the taskbar's notification area, and then click **Disconnect.**

The Least You Need to Know

➤ **Getting to the network**   Open **My Network Places** and then launch the **View workgroup computers** icon.

➤ **Sharing your stuff**   To share a resource, highlight it, select **File, Sharing and Security,** and then activate the **Share this folder on the network option.**

➤ **Creating a network place**   In the **My Network Places** folder, click the **Add a network place** link.

➤ **Mapping a network folder or drive**   Open the workgroup computer, highlight the folder or drive, and then select **File, Map Network Drive.**

➤ **Using a network printer**   Open the network computer, highlight the shared printer, and then select **File, Connect.**

The Jargon Jar: The Complete Archive

annotate   To add comments, graphics, highlights, or other doodles to a received fax.

attachment   A file that latches onto an e-mail message and is sent to the recipient.

Auto Hide   A feature that hides the taskbar until you move the mouse to the bottom of the screen.

AutoRun   A feature that automatically launches a program's setup routine after you insert its CD or DVD disc.

backplate   A piece of metal that covers a hole in the back of a computer beside an internal circuit board slot.

backup job   A file that specifies a few particulars about a backup: the files you want backed up, the location where the files will be backed up, and any backup options.

bad sector   A sector that is corrupted and can no longer store data properly.

Bcc   A blind courtesy (or carbon) copy e-mail message. These are copies of the message that get sent to other people, but their addresses aren't shown to the other recipients. *See also* Cc.

bit   Short for "binary digit"; it represents the most basic unit of computer information. Within your computer, data is stored using tiny electronic devices called "gates," each of which holds a single bit. These gates can be either on (which means electricity flows through the gate) or off (no electricity flows through the gate). For the likes of you and me, the number 1 represents a gate that's on, and the number 0 represents a gate that's off.

boot   To start your computer.

bps   Stands for bits per second, and is used to measure the speed at which the modem spews data through a phone line.

browser   *See* Web browser.

bus structure   A network structure in which each network interface card is connected to the network interface card in the computer "beside" it via coaxial cable. *See also* star structure.

byte   Eight bits strung together, which represents a single character of data. For example, the letter "X" is represented by the following byte: 01011000. Weird, I know. Further, the mathematicians tell us that a byte can have 256 possible combinations of ones and zeros (prove it for yourself by raising 2 to the power of 8), and those combinations represent all possible characters: lowercase letters, uppercase letters, numbers, symbols, and so on.

Cc   A courtesy (or carbon) copy. These are copies of an e-mail message that get sent to other people. *See also* Bcc.

circuit board   A device that fits into a slot inside your computer.

click   To quickly press and release the left mouse button.

client   In a client/server setup, a computer that has no special privileges or duties. *See also* server.

client/server   A network configuration in which one machine—called the server—acts as kind of "boss" to all the other machines—the clients. For example, the server usually won't let you and your client computer on the network unless you enter an approved username and password. For this to work, the server computer must use a special network operating system designed for servers.

coaxial cable   A cable that uses a bayonet-style connector to attach to a T-connector, which then attaches to a BNC port in the network interface card. *See also* twisted-pair cable.

color quality   The number of colors Windows XP uses to display stuff on your screen. *See also* screen resolution.

cursor   *See* insertion point cursor.

cutout   A selected section of a Paint drawing.

daily backup   A backup type that includes only files that were changed on the day you run the backup. *See also* incremental backup.

data transfer rate   The maximum (theoretical) speed at which a *modem* can send data, and it's measured in bps. Most modern modems support one of the following data transfer rates: 28,800bps, 33,600bps, or 56,000bps. If you're looking to buy a modem, get one that supports 56,000bps (which is sometimes called V.90, for reasons too geeky to go into here).

defragment To rearrange the contents of a hard disk so that each file's sectors run consecutively. *See also* fragmented.

desktop The part of the Windows XP screen above the taskbar. It's called a "desktop" because it's where your documents and tools appear.

device driver A wee chunk of software that enables Windows XP to operate and talk to a device.

dial-up A connection to a network (or an Internet service provider) that occurs via a modem over a phone line.

dialog box A box that shows up when Windows XP or a program requires more information from you.

differential backup Backs up only files in the current backup job that have changed since the last full backup. *See also* incremental backup.

digital camera A film camera-like device that takes pictures of the outside world and stores them digitally for later downloading to a hard disk.

directory *See* folder.

document scanner A photocopier-like device that creates a digital image of a flat surface, such as a piece of paper or a photograph.

double-click To quickly press and release the left mouse button twice in succession.

download To receive data from a remote computer. *See also* upload.

drag To move an object using your mouse. You do this by placing the mouse pointer over the object, holding down a mouse button (usually the left button), and then moving the mouse.

drag-and-drop A technique you use to move things from here to there; you use your mouse to drag files or icons to strategic screen areas and then drop them there.

drop To use your mouse to place an object in a new location. You do this by releasing the mouse button after you have dragged the object to its new home.

Explorer bar A pane that shows up on the left side of the My Computer window, and that's used to display bars (such as the handy Folders bar).

favorite A Web page name and address saved within Internet Explorer for easy recall down the road.

fax/modem A special type of modem (although it's by far the most common type these days) that can handle fax transmissions as well as its usual data duties.

folder A storage location for files and other folders (subfolders).

font A style of text that includes the typeface (a unique design applied to every character), the type style (such as **bold** or *italic*), the type size, and possibly some type effects (such as underlined).

433

fragmented   When a file is stored on the hard disk using multiple sectors that are scattered throughout the disk. *See also* defragment.

full backup   Backs up all the files in the current backup job. *See also* differential backup and incremental backup.

gigabyte   1,024 megabytes. Those in-the-know usually abbreviate this as "GB" when writing, and as "gig" when speaking. *See also* byte, kilobyte, and megabyte.

hard disk   The main storage area inside your computer.

hibernate   To shut off power to most systems on the computer while still maintaining the current state of the open windows and programs. *See also* standby.

hot swapping   Inserting and removing PC Card devices without having to shut down Windows XP.

hub   A central network connection point used in the star structure.

idle time   Time during which a network or Internet connection isn't used.

incremental backup   Backs up only files in the current backup job that have changed since the last full backup or the last differential backup.

insertion point cursor   The blinking vertical bar you see inside a text box or in a word processing application, such as WordPad. It indicates where the next character you type will appear.

Internet service provider   A company that takes your money in exchange for an Internet account, which is what you need to get online.

IP address   An address (which will look something like 123.234.45.67) that serves as the location of your computer while you're connected to the Internet.

ISP   *See* Internet service provider.

Jaz drive   A special disk drive that uses portable disks (about the size of floppy disks) that hold either one or two gigabytes of data. *See also* Zip drive.

Kbps   Kilobits per second, or thousands of bits per second. Data transfer rates are often measured this way, so the three main rates are also written as 28.8Kbps, 33.6Kbps, and 56Kbps.

kilobyte   1,024 bytes. To be hip, always abbreviate this to "K" or "KB." *See also* megabyte and gigabyte.

LAN   *See* local area network.

link   In a Web page, a chunk of text or an image that, when clicked, takes you to another Web page.

local area network   A group of computers located relatively close together and that are connected via network cable.

log on   To provide your Internet service provider with your username and password, and so gain access to the wonder that is the Internet.

mail server   A computer that your ISP uses to store and send your e-mail messages. *See also* server.

map   To set up a shared network folder or disk drive so that it has its own drive letter on your system. *See also* shared resource.

megabyte   1,024 kilobytes, or 1,048,576 bytes. The experts write this as "M" or "MB" and pronounce it "meg." *See also* gigabyte.

message body   The text of an e-mail message.

message rules   Specific instructions that tell Outlook Express how to handle certain incoming messages.

MIDI   A sound file that plays music generated by electronic synthesizers.

modem   An electronic device that somehow manages to transmit and receive computer data over telephone lines. Modems come in three flavors: external, internal, and PC Card.

modem cable   A special data cable that connects an external modem to a PC. The cable attaches to a port in the back of the modem on one end, and to a serial port in the back of the computer on the other end.

multimedia   Using a computer to play, edit, and record sounds, animations, and movies.

multitasking   The capability to run two or more programs at the same time.

Musical Instrument Digital Interface   *See* MIDI.

network   *See* local area network.

network interface card   A circuit board, PC Card device, or USB device into which the network cable is plugged.

network operating system   A special operating system designed for server computers. An example is Windows .NET Server, the big brother of Windows XP.

network place   A shared resource that has its own icon in your My Network Places folder.

newsgroup   An online discussion forum devoted to a particular topic.

NIC   *See* network interface card.

null-modem cable   A special communications cable designed for direct connections between two computers.

page   *See* Web page.

PC Card   A small, credit card–sized device that slips into a special socket on your notebook. There are PC Card devices for modems, network adapters, hard disks, and much more.

pixels   The individual pinpoints of light that make up a Paint drawing (and, for that matter, everything you see on your screen).

port   A receptacle in the back of a computer into which you plug the cable used by an external device. *See also* modem cable, printer port, and serial port.

post   To send a message to a newsgroup.

print job   A document for which the Print command has been issued.

print queue   The list of pending print jobs.

printer port   On the back of the computer, the receptacle into which you plug the printer cable. On most systems, the printer port is named LPT1.

RAM (Random Access Memory)   The memory in your computer that Windows XP uses to run your programs.

Recycle Bin   The place where Windows XP stores deleted files. If you trash a file accidentally, you can use the Recycle Bin to recover it.

Registry   The crucial configuration files that are the lifeblood of Windows XP.

right-click   To click the right mouse button instead of the usual left button. In Windows XP, right-clicking something usually pops up a shortcut menu.

sans serif   A font that doesn't have cross strokes at its extremities. This type of font is most often used for titles and headings that require a larger type size. *See also* serif.

screen resolution   The number of columns and rows in the grid of pixels that Windows XP uses to display screen images. *See also* color quality.

screen saver   A feature that displays a moving pattern on your monitor after your computer hasn't been used for a while. It prevents the screen image from being "burned in" to the monitor, but most folks just like to watch the crazy psychedelic patterns they make.

screen shot   A copy of the current screen image.

sector   A storage area on your hard disk.

separator   In a toolbar, a vertical bar that separates groups of related buttons.

serial port   A plug in the back of your computer into which you insert the modem cable. If you have an internal modem, the serial port is built-in to the modem's circuit board, so you never have to worry about it and there's no cable to run. On most computers, the serial port is named COM1.

serif   A font that has small cross strokes at the extremities of each character. Serif fonts are good for regular text in a document. *See also* sans serif.

server   A computer that provides data or services to clients that request them. *See also* client/server and mail server.

shared resource   A local folder, disk drive, or printer that has been set up so that people on the network can use it.

shortcut   A file that points to another file. Also, another name for most of the commands on the various Start menus.

shortcut menu   A menu that contains a few commands related to an item (such as the desktop or the taskbar). You display the shortcut menu by right-clicking the object.

signal-to-noise ratio   In a newsgroup, the ratio of useful, on-topic posts to useless, off-topic posts.

signature   A snippet of text that appears at the bottom of an e-mail message.

spam   Unsolicited commercial e-mail, and the scourge of the Internet. To avoid spam, don't put your real e-mail address in your news account.

standby   A power mode that shuts everything down temporarily until you press a key, move the mouse, or poke the power button. *See also* hibernate.

star structure   A network structure in which each network interface card is connected to a central hub via twisted-pair cable. *See also* bus structure.

Subject line   A line of text that describes what an e-mail message is about.

surf   To jump from Web page to Web page using a Web browser.

tab stop   A spot on the WordPad ruler at which the cursor stops when you press the **Tab** key.

tape drive   A device that backs up data to tape. Unless you have a spare hard disk, this is the best kind of backup medium to use.

taskbar   The gray strip along the bottom of the Windows XP screen that's used to switch between running programs.

text editor   A program that lets you edit files that contain only text. The Windows XP text editor is called Notepad.

thumbnail   A preview of an image or HTML file (Web page).

TSID   The Transmitting Subscriber Identification, which is a short bit of text that identifies your fax/modem to the recipient.

twisted-pair cable   A cable that uses RJ-45 jacks to connect to an RJ-45 port in the NIC. *See also* coaxial cable, hub, and star structure.

Uniform Resource Locator   *See* URL.

uninstall   To completely remove a program from your computer.

Universal Serial Bus   *See* USB.

upload   To send data to a remote computer. *See also* download.

URL (Uniform Resource Locator)   The address of a Web page.

USB (Universal Serial Bus)   A relatively new way to connect all kinds of devices—including keyboards, mice, speakers, printers, modems, and network cards—to a PC. Most new computers have one or two USB ports into which these devices connect.

video adapter   An internal circuit board that grabs display instructions from the processor and then tells the monitor what to show on the screen.

wallpaper   An image or design that covers the screen background.

wave file   A standard Windows sound file.

Web browser   A program that you use to surf sites on the World Wide Web. The browser that comes with Windows XP is called Internet Explorer.

Web page   A document on the Web that contains text, images, and usually a few links.

WebView panel   A panel that appears on the left side of a folder window and that contains links to common tasks and locations related to that folder or its contents.

workgroup   In a large network, a group of related computers. In a small network, all the computers.

Zip drive   A special disk drive that uses portable disks (a little smaller than a Jaz drive disk) that hold 100 or 250 megabytes of data.

Index

441